Honor and Shame in 1 Samuel 1–7

Bin Kang

Langham
MONOGRAPHS

© 2022 Bin Kang

Published 2022 by Langham Monographs
An imprint of Langham Publishing
www.langhampublishing.org

Langham Publishing and its imprints are a ministry of Langham Partnership

Langham Partnership
PO Box 296, Carlisle, Cumbria, CA3 9WZ, UK
www.langham.org

ISBNs:
978-1-83973-603-2 Print
978-1-90771-777-0 ePub
978-1-90771-778-7 Mobi
978-1-78368-779-4 PDF

Bin Kang has asserted his right under the Copyright, Designs and Patents Act, 1988 to be identified as the Author of this work.

All rights reserved. No part of this publication may be reproduced, stored in a retrieval system or transmitted, in any form or by any means, electronic, mechanical, photocopying, recording or otherwise, without the prior written permission of the publisher or the Copyright Licensing Agency.

Requests to reuse content from Langham Publishing are processed through PLSclear. Please visit www.plsclear.com to complete your request.

Unless otherwise indicated all Scripture translations in this work are the author's own.

Scripture quotations marked (ESV) are from The Holy Bible, English Standard Version® (ESV®), copyright © 2001 by Crossway, a publishing ministry of Good News Publishers. Used by permission. All rights reserved.

Scripture quotations marked (HCSB) are taken from the Holman Christian Standard Bible®, Copyright © 1999, 2000, 2002, 2003, 2009 by Holman Bible Publishers. Used by permission. Holman Christian Standard Bible®, Holman CSB®, and HCSB® are federally registered trademarks of Holman Bible Publishers.

Scripture marked (NASB) are taken from the New American Standard Bible®, Copyright © 1960, 1962, 1963, 1968, 1971, 1972, 1973, 1975, 1977, 1995, 2020 by The Lockman Foundation. Used by permission.

Scripture marked (NCV) taken from the New Century Version®. Copyright © 2005 by Thomas Nelson. Used by permission. All rights reserved.

Quotations designated (NET) are from the NET Bible® copyright ©1996, 2019 by Biblical Studies Press, L.L.C. http://netbible.com. Scripture quoted by permission. All rights reserved.

Scripture quotations marked (NIV) are taken from the Holy Bible, New International Version®, NIV®. Copyright © 1973, 1978, 1984, 2011 by Biblica, Inc.™ Used by permission of Zondervan.

Scripture quotations marked (NKJV) are taken from the New King James Version (NKJV). Copyright © 1982 by Thomas Nelson, Inc. Used by permission. All rights reserved.

Scripture quotations marked (NLT) are taken from the Holy Bible, New Living Translation, copyright © 1996, 2004, 2007, 2013, 2015 by Tyndale House Foundation. Used by permission of Tyndale House Publishers, Inc., Carol Stream, Illinois 60188. All rights reserved.

Scripture quotations marked (NRSV) are from the New Revised Standard Version Bible, copyright © 1989 National Council of the Churches of Christ in the United States of America. Used by permission. All rights reserved.

British Library Cataloguing-in-Publication Data
A catalogue record for this book is available from the British Library

ISBN: 978-1-83973-603-2

Cover & Book Design: projectluz.com

Langham Partnership actively supports theological dialogue and an author's right to publish but does not necessarily endorse the views and opinions set forth here or in works referenced within this publication, nor can we guarantee technical and grammatical correctness. Langham Partnership does not accept any responsibility or liability to persons or property as a consequence of the reading, use or interpretation of its published content.

Contents

Acknowledgements ix

Abbreviations xi

Chapter 1 1
Introduction
    1.1 Background to and Reason for This Research 1
    1.2 Honor and Shame Defined 9
    1.3 A Review of the Research on Honor and Shame 11
        1.3.1 A survey related to Old Testament in general 12
        1.3.2 Literature reviews related to Deuteronomistic History 18
        1.3.3 Literature reviews related to the book of First Samuel 23
    1.4 The Justification for This Study 32
    1.5 Research Methodology 33
    1.6 Scope and Delimitation 44
    1.7 The Structure of Our Study 45

Chapter 2 47
The Language of Honor and Shame in 1 Samuel
    2.1 Introduction 47
    2.2 Honor and Shame Terms in the Song of Hannah
        (1 Sam 2:1–10) 48
        2.2.1 רום, "be high, exalted" (2:1, 7, 8, 10), vs. שפל, "to
        bring low" (2:7) 49
        2.2.2 עשר I, "to make rich" (*hiphil*, 2:7), vs. רוש, "to make
        poor" (*hiphil*, 2:7) 51
    2.3 The Use of כבד 52
    2.4 Shame/Shaming Terms in 1 Samuel 54
        2.4.1 רעם II, "to humiliate" (1 Sam 1:6) 54
        2.4.2. נאץ, "to treat disrespectfully" (1 Sam 2:17) 56
        2.4.3 קלל I, "to be insignificant" (*qal*, 1 Sam 2:30), "to be
        considered insignificant" (*niphal*, 1 Sam 18:23), "to
        curse" (*piel*, 1 Sam 3:13; 17:43) 58
        2.4.4 בזה, "to despise" (1 Sam 2:30; 10:27; 17:42) 60
        2.4.5 חרף II, "to taunt" (1 Sam 17:10, 25, 26, 36, 45);
        חרפה, "reproach" (1 Sam 11:2; 17:26; 25:39) 61
        2.4.6 כלם, "be humiliated" (1 Sam 20:34; 25:7, 15) 63
        2.4.7 באש, "to stink" (1 Sam 27:12) 65

2.5 A "Seat" (כסא) of Honor (1 Sam 1:9; 2:8; 4:13, 18) 66
2.6 The Honor of a "Chief Position" in a Meal (1 Sam 9:22)...............70
2.7 A Monument (יד), the Proclamation of Honor (1 Sam 15:12) 71
2.8 David's Esteemed Name (1 Sam 18:30) 74
2.9 The Disgrace of Nakedness (1 Sam 19:24; 20:30)...........................75
2.10 The Face of Abigail (1 Sam 25:35) 80
2.11 Uncircumcision as a Sign of Disgrace (1 Sam 14:6; 17:26, 36; 31:4) 86
2.12 The Stigmatized Metaphors: A Dog, a Flea (1 Sam 17:43; 24:14; 26:20) 88
2.13 A Disfigured Body as a Sign of Shame (1 Sam 31:8–13).............90
2.14 Conclusion 92

Chapter 3 93
Hannah – Competing for Honor, from the Ashamed to the Honored (1 Samuel 1:1–2:11, 18–21)

3.1 Hannah Ashamed of Her Barrenness (1 Sam 1:1–8).....................93
3.2 God Clears Hannah's Shame by Giving Her a Child (1 Sam 1:9–20) 103
3.3 Hannah Honors God by Offering Samuel to the Lord (1 Sam 1:21–28)..111
3.4 Hannah's Thanksgiving Song: The Lord Who Oversees Men's Honor and Shame (1 Sam 2:1–10) 117
3.5 The Lord Honors Hannah by Giving Her Many Other Children (1 Sam 2:18–21) 132
3.6 Conclusion 133

Chapter 4 135
The Elides and Samuel – Honoring Selves versus Honoring God (1 Samuel 2:12–17; 2:22–4:18; 7:2–17)

4.1 Eli Honors His Sons More than the Lord (1 Sam 2:12–17, 22–25, 27–36)..135
4.2 Samuel Honors the Lord by His Faithful Service (1 Sam 3:1–10) 155
4.3 Eli's Family Judged with Shame (1 Sam 3:11–18; 4:12–18).........163
4.4 Samuel Honors the Lord by Establishing a Stone Monument (1 Sam 7:2–12) 168
4.5 God Honors Samuel by Establishing Him as a Prophet (1 Sam 3:19–21)..171
4.6 Conclusion 176

Chapter 5 177
The Ark Narrative – YHWH Defends His Own Glory (1 Samuel 4:1–7:1)
    5.1 The Glory of the God of Israel Is Not Present at the
        Capture of the Ark of the Lord (1 Sam 4:1–22)............................179
    5.2 The God of the Philistines Shamed Before the God of
        Israel (1 Sam 5:1–5)..190
    5.3 The Hand of the Lord Is "Heavy" upon the Cities of the
        Philistines (1 Sam 5:6–12)...194
    5.4 The Unusual Return of the Ark of the Lord (1 Sam 6:1–18) 198
    5.5 God's Glory Is Not to Be Offended (1 Sam 6:19–7:1)..................206
    5.6 Conclusion 212

Chapter 6 215
Conclusion and Implications
    6.1 Conclusion 215
    6.2 Implications of This Study...220

Appendix 1 229
    Notes on אפים *in 1 Samuel 1:5*

Appendix 2 235
    Notes on תַּכְעִסֶנָּה *in 1 Samuel 1:7*

Appendix 3 237
    Notes on אַחֲרֵי אָכְלָה בְשִׁלֹה וְאַחֲרֵי שָׁתֹה *in 1 Samuel 1:9*

Appendix 4 241
    Notes on מָעוֹן *in 1 Samuel 2:29*

Bibliography..247

Acknowledgements

I am deeply grateful to my supervisor Dr. Tim Undheim who offered me his wisdom, criticism and support. This dissertation would not have been possible without his meticulous guidance, his speedy attention to every detail and his remarkable patience. I have benefited greatly from his wide knowledge in many ancient languages as well as his example of humility.

I also wish to express my gratitude to Dr. Michael Malessa, Dr. Rico Villanueva and Dr. Bill T. Arnold (readers of my dissertation) for contributing their stimulating insights and comments. I have been very fortunate to have them on the committee.

I am deeply indebted to Dr. Joel Williams who proofread the entire manuscript and offered his valuable suggestions and comments. His expertise on the ideological point of view was a tremendous help. I cannot forget that he and his wife Becky also coordinated and raised funds for my research at Wheaton College for a semester during a very challenging time. I also want to thank Anthony and Genia Solis (College Church) who opened their house to host us during our time in the States.

The writing of this dissertation was supported by grants from the Biblical Seminary of the Philippines (BSOP); thanks go to the BSOP leadership, particularly Dr. Joseph Shao (President Emeritus), President Rev. Anthony Hao, Vice President Mark A. Chua, Dr. Samson L. Uytanlet and Rev. Philip Co, for their blessings and encouragement.

Prof. Linda Tue helped by reading the first chapter of this manuscript and offered some good suggestions. Raquel D. Cruz, Liu Jia (Grace) and my fellow students Hwa Jin Kim and Rufus Samuel in AGST were a great help in acquiring some of the much-needed resources. Zhang Rong helpfully prepared the illustrational chart in chapter 5.

I would like to extend my sincere gratitude to Clark Cheng and his wife Susanna Zhang for their kindness, friendship and financial aid over the past many years. My parents have been a great support. They have encouraged me to pursue my passions despite their illness and inconveniences.

Finally, I am tremendously thankful to my wife Hanxing for her love, prayers, encouragement and patience. She indeed suffered with me as I continued my writing in this pandemic period. 寒星，谢谢你的爱、祷告、鼓励和忍耐！

Soli Deo Gloria!

Abbreviations

Ant.	*Jewish Antiquities* by Josephus
ASV	American Standard Version
BBRSup	Supplements to *Bulletin for Biblical Research*
BDB	*Hebrew and English Lexicon of the Old Testament* edited by Brown, Driver, and Briggs
BHS	*Biblia Hebraica Stuttgartensia* edited by Elliger and Rudolph
CAD	*The Assyrian Dictionary of the Oriental Institute of the University of Chicago*
CBQMS	*Catholic Biblical Quarterly* Monograph Series
CD	Cairo Damascus Document
c.s.	Common singular
DCH	*Dictionary of Classical Hebrew*, 8 vols., edited by Clines
DDD	*Dictionary of Deities and Demons in the Bible* edited by Van der Toorn, Becking and Van der Horst
DJD	Discoveries in the Judaean Desert
Elephantine Papyri	*Aramaic Papyri of the Fifth Century B.C.* edited by Cowley
ESV	English Standard Version
Ges[18]	*Hebräisches und Aramäisches Handwörterbuch über das Alte Testament,* auflage 18, by Gesenius
GKC	*Gesenius' Hebrew Grammar*, 2nd ed., edited by Kautzsch, translated by Cowley
HALOT	*The Hebrew and Aramaic Lexicon of the Old Testament,* study ed., 2 vols., by Koehler, Baumgartner, and Stamm

HtD	*Hitpael*
HCSB	The Holman Christian Standard Bible
IBHS	*An Introduction to Biblical Hebrew Syntax* by Waltke and O'Connor
JNSLMS	Journal of Northwest Semitic Languages Monograph Series
Joüon-Muraoka	*A Grammar of Biblical Hebrew* by Joüon and Muraoka
JSNTSup	Supplements to *Journal for the Study of the New Testament*
JSOTSup	Supplements to *Journal for the Study of the Old Testament*
KJV	King James Version
LEB	Lexham English Bible
Life	*The Life* by Josephus
LXX	Septuagint
m.p.	Masculine plural
m.s.	Masculine singular
MT	Masoretic Text
NASB	New American Standard Bible
NCV	New Century Version
NET	New English Translation
NIV	New International Version
NJPS	New Jewish Publication Society of America Tanakh
NKJV	New King James Version
NLT	New Living Translation
NRSV	New Revised Standard Version
NT	New Testament
OT	Old Testament
OTL	Old Testament Library
RSV	Revised Standard Version
2 s.f.:	Second singular feminine
SBL	Society of Biblical Literature
SBLDS	Society of Biblical Literature Dissertation Series
s.f.	Singular feminine

TDNT	*Theological Dictionary of the New Testament*, 10 vols., edited by Kittel and Friedrich, translated by Bromiley
TDOT	*Theological Dictionary of the Old Testament*, 8 vols., by Botterweck and Ringgren, translated by Willis, Bromiley and Green
3 s.f.	Third singular feminine
VTSup	Supplements to *Vetus Testamentum*
WYC	Wycliffe Bible
YLT	Young's Literal Translation
1QS	Rule of the Community
1QH	Thanksgiving Hymns
11Q13	Melchizedek

CHAPTER 1

Introduction

1.1 Background to and Reason for This Research

Reading through the book of 1 Samuel (especially the Hebrew texts), one can hardly ignore the notion of honor and shame communicated to us through its key vocabulary and terms, for example the root כבד (with the primary meaning "to be honored") appearing six times and קלל I (with the meaning "to be insignificant") occurring four times in 1 Samuel.[1] The importance of such a concept of honor and shame has been duly noted by some scholars. For instance, in *A Biblical History of Israel*, the authors highlight "the aforementioned key word *kbd*, 'weight, honor,' that is introduced in 2:29–30 and continues to recur throughout chapters 4–6, thus effectively (if subtly) tying the sections together."[2] In addition, Kasle observes that the book of 1 Samuel contains a large number (sixteen occurrences total) of various explicit terms denoting shaming/shame.[3] Thus, there is no doubt that giving attention to

---

1. See כבד (with the meaning "to honor") in 1 Sam 2:29 (3x), 9:6, 15:30 and 22:14; and קלל I (with the meaning "to be insignificant") in 1 Sam 2:30, 3:13, 17:43 and 18:23. I have not included כבד with the literal meaning "to be heavy," occurring five times (1 Sam 5:6, 11; 6:6 [2x]; 31:3), and קלל I, occurring one time relating to physical lightness (1 Sam 6:5), in these totals. A word can possibly have different homonymic values, i.e. different semantic meanings. I refer to *HALOT* for its different homonymic values in this dissertation. Since *HALOT* does not differentiate the homonyms for קלל, I refer to *DCH*. Only *DCH* lists two homonyms for קלל. See "קלל," *DCH*, 7:256–258.

2. Provan, Long, and Longman, *Biblical History of Israel*, 205.

3. According to Kasle, these shaming/shame terms in 1 Samuel are בזה and קלל in 2:30; קלל in 3:13; מאס in 8:7; מאס in 10:19; בזה in 10:27; חרפה in 11:2; מאס in 15:23; מאס in 15:26;

1

honor and shame, as important cultural background entities in ancient Israel,[4] is indispensable for a better understanding of the message of 1 Samuel. It should be stated at the forefront that this study does not rely simplistically on word studies or lexical data in forming its theological discussion, as would be the concern of James Barr.[5]

Although 1 Samuel 1–7 has been studied extensively by biblical scholars using historical-critical and literary-critical methods,[6] particularly the latter in the last few decades,[7] not many scholars have reflected the social-cultural dynamics of honor and shame in their analyses.[8] This is not too surprising though, since biblical scholars are predominantly from the West, where the culture is more guilt driven rather than honor/shame oriented.[9]

In view of this background, in this dissertation I will study 1 Samuel 1–7 from a social-cultural perspective of honor and shame. Moreover, it is my

---

מאס in 16:1; בזה in 17:42; קלל in 17:43; בשת in 20:30 (2x); כלם in 20:34; and חרפה in 25:39. See Kasle, "Analysis," 46.

4. That honor and shame are important aspects of the social culture of the ancient Near East has been widely accepted by scholars. For instance, Olyan comments on honor and shame in ancient Israel: "Yet these concepts are not at all alien to the worldview of ancient Israelites or their neighbors. On the contrary, they are common almost to the point of banality, occurring in discourses concerning many aspects of social relations: war, international diplomacy, marriage, the family, the penal system, and death and the afterlife." Olyan, "Honor, Shame, and Covenant," 203.

5. Barr, *Semantics*, 6.

6. Frolov has given a good summary of the adherents of these two camps of methodology, though with different preferred terminology: "Diachronic Approaches" and "Synchronic Approaches." See Frolov, *Turn of the Cycle*, 6–24. Both approaches have contributed to sharpening our understanding of 1 Samuel with regard to its structure, source, tradition, social setting, and narrative art. Historical-critical studies of 1 Samuel are subdivided into the classifications of source-critical, form-critical, tradition-critical and redaction-critical approaches. For source criticism, see Wellhausen, *Die Composition*; Miller and Roberts, *Hand of the Lord*. For works of form/traditional criticism, see Campbell, *Ark Narrative*; Gnuse, *Dream Theophany of Samuel*; Hertzberg, *I and II Samuel*. For books on redactional criticism, see Weiser, *Old Testament*; Birch, *Rise*; McCarter, *I Samuel*; Campbell, *Of Prophets and Kings*. For those who espouse a literary-critical method, see Eslinger, *Kingship of God*; Garsiel, *First Book of Samuel*; Miscall, *I Samuel*; Polzin, *Samuel and the Deuteronomist*; Fokkelman, *Narrative Art*; Jobling, *1 Samuel*; Tsumura, *First Book of Samuel*; Firth, *1 & 2 Samuel*; Alter, *David Story*; Bodner, *1 Samuel*; Brueggemann, *First and Second Samuel*; Arnold, *1 and 2 Samuel*; Hoffner, *1 & 2 Samuel*.

7. Dillard and Longman comment that "no book of the Bible has been the object of such intense interest to literary analysts as has Samuel." See Dillard and Longman, *Introduction*, 158.

8. For more information, see section 1.3.3 in this chapter.

9. A guilt-driven culture emphasizes the "internal sanction of guilt and the conscience," as Western cultures often focus on the welfare and dignity of the individual. See Bechtel, "Shame as a Sanction," 50–51.

contention that 1 Samuel 1–7, and even the entire book of 1 Samuel, can be arguably read from a narrated ideological point of view[10] that highlights the thematic centrality of honor and shame.[11] Such a focus on honor and shame is used by the narrator to provide a standard of judgment with regard to the divine election of leadership in the Eli/Samuel and Saul/David episodes.[12] To be more precise, one's attitude of either honoring or dishonoring God (as a reflection of one's spiritual character) determines the rise and fall, the election and rejection, of God's chosen leadership, be he a priest or king, in 1 Samuel. But, of course, this claim requires further justification.

Admittedly, identifying the narrator's ideological point of view (sometimes referred to as the narrator's "value scale")[13] can be a difficult or even elusive task. However, it is still possible to do so with some methodological orientation and careful attention to specific textual features.[14] In 1 Samuel 1–7,

---

10. Readers can acquire knowledge of this from the perspective of the narrator, who orchestrates all things to happen according to his design. The narrator's ideological point of view is communicated explicitly or implicitly to the reader through the development of story and the shaping of characters. Uspensky, a Russian linguist, was probably the first one to introduce the concept of the ideological point of view to the public; see Uspensky, *Poetics of Composition*, 8–16. This concept, in turn, has been applied to biblical studies, especially by Fokkelman, *Reading Biblical Narrative*, 139–155; Bar-Efrat, *Narrative Art*, 15–16; Yamasaki, *Watching a Biblical Narrative*.

11. I will support this argument with more detail in the following paragraphs.
Jumper was the first to observe honor and shame playing an important role in both 1 Samuel 1–7 (the priestly episode) and 8–31 (the king's episode). Without stating further reasons, he suggests that honor and shame should be employed as a standard of judgment in the divine election of leadership in Israel. However, Jumper's reading, in my view, has a serious flaw in that he interprets 1 Samuel 1–7 as drawing a contrast between Eli and Zadok (rather than between Eli and Samuel). See Jumper, "Honor and Shame," 164–212. I will review his work in further detail shortly.
Long considers the weight (glory) of God as the theological center of the book of Samuel; see Long, *1 and 2 Samuel*, 63–64. Hanley also notices the contrast between Saul and David in their concern to honor YHWH; see Hanley, "Use of Nakedness Imagery," 133–150.

12. It is the point of view from which the narrator judges or evaluate the characters in the story. Sometimes, it is also called the narrator's ideological or evaluative point of view. See Rhoads and Michie, *Mark as Story*, 39–40; Powell, *What Is Narrative Criticism?*; Andersson, *Untamable Texts*, 210–212; Sternberg, *Poetics of Biblical Narrative*, 129–52.

13. Fokkelman, *Reading Biblical Narrative*, 143.

14. Fokkelman offers the suggestion that in order to understand the narrator's value scale, these questions should be asked to clarify the situation: What is the narrator's faith and moral standard? Where is the text's ideological focus? What is his value in pronouncing a judgment? See Fokkelman, 139–155.
Similarly, Bar-Efrat advises that, if a narrative is comprised of the combination of "what" (what is related) and "how" (how this is done), then the point of view centers on the most important "how" factor. See Bar-Efrat, *Narrative Art*, 16.

however, pinpointing the narrator's ideological point of view is not, I would say, a particularly challenging task.

First, we seek to determine the narrator's assessment of the main characters. The main contrast in 1 Samuel 1–7 is between Samuel and Elides.[15] The narrator's attitudes (pro or con) toward Samuel and Eli's household are fairly obvious. For instance, when the narrator calls the sons of Eli בני בליעל in 1 Samuel 2:12 ("sons of without profit"; many rendering it more comprehensibly as "worthless men" or "scoundrels"),[16] he has made clear his resentment pertaining to Eli's sons.[17] In this case, the narrator's value judgment is explicit. Likewise, the narrator's disfavor of Eli can be seen from the directly and indirectly pronounced judgment of God's rejection of his household from the priesthood (1 Sam 2:31–36; 3:12–14). The narrator's portrayal of Eli's eye defect (1 Sam 3:2; 4:15), in its context, is also an implicit tactic to foreground his lack of spiritual vision. In contrast, the narrator's favor of Samuel is without restraint. Samuel is depicted as a servant of the Lord (1 Sam 3:10) who has God's favor and presence (1 Sam 2:26; 3:19). As such, the narrator reveals to us his value scale in viewing the different main characters.

Second, proceeding further, we seek to identify the narrator's ideological point of view,[18] the deeper basis for his standard of judgment. We discover that the ultimate reason that God rejects the Elides is because they have belittled the Lord in their services. Eli is accused of honoring his sons more

---

Brown, in his study of the point of view in Ezra, suggests that both the narrator's intrusions and his portrayal of characterization reflect his point of view. See Brown, "Point of View," 314–329.

15. The Elkanah/Hannah episode, as a prelude, is only preparatory for the Samuel/Eli story to come. The Samuel/Eli story, in turn, prepares for the Saul/David story.

16. The same word is used to describe Saul's opponents who refuse to embrace his reign (1 Sam 10:27). This indicates that Saul is at least temporarily in the narrator's favor at the beginning of his kingship. For a detailed analysis, see Fokkelman, *Reading Biblical Narrative*, 151–153.

17. Eli's sons should be seen as literary foils to the main characters of the story. The blaming finger points to Eli, who, as the father, is at least partly responsible for the corruption of his sons (1 Sam 3:13).

18. The narrator may have different ways to express his points of view. What I seek to establish here is that the centrality of honor and shame is at least one of his means of conveying perspective.

For instance, in Eslinger, "Viewpoints," 61–76, Eslinger argues that the narrator maintains "a steadfast neutrality towards the subject of monarchy" in the presence of many different voices of pro- and anti-monarchic opinions in 1 Samuel 8–12. Polzin believes that in 1 Samuel the author's ideological perspective involves the institution of kingship. See Polzin, *Samuel and the Deuteronomist*, 71–72.

than God (1 Sam 2:29; ותכבד את בניך ממני). The statement is even clearer in the end of the next verse (v. 30): "For those who honor me I will honor, but those who despise me shall be insignificant" (כי מכבדי אכבד ובזי יקלו).[19] Eli's family, unfortunately, belongs to the latter group that despises (בזה) the Lord. Eli's sons are said to treat the Lord's offering with contempt (1 Sam 2:17; נאצו) and to blaspheme (1 Sam 3:13; מקללים) God; thus, the Elides are judged accordingly by the Lord, resulting in their demise. Having said that, it should be noted here that this judgment against the Elides is expressed through God's own words with "absolute validity."[20] Though it directly reflects God's value system, the narrator's point of view in these cases is obviously identical to God's value standard.[21] Anyone who is familiar with the semantics of the Hebrew words just mentioned will realize that we are entering the realm of honor and shame.[22]

The above discussion, in brief, suggests to us an ideological picture in which the Elides shame the Lord through their service and are thus judged with shame.[23] The notion of honor and shame is what motivates God to favor some with honor and judge others with shame. Those who honor God, God will also honor them; those who treat God with light esteem (i.e. those who dishonor God), God will likewise dishonor them. This insight brings us close to the narrator's ideological point of view in 1 Samuel 1–7.

If the Elides are those who dishonor God, who are those who honor him? 1 Samuel 2:35 hints that God will raise up a faithful (נאמן) priest to replace the Elides. In view of the frequent contrast between Samuel and the Elides in 1 Samuel 1–3, readers will understand implicitly that the one who honors

---

19. I consider this the key verse in 1 Samuel in expressing the narrator's ideological point of view.

20. Characterization voiced by God carries "absolute validity." See Bar-Efrat, *Narrative Art*, 54.

21. To apprehend the narrator's ideological point of view is to discover "the norms, values, beliefs, and general worldview that the narrator wants the reader to adopt or reject." See Resseguie, *Narrative Criticism*, 167. The narrator of 1 Samuel, in this case, certainly endorses the value of honoring God to his readers. Likewise, Bar-Efrat affirms that here the author fully identifies with the prophet sent by God. See Bar-Efrat, *Narrative Art*, 84.

22. That is to say, כבד ("to honor"), קלל I ("to be insignificant"), בזה ("to despise") and נאץ ("to have contempt for").

23. Interestingly, Saul seems to fall into the same trap as the Elides in honoring himself above the Lord (1 Sam 15:30; כבדני) and is judged by God.

God is Samuel (contra the Elides who dishonor God),[24] and, accordingly, he will be honored by God. Indeed, Samuel honors God through his humble and faithful services.[25] Consequently, God also honors Samuel by revealing his precious words to him and establishing him as a prophet in Israel.[26] Those who honor God will also be honored.

In 1 Samuel 7, Samuel continues to honor YHWH by erecting a stone monument (7:12) as a reminder of God's miraculous deliverance of the Israelites from the impending threats of the Philistines. The name of the place is thus called "Ebenezer," a conspicuous symbol that reminds the Israelites of a reversal of their previous humiliating defeat in a place with the same name (4:1).[27]

Now, we have come to discover a fuller picture of the narrator's ideological point of view in 1 Samuel 1–7 and the centrality of honor and shame in that point of view. The topic of honor and shame ties the threads together in the narratives.

Then the ark narrative (1 Samuel 4–6) seems to jump out of the box of the narrator's ideological perspective. The ark ostensibly has no direct contrast. At least, this appears to be true at first sight. As a result, source critics often treat this unit as derived from a different source, and, hence, irrelevant to the

---

24. Although Samuel's identity is more than a priest, his priestly position is still prominent (1 Sam 2:18; 7:9; 9:13; 10:8; 16:5). Besides which, Samuel is described as faithful (1 Sam 3:20; נאמן); the same key word נאמן also appears in 1 Samuel 2:35. For discussion of Samuel's identity as a judge, priest and prophet, see Leuchter, *Samuel*.

25. Though less explicitly, Samuel's faithful and humble service can also be seen from some detailed descriptions, e.g. the repetition of הנני (1 Sam 3:4, 6, 8, 16) showing his availability to serve; Samuel *ran* (1 Sam 3:5; וירץ) at Eli's call (though it turned out to be God's call); Samuel opens the temple gate as usual despite a disturbing night (1 Sam 3:15); Samuel leads a national repentance from idolatry (1 Sam 7:3-6). Such characterization (through action and speech) is also a means by which the narrator expresses his own point of view. See Brown, "Point of View," 324–329.

Also relevant here (although not directly God's assessment of Samuel) is the narrator's portrayal of the words a man of God speaks to Eli in 2:29 (ותכבד את בניך ממני) that tacitly put Samuel into the category of honoring God – as well as כי מכבדי אכבד in the following verse. I thank Dr. Tim Undheim for bringing this to my attention.

26. Saul's servant reminds Saul that Samuel, a man of God, is a man honored (1 Sam 9:6; האיש נכבד). Samuel's good reputation must have sufficiently spread to the degree that even Saul's servant is aware of it, though it seems that Samuel's honorable status here is a mixture of honor as conveyed by the community and by God honoring him by fulfilling the words he says ("All that he says surely comes true"; the use of the infinitive absolute בוא יבוא here being emphatic).

27. For more discussion on "Ebenezer" (אבן העזר) and its the significance, see section 4.4.

story of Samuel.²⁸ But, examined more closely, the centrality of honor and shame is still prominent in these chapters. The defeat of the Israelites before the Philistines, despite the coerced presence of the ark of God, is a scandal that ironically reveals the tragedy of the absence of the glory of God, hence the naming of the child of Eli's daughter-in-law "Ichabod" (אי־כבוד).²⁹

With the ark being captured, the Philistines shame the Lord by placing the ark as a trophy in the house of Dagon (the deity of the Philistines). In response, YHWH, the God of Israel, defends his own honor for his own sake. Eventually, Dagon is shamed before YHWH (1 Sam 5:3, 4). The Philistines also suffer severe plagues (1 Sam 5:6–12) under the heavy (1 Sam 5:6, 11; כבד) hand of the Lord and are forced to return the ark to Israel with precious golden guilt offerings to acknowledge and restore YHWH's honor (1 Samuel 6).³⁰ The centrality of honor and shame in the narrator's ideological point of view still works adequately to bring the pieces together.

For the sake of spatial limitation, I choose not to speak here any further on the Hannah episode, which is also permeated with the centrality of honor and shame, as can be shown in my outline. Therefore, the voice of the narrator, utilizing the ideological perspective of honor and shame, ties together all of the narrative plots in 1 Samuel 1–7.

To push further, although not a direct concern of our study of 1 Samuel 1–7, it is very likely that the centrality of honor and shame in the narrator's ideological perspective also extends to the later Saul/David story (1 Samuel 8–31) as well. Initially, King Saul seems to have God's favor (1 Sam 10:6–7; 11:5–15).³¹ However, when he exalts himself over God's commandment through his disobedience in the offering of sacrifices (1 Sam 13:8–13), and the sparing of King Agag's life and his best animals (1 Sam 15:9), God, through the prophet Samuel, pronounces his judgment on him, rejecting Saul from being king of Israel (1 Sam 13:14; 15:28). Yisca Zimran insightfully comments on these actions: "Saul's violation of the order because he prefers to heed the people demonstrates the significance he attaches to the people's attitude and authority over him, and attests that human considerations are more important

---

28. Schulz, "Narrative Art," 122.

29. The exact meaning of this phrase will be discussed later in sections 1.3.3.2 and 5.1.

30. The wordplay of כבד with its different semantic values ("honor or heavy") is obvious. The glory of YHWH is too heavy for them to bear.

31. For more discussion, see Edelman, *King Saul*.

to him than God's authority over him as king."³² It is a tragedy that Saul clings so much to his own prestige that, even in the moment of God's judgment for his disobedience, he pathetically begs Samuel to honor him before all the elders and the people (1 Sam 15:30; כבדני). God thus replaces Saul with David who seeks after God's honor above all,³³ and he establishes him as the new king of Israel. In the end, David is the one being honored as the king of Israel. Again, the perspective of honor and shame permeates the Saul/David story.

After seeing the whole picture, it is clear that the narrator's ideological perspective of honor and shame is consistent throughout the book of 1 Samuel. Just as a reader can read the Deuteronomistic History from the perspective of Deuteronomy, one can also read 1 Samuel from the perspective of honor and shame. From an honor and shame perspective,³⁴ I suggest that the Elides/Samuel episode in 1 Samuel 1–7 serves as a paradigm for the later Saul/David episode. In both places, we have two leaders, one who dishonors God, and one who honors God. The ones who dishonor God are judged with shame and are deposed from their leadership positions, while the ones who honor God are established as leaders. The ones who dishonor God are superseded by those who honor God. The paradigm, as discussed, seems to be plausible. Thus, it motivates us to study 1 Samuel 1–7 with more purpose and significance.

Interestingly, one of the important themes of 1 Samuel is considered to be kingship,³⁵ or, more precisely, the election and rejection of kingship.³⁶ But on what ground does God choose David and reject Saul? Some scholars

---

32. Zimran, "Divine vs. Human Authority," 404.

33. David's utmost concern, in the face of Goliath's challenge, is that God's honor is put at stake when Goliath shames the army of the living God (1 Sam 17:26, 36). As a result, when he volunteers to take on Goliath, he declares publicly that he comes in the name of the Lord and fights for the Lord's honor (1 Sam 17:45–47). The fact that David, while being pursued, spares Saul's life twice when it is at his disposal also suggests that David honors God's commandment even in critical situations (the reason David dares not act against Saul is that he sees him as God's anointed one [1 Sam 24:6; 26:11]). But, of course, we do not deny that David does not meet all the expectations of the ideal king. He also is a person with flaws and shortcomings.

34. The narrator's point of view can be summarized in this key verse, "For those who honor me I will honor, and those who despise me shall be insignificant" (1 Sam 2:29). As the Elides dishonor God in their service, so God rejects them from being priests. In contrast, Samuel honors the Lord in his faithful service, and God honors him exceedingly.

35. Dillard and Longman, *Introduction*, 163; Howard, *Introduction*, 158–165; Arnold, *1 and 2 Samuel*, 35–37; Firth, *1 & 2 Samuel*, 43–45.

36. Dietrich, *Early Monarchy in Israel*, 326; Soggin, *Introduction*, 219. Both consider the election and the rejection of certain people to be one of the fundamental theological problems appearing in 1 Samuel.

express their sympathy for Saul and accuse God of being too harsh on Saul in showing a preference for David.[37] The following comment by Walter Dietrich reflects this concern:

> This sharp contrast between election and rejection that determines the commonly held evaluation of David and Saul does not match the texts of the first book of Samuel. . . . The one is covered in good fortune, whereas the other is burdened with misfortune. The rise of the one seems as unstoppable as the fall of the other. Why does David exude such assurance and Saul such resignation? Is Saul truly so much worse than David? Why does God discriminate against Saul and favor David? Does he reject without reason; is he arbitrary, even cynical?[38]

Though not agreeing with Dietrich's statements, one can affirm that he indeed asks a relevant question: What is the basis of God's election and rejection? As discussed in this dissertation, the concept of honor and shame offers the most plausible criterion for understanding the narrative dynamics of 1 Samuel 1–7.

The above roundabout discussion is not without purpose. I am trying, as much as possible, to explain why I approach 1 Samuel 1–7 from the perspective of honor and shame. It is not so much that I want to choose to work on honor and shame in 1 Samuel 1–7; rather, it is the text and the narrator's perspective of honor and shame that lead us to the study of this topic.

1.2 Honor and Shame Defined

While most contemporary readers may perceive honor and shame as a psychological state reflecting a person's character, the ancient biblical world saw honor as an evaluation of one's identity and social status.[39] It is also a reality that modern readers perhaps have often downplayed the value of reading the biblical text against a backdrop of honor and shame. Honor and shame, as a

---

37. Gunn, *Fate of King Saul*; Exum, *Tragedy and Biblical Narrative*; McKenzie, *King David*; Halpern, *David's Secret Demons*; Tushima, *Fate of Saul's Progeny*; Gilmour, *Representing the Past*, 110.

38. Dietrich, *Early Monarchy in Israel*, 328–329.

39. Pedersen, *Israel*, 213–244. The book of Job portrays how Job's life is woven with honor and shame. Honor is identical with the very being of this man.

binary opposite pair,⁴⁰ are often thought by the Mediterraneanists⁴¹ to be the "pivotal values" of the ancient Mediterranean world.⁴² This theory appears to be true in our analysis of the honor-shame culture in 1 Samuel.

What then are "honor" and "shame"? This is not a simple question to answer. Malina defines honor as "the value of a person in his or her own eyes (that is, one's claim to worth) *plus* that person's value in the eyes of his or her social group."⁴³ This seems to be a good definition, as it involves both the personal and communal acknowledgement of such a value. Indeed, the discussion of honor and shame is often put in a social relationship where the

---

40. The dichotomy of "honor" and "shame," for the most part, seems to be true from Hebrew terms such as כבד (signifying heavy esteem) and קלל I (expressing light esteem), though not every shame term may strictly find its pair with a proximate opposite. The presence of shame/shaming terms is far more pervasive than honor/honoring terms in the Hebrew Bible. For instance, shaming/shame terms may include בוש I ("shame"), חרף II ("taunt"), כלם ("be humiliated"), בזה ("despise") and מאס I ("reject").

I understand that sometimes shame can function as a positive value in a society. For instance, Lapsley points out that shame plays an important positive role in understanding the exiled community. The recognition of Israel's shamed status, as shown in the metaphor of an adulterous woman in Ezekiel 16 and 23, would guide them to a right evaluation of their past shameful practices, orient them to the good and ultimately lead them to a restoration of relationship with YHWH. See Lapsley, "Shame and Self-Knowledge," 143–173. I also talk about the positive function of shame for the post-exilic returnees in Ezra/Nehemiah in a recent article (see Kang, "Positive Role of Shame," 250–265), but the discussion is more about shame as the positive value of a social control, i.e. the value of having a right sense of shame.

41. Those who promote modern anthropological studies about the Mediterranean world, especially honor and shame, can have great influence over our understanding and interpretation of the Scriptures. In other words, the term "Mediterraneanists" (alias "The Context Group") refers to modern scholars of Mediterranean culture who export upon the ancient Mediterranean world interpretations based upon observations within a modern model. My use of this term is consistent throughout this dissertation. For more on the definition of "Mediterraneanist," see section 1.5.

42. See Malina, *New Testament World*, 25–51. Even within the Mediterraneanists, there seem to be diversified opinions concerning how pivotal these values are; for example, they are described as "core (Plevnik)" or "central (Moxnes)" social values of the ancient Mediterranean world. See Botha, "Isaiah 37:21–35," 269; Crook, "Structure versus Agency," 252.

43. See Malina, *New Testament World*, 30. Similarly, Neyrey later refines the definition and clarifies it as "the worth or value of persons both in their own eyes and in the eyes of their village or neighborhood." Neyrey, *Honor and Shame*, 5. The latter, a person's value in the eyes of his/her community, appears to be stronger than the former in community-oriented cultures in many parts of Asia. Malina classifies honor into the categories of "ascribed honor" and "acquired honor" (p. 33–37). Ascribed honor refers to the inherited honor with which one is born, and acquired honor is the honor one acquires throughout his or her life. The latter is more dynamic, as people may win or lose honor over the course of their lives. Similarly, Crook refines the ascribed/acquired honor language to "attributed honor" and "distributed honor." Crook, "Honor," 610.

presence of an audience is noted.[44] Honor, as a positive value, can be associated with the acquisition of wealth, a high position and status, the adherence to good morality, diligence in works, hospitality to visitors, victory in wars, the reception of divine blessings, the bearing of children and having a good name (reputation).[45] Shame, possibly paired binarily with honor, can be defined as a failure to attain such desired values.[46]

1.3 A Review of the Research on Honor and Shame

A review of research concerning honor and shame in Old Testament (OT) studies is necessary for various reasons. First, it prepares us to become familiar with what others have contributed to the topic. Second, it justifies the necessity of our discussed topic of honor and shame in 1 Samuel 1–7. Nevertheless, it should be said that many others have done similar literature reviews. In fact, works of notable scholars on the topic of honor and shame have been extensively and repeatedly reviewed – for instance, the work of Klopfenstein,[47] Betchel,[48] Laniak,[49] and Stiebert.[50] It does not make sense to repeat contributions already made by others. Thus, in my literature reviews, I will, as much as possible, avoid such repetition; instead, I will outline the general picture of past scholarship on honor and shame and focus more on the research most relevant to my topic. Hence, the following discussion is organized in this

---

44. For instance, Daube points out that Deuteronomy 25:5–10 is an implicit law code where the punishment for the unfaithful brother who refuses to fulfill the obligation of levirate marriage consists of the public degradation of spitting and the loosing of his sandal. Many of the other shame-provoking scenarios Daube notes in Deuteronomy also involve the presence of an audience within the community. See Daube, "Culture of Deuteronomy," 995–1013. Stiebert, while seeing shame as primarily a "negative self-evaluation," also believes the presence of an audience is a frequent catalyst of shame. See Stiebert, "Shame and Prophecy," 256–257.

45. Pedersen, *Israel*, 213–244.

46. Stiebert, "Shame and Prophecy," 257. Similarly, Bechtel, "Shame as a Sanction," 49.

47. See reviews in Huber, "Biblical Experience," 24–29; Stiebert, *Construction of Shame*, 44–50; Jumper, "Honor and Shame," 11–12; Kasle, "Analysis," 18–20.

48. See reviews in Jumper, "Honor and Shame," 14–16; Kasle, "Analysis," 21–25.
Betchel's last name first appears as "Huber" (Lyn Betchel Huber) in her dissertation in 1983; however, she consistently uses "Betchel" in all her later publications. See Bechtel, "Perception of Shame"; Bechtel, "What if Dinah," 19–36. Thus, I will refer to her last name as Betchel throughout this dissertation.

49. See reviews in Jumper, "Honor and Shame," 25–27; Kasle, "Analysis," 37–39.

50. See reviews in Jumper, "Honor and Shame," 33–36; Kasle, "Analysis," 25–28; Wu, *Honor, Shame, and Guilt*, 52.

order: (1) An introduction of honor and shame related to the Old Testament in general will be briefly reviewed. (2) Literature related to honor and shame in Deuteronomistic History will be examined.[51] (3) Literature related to the book of First Samuel will be discussed in further details.

1.3.1 A survey related to Old Testament in general

The study of honor and shame in biblical studies is not confined to the realm of the Old Testament. As a matter of fact, scholars studying the New Testament initially spearheaded the research, partly due to the effort of the Mediterraneanists. As a result, a wide range of books[52] and journal articles[53] have contributed to the study of honor and shame in the New Testament. Gradually, scholars studying the Old Testament have also begun to utilize honor and shame as a heuristic tool[54] or a framework of interpretation[55] in biblical studies. Now we shall turn to the trajectory of its development in Old Testament studies.

Johannes Pedersen, in his book *Israel, Its Life and Culture*,[56] has lit the spark of interest in employing honor and shame in biblical studies. Nevertheless, succeeding scholars have adopted different approaches in their studies of honor and shame. As far as we can summarize, there are cultural, semantic, psychological, anthropological, covenantal and canonical approaches.[57] I

---

51. The reason to incorporate Deuteronomistic History into our discussion is because the book of First Samuel is often regarded as part of the Deuteronomistic History. For more information on the hypothesis of Deuteronomistic History and its relationship to 1 Samuel, see Noth, *Deuteronomistic History*; Polzin, *Samuel and the Deuteronomist*; Auld, *Samuel at the Threshold*.

52. Among many others, see Duff, "Honor or Shame"; deSilva, *Despising Shame*; deSilva, *Bearing Christ's Reproach*; deSilva, *Hope of Glory*; Neyrey, *Honor and Shame*; Campbell, *Honor*; Jewett, *Saint Paul Returns*; Lendon, *Empire of Honour*; Elliott, *Conflict, Community, and Honor*; Levasheff, "Jesus of Nazareth."

53. For instance, Marshall, "Metaphor of Social Shame," 302–317; Corrigan, "Paul's Shame," 22–27; Moxnes, "Honor and Righteousness," 61–77; Daley, "Position and Patronage," 529–553; McVann, "Reading Mark Ritually," 179–198; Neyrey, "Despising the Shame," 113–137; Landry, "Honor Restored," 287–309; Hellerman, "Challenging the Authority," 213–228; Lawrence, "For Truly," 687–702; Daniels, "Engendering Gossip," 171–179.

54. Downing, "'Honor' among Exegetes," 53–73; Mahlangu, "Ancient Mediterranean Values," 85–100; Mbuvi, "Ancient Mediterranean Values," 752–768.

55. Simkins, "Return to Yahweh," 52; Botha, "Honour and Shame," 392–403.

56. Pedersen, *Israel*, 213–244.

57. These categories of approaches may not be coined by the authors in their writings; nevertheless, I use such terms for the convenience of our discussion (of course, they also reflect my own evaluations), and they should not be understood rigidly, as authors may use multiple

will follow this sequence in my brief survey. It should be noted that I rely, for my materials, on books *and* journal articles,[58] which are equally important in informing us about the broad landscape of past research on honor and shame in the Old Testament.

1.3.1.1 Cultural approach

The aforementioned Johannes Pedersen was the first one to study the cultural concept of honor and shame as it relates to the Old Testament. He thinks honor is equal to the soul's weight, filled with the "heaviness" of blessing, prosperity, wealth and strength, whereas shame is the opposite, a lack of "heaviness," the emptying of the soul (making it inferior) through defeat, misfortune and reproach. In the book of Job, Job is a character who portrays the change of honor and shame in his life. Pedersen believes a person with honor is harmonious with God and their community, but a shamed person is rejected, humiliated and derided by others. One other who follows Pedersen's footsteps is D. Daube. In his short yet important article "The Culture of Deuteronomy," he proposes that there are strong elements of shame culture in the book of Deuteronomy.[59] I will save his essay for later discussion when I do literature reviews (see section on 1.3.2).

1.3.1.2 Semantic approach

Martin Klopfenstein's *Scham und Schande nach dem Alten Testament* is the first significant work that analyzes three shame related words (בוש, כלם and חפר II) in the Hebrew Bible, exploring the relationship of shame and guilt.[60] He concludes that shame can be defined objectively as a consequence of being guilty and subjectively as an expression of guilt consciousness.[61]

In the article "בוש in the Psalms: Shame or Disappointment?,"[62] Avrahami's investigation of the multi-faceted meaning of בוש is an interesting theory. The

---

approaches in their works.

58. Most scholars have failed to integrate many available journal articles into their contributions.

59. Daube, "Culture of Deuteronomy," 995–1013.

60. Klopfenstein, *Scham and Schande*. Regrettably, this German work has not been translated into English. Sometimes, Klopfenstein's approach is named as "philological," a slightly different and less familiar term. See, Bechtel, "Biblical Experience," 24.

61. See Klopfenstein, *Scham and Schande*, 32–33.

62. Avrahami, "בוש in the Psalms," 295–313.

contention is that בוש I should be translated as "disappointment" rather than "shame" in some of the contexts where it appears in Psalms. Her proposition, interesting as it may be, seems to be not fully convincing.[63] Therefore, Avrahami's challenge against the traditional reading of the meaning of the commonly used word (בוש I) should be treated with caution.

Others who adopt the semantic approach include H. Seebass,[64] J. W. Olley[65] and Jerry Hwang.[66]

1.3.1.3 Psychological approach

Bechtel, in her unpublished dissertation in 1983, "The Biblical Experience of Social Shame/Shaming," explores the significance of shame in the Hebrew Bible. In particular, she analyzes how shame functions as a major behavioral

---

63. Ascribing "disappointment" to the meaning of בוש I in some lament Psalms is partly grounded in Avrahami's speculative study of its synonyms (e.g. ריק in 25:3 and שוב in 6:11 and 70:4) and antonyms (e.g., בקש in 69:7; קרא in 31:18). However, words put together in a sentence are not, by default, synonyms or antonyms. It is, therefore, very inaccurate and problematic for Avrahami to use these terms in such ways. The challenge in reading בוש I as "disappointment" also encounters a serious problem wherein its derived noun בשת in the Psalms is obviously "shame" (often used in parallel with other shaming/shame terms; e.g. Ps 35:26; 44:16; 69:20; 109:29). Her contextual analysis is also not persuasive. In my opinion, the word בוש I in Psalm 71:1, instead of being rendered "be disappointed," can arguably be read "put to shame," since shame is exactly what the psalmist encounters (v. 7), and his prayer is that his enemies, by a reversal of fate, will suffer the same (note חרפה and כלמה in v. 13; בוש I and חפר in v. 24). In Psalm 25:2–3, 20, though not denying the existence of shame, Avrahami proposes that this notion of shame is "consequential"; i.e. shame is the aftermath of disappointment/failure (disappointment/failure leads to shame). Nevertheless, there is no reason to see why the emotion of disappointment has to appear before the existence of shame in the text. Divine and social rejection, first and foremost, leads to shame rather than disappointment. See Bechtel, "Perception of Shame," 82–84. Moreover, if the word בוש I connotes the meaning "disappointment" in some lament Psalms (as Avrahami suggests), such a meaning should be also reflected in its usage in other prose texts in the Old Testament. Unfortunately, Avrahami simply imposes her alternative meanings (against the conventional meaning "be ashamed") for בוש I in some prose texts (e.g. Ezra 8:22 and 2 Sam 19:6) without much explanation. Thus, the argument is hardly convincing. In addition, there seems to be an error in her method of treating יתבששו in Genesis 2:25 as a *hapax*. Whereas certainly the *hitpolel* as a stem for בוש is a *hapax*, it is still from the verb בוש, which arguably preserves the broader lexical semantic of the verb and derived nouns, but in a modified stem – here, the differentiation of verbal voice "being ashamed before one another" (reciprocality being one function of the HtD stem). I am indebted to my mentor Dr. Tim Undheim for this insight.

64. Seebass, "בוש," *TDOT*, 2:50–60.

65. Olley, "Forensic Connotation of *bôš*," 230–234. Olley argues that בוש has a forensic aspect in some contexts rather than the state of "shame."

66. Hwang, "How Long," 684–706. Hwang explores the semantic richness of honor and shame in various kinds of OT poetic laments, as well as penitential prayers in the prose of the post-exilic era.

sanction within the society of ancient Israel – for example, in legal processes, warfare, and diplomacy. On a religious level, shame functions as an important tie between YHWH and his people. On the one hand, Israel felt shamed by God through his divine abandonment; on the other hand, Israel believed it was YHWH's covenantal obligation to protect them from being shamed before their enemies. Shame is not confined to the human sphere; even God can possibly be shamed. Bechtel considers her work as mainly modern psychoanalytic in approach. She recognizes that there is a subtle but distinct difference between guilt and shame. Shame functions best in a group-oriented society whereas guilt in an individual-oriented association.[67]

Stiebert, with her psychological approach (which sees an overlap between shame and guilt and thus deviates from Bechtel's clear distinction between shame and guilt), analyzes the role of shaming/shame in the prophetic texts (esp. Isaiah and Ezekiel). She finds that the Mediterranean honor/shame model is difficult to establish in her study of shame in prophetic literature. Stiebert discovers that shame is often associated with offensive sexual imagery in the Prophets. The context of the exile is important for understanding the depiction of shameful sexuality. She believes that shame emerges as both an outward mechanism of social control and an internalized self-restraining ethical function. Stiebert's discussion of God's susceptibility to shame is also a helpful contribution following Betchel's insight on the subject.[68]

1.3.1.4 Anthropological approach

Another name for this approach is the Mediterranean model.[69] The Mediterraneanists, among other things, believe that honor and shame, as an opposite binary pair, are the pivotal social values of the ancient Mediterranean world. Shane Kirkpatrick, in his book *Competing for Honor: A Social-Scientific Reading of Daniel 1–6*, employs this approach in his research. He contends that the cultural context of honor and shame is important to analyze the tale of Daniel for the second-century BCE Judean audience.[70] Similarly, Timothy S. Laniak utilizes this approach in his fruitful research *Shame and Honor in*

---

67. Huber, "Biblical Experience."
68. Stiebert, *Construction of Shame*.
69. I will evaluate this approach in further detail when I discuss my methodology (see section 1.5).
70. Kirkpatrick, *Competing for Honor*.

the Book of Esther.[71] Scholars who have embraced this approach are many, including Charles Muenchow,[72] Victor H. Matthews,[73] Gale A. Yee,[74] Andrew M. Mbuvi,[75] Leonard P Maré[76] and others.[77]

1.3.1.5 Covenantal approach

Bechtel was probably the first to show great interest in placing honor and shame in the covenantal context.[78] Following her lead, Saul M. Olyan formalizes the specifics of honor and shame in covenant settings.[79] In an unpublished dissertation, Jumper defines this new approach by studying honor and shame in the context of Israel's covenantal relationship with YHWH in Deuteronomy 28 and other covenantal texts, though an important chapter of his dissertation (ch. 2) is also devoted to semantic studies.[80] Jumper's work is particularly important in relation to my research topic. Thus, I will evaluate his work twice (but from different perspectives) in my later literature reviews concerning Deuteronomistic History and the book of 1 Samuel.

1.3.1.6 Canonical theology approach

Daniel Wu analyzes the relationship of honor, shame and guilt in the book of Ezekiel. Accordingly, he scrutinizes three important Hebrew words, בוש, כבד and עוה,[81] and shows how these concepts are integrated for a better

---

71. Laniak, *Shame and Honor*. I will comment more on this book later, when introducing social-scientific criticism.
72. Muenchow, "Dust and Dirt," 597–611. Muenchow argues that dust and dirt reflect shame in the context of Job 42:6.
73. Matthews, "Honor and Shame," 97–112.
74. Yee, *Poor Banished Children*.
75. Mbuvi, "Ancient Mediterranean Values," 752–768.
76. Maré, "Honour and Shame," 1–12.
77. For example, Bergant, "My Beloved," 23–40; Simkins, "Return to Yahweh," 41–54.
78. Bechtel, "Perception of Shame," 79–92.
79. Olyan, "Honor," 201–228
80. Jumper, "Honor and Shame."
81. The word עוה, broadly speaking, can be understood as the "focal point of the concept sphere associated with 'guilt'" (p. 132) due to its frequent association with priestly conceptions of defilement in Ezekiel. While עוה (as a verb) has the most basic physical concept of "to bend/twist/distort," the concept "twisting" leads naturally to "sin/iniquity/offense" (the major use of עוה in the OT). It would be better if Wu could distinguish between the different homonyms of עוה (*HALOT* lists just one verb, עוה, but both BDB and *DCH* list two). BDB identifies עוה I, "to bend, twist" and עוה II, "to commit iniquity, err." *DCH* reverses the homonym designations

understanding of the message. Though often perceived as a social-scientific approach, Wu's work is fundamentally guided by "a judicious use of canonical theology." Indeed, Wu extensively examines themes across the OT as comparative data to reconstruct the cultural conceptions behind the use of בוש, כבד and עוה in Ezekiel.[82] In other words, Wu's analyses of these key terms is set within the context of canonical theology, and Kasle follows suit by naming his approach a "Canonical Theology" approach.[83] Likewise, Kasle's own dissertation in 2019, "An Analysis of the Role of Shaming and Shame in the Tanakh," follows this approach. Her extensive literature review in chapter 1 is extremely helpful. In the main body, she examines the main shame/shaming terms in the whole canonical context; that is, the whole Tanakh has been taken into consideration as she analyzes terms like בוש and כלם. One interesting phenomenon is that she compartmentalizes the "terms of disparagement" (e.g. קלל and מאס) as part of the larger complex of shame/disgrace.[84] Her interactions with other scholars on the analysis of related terms are also valuable and up to date.

The works of Walter Brueggemann and David A. Glatt-Gilad may also be considered as falling within a canonical theology approach.[85]

---

of BDB so that readers can understand clearly which homonym of עוה is linked to "guilt" (according to BDB, it is עוה II). Wu argues that עוה can also possibly have other meanings of "to bear/bear responsibility for sin," "debt" or "punishment" in the OT. עוה, with the meaning "sin," can be viewed as a legal "breach of covenant terms" against YHWH, leading to "culpability for judgment" due to a rejection of YHWH, expressed as a breach in the covenantal relationship. Wu also believes that עוה, as a term associated with "guilt," can potentially connote shame (it spans both guilt and shame concepts). Admittedly, none of the three occurrences of עוה (as a noun) in Ezekiel 21:32 falls under the category of guilt language in Ezekiel. The appearances of עוה there can only mean "ruin" – the destruction of Jerusalem (a more metaphorical use of "distorting"). Wu also notices the presence of other guilt-related terms in Ezekiel, i.e. חטא, אשם, פשע. For further details, see Wu, *Honor, Shame, and Guilt*, 132–167.

82. Wu, *Honor, Shame, and Guilt*, 63.
83. Kasle, "Analysis," 34.
84. Kasle, 78.
85. Brueggemann, *Ichabod toward Home*; Glatt-Gilad, "Yahweh's Honor at Stake," 63–74. From a canonical perspective, Brueggemann interacts extensively with other relevant texts in Psalms, Ezekiel, Jeremiah, Deutero-Isaiah and Lamentations as supporting references for his discussion of the topic. I will review this work shortly. Glatt-Gilad explores the theme of YHWH acting for the sake of his reputation in the face of Israel's adversaries in a large variety of biblical texts (Psalms, Deut 32, Deutero-Isaiah and Ezekiel). The conception of Israel's military successes or failures reflects the power or impotence of their God. YHWH is concerned with his own honor in the eyes of the nations. As such, YHWH's decision to act/save is often derived from his concern for the sake of his reputation. Israel's fortunes are tied to God's manifestation of his "name."

Though not all works concerning honor and shame can rigidly fit into the above-mentioned categories, they are still helpful categories for succinctly summarizing past scholarship on the topic of honor and shame in the Old Testament. Next, we shall move to the literature reviews which I consider important to my topic, and I will discuss them in greater detail.

1.3.2 Literature reviews related to Deuteronomistic History

1.3.2.1 D. Daube: "The Culture of Deuteronomy"

In this short article, published in 1969,[86] Daube, proposes that the book of Deuteronomy contains some strong elements of shame culture.[87] He argues that such a shame culture may be affiliated, in a general sense, with wisdom literature,[88] which often teaches people how to attain honor and avoid disgrace.

Daube suggests that many passages in the Deuteronomic code should be understood from the embedded culture of shame. Shame-provoking scenarios include the proclamation in a war context that any man who is fearful and faint-hearted is permitted to return to his house (Deut 20:8);[89] the warning against "hiding yourself" (Deut 22:1, 3, 4);[90] the charge by the groom against the bride pertaining to her virginity (Deut 22:13–21);[91] the command to exclude eunuchs and Ammonites, Moabites and Edomites from "the assembly of the Lord"; the phrase "nakedness of a thing" in relation to camp hygiene and remarriage (Deut 22:14; 24:1); the rule regarding leprosy (Deut 24:8); the command to remain outside while collecting the pledge when making a

---

86. Daube, "Culture of Deuteronomy," 995–1013.

87. This is not to deny that the culture of guilt may be dominant in Deuteronomy. But one cannot accurately interpret the theological message of the book without treating both guilt and shame culture as an admixed whole. See Daube, 996.

88. Daube, 1013.

89. Anyone who slips away from the battlefield is prone to the infliction of shame. See Daube, 996.

90. Unwillingness to see and be seen involves a shame aspect. See Daube, 997.

91. The whole incident centers on the reputation of the woman and her insulted family. If the charge proves to be wrong, the man shall be fined to restore the honor of the woman and her father's house. If the charge succeeds, the bride shall be stoned to death at the door of her father's house to do away with the public dishonor for such a shameful thing in the house where she once lived. See Daube, 997–998.

loan (Deut 24:10);[92] the warning against beating the wrongdoer more than is exacted (Deut 25:3); a woman's seizing of a man's genitals in fighting (Deut 25:11–12); the treating of parents with contempt (Deut 27:16); and others. Among all these shame related uses of language, Daube thinks the only law in the whole Pentateuch with a punishment consisting of public degradation is the law concerning levirate marriage (Deut 25: 5–10).[93] Some precepts – for instance, "thou/he cannot do so-and-so"[94] and "if there be found"[95] – also appeal to shame. God's concern for his own name in his relationship with Israel (Deut 9:27–29) is also considered an appeal to shame.[96]

Some of the above-mentioned scenarios are uniquely Deuteronomic – that is, no other parallels are found outside Deuteronomy. The conclusion is that the editor of Deuteronomy is perhaps more perceptive of the "shame-cultural bias."[97] Unfortunately, Daube does not state if such a shame culture "bias" is also explicit in the Deuteronomistic History.

Daube's research of the shame culture in Deuteronomy is extensive in its scope, though he does not cover every subject in depth. But, as a pioneer, he has brought up an important topic for future biblical scholarship. Indeed, Daube's topic of the shame culture in Deuteronomy has paved the way for Bechtel's[98] and Jumper's[99] fruitful research.

---

92. If the creditor steps inside the home, it will incur dishonor for the debtor. See Daube, 1000.

93. If two brothers live together and one dies, the other survivor is obligated to marry the widow of the deceased in order to carry on his name. If he does not take up the responsibility in front of all the elders of the city, the widow will come forward and spit on his face and pull off his sandal. Then he will be subject to the shame of perpetual infamy: "The house of him who had his sandal pulled off." See Daube, 1001–1002.

94. Daube argues this is different from "thou shalt not" or "he shall not," though commonly treated by scholars as identical. The difference is that "thou/he cannot do so-and-so" (Deut 12:17; 16:5; 17:15; 21:16; 22:3; 22:19; 24:4) refers to customs and beliefs of the society, not the cultic law. See Daube, 1006–7.

95. Such a phrase emphasizes the fearfulness of being seen in the eyes of the beholder – God above all. See Daube, 1007–1012.

96. Daube, 1013.

97. Daube, 1009.

98. Among many other topics, Bechtel analyzes shame as a sanction of social control in biblical Israel. See Bechtel, "Shame as a Sanction," 47–76.

99. Jumper touches on the topic of honor and shame in the Deuteronomic covenant; we will review his work shortly.

1.3.2.2 *Ken Stone:* Sex, Honor and Power in the Deuteronomistic History

As the title may suggest, the book by itself is not a study about honor and shame. Rather, Stone examines the sexual practices in the Deuteronomistic History within the social and cultural ideology of gender, honor and power. In other words, the analysis of sexual activity cannot be isolated from all other important features of the story, such as gender, honor and power. Honor and shame have only been used as a heuristic lens to uncover the issues around sex and gender.[100] Stone's main thesis is that male and female sexual activity in the biblical narratives functions primarily for the interest of the male-male struggle for honor and power.[101]

The first chapter is devoted to a list of literature reviews pertaining to past research on the topic of sex and culture in biblical narratives. Chapters 2 and 3 handle the methodology. Stone thinks a single methodological approach, whether purely literary or a social-scientific approach, is not adequate enough to offer an interpretation of sexual practices in biblical narratives. Thus, an integration of an anthropological framework and a narratological method[102] will facilitate a better reading. In chapter 4, going into the core of his argument, he analyzes the details of six selected texts concerning sexual activity within the Deuteronomistic History in light of the previous methodological discussions.[103] Stone's approach offers a fresh but sometimes questionable reading of these texts. Taking Judges 19 for example, the violent treatment of the Levite's concubine is bizarre, and scholars tend to treat this problem with an emphasis on the "hospitality protocol."[104] Stone, however, utilizes Mediterranean honor and shame as a heuristic model to address the question. In such a lens, the men of Gibeah's homosexual desire toward the Levite

---

100. Stone, *Sex, Honor and Power*, 42.

101. Stone, 135–136. Sexual acts are often initiated by men and evaluated in the opinions of the male characters. The narrator is concerned about sexual activity because of the possible consequences it may bring to the relationships between men.

102. Stone adopts Mieke Bal's narratological method (see Bal, *Narratology*), connecting literary analysis with the interest of cultural context. Stone, 50.

103. The six texts include the story of the Levite and his concubine in Judges 19; Ishbaal's challenge of Abner over Rizpah (his father's concubine) in 2 Samuel 3:6–11; the David and Bathsheba episode in 2 Samuel 11–12; Amnon's rape of Tamar in 2 Samuel 13; Absalom's sexual relations with David's concubines in 2 Samuel 16:20–23; and Adonijah's failed attempt to acquire Abishag (the virgin maid for David) in 1 Kings 2.

104. Stone, "Gender and Homosexuality," 88.

is interpreted as their challenge over his masculinity and honor. Instead, the Levite offers his concubine as a substitute to buffer such an offense.[105] Eventually, the Levite's call for retaliation has little to do with the welfare of the woman (her body was cruelly cut up into twelve pieces), but instead, the restoration of his own honor.[106] In this way, the story is illuminated by the play of honor and power behind the scenes.

Stone's insightful analyses open a fresh cultural perspective on honor and shame that penetrates into many of the sex-related texts. It should be noted that most of Stone's studied texts are found in 2 Samuel, which shows us, to say the least, that the book of Samuel is a book replete with strong elements of honor and shame.[107] However, since Stone's research is built up, to a certain degree, on the anthropological model, one still needs to be cautious in evaluating the data acquired.[108]

1.3.2.3 James N. Jumper: Honor and shame in the Deuteronomic covenant

In the unpublished dissertation "Honor and Shame in the Deuteronomic Covenant and the Deuteronomistic Presentation of the Davidic Covenant," Jumper explores the relationship between the notion of honor and shame and the Israelite covenant. His main thesis is that honor and shame are pivotal to understanding Israel's covenantal relationship with YHWH in Deuteronomy 28 and 2 Samuel 7.[109] To be more specific, with regard to Deuteronomy 28, honor is portrayed as corresponding to Israel's high status of military power and economic prosperity among the nations, whereas shame is depicted as the loss of such a pre-eminent status and also the loss of social existence. To support his argument, Jumper devotes a whole chapter (ch. 2) to analyze the semantics of honor and shame in the whole Hebrew Bible. He divides the semantics of honor and shame into categories of importance and unimportance,

---

105. The men of Gibeah accept this woman (who belongs to the Levite) but not the host's virgin daughter, as they do not intend to offend the host's honor. By raping the Levite's concubine, they implicitly challenged the Levite's honor. See Stone, 100.

106. Stone, 101.

107. There is doubt whether the assumed patterns about sexual practices mentioned conform to a "Deuteronomistic" perspective. See Stone, 144.

108. I will address the limitations of the anthropological model in the methodology (see section 1.5).

109. Jumper, "Honor and Shame," iii.

lofty and low, making a great or valuable name for oneself and other miscellaneous "shame" vocabulary. Jumper's study finds that honor and shame seem to be binary social values, as claimed by Mediterraneanists.

To continue, Jumper contends that blessings and curses in Deuteronomy 28 should be seen as expressions of Deuteronomic covenantal honor and shame. If Israel honors YHWH through its obedience to the covenant, the Lord will bless Israel with a place of honor (economic and military superiority) among the nations for its loyalty. On the contrary, if Israel fails to abide by the stipulations of the covenant, Israel will be shamed by YHWH through the diminishment of her status (loss of economic and military strength) among the nations.[110] Israel is bound to YHWH by an "honor-for-honor/shame-for-shame" exchange pattern based on Israel's covenantal loyalty.[111] Jumper's study also finds that, despite Israel's possible adoption of patterns of other Near Eastern treaties, the Israel-YHWH covenant in Deuteronomy 28 remains uniquely Israelite.[112]

The rest of Jumper's dissertation focuses on the discussion of shame and honor in the Deuteronomistic conception of the Davidic covenant,[113] but I will save most of it for later discussion in my literature reviews relating to scholarship on 1 Samuel (see section 1.3.3). The Davidic covenant in 2 Samuel 7, central to the Deuteronomistic History, reflects the Deuteronomistic value of honor and shame. While it is conventional to see 2 Samuel 7 as a covenant relationship between David and YHWH, it is strange that Jumper even includes Zadok as part of the Davidic covenant. This is clearly reflected in his summary statement in the abstract: "With regard to the [sic] 2 Samuel 7, we argue YHWH honors David and Zadok with eternal royal and priestly positions."[114] The problem is Zadok's name does not even occur in the Davidic covenant in 2 Samuel 7, neither does Jumper mention his name in the analysis of it.

In summation, Jumper's research is historical inasmuch as he ventures into a terrain that integrates honor and shame with Israel's covenant. His

---

110. Jumper, 133–134.

111. Jumper, 133–134.

112. In comparison with other ancient Hittite and Assyrian treaties, an accentuation of the vassal's (Israel's) wellbeing and blessing is emphasized. See Jumper, 132–133.

113. Jumper holds the view that the Davidic covenant in 2 Samuel 7 is integral to Deuteronomistic History. See Jumper, 214.

114. Jumper, iii.

semantic study of honor and shame offers a fresh perspective to perceive honor and shame terms in ancient Israel. Nevertheless, Jumper's presentation of the Deuteronomistic conception of the Davidic covenant raises questions and criticisms that need to be answered.

1.3.3 Literature reviews related to the book of First Samuel

1.3.3.1 Gary Stansell: "Honor and Shame in the David Narratives"

Gary Stansell's article seeks to apply the cultural values of honor and shame favored by the Mediterraneanist to the David narratives and investigates the trajectory of honor and shame in David's life. Stansell seeks to demonstrate that honor and shame are significant in understanding David's rise to power, his friendship with Jonathan, his family life and his political career. However, it should be said that Stansell does not limit his discussion to 1 Samuel but extends it to 2 Samuel and 1 Kings 1–2 since it is a thematic approach, covering both the period of the history of David's rise and the succession narrative.[115]

At the outset, David started as a shepherd boy, a person of no honor and significance, and was later promoted to Saul's son-in-law, a higher status of honor.[116] Stansell contends that the challenge-response pattern is essential to understanding the narrative in 1 Samuel 25. On the one hand, David's response of seeking revenge against Nabal is an attempt to remove the shame David suffered when he was rejected by Nabal in his collection of gifts (seen as a challenge to Nabal). On the other hand, Abigail's response to David's challenge of revenge was to act as a mediator between the two disputing parties.[117] Eventually, David married Abigail, a woman of wisdom, and thus gained additional honor through such a marriage. Likewise, the challenge-response pattern can be seen through David's marriage relationship with Michal, the daughter of Saul.

To continue, Stansell shows that honor and shame play important roles in two of the political contexts: the disgrace of having David's messengers' beards shaved and David's risk of bringing dishonor to his troops in his

---

115. See Stansell, "Honor and Shame." This was one of the contributed articles to *Semeia 68* in which scholars attempted to integrate social-scientific method and biblical studies to examine the biblical concept of honor and shame.

116. Stansell, "Honor and Shame," 57–59.

117. Stansell, 61–65.

grievous lamentation over Absalom's death.[118] At last, David's own family is tainted with the shameful acts of rape and incest.[119]

Stansell contends that the honor and shame theme plays a significant role in David's ascent to power. David, though at the beginning a person of no honor, seeks and gains honor on the way to the position of highest honor in Israel.[120] Honor and shame also entangle David's relationships in his marriages, his family, his friendships and his reign.

To sum up, one can say that Stansell's work provides "valuable insights to the application of the Mediterranean model" to these Davidic narrative texts.[121] Stansell's strength is also found in his analysis of many Hebrew terms communicating honor and shame (e.g. the wordplay between כבד, "honor" and, קלל I, "to be insignificant," and באש, "stink") in these narratives. However, the limitation of Stansell's work can be seen in that he offers no discussion, even briefly, pertaining to the rest of themes of honor and shame in the book of Samuel.

1.3.3.2 Walter Brueggemann: Shame and honor in the ark narrative

The next person that touches on the topic of honor and shame in 1 Samuel is Walter Brueggemann in his book *Ichabod toward Home: The Journey of God's Glory*.[122] This is an interesting book that focuses on the ark narrative in

---

118. Stansell, 68–70.

119. Stansell, 70–73. For instance, Amnon's rape of Tamar and Absalom's sexual relationship with David's concubines.

120. Stansell, 73.

121. Kasle, "Analysis," 20.

122. The term Ichabod is taken from 1 Samuel 4:21 where the name is given to the newborn child by Eli's dying daughter-in-law to commemorate the tragedy of the capture of the ark. The Hebrew, אי־כבוד, possibly means "Where is the glory?" (Brueggemann supports this reading; *Ichabod toward Home*, 8). Alternatively, it could be אי IV "woe" according to the LXX Οὐαὶ βαρχαβωθ ("Woe, Barchabod") or Ουαι χαβωθ ("Woe, the Chabod" = "Woe, the Glory") in Codex Alexandrinus – as in Ecclesiastes 10:16, אי לך ארץ, "Woe to you, O Earth." Reading it this way, it would fit the language of the *qinah* (funeral dirge). Alternatively, the component אי could be אי III for the translation ("no glory," meaning glory no longer exists in Israel). BDB (p. 33) reads the child's name as "inglorious." *HALOT*'s preferred interpretation seems to be אֲחִי/אֲבִיכָבוֹד, "the father (brother) is honour" with the alternative "Where is the honour?" (*HALOT* 1, 39). Ges[18] (p. 46) suggests that איכבד could be a pejorative version of יוכבד because of Ιωχαβηδ in LXX 1 Reg 14:3.

1 Samuel 4–6,[123] particularly the journey of God's glory in these chapters. In the first chapter, "Ichabod Departed," Brueggemann acknowledges that the ark narrative is a tale of loss. He comments, "The narrative moves, sentence by sentence, deep into loss, clear to the bottom of loss, as far as the narrative is able to imagine loss."[124] This "descent into loss" can be seen in Israel's loss in battle against the Philistines. More importantly, this loss can be explained in the captivity of the ark of the covenant. The gravity of this loss can be found in the capture of the ark being reported as many as five times by the end of 1 Samuel 4. Brueggemann argues that it was not just Israel's loss but YHWH's: "It is YHWH who has been shamed and humiliated, and who has lost credence."[125] The question of God's vulnerability to shame is brought up. He also contends that the loss in battle is not simply a consequence of Israel's guilt and disobedience against the Lord. In the second critical defeat against the Philistines, the loss is hard to explain in terms of guilt because "the loss has broken well beyond any thinkable guilt."[126]

In the second chapter, "Joy Comes in the Morning," the God of Israel, exiled in humiliation, paradoxically mocks the god of the Philistines through his mighty works of bringing Dagon down to YHWH's feet. The purpose is to prove who the true God is, and who is the fake one. The Lord, out of concern for his own reputation,[127] acts to fight against Dagon, the god of the Philistines. Such an act is not even grounded in God's covenantal obligation with Israel,[128] but out of his own free will and the concern for his own honor in front of other gods. YHWH is a "glory-seeking, glory-getting God."[129] Ironically, the hand of the Lord was so "heavy" that the Philistines could not take its burden but cried for help due to the existing plagues in their midst. Brueggemann has duly noted the wordplay of the root כבד in these texts:

---

123. Jumper also talks briefly about the "Deuteronomic honor and shame" within the ark narrative. In his view, honor and shame is discussed in the context of the covenantal blessings and curses. See Jumper, "Shame and Honor," 147–155.
124. Brueggemann, *Ichabod toward Home*, 2.
125. Brueggemann, 9.
126. Brueggemann, 22.
127. Brueggemann, 48.
128. Brueggemann, 47.
129. Brueggemann, 39.

YHWH's exiled glory (*kabod*) is inseparable from the heaviness (*kabod*; 1 Sam 5:6, 11) of the disasters.

The Lord showed his primacy over the god of the Philistines by cutting off Dagon's hands and head. Eventually, the God of Israel will regain his glory. Accordingly, the shamed Israel will also be restored due to its attached covenantal relationship with YHWH. In the third chapter, "Kabod Homeward," Brueggemann depicts the journey of God's glory back to Israel from the land of the Philistines. The Philistines had to offer golden items as guilt offerings to acknowledge the glory (כבוד) of the God of Israel so that he would lighten (קלל) his hands from them. The God of Israel was exalted as the ark of the Lord was triumphantly transported back to Israel. In the end, the destination of the ark of the Lord was Jerusalem, the city of David (2 Sam 6:12). From the departure of glory to the return of glory, the journey shows YHWH's sovereignty and dominion in the midst of chaos, defeat, despair, shame, hope, joy and honor.

Of course, Brueggemann's focus is not just on the ark narrative per se; his larger concern is how the Christian church as a whole should respond to the texts. Thus, in the next two chapters, he attempts to challenge the church to reflect upon Western culture, dominated by reason and rationality. Brueggemann criticizes the modern dominant culture that puts emphasis on self-indulgence, narcissism and self-sufficiency. One can say this is not a book just about biblical theology but an exercise in social criticism.[130] If the ark narrative is a "guerrilla theater,"[131] then it will have its subversive attack upon the lives of God's people.

Several comments can be made concerning Brueggemann's work. First, Brueggemann makes a unique contribution in reading the ark narrative from a social-literary perspective. His sensitivity to the purview of honor and shame in the ancient Near East brings fresh perspectives for reading the story. However, Brueggemann's work is more like a theological reflection of the ark narrative than a conventional exegetical piece of work, as he spends the last two chapters on contemplating Christian issues. No wonder Robert Gnuse, in his review of the book, calls it "a poetic sermon cast in the form of

---

130. Brueggemann, 22.
131. Brueggemann, 115.

exegetical exposition."¹³² Indeed, Brueggemann's interaction with other contemporary scholars on related topics is surprisingly scarce. This is intentional, as he wants to resist the traditional criticism of "history, reasonableness, or doctrinal consensus."¹³³ Of course, there is nothing wrong about his approach. Brueggemann is known for such a creative and iconoclastic style of writing. But such a choice may result in a lack of length and depth for a critical treatment of the texts. Brueggemann does note that shame and honor functions as an important theme in the ark narrative (and even in 1 Samuel 1–6), but how important such a theme is or how it is further connected to the message of the rest of the book are issues that are left unaddressed.

Second, Brueggemann's broad scope in intertextual reading also comes with "freshness of imagination." Throughout the book, he dialogues extensively with other parallel texts in the Old Testament, particularly Psalms, Ezekiel, Deutero-Isaiah and Lamentations. The exile of the ark among the Philistines is paralleled to the Israelite exilic experience after 586 BCE. Interestingly, most of the quotes are references to exilic texts.¹³⁴ This raises the question of whether it is appropriate to draw comparisons between the quoted texts and the ark narrative and its context.

1.3.3.3 James N. Jumper: Honor and shame in the Hannah-Eli episode and in the houses of Saul and David

Though Jumper's main focus in his dissertation is honor and shame in the Deuteronomic covenant (Deuteronomy 28), as I have briefly reviewed, he does spend some time discussing the Deuteronomistic presentation of the covenant. The book of 1 Samuel, which is often considered to be part of the Deuteronomistic History, reflects the value of Deuteronomic honor and shame. In the fourth chapter, "Shame and Everlasting Honor in Deuteronomistic Conception of the Davidic Covenant," Jumper covers a broad range of texts (1 Samuel, 2 Samuel 7, 1 Chronicle 17 and Psalm 89) to explicate how honor and shame relate to the Deuteronomistic presentation of the Davidic covenant.¹³⁵ Nevertheless, it is honor and shame in the

---

132. Gnuse, review of *Ichabod toward Home*, 104.
133. Brueggemann, *Ichabod toward Home*, 89.
134. Firth, review of *Ichabod toward Home*, 254.
135. Jumper, "Shame and Honor," 165.

Hannah-Eli episode and in the houses of Saul and David that we are going to review here.

Jumper argues that the Deuteronomist tries to legitimize the shifting of power from the northern priestly and royal houses (Eli and Saul) to the southern ones (Zadok and David) in view of the Davidic covenant (2 Samuel 7).[136] The standard of evaluation for such a change of status can be seen in whether or not these powers publicly honor YHWH in the cult.[137] In his view, the reason that the northern centers of power lose their distinguished position is because they have treated the Lord with "low regard." The Song of Hannah, according to Jumper, adumbrates a loss of the status of the northern priestly and royal houses.[138] Jumper argues two important things in this song: (1) The focus of the song is about the exchange of honor (2:3–8) between those in high and low positions, bracketed with the glory of YHWH in its structure. (2) The obvious "anachronisms" concerning the exaltation of the king in 2:10 should be understood as "a type of foretelling of what was to come for all of the major characters of the book."[139] Thus, the Song of Hannah can be said to play a proleptic function and to set up the contrast between the main characters noted in the story: Hannah, Eli/Zadok and on to Saul/David.[140]

Furthermore, the attitude of dishonoring God also reflects a person's character (informally expressed as "heart"); such an attitude of treating YHWH with honor or low regard in 1 Samuel serves as God's criteria of electing leadership in Israel.[141] Hannah's positive character is portrayed as honoring the Lord by giving up her firstborn to the Lord in her vows, and indeed fulfilling her promise by dedicating Samuel her only son to YHWH. In

---

136. Jumper, 166.

137. Jumper, 167.

138. Jumper, 168. The song, by itself, is a contrast between Hannah and her rival Peninnah in their change of fortunes. Hannah's household is to be exalted by the Lord whereas Hannah's rivals are to be judged with lowliness. Yet, one could potentially argue it sets a tone for the unfolding of the rest of the book. The exaltation of Hannah over her rival wife and the increasing ascendancy of her son Samuel could be seen as repeating in the David/Saul story. Peninnah and her "high" position of bearing children could parallel Saul's high status in the sight of men, with Hannah's low position being similar to David's, who was a mere shepherd. The role reversal is experienced by Saul and David as well. I thank Dr. Tim Undheim for this valuable comment.

139. Jumper, 179.

140. Surprisingly, Jumper replaces Samuel with Zadok. I will comment on this issue very shortly.

141. Jumper, 167.

contrast, Eli's negative character is underscored by having "bad eyes," failing to perceive the spiritual reality of his times and belittling the Lord in service (1 Sam 2:29; 3:13).[142] Meanwhile, the houses of Saul and David are put into contrast. Saul – resembling Eli's house in its bad character of dishonoring YHWH – was judged with a diminishment in his "position, progeny, and prosperity."[143] Jumper thinks such a common trait of negative character of the leaders leads to the decline of the northern kingdom. While the men of Israel look on Saul's lofty "height" (outward appearance) for the election of a king, God looks on David's "heart" (inner character). The honor of David and the dishonor of Saul can be clearly seen from the Goliath episode as the two demonstrate dramatic character differences in their concerns for God's honor. Such a theme of contrast accounts for the justification of the decline of Saul's house and the establishment of David's house.[144] The shifting of power and fate and the election of dynasty are tied to their character in the context of honoring or belittling YHWH.

Jumper claims that the Hannah-Eli narrative serves a greater purpose for the later Saul/David narrative: the similar pattern of how God raises the lowly faithful and lowers the unfaithful leader is found in both narratives.[145] However, the foreboding pattern set up in 1 Samuel 1–7 is not the contrast between Eli and Samuel but the contrast between Eli and Zadok. This is clearly testified in Jumper's own words: "What is true of the houses of Eli and Zadok will also be true of the houses of Saul and David."[146]

It is fair to say that Jumper's contribution on the study of honor and shame in 1 Samuel 1–7 is significant and unprecedented. His broad view of seeing the message of the whole book of Samuel through the lens of honor and shame is enlightening. He insightfully proposes that the divine election of leadership and dynasties in the book of Samuel is closely related to the leaders' honoring or not honoring YHWH sufficiently. Having said that, the theory has the following weaknesses: (1) While each individual is evaluated according to their character, and God's election of leadership occurs

---

142. Jumper, 169–178.
143. Jumper, 194–195.
144. Jumper, 200.
145. Jumper, 169.
146. Jumper, 194.

accordingly,[147] it was never confined to any geographical preference. Though historically speaking, the shift of power from the north to the south is true, it was not the intention of the narrator to emphasize such a point. Samuel, the faithful judge, priest and prophet (seer), is from Ramah, in the northern part of Israel. Most of Samuel's ministry also centers around northern cities such as Bethel, Gilgal and Mizpah (1 Sam 7:15). If the shift from north to south is being emphasized, the faithful Samuel, who is a prominent leader from the north, would stand out against the trend. Of course, Jumper trivializes this problem by replacing Samuel with Zadok (a priest of David, thus a southern associate).[148] (2) Jumper's reading of 1 Samuel 2:34–36 as exclusively referring to Zadok is unlikely.[149] In fact, the first occurrence of a clear reference to the priest Zadok is far later in 2 Samuel 8:17. Meanwhile, frequent contrasts between the priest Eli (or his sons) and Samuel in 1 Samuel 1–3 is very obvious.[150] Such contrasts, from both the narrator and readers' point of view, bring the unavoidable conclusion that Samuel is the one being referred to. The allusion of 1 Samuel 2:34–36, in the immediate context of bringing a contrast to the priest Eli, cannot be to anyone other than Samuel,[151] although eventually the Zadokite priests did completely replace Eli's line.

Indeed, God's dishonoring of the Elides and honoring of Samuel is contrasted in 1 Samuel 1–7. But such a contrast of fate is due to the difference between their characters – that is, their attitude of honoring or dishonoring God in their lives. Samuel's attainment of honor is not what Jumper calls a "resultant honoring,"[152] consequentially inheriting from the credits of the mother, faithful Hannah, but is based on Samuel's personal commitment to honoring the Lord in his own service. Jumper himself admits that the divine

---

147. God will raise up one who will do according to what is in his heart and soul (1 Sam 3:35).

148. Because of such a problematic presupposition, Jumper rarely mentions the ministry of Samuel in his analysis of the Hannah-Eli narratives.

149. Jumper, 168.

150. For instance, in 1 Samuel 3, Eli, the old priest whose eyes are dim (such a description of the character also reveals his failure of spiritual perception), is without the word of God; young Samuel, though in his priestly apprenticeship, faithfully serves YHWH and has the word of the Lord revealed (נגלה; v. 21) to him.

151. See, Eslinger, *Kingship of God*, 138–140; Arnold, *1 and 2 Samuel*, 75–76; Leuchter, *Samuel*, 40; Bar-Efrat, *Narrative Art*, 112; Firth, "Play It Again," 8.

152. Jumper, "Shame and Honor," 184.

election of leadership in Israel has a "causal connection"[153] to the character of the leaders of Israel. If Jumper has to read 1 Samuel 2:34–36 as exclusively referring to the priest Zadok, then readers will be left in bewilderment, as Zadok's name is not even mentioned in 1 Samuel, let alone there being any hints of his character. Jumper thus foregrounds Hannah's good character (not Zadok's) as a contrast to the bad character of the priest Eli and his two sons.[154]

In sum, we have noted that Stansell, Brueggemann and Jumper have contributed greatly to the discussion of honor and shame in 1 Samuel from different perspectives. Due to spatial limitation, I have not included the works of Kasle,[155] Olyan,[156] Lemos[157] and Hanley,[158] scholars who have also touched briefly on the topic of honor and shame in 1 Samuel. In light of my focus on 1 Samuel 1–7, I found Brueggemann and Jumper's research to be most beneficial to my study.

1.4 The Justification for This Study

As can be seen, only limited works have been done concerning honor and shame in the book of 1 Samuel, let alone 1 Samuel 1–7. The lack of research on this subject has already shown the justification for someone to pursue further study on such a topic.

In the past, studies of honor and shame terms tended to follow a thematic/systematic approach; that is, a word was selected to analyze its meaning and significance by reviewing its occurrences throughout the Hebrew Bible.[159] In

---

153. Jumper, 194.

154. Jumper, 169–174. Hannah's aforementioned good character may have its potential consequence in the honoring of Samuel her son, but not Zadok, a remote figure. In fact, 1 Samuel 1–7, for the most part, puts Samuel and Eli and his two sons in contrast. The reason that Jumper coercively contrasts Zadok with Eli is probably due to his self-imposed constraint that everything in 1 Samuel must conform to the lens of the Davidic covenant. Zadok, as a priest for David, better fits into the language of God's covenantal favor for the Davidic dynasty than does Samuel.

155. Kasle, "Analysis," 125–132.

156. Olyan talks about honor and shame in covenant settings, with most of his analysis covering texts in 2 Samuel. Nevertheless, he does mention the notions of honor and shame with reference to the death and burial of Saul and his sons in 1 Samuel 31. See Olyan, "Honor," 214–215.

157. Lemos analyzes Nahash the Ammonite's use of mutilation as a shaming tactic against Jabesh-Gilead in a war context in 1 Samuel 11. See Lemos, "Shame and Mutilation," 229–232.

158. Hanley, "Use of Nakedness Imagery," 133–50.

159. See, for instance, Klopfenstein, Jumper and Kasle's work.

this dissertation, the present writer will focus more on the study of honor and shame terminology in their context in Samuel rather than in the whole Hebrew Bible. In other words, I will make room for an inductive approach to a study of these terms.[160] By doing so, I hope to help readers see the uniqueness of some honor and shame terminology in 1 Samuel. For instance, one idiom in 1 Samuel denoting vulgar mocking is to address others as a dog or flea (1 Sam 17:43; 24:14; 26:20). The stigmatized metaphors are used to undermine one's significance and thus trigger shame. In addition, the erection of a monument (1 Sam 15:12) has to do with the proclamation of one's name and reputation; hence, honor is involved behind the scene.

Furthermore, the covenant relationship between YHWH and Israel seems to bind YHWH and Israel together in a mutual "honor-for-honor/shame-for-shame" relationship.[161] But the capture of the ark does not seem to comply with such a conceptual framework. Israel is shamed at her defeat and the ark's capture, but the God of Israel seems to sit tight and displays no care about his subdued people. It appears that YHWH's subsequent action against Dagon and the Philistines has nothing to do with the covenant relationship between YHWH and Israel but displays concern for God's own honor. These topics, along with some other issues, can be part of our investigations. Conversely, the study of honor and shame in 1 Samuel can test the theory of whether honor and shame is really the "pivotal" value in the study of ancient Israel as claimed by the Mediterraneanists.

I propose that honor and shame are central to the narrator's ideological point of view in 1 Samuel.[162] Such an ideological perspective is fundamental to understanding the narrator's presentation of the structure, plot, characterizations and message of the book. The Elides/Samuel and Saul/David episodes seem to demonstrate the same honor and shame pattern in which we see God honoring those who honor him and, likewise, dishonoring those who dishonor him. The perspective of honor and shame can be plausibly connected

---

160. The discussion of honor and shame terminology will be based on their own context in texts selected from 1 Samuel rather than generalized observations from the Old Testament.

161. Jumper, "Shame and Honor," 133–134.

162. The author may have other points of views in mind. For example, Halbertal and Holmes discuss the book of Samuel from a political perspective. See Halbertal and Holmes, *Beginning of Politics*.

to the theological theme (the election and rejection of leadership) of the whole book of 1 Samuel.

This stimulating journey starts with an expectation that a socio-literary study of 1 Samuel 1–7 brings us to a deeper understanding of the text in its broader social-cultural context of honor and shame. As an Asian who is immersed in such a culture of honor and shame, I am, perhaps, in a more advantageous position to recognize such nuances and highlight such a cultural influence over the meaning of the text.

1.5 Research Methodology

The proliferation[163] and interdependence[164] of different interpretive approaches and methodologies make it a very difficult task for one to choose an appropriate method in doing biblical studies. In fact, it is almost impossible for one to study a portion of text with one single approach, isolating the work of other approaches. To simplify the complexity of the problem we are facing, it should be stated at the forefront that I adopt socio-literary criticism for this study.[165] To be more exact, the current study is an amalgamation of socio-cultural and literary-narrative analysis. But of course, this is a statement that requires further explanation.

The goal of this dissertation is to study 1 Samuel 1–7 with a focus on examining the development of honor and shame and understanding how

---

163. For a survey of different approaches, see LeMon and Richards, *Method Matters*; Hasel, *Old Testament Theology*.

164. "The interdependence of the methods . . . connects all of the methodological steps to an over-arching system of correlation." Steck, *Old Testament Exegesis*, 17.

165. Gottwald sees that socio-literary criticism, as an integration of new literary criticism and social scientific criticism, is a response to the limitation of the confession-religious approach and historical-critical approach in studying the Scriptures. See Gottwald, *Hebrew Bible*, 29. I do not side with Gottwald in perceiving *new* literary criticism and social scientific criticism as the two separate components of socio-literary criticism in my application of the method in this dissertation. Rather, a slight modification is that I consider socio-literary criticism as a convergence of literary criticism and social scientific criticism. The reason for this slight change is that the present writer believes that *new* literary criticism may have gone too far in rejecting reference to the author's intention. See Barton, "Reflections on Literary Criticism," 528–529. I actually prefer naming "cultural-literary" as my method of approach (perhaps to avoid the debates of the Mediterraneanist model, whose affinity to social-scientific criticism can be hardly isolated), but that seems to be a new invention of terminology. For the sake of consistency within circles of scholarship and for the readers' benefit, I concede to the use of socio-literary criticism for this dissertation.

it functions in these chapters. Since honor and shame are closely related to the socio-cultural dimension which belongs to the sphere of social-scientific criticism,[166] I will need to spend some time to introduce this methodology for consideration.

Social-scientific criticism is a relatively new player in biblical methodology.[167] John Elliott defines social-scientific criticism as "that phase of the exegetical task which analyzes the social and cultural dimensions of the text and of its environmental context through the utilization of the perspectives, theory, models, and research of the social sciences."[168] In other words, social-scientific criticism seeks to discover the social-cultural perspectives (in Malina's term, "the social system"[169]) of the text in order to facilitate its interpretation. Elliott sees social-scientific criticism as a method that closely ties in with the historical-critical method, literary criticism, rhetorical criticism and, of course, the social-cultural paradigm.[170]

It should be noted that practitioners of social-scientific criticism, since the very beginning of the discipline, have believed that the field research of cultural anthropologists can contribute to an understanding of the biblical concept of honor and shame. This can be clearly gleaned from the works of early pioneers of social-scientific criticism.[171]

Proponents of social-scientific criticism, in particular, are those of the Context Group (so called pan-Mediterraneanists or Mediterraneanists). Their representatives, among many others, are John H. Elliott, Bruce Malina, Jerome H. Neyrey, John J. Pilch and Richard L. Rohrbaugh.[172] Mediterraneanists

---

166. The broader scope of social sciences includes anthropology, sociology, political science and economics, as well as those typical of the humanities. However, social-scientific criticism, in the narrow sense as a biblical methodology, refers to the limited subsection of "cultural anthropology," where the main concern is how the study of the interaction between people influences the interpretation of texts. See Berding, "Hermeneutical Framework," 5.

167. For a recent book that introduces social-scientific criticism and its practice, see Chalcraft, Uhlenbruch, and Watson, *Methods, Theories, Imagination*.

168. Elliot, *What Is Social-Scientific Criticism?*, 37.

169. Malina, "Rhetorical Criticism," 6.

170. Elliot, *What Is Social-Scientific Criticism?*, 7–11.

171. Stiebert has helpfully reviewed some of the pioneers and their works, which include Campbell, *Honour, Family and Patronage*; Peristiany, *Honour and Shame*; Pitt-Rivers, *Fate of Shechem*. See Stiebert, *Construction of Shame*, 14–29.

172. See, for example, Elliott, *Home for the Homeless*; Malina, *New Testament World*; Neyrey, *Social World of Luke-Acts*; Malina and Pilch, *Social Scientific Models*; Rohrbaugh, *Social Sciences*.

argue that honor and shame as binary concepts were the pivotal forces that functioned in the ancient Mediterranean social order. Such a collective social value is in contrast to the values of modern Western individualistic societies. Another thing most Mediterraneanists defend is that honor and shame were closely related to a person's gender identity. In their opinion, men could be said to embody honor and women to embody positive shame.[173] The contest for honor among men occurred through the challenge and riposte pattern and was thereafter evaluated by the "Public Court of Reputation," whereas a woman's honor was defined in the protection of her sexual chastity and modesty.[174] In other words, there was great distinction in the play of honor and shame among males and females in the ancient Mediterranean world. Such propositions of the Mediterraneanists, especially the gender distinction concerning honor and shame, engender many critical responses. Critics usually do not buy into the concept that a woman's value was exclusively based on her sexuality,[175] and our analysis of women's worth in 1 Samuel seems to confirm that women's honor was more complex than such a reduction would imply.

Without denying the contributions proponents of social-scientific criticism have brought into the arena of biblical interpretation, this approach is beset with challenges and doubts within critical scholarship.[176] For example, Kenneth Berding, in his article, "The Hermeneutical Framework of Social-Scientific Criticism: How Much Can Evangelicals Get Involved?,"[177] has addressed a list of limitations or weaknesses of this approach. To name a few of the obvious disagreements: First, the problematic presupposition that "reality is socially interpreted"[178] considers that there is no other lens through which

---

173. In one sense it was understood as modesty, shyness or deference. Moxnes, "Honor and Shame," 21; Peristiany, *Honour and Shame*, 68–69; Malina, *New Testament World*, 48.

174. Rabichev, "Mediterranean Concepts," 53–56.

175. See Crook, "Honor," 591–611; Yee, *Poor Banished Children*, 41–42; Jumper, "Shame and Honor," 44; Stiebert, *Construction of Shame*, 166; Downing, "'Honor' among Exegetes," 58–59. It is not my intention in this dissertation to argue against the Mediterraneanist model.

176. See Wilson, "Reflections," 515–517; Rodd, "On Applying," 29–30; Kirkpatrick, while employing social-scientific criticism in his book *Competing for Honor*, still acknowledges the weaknesses that historical and literary critics have raised against this method. Nevertheless, Kirkpatrick's defense of social-scientific criticism is that it *can* contribute to the biblical interpretation through its richness of "cultural contrast." See Kirkpatrick, *Competing for Honor*, 8–12, 19.

177. Berding, "Hermeneutical Framework," 3–22.

178. Malina, "Bible, Witness, or Warrant," 86. Likewise, Elliott says that "all knowledge is socially conditioned and perspectival in nature." See Elliott, *What Is*, 37.

one can interpret reality; that is, it upholds social-scientific criticism with such a high degree of subjectiveness that it rejects all other approaches.[179] Second, it has a tendency to limit and discourage the presence of supernatural causes in the biblical world, since divine intervention disturbs the sociological analysis as a horizontal social order. Third, it assumes that the culture of the ancient Near East is very similar to that of the modern Mediterranean world, where contemporary cultural anthropologists base much of their research. In other words, there is a tendency to take a study of some part of the modern Mediterranean world and apply it without discreetness to the study of the ancient biblical world.[180] These concerns seem to be legitimate. Nevertheless, Berding's purpose was not to reject social-scientific criticism but to admonish biblical scholars to treat it with caution as they employed it in their interpretations of specific passages. He thus concludes with a positive spirit: "Social-scientific Criticism, at least if done carefully along the lines suggested above, holds promise for the evangelical biblical scholar."[181]

Interestingly, the main camp for the early practice of social-scientific criticism was in the field of New Testament (NT) studies.[182] Later, scholars in Old Testament studies also came to realize that the concepts of honor and shame were not limited to the New Testament but were also embedded ideas in the Old Testament. *Semeia 68: Honor and Shame in the World of the Bible*, a production of the 1991 SBL meeting, is an important step that embraces the anthropological discipline into the study of honor and shame in the Old Testament.[183] Since then, social-scientific criticism has also developed in Old

---

179. They tend to claim that one reading is right while all others are wrong.

180. Berding, "Hermeneutical Framework," 6–19.

181. Berding thinks a good example among the evangelical circle in NT study of someone who has made good use of cultural background is deSilva in his book *Honor, Patronage, Kinship & Purity*.

182. Its works are massive. For an introduction to social-scientific criticism and its supporters, see Horrell, *Social-Scientific Approaches*.

183. Matthews, Benjamin, and Camp, *Semeia 68*, 23–113. For essays in the *Semeia* volume directly related to Old Testament studies, see Bergant, "My Beloved Is Mine," 23–40; Simkins, "Return to Yahweh," 41–54; Stansell, "Honor and Shame," 55–79. Prior to the publication of *Semia 68*, Matthews and Benjamin had already co-authored an important book, *Social World of Ancient Israel, 1250–587 BCE* (one would also be remiss not to mention Neyrey's NT counterpart, *The Social World of Luke-Acts*).

Testament studies.[184] One notable example is Daniel Wu's *Honor, Shame, and Guilt: Social-Scientific Approaches to the Book of Ezekiel*, which I consider to be a good model in using social-scientific criticism for doing biblical studies in the OT. Wu's embrace of the social-scientific approach is obvious throughout the book. He adopts the anthropological terminology of *emics* and *etics* (i.e. the viewpoint of insiders and outsiders) as the paradigm for his analysis of כבד (honor), בוש (shame) and עוה (guilt) in Ezekiel.[185] Nevertheless, Wu has certainly kept a fair distance from the Mediterraneanists by critically examining their data throughout the development of this theory. It is a valid evaluation that Wu considers social-scientific approaches in a "critically appreciative manner."[186]

Some other OT scholars have also been critical in their treatment of social-scientific approaches. While employing a psychological approach in *The Construction of Shame in the Hebrew Bible: The Prophetic Contribution*, Joanna Stiebert does use a great amount of anthropological data to inform her research (esp. in ch. 1). Nevertheless, she constantly criticizes social-scientific models. Although the social dynamics of human honor appear often in the narratives of Genesis and the Deuteronomistic History, they cannot accommodate an analysis of prophetic literature. Stiebert contends that the prophetic books give prominence to the description of YHWH's honor instead of human honor on a horizontal level.[187]

---

184. For examples of other works on honor and shame in the Old Testament since the time of the *Semeia* volume, see Matthews, "Honor and Shame"; Olyan, "Honor," 201–228; Chalcraft, *Social-Scientific*; Laniak, *Shame and Honor*; Simkins, Cook, and Brenner, *Social World*; Kirkpatrick, *Competing for Honor*; Esler, *Ancient Israel*; Pilch, *Introducing*; Mbuvi, "Ancient Mediterranean Values," 752–768; Wu, *Honor, Shame, and Guilt*, 31–36.

185. Wu often connects עוה to עון when he discusses the meaning of עוה; sometimes he even treats these two words interchangeably. As discussed before, it is probably better if we treat עוה as two different homonyms, namely, עוה I, "to bend, twist" and עוה II, "to commit iniquity, err" (as per the BDB). Both עוה II and עוה I are guilt-related terms. See Wu, *Honor, Shame, and Guilt*, 145–161.

186. Wu, *Honor, Shame, and Guilt*, 168. The book's whole second chapter is devoted to the evaluation of anthropological approaches.

187. Stiebert, *Construction of Shame*, 88–90, 166. Honor pertaining to humans (primarily to men), as depicted by the anthropological pattern, is not well attested in Isaiah. Instead, honor in Isaiah is attributed primarily to YHWH. The competition for honor (the so-called challenge-riposte pattern) is also absent in Isaiah. Stiebert's critique against the Mediterraneanists is so extensive one gets the impression that much of her work is to prove that the anthropological model of honor/shame does not work.

Apparently, Jumper also treats social-scientific criticism with much caution but allows himself to have the freedom to engage with it. He says, "But when we use anthropological models, we try to show that such ideas exist in many places in the Hebrew Bible. That is, we try to provide textual justification when use [sic] the anthropological models."[188] Several other biblical scholars have expressed similar concerns about social scientific criticism.[189]

In view of such a background, my reference to the social-cultural approach throughout this dissertation is also made with reservation (i.e. we will use the insights from social science only when such information can be justified by biblical data). For this reason, the entire second chapter of this dissertation will be devoted to the study of the semantics of the terms for honor and shame in 1 Samuel. The purpose is to delve into the Old Testament culture of honor and shame in its own texts and contexts so that the discussion of honor and shame in 1 Samuel as a social-cultural context can be built up on more solid grounding. In this way, the risk of modernizing the ancient biblical text can be minimized.

Since socio-literary criticism integrates both the social and literary aspects of analysis, I shall now move to the literary part of the methodology. As we have discussed before, scholars in the past have often tried to study 1 Samuel through historical-critical criticism. Nevertheless, with the exception of Hannah's prayer, which is a distinct poetic song (1 Sam 2:1–10), the nature of 1 Samuel 1–7 is narrative text throughout – that is, the telling of stories through narration.[190] As such, the narrative genre determines that the utilization of literary-narrative analysis is clearly necessary. Such thoughts can be gathered from Bar-Efrat in the introduction of his classic book *Narrative Art in the Bible*:

> The various historical approaches have undoubtedly contributed greatly to our knowledge of the world and literature of the Bible. The literary approach and methods are no less important than

---

188. Jumper, "Shame and Honor," 45–46.

189. Schwartz, *Were the Jews*, 23–24; Avrahami, "בוש in the Psalms," 295–313; Kasle, "Analysis," 12–16. Kasle is implicit in stating her own criticisms here, but her critique against the Mediterraneanists' model can be detected throughout the dissertation.

190. The telling of stories as experiences are meant to communicate meaning/significance to the readers, since the author/narrator is often implicit in stating his own point of views within the narratives.

> the historical ones, however, since the being of biblical narrative is equally as interesting as its becoming. Anyone who wishes to study its being must use the avenue of literary analysis, for it is impossible to appreciate the nature of biblical narrative fully, understand the network of its component elements or penetrate into its inner world without having recourse to the methods and tools of literary scholarship.[191]

Bar-Efrat means to say that despite the abundance of various historical approaches ("becoming") in biblical scholarship, literary analysis is equally important and indispensable for the study of the text as it is ("being"). While the struggles between historical viewpoints and literary criticism in the study of biblical narratives will continue,[192] it is the latter approach that will strengthen not only our understanding of the text but also the faith of God's people.

Literary criticism, treating the final form of the text as a literary whole,[193] is not a novelty to biblical scholars.[194] Nevertheless, Robert Alter's *The Art of Biblical Narrative* in 1981 reached a large audience with a widespread understanding of reading biblical narratives. In this book, he defines the literary approach as follows:

> By literary analysis I mean the manifold varieties of minutely discriminating attention to the artful use of language, to the shifting play of ideas, conventions, tone, sound, imagery, syntax, narrative viewpoint, compositional units, and much else; the kind of disciplined attention, in other words, which through a whole spectrum of critical approaches has illuminated, for example, the poetry of Dante, the plays of Shakespeare, the novels of Tolstoy.[195]

---

191. Bar-Efrat, *Narrative Art*, 10. The last chapter of the book presents a very helpful illustration of analyzing the story of Amnon and Tamar (2 Sam 13: 1–22) with all the narrative tools employed.

192. For the relationship between these two, see Dunn, "New Directions," 412–422.

193. Muilenburg, "Form Criticism and Beyond," 1–18. See also Childs, *Introduction*, which has an emphasis on the canonical context of the biblical text.

194. For a further introduction to the history of literary criticism and its development, see Barton, "Reflections on Literary Criticism," 523–559.

195. Alter, *Art of Biblical Narrative*, 12–13.

Alter's critical definition of this approach brings attention to the text and its appreciation,[196] rather than its history/the history behind it, which would be the interest of the proponents of the historical-critical approach. Indeed, a synchronic reading will be more beneficial for us to grasp the meaning of the text than a diachronic reading. Literary-narrative criticism often focuses on the discussion of literary features such as the story scenes, the plot, the characters, the action, the repetition and the style.[197] It is my expectation that such a focus on the text and its literary features in the narrative analysis will guide us toward a right direction in interpreting 1 Samuel 1–7. In my literary analysis, I will focus on how honor and shame are used in the narratives to help portray characters, and how the narrative perspective of honor and shame creates a standard of judgment by which we are able to evaluate people in the narrative. I will also examine literary features such as the use and manipulation of type scenes and the use of foreshadowing in the Song of Hannah.

Thus far, I have briefly introduced socio-literary criticism through its two compartments: social-scientific criticism and literary criticism. As may be seen, the socio-literary criticism approach embraces both the social-cultural and the literary aspects in interpreting texts. Though the approach is not new in biblical scholarship, in practice, strangely, not many works have ostensibly been done using such a method.[198] In NT studies, Betsworth, by comparing

---

196. Alter, 5–10. Alter illustrates this through his discussion of Genesis 38. The story of Judah and Tamar, according to Alter's literary analysis, is not a clumsy interpolation, as claimed by many commentators, but a thematic unity within the rest of the Joseph story. This can be established by the repetition of the key verb נכר ("recognize") in Gen 38:25–26, 37:32–33 and 42:7–8. Jacob was deceived by his sons as he could not recognize the lie of Joseph's death (Genesis 37). Later Judah, the deceiver, as a representative of his brothers, would be deceived as he recognized his personal items (Genesis 38). In the end, Joseph, the one who was sold in Egypt, would recognize his brothers in Egypt without them recognizing him (Genesis 42). All these stories are intentionally framed by the narrator to emphasize their ironies.

197. For an introduction to more books on narrative analysis, see Fokkelman, *Reading Biblical Narrative*; Amit, *Reading Biblical Narratives*; Jobbling, *Sense of Biblical Narrative*; Funk, *Poetics of Biblical Narrative*; Andersson, *Untamable Texts*; Powell, *What Is Narrative Criticism?*; Williams, *Other Followers of Jesus*. The latter two emphasize NT studies.

198. This is perhaps because social-scientific criticism has already claimed its close relationship with literary criticism. Thus, many choose to use social-scientific criticism instead.

It seems that Ken Stone's *Sex, Honor and Power in the Deuteronomistic History* also implicitly uses socio-literary criticism, though he presents his methodology somewhat differently as "an anthropological framework and a narratological method." See Stone, *Sex, Honor and Power*, 11. In one other shorter article, Stone presents his methodology in a clearer shape by saying that

attitudes toward daughters in the Greco-Roman world, analyzes the scenes of daughters in the Gospel of Mark and concludes that these minor characters demonstrate the nature of the reign of God.[199] Betsworth's use of the social-historical data about the life of girls in the ancient Greco-Roman world is supplementary to her literary analysis of the Gospel of Mark. Though she does not discuss her methodology openly within the book (only the book title suggests it), the use of socio-literary analysis is still obvious. Betsworth's application of the method is commendable, for she does not establish the social context of the life of daughters through modern anthropological data but through other literature around the time of the NT. As such, the social location she presents in the book provides a solid bedrock for her discussion of the daughters in the Gospel of Mark.

One notable scholar in OT studies who has adopted socio-literary criticism is Timothy Laniak in his work *Shame and Honor in the Book of Esther*. Adopting many of the anthropological theories of the Context Group, Laniak investigates the theme of honor and shame in the post-exilic Israelite community through a socio-literary analysis. Laniak's work brings readers to a more sensitive understanding of those social-cultural values in the story. His contribution is often identified as the product of the two plot patterns in the Hebrew Bible: "sin-alienation-reconciliation" and "challenge and honor."[200] However, Laniak's work has also engendered many critics. Jumper criticizes that Laniak's discussion of honor and shame in Esther lacks lexical support and analysis.[201] Furthermore, Laniak's utilization of Mediterraneanists' anthropological insights to conjecture the social location of the exilic Jewish community is thought to be not too convincing.[202]

"literary meaning and reading need not be isolated from questions of context and of cultural context." Stone, "Gender and Homosexuality," 89.

199. Betsworth, *Reign of God*.

200. It is the latter pattern that Laniak applies to the book of Esther. The "challenge and honor" pattern comprises four parts: (1) Honor granted (e.g. Esther 1–2), (2) honor challenged (e.g. Esther 3–5), (3) honor vindicated (e.g. Esther 6–7), and (4) honor enhanced (e.g. Esther 8–10). One may see it is a modification of Neyrey and Malina's "challenge-riposte" pattern. See Laniak, *Shame and Honor*, 12.

201. Jumper, "Shame and Honor in Deuteronomy," 27. None of the "shame" words Laniak listed appears in Esther.

202. Jobes, review of *Shame and Honor*, 273–275.

Occasionally, the use of socio-literary criticism is also found in journal articles.[203] In my observations, most, if not all, who have adopted socio-literary criticism are those who engage in the analysis of narrative texts. This is understandable, since literary criticism is a very good and natural option for treating narrative texts. If the authors want to address the social-cultural concerns in the texts, then socio-literary criticism is a good choice, as it emphasizes both the literary and socio-cultural concerns. Having said so, it is a reasonable conclusion that my treatment of 1 Samuel 1–7 is an example of socio-literary criticism.

It should be also noted that my study of 1 Samuel 1–7, following Jumper's approach,[204] will be restricted to the discussion of *biblical* Israel, not historical Israel. There are reasons for such an arrangement. Historical-critical analysis often deals with "the world behind the text." Whereas examining both written and non-written data is critical to determining the state of affairs of a region, practitioners of historical-critical analysis often do not give sufficient attention to the literary features of the biblical text, particularly salient elements in penetrating the honor-shame narrative of the region under study. Thus, historical criticism is not the focus of my attention in this dissertation. Some historical-critical scholars even go to the extreme of sifting out the presence of God in their study. For example, Walter Dietrich writes in *The Early Monarchy in Israel*: "Statements about God are above historical evaluation – except as information about those who made these statements. In the modern age, history must be understood and described *etsi deus non daretur* ('as though God did not exist')."[205] Such an interpretative grid can be easily detected in some books that speak about the history of Israel.[206] In rebuttal, conservative scholars, such as Iain Provan, V. Philips Long and Tremper Longman in their joint work *A Biblical History of Israel*, defend the notion that the testimony of Old Testament narratives should be accepted as historically accurate unless it

---

203. Joubert, "Jerusalem Community," 49–59; Houston, "Tragedy in the Courts," 31–39. In this short article, Houston presents Aaron as a tragic hero exploiting the honor of the Lord, who is thus judged in disgrace by the death of his two sons.

204. Jumper, "Shame and Honor," 41.

205. Dietrich, *Early Monarchy in Israel*, 102. In relation to 1 Samuel, for example, Dietrich does not believe that the ark was exiled and caused disease and death in the land of Philistines (pp. 103, 251).

206. For example, Soggin, *Introduction*; Lemche, *Ancient Israel*.

is proven to be falsified.²⁰⁷ These debates will continue and will not end soon. In the end, the attempt to find out "as it actually happened" ("*wie es eigentlich gewesen*")²⁰⁸ in antiquity seems to be a difficult, if not impossible, task. In view of the complexities of the problems we are facing, I have chosen to limit my discussion of 1 Samuel 1–7 to biblical Israel as depicted in the biblical texts (regardless of the reconstruction of historical Israel) and focus on the social-cultural values of honor and shame within the book of 1 Samuel itself.

Besides socio-literary criticism, some other supplementary approaches will also be considered. The Hebrew MT text of 1 Samuel is a text that displays various signs of textual corruption.²⁰⁹ Credible though the MT is, it suffered certain alterations in transmission, albeit relatively minimally, from the original textual compositions. As such, the MT is one textual source connecting us to the past, but which must be evaluated in light of other ancient source witnesses and internal evidence. Thus, we will need to respond to some textual-critical issues along the way, especially when textual criticism is determinative in the interpretation of our discussed topic. The second chapter of the dissertation will be devoted to a semantic analysis of key words (terms) of honor and shame in 1 Samuel. Semantic analysis is a critical part of this study. The book of Samuel is often considered to be part of the Deuteronomistic History. Its connection with the Deuteronomistic History or other parts of the Scriptures is inseparable; thus, the utilization of inter-textual criticism is also expected. Since writings about the ancient Near East will inform our understanding of the social-cultural background of biblical Israel, extra-biblical criticism will also surface in the studies.

1.6 Scope and Delimitation

The book of Samuel, according to its Jewish origin, belongs to the section of Scripture known as the Former Prophets, which narrates the history of

---

207. Provan, Long, and Longman, *Biblical History of Israel*, 73; for a similar view, see Kaiser, *History of Israel*.

208. von Ranke, *Geschichten der romanischen*, v–vi. For some recent refutation of the way von Ranke's approach was used in the latter nineteenth and early twentieth-centuries, see Provan, Long, and Longman, *Biblical History of Israel*, 21–23.

209. The discovery of the Qumran Scrolls testified to that corruption. See Driesbach, *4QSamuelᵃ*; Tov, *Textual Criticism*, 301–304.

Israel from the entry to the promised land to the exile of Israel, covering the books of Joshua, Judges, Samuel and Kings. Its theological connection with the book of Deuteronomy has led scholars to postulate a theory that these books, formed together, constitute the so-called Deuteronomistic History.[210] The redactors of the Septuagint first divided the book of Samuel into two parts: 1 and 2 Samuel.[211] Since then, the Christian canon has followed suit. In this dissertation, I have delimited the scope of the study to 1 Samuel, though we may occasionally bring up some issues in 2 Samuel should the need arise.

To maintain a relative depth in this study, I have decided to focus on the discussion of honor and shame within 1 Samuel 1–7. I am aware of the disagreement among scholars as to whether chapter 7 (to be exact, 7:2–17), as a literature unit, should align with the previous story of Samuel (chs. 1–7) or as a prelude to the later story of Saul.[212] The disagreement is not likely to be completely resolved. But it seems to me that the unit division of 1 Samuel 1–7 is most reasonable since chapter 7 offers a resolution to the previous conflicts and chapter 8 brings out a different theme, which is the institution of kingship.

This study will not examine the history of the texts and what is behind them. Thus, I will not give attention to source criticism, form/tradition criticism or redaction criticism in order to concentrate clearly on the cultural and literary aspect of the study.

1.7 The Structure of Our Study

The structure of this dissertation is presented as the following:

---

210. Since this hypothesis is widely accepted by scholars, I hereby comply with the use of such terms. According to this theory, an editor, the so-called Deuteronomist, used various available sources, freely edited from them and finalized the overall structure of the Deuteronomistic History during Israel's exile in Babylon in the sixth century BCE – though traditionally the authorship of 1 Samuel was accredited to the prophet Samuel. For a further introduction on the Deuteronomistic History, see Noth, *Deuteronomistic History*; Gordon, *1 and 2 Samuel*, 14–22.

211. The reason the LXX divides the book in such a way is probably because 1 Samuel ends with the death of King Saul and his sons, and 2 Samuel begins with the emergence of David as the new king of Israel. Thematically speaking, there is good logic in such a division.

212. For scholars who argue for the unity of 1 Samuel 1–7, see Willis, *1 & 2 Samuel*; Eslinger, *Kingship of God*; Miscall, *I Samuel*; Polzin, *Samuel and the Deuteronomist*, 5; Tsumura, *First Book of Samuel*, 244; McCarter, *I Samuel*, 148–150; Kim, "Paragraph Delimitation," 238; Firth, "Play It Again," 1–17.

For those who contend for chapter 7's connection to the story of Saul, see Hertzberg, *I and II Samuel*, 66; Gordon, *1 and 2 Samuel*, 41.

In chapter 1, as may be seen, I lay the most fundamental groundwork for my research on this topic. To do that, I first define the terminology of honor and shame and survey the scholarly literature on honor and shame, particularly the works pertaining to the Deuteronomistic History and the first book of Samuel. By doing so, I justify the necessity of pursuing further research on this topic. To continue, the method of socio-literary criticism is clarified. Both the social and literary part complement each other in forming a better interpretation of the texts. Meanwhile, I urge caution in adopting modern anthropological influences through social-scientific criticism in this study. Lastly, some delimitations of the study are introduced.

In chapter 2, the vocabulary of honor and shame is investigated for their semantics and significance in 1 Samuel. The purpose is to analyze each of these terms in the texts where they actually occur, so that we may be able to have a better grasp of the culture of honor and shame within the book of 1 Samuel. By doing so, we shield ourselves, as much as possible, from other outside cultural influence that may not be relevant to the text of 1 Samuel. The study finds that honor and shame appear to be prevalent cultural features with their own uniqueness in ancient biblical Israel.

In chapters 3–5, going to the core of my study, I examine 1 Samuel 1–7 through the social-cultural norm of honor and shame. The centrality of honor and shame, as the narrator's ideological perspective, proves to be significant in understanding the structure, plot, characterization and message of the book. The narrator's ideological perspective of honor and shame can be used as a standard of judgment for God's election of Samuel and the rejection of the Elides. Such a standard of judgment in the Elides/Samuel episode can be even considered as a paradigm for the later Saul/David episode. Thus, it is obvious to see how honor and shame work behind the scenes and serve as a driving force in forging the story in 1 Samuel 1–7. It should be noted that my study does not follow the sequential order of the text but is organized according to thematic interests – for example, the ark narrative (chs. 4–6) is not analyzed in the middle of the narrative analysis chapters but in chapter 5 (the last chapter before the conclusion), since the ark narrative is the climax of the story and is of greatest theological significance in 1 Samuel 1–7.

Finally, in the last chapter, I will review the study and make some conclusions. I will also draw out some implications for an Asian cultural context. Some suggestions will also be provided for future studies.

CHAPTER 2

The Language of Honor and Shame in 1 Samuel

2.1 Introduction

This chapter examines conspicuous vocabulary and terms denoting honor and shame, exposing their semantics and significance in 1 Samuel. The purpose of the chapter is to use the lexical information to provide some information on where the text of 1 Samuel deals with honor and shame issues. By doing so, we hope to adumbrate the social-cultural honor-shame system in biblical Israel as communicated in 1 Samuel.[1] This is an important preparatory step that will facilitate our further analyses of 1 Samuel 1–7 from the perspective of honor and shame. I do not press to say that everything is about honor and shame in 1 Samuel. Instead, there are lexical indicators where honor and shame issues rise to the forefront. The study finds that the honor-shame culture is pervasive, with its own unique manifestations, in 1 Samuel. Honor and shame permeate all areas of life in biblical Israel, including politics, family, friendship, war, sex, meals, daily language and even death. Thus, the notion of honor and shame is an important aspect of social culture that governs the thoughts, the words and the deeds of the people in biblical Israel. One also needs to expect that there will be some overlap and redundancy in my discussion of some honor

---

1. This is a response to Stiebert's concern that "few biblical interpreters have chosen to focus on the texts where such vocabulary actually occurs." See Stiebert, *Construction of Shame*, 166.

and shame terms. Meanwhile, my discussion of the terms denoting honor and shame, due to limits of space, is selective.[2]

Though not a direct concern of this dissertation, a distinction between shame and guilt is often debated.[3] It should be acknowledged at the very beginning that the term "shame" in this dissertation is used distinctively from "guilt." The difference between shame and guilt is subtle but important.

2.2 Honor and Shame Terms in the Song of Hannah (2:1–10)

The Song of Hannah (2:1–10), as a poetry inset within the narrative, has an impact on the development of the entire narrative. As I have discussed in chapter 1, the song sets a tone for the unfolding of the rest of the story, the Eli/Samuel and Saul/David episodes. Though Hannah is initially shamed, she is eventually exalted by the Lord above her rival; likewise, Samuel and David will also ultimately gain their ascendancy over Eli and Saul. In view of the thematic connections, Robert Polzin contends that Hannah's multi-voiced song is a "proleptic summary" of David's song in 2 Samuel 22.[4] Many others notice that the songs of both Hannah and David serve as an *inclusio* for the entire narrative of 1 and 2 Samuel.[5] Meanwhile, the exchange of honor between those in high and low positions in the Song of Hannah is duly noted

---

2. For example, the noun בשׁת ("shame") in 1 Samuel 20:30 and the repeated occurrence of בליעל ("worthless person," possibly as a shamed term) in 1 Samuel 1:16, 2:12, 10:27, 25:17, 25:25 and 30:22 are not discussed here. For shame/shaming terms in 1 Samuel, I delimit myself to the most relevant verbal terms.

3. Most scholars today regard "shame" and "guilt" as two different categories of emotions: "shame" as an emotion in response to "negative self-evaluation" and "guilt" as an emotion related to the transgression of laws. There are still debates as to whether one should separate shame and guilt in practice. See Stiebert, "Shame and Prophecy," 255–259. Likewise, Bechtel defines shame as "failure or inadequacy to reach or live up to a socio-parental goal or ideal" (p. 49) and guilt as "the act of transgression" (p. 53). Shame often has an impact on "who a person is," while guilt often points to the aftermath of a certain action that is wrong. Bechtel, "Shame as a Sanction," 48–53. Wu summarizes that "it seems reasonable to view both shame and guilt as part of a common concept sphere denoting an actual or potential ascription of disconnection between expectation and reality." Wu integrates both shame and guilt as a disconnection between expectation and reality, but such ascription may be given by the person him/herself, the community or by God. See Wu, *Honor, Shame, and Guilt*, 57.

4. Polzin, *Samuel and the Deuteronomist*, 33–34.

5. Tsumura, *First Book of Samuel*, 135; Polzin, *Samuel and the Deuteronomist*, 31; Arnold, *1 and 2 Samuel*, 69; Brueggemann, "I Samuel 1," 46; Bailey, "Redemption of YHWH," 213–231; Fokkelman, *Reading Biblical Narrative*, 186.

2.2.1 רוּם, "be high, exalted" (2:1, 7, 8, 10), vs. שׁפל, "to bring low" (2:7)

In Hannah's song, the frequent change of one's status can be seen from the fact that God will exalt some and humble others. The root רוּם, occurring four times in this song (2:1, 7, 8, 10), is noticeable and is even regarded as the "theme verb" of this song.[7] The verb רוּם literally means "to be high." In the figurative sense when applied to persons, it conveys the idea of "being exalted."[8] The meaning of "being exalted" certainly denotes an elevated status. It magnifies the value and supremacy of related persons and is thus considered as a word associated with honor.[9]

After dedicating Samuel to the Lord in Shiloh, Hannah praised God that her horn, a symbol of visible strength, was exalted (1 Sam 2:1; רמה) in the Lord.[10] After a long period of barrenness, it is the Lord who granted her the blessing to conceive a child and bring him into this world so that she could stand before her rival without being shamed. Indeed, it is the Lord's sovereignty to humble some and exalt (1 Sam 2:7; מרומם) others. In particular, the Lord elevates (1 Sam 2:8; ירים) those who are poor and needy and grants those in low positions a seat of honor. People's fates are reversed with a change of their status.[11] God's exaltation falls under a certain principle: his faithful ones (חסידיו)[12] he will keep, but the wicked (ורשעים) shall be cut off (1 Sam 2:9).

---

6. Jumper, "Honor and Shame," 179.

7. Lewis, "Textual History," 25.

8. "רוּם," BDB, 926–927.

9. Such is the case in God's elevation of Jeroboam and Baasha, his chosen kings, in 1 Kings 14:7 and 16:2, as well as the exaltation of the servant of YHWH (Isa 52:13). A parallel and synonymous term, קום ("arise, stand up") in v. 8, also suggesting honor in the context, will not be discussed here.

10. Lifting up one's horn may evoke the image of boastfulness (Ps 75:4). However, Hannah's boasting confidence is in the Lord.

11. The reversal of fortunes, for example, can be seen in that the Lord raises the poor from their lowly position to an honorable one. Tsumura, *First Book of Samuel*, 147.

12. The *Ketiv* possibly reads the singular חסידו (unless a *yod*, signifying a plural form, was omitted before the 3ms suffix; i.e. -*w* can be considered a spelling variant of -*yw*). I thank Dr. Michael Malessa for this reminder.

From a shamed barren woman to a rejoicing and honorable mother, Hannah has personally experienced such a reversal of her status.

More importantly, what grants Hannah special honor is not just the number of children she would continue to bear, but that she would have a part, albeit indirectly, in the exaltation (1 Sam 2:10; וירם) of God's anointed one (as a royal title).[13] For this reason, it is often believed that there is a prophetic element to Hannah's song since kingship as a system was not yet established in Israel during that time.[14]

In antithesis to רום, the root שפל occurs only once as a *hiphil* participle (1 Sam 2:7). The word שפל, with the literal meaning of "to be low" in the *qal* stem, can have the figurative sense of "to abase" in the *hiphil*.[15] It is obvious that the Lord abases (משפיל) some and exalts others pertaining to their status. Though humans struggle to secure their primacy, it is the Lord who sets and maintains the social ranking order to elevate some and abase others.[16] Despite Peninnah being initially elevated because of her having many children, the Lord would bring her low due to her arrogance. Indeed, her name is not remembered anymore after 1 Samuel 1:8. In a similar vein, the reversal of high status is shown in Eli's household.[17] The diminishment of the house of Eli is unavoidable as God judges its members for not paying due honor to God.

---

13. Hannah's son, Samuel, is given the honor of anointing both Saul and David, two of God's anointed ones (1 Sam 10:1; 16:13).

14. Tsumura, *First Book of Samuel*, 150; Arnold, *1 and 2 Samuel*, 70; Auld, *I & II Samuel*, 38.

15. "שפל," *HALOT* 4, 1632. Here the opposite of מרומם in 2:7 is "to abase" (משפיל, to commit a "lowly status" upon someone) rather than literally "make low." See also "שָׁפֵל," BDB, 1050. Its counterpart in the LXX reads ταπεινόω which generally means "to bow down, to make low, to humble" in the active voice. See Walter Grundmann, "Ταπεινός, Ταπεινόω, Ταπείνωσις, Ταπεινόφρων, Ταπεινοφροσύνη," *TDNT*, 8:4–6.

16. Keddie notices the connection to Psalm 75:7–8 in the canonical context (both verbs שפל and רום in their *hiphil* forms, with God as the subject, occur there). See Keddie, *Dawn of a Kingdom*, 34.

17. Jumper compares שפל and קלל as words that describe the reversal of status, themes presented in Hannah's song and the judgment oracle of the house of Eli (1 Sam 2:30–36). See Jumper, "Honor and Shame," 192.

2.2.2 עשׁר I, "to make rich" (hiphil, 2:7), vs. רושׁ,[18] "to make poor" (hiphil, 2:7)

Further on, honor and shame are communicated in the song by the gaining or losing of wealth. Wealth, as a sign of blessing from the Lord, is often seen as a token of honor. Thus, Job loses his honor when his possessions are taken away from him because wealth forms an essential part of his honor.[19] Likewise, according to the Deuteronomic covenant (Deut 28), God's blessings, such as prosperity and increase of wealth, are granted to those who obey his words; on the contrary, curses, such as failure and decrease of wealth, will follow those who disobey. Jumper affirms that such covenantal blessings and curses are reflections of honor and shame.[20]

In 1 Samuel 2:7, the Lord is the one who makes one poor (מריש) or rich (מעשׁיר) – both *hiphil* participles render the agency of causation. The Lord brings about wealth and poverty. Hannah's greatest wealth is the gift of her son Samuel (Ps 127:3). This is also a foreshadowing of the later story when the Elides will be impoverished due to their unfaithfulness in serving the Lord. The Elide priests, once well-off in their economic standing, will become so destitute that they will even have to beg for meager food for bare survival (1 Sam 2:36). The Lord will strip away their honor as they are humbled in their material shortage. David, meanwhile, once a shepherd and a poor man (1 Sam 18:23), will be granted abundance of material possession (1 Sam 27:8–12) so that he can even share his blessings with his friends, the elders of Judah (1 Sam 30:26). One can assume that Nabal's great wealth (1 Sam 25:2) is also ascribed to David as he marries Abigail after Nabal's death. David's honor increases as his wealth multiplies.

---

18. MT reads מוֹרִישׁ, "to dispossess." Although there is no textual variant in *BHS* concerning מוֹרִישׁ, *HALOT* 2, 442 suggests the verb may be רושׁ ("to be poor"; H-stem, "to make poor" – מֵרִישׁ). The obvious problem is the *waw mater lectionis*, suggesting a 1-*yod* verb as mediated by the Masoretes. One could perhaps postulate, however, the misinterpretation of an ō vowel, מֹרִישׁ (without vowel pointing: מרישׁ), when it should have been an ē vowel, written מֵרִישׁ. See מֹרֶה in Proverbs 6:13 as an example of a *hiphil* 1-*yod* participle without the standard *waw mater*. The LXX also renders it πτωχίζω ("to make poor") rather than other verbs associated with the H-stem of ירשׁ (e.g. ἐξολεθρεύω in Josh 13:13; ἀπόλλυμι in Num 32:39; ἐξαίρω in Judg 2:23; ἐκβάλλω in Num 21:32). Likewise, the Vulgate's *"pauperem facit"* ("makes poor"), the Targum's מסכן ("to make poor"), as well as the same in the Syriac, ܡܣܟܢ. I thank Dr. Tim Undheim for sharing this valuable insight.

19. Pedersen, *Israel*, 224.

20. Jumper, "Honor and Shame," iii.

The Lord makes poor and makes rich. The Lord adds honor to certain individuals through granting material prosperity, but he also has the right to take it away, especially if a person exalts himself above God.[21]

In short, the Song of Hannah allows us to see that the Lord is the source of honor. He grants wealth, prosperity and elevation to those he pleases. On the contrary, as for the wicked ones (the enemies), the Lord judges them with poverty, lowliness and shame. The Lord, who is enthroned on high, oversees all humans in this world for their honor and shame.

2.3 The Use of כבד

As I have discussed in chapter 1, the word כבד, occurring eleven times with its meaning "be heavy, honored," is a noticeable term in 1 Samuel. The frequent repetition of this root is an important feature of the book. Bar-Efrat, following Buber, suggests that a word can be considered a key word when it brings separate stages of a narrative together in a close relationship and directly conveys its essential point.[22] It is plausible to say that כבד is one such key word in 1 Samuel.[23]

The position of priesthood is a privilege given by God to the house of Eli among all the tribes of Israel (1 Sam 2:27–28), but they have abused such an honor. In God's judgment of Eli's household, a grave problem God points out is that Eli honored his sons, Hophni and Phinehas, more than the Lord (1 Sam 2:29; ותכבד את בניך ממני), as he tolerated their robbing the choicest parts of every offering (1 Sam 2:13–14). By doing so, the Elides had profaned the position of priesthood and despised the Lord in their service. The offense was so grievous that the Lord decided to forfeit his earlier promise to keep them as priests forever. God is not to be taken lightly because God only honors those who honor him, and those who despise him shall be insignificant (1 Sam 2:30).

The narrator's description of Eli's outward appearance as an "old and heavy man" (1 Sam 4:18; זקן האיש וכבד) is very unusual because the heaviness of his

---

21. The king of Tyre is an example in his change of wealth and honor after he boasts himself as a god (Ezek 28:1–19).

22. Bar-Efrat, *Narrative Art*, 213.

23. I discussed the importance of כבד in different narrative sections of 1 Samuel when I discussed the ideological point of view in section 1.1.

weight contributes to the tragedy of his death: Eli was so heavy that he could hardly control his balance, fell backward, and broke his neck upon hearing the sad news of the death of his two sons and the captured ark. It is ironic that the heaviness of his body partly leads to his death. Readers will not forget that Eli was accused of honoring his sons more than God by allowing their fattening (ברא II)[24] of themselves on the choicest parts of every offering. One can assume Eli, though not directly involved in robbing the sacrificial meat, conceivably benefited from the share of such spoils. Thus, Eli's indulgence of his two sons would most likely contribute to his extraordinary weight, which, in turn, caused his death. The implicit use of כבד is ironic in the context and it serves to give prominence to Eli's culpability. The unusual means of his death cautions the consequence of anyone who honors people rather than God.

In the wars against the Philistines, Israel brought the ark to the battlefield in the hope that the Lord would grant them victory (1 Sam 4:3–5). Sadly, this did not change the tide of fortune. Israel was defeated again and, even worse, the ark was captured. This brings a theological crisis: how shall Israel perceive its "impotent" God when the glory (כבוד, the noun form of כבד) has been exiled (4:21–22) from Israel? The "failure" of the כבוד for Israel in the battle paradoxically betokens a shamed and humiliated God.[25] The Philistines tried to further shame YHWH by placing the ark in the temple of Dagon as a trophy. However, YHWH overpowered Dagon in the secret scene and spoke for himself by showing his heavy (1 Sam 5:6, 11; the same root כבד) hand against the cities of the Philistines.[26] Unlike the Pharaoh and Egyptians who hardened (1 Sam 6:6; כבד) their hearts and suffered badly, the Philistines had to acknowledge that sacrilege against YHWH must be compensated for by returning the ark in a proper way to restore his glory.

Contrary to Eli, who suffered a disgraceful end as a consequence of divine judgment against his sin of honoring his sons above God, Samuel, who was faithful in his service to God, was held in honor (1 Sam 9:6; נכבד) by the

---

24. However, 4QSam[a] reads להבריך מראש כול מנחות ("by giving a blessing from the best of all the offerings"). Similarly, the LXX reads ἐνευλογεῖσθαι ἀπαρχῆς πάσης θυσίας Ισραηλ ("by blessing themselves with the first-fruits of every sacrifice of Israel").

25. Brueggemann, *Ichabod toward Home*, 9.

26. The wordplay of כבד with its different semantic values ("honor or heavy") is obvious. The exiled glory of YHWH was too heavy for them to bear.

Israelites. Samuel was highly respected as a prophet (a man of God) who proclaimed the word of God.

Another comparison in 1 Samuel is between Saul and David. Saul sought to promote his personal honor (1 Sam 15:30; כבדני) before all Israel despite his disobedience to the Lord. God thus replaced Saul with David as the new anointed one of Israel. Though the new anointed one came from a humble origin as a shepherd boy (1 Sam 16:11), he was a man after God's heart (1 Sam 13:14), and thus God also elevated him in due course. David was also respected with honor (1 Sam 22:14; נכבד) as the king's son-in-law, an elevated status rendered by the community. Eventually, he would attain the true honor as the king of all Israel (2 Sam 5:1–5).[27]

As can be seen, the root כבד, as a key word in 1 Samuel, ties different stages of the narrative together in nuanced and meaningful ways and very often evinces the notion of honor or shame in its context.

2.4 Shame/Shaming Terms in 1 Samuel

2.4.1 רעם II, "to humiliate" (1 Sam 1:6)

Notwithstanding Elkanah's special love and favoritism toward Hannah (1 Sam 1:5),[28] this does not change the fact that Peninnah had children and Hannah had none (1 Sam 1:2). Barrenness, signifying the incompleteness and infertility of a woman's womb, triggers the emotion of inferiority and thus brings shame to the barren person. In the ancient Near East, women without children were subject to shame.[29] In practice, if a barren woman was not able to multiply and continue the name of her husband through posterity, she would be dishonored due to her failure to become a mother.[30] If the Deuteronomic covenant (Deut 28:18) is taken into consideration, barrenness also showed the consequence of God's disfavor on a person due to his/her disobedience. Naturally, a barren woman often suffered constant ridicule and taunts from

---

27. The leaders of Israel acknowledged God's divine appointment of David as the new king of Israel. David's superior gift of leadership was conspicuous even when Saul was king over them.

28. The textual problem pertaining to מנה אחת אפים in 1 Samuel 1:5 will be addressed shortly.

29. Kasle, "Analysis," 156; Stiebert, "Shame and Prophecy," 257; Jumper, "Honor and Shame," 12. In many parts of Asia today, the phenomenon that barrenness elicits shame still rings true.

30. Petersen, *Israel*, 231.

others in the community, and her position and value as a wife in her family would also be challenged. This is especially so for a family with two striving wives.

Peninnah, who is clearly described as Hannah's rival (צרתה), provoked Hannah to extreme anger for her barrenness. The *piel* verb (ובעסתה) should be rendered as factitive for such a stative root, thus, Peninnah "would make her angry." The cognate accusative (כעס) certainly reflects the intensity of the anger, functioning as an adverbial adjunct – thus, "severely." The purpose (בעבור) is to הַרְעִמָה. While some translations (ESV, NASB, NRSV, NIV) render this verb רעם, together with the 3f.s. suffix, as "to irritate her," it fails to capture Peninnah's real intention. It does not make sense that Peninnah made Hannah angry in order to merely irritate her per se. Note that the conjunction בעבור often implies a purpose with the intention to bring about a presumably new event to be introduced.[31] Indeed, the context also suggests the reading of רעם II, "to humiliate." Elkanah used to give מנות (most probably the meat portion after the sacrifice) to Peninnah, her sons and daughters. For Peninnah, it was a family union and a demonstration of her strength. But Hannah had to eat her own portion alone. Though Elkanah may have given Hannah one (special) portion, (gaining) face (אפים)[32] because of his special love toward her, it could have only triggered greater jealousy for Peninnah, giving her even better reasons to inflict Hannah with ridicule. Hannah's song in chapter 2 also suggests that her arrogant enemy had been speaking haughtily (2:3; גבהה גבהה) against her, insinuating that Hannah was brought low in the verbal abuse she endured.

While the verb רעם has the most common meaning of "to thunder, to rage,"[33] *HALOT* places the meaning of this infinitive (הַרְעִמָה) under the category of רעם II, meaning "bring low, humiliate" or perhaps "to appear downcast, show oneself oppressed."[34] The translation of "to irritate" (ESV, NIV, NASB, NRSV, NET [2nd ed.]), albeit implicitly, seems to align itself with

---

31. Van der Merwe, Naudé, and Kroeze, *Biblical Hebrew Reference Grammar*, § 40.19.

32. See appendix 1 for details. It is our conjecture that there is an ellipsis of a Hebrew term before אפים, so "(gaining) face" reflect the literal translation of such a theory, albeit awkward in English grammar.

33. "רָעַם," BDB, 947.

34. "רעם II," *HALOT* 3, 1267.

homonym #2 (רעם II, "to bring low, to humiliate")³⁵ but not homonym #1 (רעם I, "to thunder, to rage"). Though the latter can potentially and conceivably connote shaming,³⁶ it is the former that conspicuously exhibits such an aspect of shame. Peninnah's true intention was perhaps to humiliate Hannah by reminding her of the indelible fact that she was childless. Interestingly, some other translations do bring out the sense of shame in the context, thus "to make her miserable" (NJPS), "make fun of her" (NLT), "to upset her" (NCV), τὸ ἐξουθενεῖν αὐτήν (the Lucianic recension, "to disdain her"). Likewise, many scholars also acknowledge the presence of humiliation being stressed here.³⁷ Having said this, it makes more sense to read רעם as homonym #2 ("to humiliate") in this context.

2.4.2. נאץ, "to treat disrespectfully" (1 Sam 2:17)

The two sons of Eli, as priests of the Lord (1:3), surprisingly, are described as worthless men (1 Sam 2:12; בני בליעל).³⁸ The narrator's negative portrayal of their character prepares the reader to surmise their evil and offensive practices against the Lord.

When people came to Shiloh to offer their sacrifices to the Lord, the young servant (נער הכהן)³⁹ of Eli's sons would bring his fork and take away the choicest meat, if necessary by force, even before the meat and the fat were offered to the Lord. Eli's two sons were obviously endorsing the action

---

35. This appears to be true for the author of this portion of the NET Bible (2nd ed.) notes. The author comments that the earlier action of provocation is "for the purpose of troubling her" and explains that רעם means to "disturb, humiliate, or provoke to anger." In my opinion, a problem with the translation of "to irritate" is that its meaning can be easily confused with רעם I, "to thunder, to rage."

36. Irritation is frightening ("making her tremble," YLT). Verbal abuse can be a competition between social equals (both were wives of the same man) as a challenge to obtain greater honor (i.e. shaming the rival as a consequence of making one miserable could be an attempt to regain honor).

37. Hertzberg, *I and II Samuel*, 24; Tsumura, *First Book of Samuel*, 114; Jobling, *1 Samuel*, 132, 182; Polzin, *Samuel and the Deuteronomist*, 20, 31; Alter, *Art of Biblical Narrative*, 83; Bergen, *1, 2 Samuel*, 67; Bodner, *1 Samuel*, 15; Fokkelman, *Vow and Desire*, 26; Cartledge, *Vows*, 187; Eslinger, *Kingship of God*, 73.

38. Ironically, Eli mistakenly applied the same term to Hannah earlier (1 Sam 1:16).

39. Possibly נער should be rendered adjectivally in English as a construct noun, thus "the young priest," lit. "the young one of the priest." נער is also used to refer to Samuel (2:18, 21; 3:1). See Tsumura, *First Book of Samuel*, 157.

of the young servant.⁴⁰ Of course, the law decreed that priests could have their portion of meat (Lev 7:28–36). But much of the offered meat was to be left for the offerer so that he could share it with his family and friends as a feast (1 Sam 1:4–5).⁴¹ Yet people had to tolerate the priests' offense to such a point that it became a custom (1 Sam 2:13; משפט) that the priests would rob from them. Even when people succumbed to the unreasonable demand that the priests could select whatever portion of the meat they desired, the young servant could not even wait until the fat was burned and sacrificed to the Lord. Instead of taking the boiled meat, the priests favored a different taste in having the raw meat roasted. Eli's sons robbed even the part due to God.⁴² It is ironic that even ordinary worshipers of the Lord had to teach the priests (2:16) about the value of worship.

The narrator summarizes, saying that the sin of the young lads (הנערים, i.e. Eli's two sons)⁴³ was great before the Lord, for they (האנשים) disdained the gifts offered to the Lord. האנשים is better read as synonymous with הנערים. The sons of Eli did not make the offerers treat with disrespect the offerings – rather they themselves treated the offerings with disrespect. The verb נאץ, used in the *piel* stem, indicates pluralitive activity, treating disrespectfully in a variety of situations or with reference to a variety of objects. Thus, the sons of Eli dishonored the gifts offered to the Lord.

Being priests, Eli's two sons inherited these honorable positions because of their father. But they dishonored the Lord by taking advantage of their given positions as a means for their personal gain and thus profaned the Lord's offerings. Interestingly, the same verb נאץ is used in Deuteronomy 31:20 in the context of Israel breaking the covenant with the Lord by falling

---

40. The young servant said he would take this meat for the priest (not for himself) and the 3ʳᵈ masculine singular verb (1 Sam 2:15; יקח) also suggests he served the interest of the priest.

41. Meat, being an uncommon food, was rarely consumed in those days.

42. The choicest parts of every offering belonged to the Lord (1 Sam 2:29). The first fruits of every produce from the ground (Exod 34:26) or animal (Exod 34:19) belonged to the Lord.

43. There is a switch from the singular נער in v. 13 and 15 to the plural נערים in v. 17. There is lack of accord on the identity of the נערים, as to whether it refers to Eli's sons or not. However, it seems that the use of the plural נערים in v. 17 condemns not just the earlier singular young servant but, most importantly, Eli's two sons, as the young servant only served the interests of Eli's sons. The main point is to make a contrast between Eli's sons and Samuel, who is a different class of נער. For a detailed discussion of this problem, see Klein, *1 Samuel*, 24–25; Tsumura, *First Book of Samuel*, 157–158; Brueggemann, *First and Second Samuel*, 22–23; Hertzberg, *I & II Samuel*, 35. Hertzberg even suggests that נערים is a belittling term.

into idolatry. Likewise, Eli's two sons exalted themselves above the Lord. Their gods, however, were their own bellies. The wicked practices of Eli's sons were condemned since they expressed contempt for the Lord's offering.

2.4.3 קלל I, "to be insignificant" (*qal*, 1 Sam 2:30), "to be considered insignificant" (*niphal*, 1 Sam 18:23), "to curse" (*piel*, 1 Sam 3:13; 17:43)

In semantic antonymy to כבד,[44] the verb קלל I, with the meaning "to be insignificant" in the *qal* (1 Sam 2:30), "to be considered insignificant" in the *niphal* (1 Sam 18:23), or "curse" in the *piel* stem (1 Sam 3:13; 17:43),[45] is a conspicuous term denoting shame in 1 Samuel. Jumper places קלל I in the larger category of "unimportance" that denotes insignificance.[46] Likewise, Kasle considers it a term of "disparagement."[47]

In God's judgment of Eli's household, he says emphatically, "Far be it from me, for those who honor me I will honor, but those who despise me shall be insignificant (קלל I)" (1 Sam 2:30). The term קלל I,[48] however, is given a specific connotation in pointing to the demise of Eli's family as a result of God's judgment (1 Sam 2:31–36). To be more specific, Eli's descendants will suffer an untimely and tragic death. Eli's two sons, Hophni and Phinehas, shall die on the same day. The Elides' priesthood will be replaced by a new faithful priest. Eli's descendants will suffer a shortage of food and a humbled status.

In 1 Samuel 18:23, as a response to the cheering and alluring words of Saul's servants that David would be the best candidate for the king's son-in-law, David said, "Is it insignificant (הנקלה) in your eyes to become the king's son-in-law? Since I am a poor man (איש רש) and am of little account

---

44. It should be said antonymic overlap between the honor side of כבד and other verbs denoting shame is arguably possible. For instance, קלה II (*niphal* – "to be considered insignificant, dishonored," a biform of קלל I); בוש I (*qal* – "to be ashamed of, put to shame"; *piel* – "to dishonor" [post biblical]; *hiphil* – "put to shame, act shamefully"; *hitpolel* – "be ashamed before one another"); חסד II ("to bring shame/reproach on someone"); חפר II ("ashamed, bring shame") and even כלם I ("be humiliated").

45. See "קלל I," *DCH*, 7:256–58.

46. Jumper, "Honor and Shame," 55–56.

47. Kasle, "Analysis," 86–87.

48. It is "shame" announced here. See Hertzberg, *I & II Samuel*, 38.

(ונקלה)." David's words (also 18:18) have often been understood as courtesy in Eastern custom.[49]

The perspective of honor and shame, however, offers a slightly different reading. Obviously, the king's son-in-law is a designation ascribed with honor in that it grants a person a connection with a royal family. David's words here seem to imply a sense of rebuke toward Saul's servants.[50] The offer to be the king's son-in-law was such a high honor that David thought that Saul's servants should not even suggest that he, someone who was a person of poor origin (איש רש)[51] and a person of "no honor" (ונקלה; cf. the LXX, οὐχὶ ἔνδοξος), was a candidate for the king's son-in-law. David's humility is revealing, given that he had already been offered the opportunity to become the king's son-in-law by marrying Saul's oldest daughter, Merab. However, David was put to shame when Saul gave her to someone else as a wife (18:19).[52] It seems that David did not hold the previous bitter experience as a grudge against the royal family but continued to fight courageously for Saul.

David's low estimation of his own honor and prestige can be clearly seen through the wordplay between הנקלה (the root קלל I) and ונקלה (the root קלה II, the by-form of קלל I, meaning "to be contemptible, dishonored").[53] Such an assessment of his honor actually reflects his status quo. Even though he was now the "commander of a thousand" (18:13), he was still often known as a former shepherd, a person of poor origin, insignificance and low status.[54] But David's status would soon change, not through the ascribed honor of royal marriage, but through his own effort and endeavor in fighting against the Philistines, thus earning a valuable name for himself (1 Sam 18:30).

---

49. Hertzberg, *I & II Samuel*, 161; Bergen, *1, 2 Samuel*, 204; Ackroyd, *First Book of Samuel*, 153–154.

50. E.g. the ESV, RSV, "Does it seem to you a little thing . . . ?"

51. Being poor, David would have been unable to afford the dowry paid to the father. In this case, pertaining to a princess, the dowry would have to be high enough to reflect her honorable status. Taking it as an opportunity to get rid of David, Saul later cunningly sets the amount of dowry as "a hundred Philistine foreskins."

52. Some scholars treat David as the one refusing the offer to marry Merab rather than the one being refused. See Bergen, *1, 2 Samuel*, 204; Firth, *1 & 2 Samuel*, 211. But this is a less likely reading since the text suggests that Saul was supposed to give Merab to David as his wife at a fixed time, which already implies mutual consent.

53. Stansell, "Honor and Shame," 57–58.

54. Stansell, 58.

In 1 Samuel 3:13, God condemns Eli because his sons were cursing (מקללים) God and he did not rebuke them.[55] The verb קלל I in the *piel* has a factitive sense;[56] that is, Eli's sons made God insignificant or contemptible in their perspective, hence "declare cursed." The blasphemous nature of Eli's sons is not strange to the readers, as it can be seen through their robbing of the sacrificial meat (1 Sam 2:12–17) and illicit sex with women who served at the entrance to the tent of meeting (1 Sam 2:22). Consequently, God would punish Eli's family for their sins.

In 1 Samuel 17:43, the verb קלל I (in the *piel*) is used in the context wherein Goliath cursed David by his gods because David carried sticks (not a common weapon) to approach him in battle. Goliath read David's gesture as treating him as an "unworthy opponent,"[57] thus insinuating shame. In response, the giant declared David cursed (קלל I) by the name of his gods. He threatened to leave David's corpse as food to the birds of the air and to the beasts of the field (17:44). The boasting of one's own strength and the scorning of the adversary was a common tactic in ancient combat.[58] However, it is obvious that only the true God, not the unknown gods, could bring both blessings and curses.

In each of these contexts, the occurrence of the term קלל I suggests that God and humans can both be the subject or the object with respect to the relationship of treating another with contempt. The widespread use of קלל I also shows that it is a conspicuous shame/shaming term in 1 Samuel.

2.4.4 בזה, "to despise" (1 Sam 2:30; 10:27; 17:42)

The word בזה usually means "despise, regard with contempt." It is contempt and arrogance shown openly in public. Considered as another term of disparagement, בזה is often relationship-based.[59] Along with קלל I and קלה II,

---

55. The MT מקללים להם is often recognized as "emendations of the scribes" of the more likely reading מקללים אלהים. The LXX ὅτι κακολογοῦντες Θεὸν has probably preserved the true reading. See Driver, *Notes*, 44; McCarter, *I Samuel*, 96; Steinmann, *1 Samuel*, 111; Klein, *1 Samuel*, 30; Tsumura, *First Book of Samuel*, 180; Adair, *Inductive Method*, 222.

56. "קלל I," *HALOT* 3, 1104.

57. Klein, *1 Samuel*, 180.

58. Klein, 180.

59. Kasle, "Analysis," 81.

Jumper places it as a semantic opposite of כבד, as בזה denotes unimportance and insignificance.[60]

The Elides were accused of belonging to those who despised YHWH (1 Sam 2:30; "those who despise me," בזי), and they were thus condemned to insignificance. The accusation of scorning the Lord definitely refers back to the robbing of the choicest meat in public from anyone who offered sacrifices in Shiloh (1 Sam 2:12–16), as 2:29 suggests.

Some worthless fellows (בני בליעל) questioned Saul's ability to bring deliverance to Israel and thus despised (1 Sam 10:27; ויבזהו) God's anointed one by refusing to bring him tribute and pay him the honor due to him. Public disgrace toward the new chosen king instigated strong resentment among the people who even suggested killing these worthless fellows in order to revenge the insult done to Saul (1 Sam 11:12).

Goliath, the mighty Philistine warrior, despised David (1 Sam 17:42; ויבזהו), who apparently looked like an inexperienced young lad at first sight and dared to confront him with only sticks and stones.

As can be seen from the above discussion, the term בזה often suggests a public belittling of someone, causing them to be despised. Such arrogance and contempt can be expressed to God or a king or ordinary people. But such a negative attitude against God or persons is denounced, as it does not comply with the teachings of the Lord and will only be judged with further diminishment.

2.4.5 חרף II, "to taunt" (1 Sam 17:10, 25, 26, 36, 45); חרפה, "reproach" (1 Sam 11:2; 17:26; 25:39)

The verb חרף II is a common term denoting shaming in the Hebrew Bible. It has the meaning "to reproach" or "to taunt." Kasle says that it refers to "actions that can cause shame."[61] The verb means to make a negative accusation about another's character.[62] The one who taunts others often seeks to actively boast of their own greatness and denigrate the significance, worth and ability of

---

60. Jumper, "Honor and Shame," 63. I tentatively place בזה in a separate category of verbs denoting shame since it only communicates the sense of shame indirectly.

61. Kasle, "Analysis," 58. Potentially, however, David did not feel ashamed when Goliath taunted (חרף II) Israel (17:45); rather, he stood up courageously to oppose him.

62. Jumper, "Honor and Shame," 97. However, it does not mean that the accusation against the opponent is true, as in the case when Goliath taunted the ranks of Israel (17:10, 25–26, 36).

others.⁶³ The nominal form חרפה, as a synonym of בשת, can be used to mean "disgrace, shame." Here, I will first address the nominal form and come back to discuss the verb, which occurs more frequently in 1 Samuel.

Nahash, the Ammonite, came up to make war against Israel and his forces besieged Jabesh-Gilead. Although the men in the city begged to make a peace treaty with them, Nahash would not do so unless all the men in the city would gouge out their right eye. The purpose was not to demonstrate the prevailing Ammonite military might over Israel but to show their superiority in status in light of Israel's mutilations,⁶⁴ thus bringing disgrace (1 Samuel 11:2; חרפה) to all Israel. As Lemos rightly says, "It is a desire to shame the Israelites that moves Nahash to mutilate them."⁶⁵ By gouging out the right eyes of the men in Jabesh-Gilead, Nahash wanted to bring shame, first and foremost, to the citizens of Jabesh-Gilead, but also to diffuse it to all the people of Israel, since it signifies the impotence of the Israelites who were too weak to aid Jabesh-Gilead.⁶⁶ Furthermore, in the context of warfare, the function of this shaming was to suppress and subdue Israel without blades, since shame was "restrictive and psychologically repressive."⁶⁷ Shame, in this case, is employed as a sanction to restrain the enemy in warfare.

The verb חרף II occurs mostly in the *piel* stem. According to *HALOT*, both the *qal* and *piel* stems have the same meaning, "to taunt." But one can assume that the *piel* stem differs in its extensiveness, here involving taunting in a variety of situations or upon multiple objects.⁶⁸ In 1 Samuel, the verb חרף II occurs five times (all in the *piel* stem) in the battle between Israel and the Philistines (1 Sam 17:10, 25, 26, 36, 45), with the combat of David and Goliath as the nucleus. The warrior Goliath, representing the Philistine army, stands

---

63. Kutsch, "חרף," *TDOT*, 5:211.

64. Elsewhere, captured kings' thumbs and big toes were cut off (Judg 1:6). Mutilation brings a defect to the body and thus makes it less attractive to behold. The lack of wholeness may also create an obstacle for people to participate in temple worship. See Lemos, "Shame and Mutilation," 230–231.

65. Lemos, 229.

66. Lemos, 230.

67. Bechtel, "Shame as a Sanction," 64. The Ammonites, as victors, would not worry about further rebellion if the Israelites were psychologically ruined and physically flawed.

68. As Goliath taunted the ranks of Israel, he defied the ranks of the God of Israel. For the pluralitive function of the *piel* (possibly involving multiple subjects, actions, or action upon multiple objects), see Joüon and Muraoka, *Grammar of Biblical Hebrew*, § 52d, pp. 144–145 (hereafter cited as Joüon-Muraoka).

out and taunts the "ranks of Israel" (1 Sam 17:10, 45). The advantage of his stature, strength and equipment (17:4–7) led him to assert his superiority over all other Israelites in any single combat and made him assume that no one would have any chance to prevail against him. Goliath's taunt suggests that all Israelites shall be slaves to the Philistines and serve them if he wins (17:9). The verb חרף II implies "not only defiance and provocation but also open contempt."[69] Jumper also suggests that taunting was a tactic of "drawing an enemy into conflict."[70] Psychological warfare has already happened before any use of swords. However, the person whom Goliath taunts is not only Israel but "the ranks of the living God," as David points out repeatedly (17:26, 36, 45).[71] The only way to remove such disgrace (17:26; חרפה) from Israel was for someone from Israel to venture out and kill Goliath. As it turns out, David's volunteering in battle and his victory over Goliath were motivated by such a concern.

The fact that חרף II is used very frequently as a shaming term in warfare should draw our attention. For example, in a similar context of war, Sennacherib, the king of Assyria, came up against Jerusalem and taunted (2 Kgs 19:4, 16, 22 [2x]. cf. Isa 37:4, 17, 23 [2x]; 2 Chr 32:17) YHWH, the living God. It seems that taunting was a prevalent anti-morale military tactic used in wars for generating shame (as a psychological threat) to the enemy. That is why the use of חרף II in the Hebrew Bible is often related to a warfare context; this is even true for most of its uses in the Psalms (42:11; 44:17; 55:13; 69:10; 74:10, 18; 79:12; 89:52; 102:9).

2.4.6 כלם, "be humiliated" (1 Sam 20:34; 25:7, 15)

The verb כלם has the basic meaning of "be humiliated, be put to shame" in the *niphal* and "put to shame, humiliate" in the *hiphil*.[72] According to Jumper, in as many as twenty verses, כלם appears in parallel with בוש I as a synonym.[73] Such information also shows the close relationship between כלם and בוש I, the latter being a conspicuous term denoting shame in the Hebrew Bible. The word

---

69. McCarter, *1 Samuel*, 293.
70. Jumper, "Honor and Shame," 96.
71. It is clear that God stands behind Israel. Ultimately, the taunt against Israel is against YHWH himself.
72. "כָּלַם," BDB, 484. The majority of the occurrences are in the *niphal*.
73. Jumper, "Honor and Shame," 95.

כלם also appears together with חרף II, both being terms of shaming/shame.[74] Wagner's observation is insightful for us to understand the meaning of כלם:

> In the Hebrew OT, the meaning of *klm* appears to stay within the realm of "disaster" and "disgrace," both active and passive. The root conveys the notion of disintegration. A person to whom *klm* is applied is degraded both subjectively and objectively. That person is isolated within his previous world, and his own sense of worth is impugned. He becomes subject to scorn, insult, and mockery, and is cut off from communication.[75]

According to Wagner, "shame" and "disgrace" are the unavoidable consequences of someone described by כלם. A person humiliated is subject to shame. כלם appears three times in 1 Samuel, two times in the *hiphil* and one time in the *hophal* stem. In the court story, Jonathan is grieved in his heart when his father Saul humiliates David (1 Sam 20:34; הכלמו, *hiphil* stem). The meaning of "insult, humiliate" is obvious in this stem. Saul's disrespect toward David can be shown in the fact that he refrained from calling David by name, only addressing him as "the son of Jesse" (20:27, 30, 31). Saul's "disgracing" acts involve the use of vocal threat and physical violence to eliminate David.[76] All these enrich the meaning of כלם in its context.

Other occurrences of כלם are found in the familiar story of Nabal, Abigail and David (1 Sam 25:7, 15). Assuming that Nabal would be generous toward those who had provided protection to his shepherds and his sheep (25:16), David sent his men to collect some gifts from him at sheep shearing, a festival season, as compensation for this contribution. The text (25:7) states that David's men did not mistreat (הכלמנום) Nabal's shepherds. The interpretation of this כלם (*hiphil* stem) is controversial. BDB renders it as "insult, humiliate."[77] But *HALOT* reads it as having a different meaning: "to harm somebody."[78] *TDOT* accords with *HALOT*'s position by pointing to the parallel clause,

---

74. Kasle argues that the nominal form of the root כלמה is often defined as "insult" through deeds whereas חרפה generally refers to verbal insult. See Kasle, "Analysis," 62.
75. Wagner, "כלם," *TDOT*, 7:186.
76. Wagner, 7:187.
77. "כָּלַם," BDB, 484.
78. "כלם," *HALOT* 2, 480.

"They have not missed anything,"[79] which seems to indicate that David's men did not rob them or take anything from them.[80] Indeed, in its context, David seems to suggest something more tangible than a sentiment of emotional harm. After all, כלם, if understood as not disgracing Nabal's servants, commendable as it may be, still does not directly contribute to Nabal's economic standing, and thus weakens David's ground for asking for gifts from him. Therefore, it is more likely that כלם here involves an element of physical mistreatment in the context;[81] that is, David's men "did them no harm" (ESV, NRSV), or even more vividly, "did not hurt them" (NKJV). Indeed, with a wandering group of six hundred men (25:13), David could have easily taken advantage of the situation by harassing Nabal's shepherds and forcefully taking away his property. Thus, the expected gift from Nabal is not groundless.

To sum up, כלם, though often defined as meaning "put to shame," should be treated with more caution, especially pertaining to its *hiphil* and *hophal* stems, where it is possibly read as "to harm" or "to suffer harm" in certain contexts, as is the case here in 1 Samuel 25:7 and 25:15.

2.4.7 באש, "to stink" (1 Sam 27:12)

During David's exile in the land of the Philistines, he was granted the land of Ziklag by Achish, the king of Gath (1 Sam 27:5–6). David and his men raided the Geshurites, the Girzites and the Amalekites,[82] left no one alive and took the booty. Upon returning from these military campaigns, at Achish's inquiry, David repeatedly deceived him by vaguely reporting the raiding location as "The Negev of Judah" or "The Negev of Jeharmeel" or "The Negev of the Kenites." All these Negev locations are closely associated with Judah's

---

79. A similar statement is confirmed again in v. 15 by a servant's words to Abigail, "And we were not mistreated (הכלמנו, *hophal*), and we did not miss anything." The meaning of כלם in v. 15 should be consistent with whatever interpretation one takes for the same verb in v. 7, since the *hophal* is the passive voice of the *hiphil* stem.

80. Wagner, "כלם," *TDOT*, 7:187.

81. Some commentators support such a reading by interpreting כלם as "molested" (Hertzberg, *I and II Samuel*, 202), "abuse" (McCarter, *1 Samuel*, 389), "harm" (Klein, *1 Samuel*, 243), and "mistreat" (Arnold, *1 and 2 Samuel*, 338).

82. The exact locations of these people are not stated, but these semi-nomadic groups may have lived close to the Negev and Sinai area. What is important is that all these people posed a direct threat to Judah's safety. By raiding these desert marauders, David showed himself as Judah's protector. See Arnold, *1 and 2 Samuel*, 361.

southern districts.⁸³ By doing so, David leads king Achish to believe that he has become an enemy of his own country and thus would spend the rest of his life serving him, when in actuality he was assaulting enemies of Judah.

The narrator captures Achish's inner thoughts for the readers: "He has acted utterly repulsively (הבאש הבאיש, literally "has exhibited an utter stench") to his people in Israel; therefore, he shall always be my servant" (1 Sam 27:12). The infinitive absolute (הבאש), preceding a finite verb (הבאיש), typically conveys an intensification of the action. Here it displays what one might not expect: in Achish's perspective, David has acted utterly repulsively towards his own people, which contradicts expected behavior toward one's people group. The stench, in this case, refers not to the odor caused by physical deterioration but David's own reputation (being a traitor to his own people). Achish assumed that David had exhibited an utter stench – that is, his reputation had deteriorated and gone bad. In this way, even if David were to think about returning to his homeland afterwards, his bad reputation among his people would make him an unwelcome person and it would only further strengthen David's allegiance to king Achish. When someone's reputation goes bad, he is exposed to shame.⁸⁴ The notion of shame is precisely captured in the LXX's rendering of Ἤσχυνται αἰσχυνόμενος (thoroughly disgraced) as a translation of הבאש הבאיש. Thus the translators of the LXX understood clearly that David would be put to shame among his people if he truly raided the south of Judah. As a matter of fact, David's positive reputation was actually enhanced as he destroyed Judah's potential threat. At one time, David even shared part of his spoils with the elders of Judah (1 Sam 30:26–30). With this effective strategy, he certainly gained the favor and support of his people.

2.5 A "Seat" (כסא) of Honor (1 Sam 1:9; 2:8; 4:13, 18)

The word כסא can have different meanings. According to *HALOT*, it can be an ordinary seat as well as a throne, a seat of honor.⁸⁵ BDB adds a third layer

---

83. Arnold points out that נגב is a Hebrew term to refer to the desert south of the Judean hills. See Arnold, *1 and 2 Samuel*, 361.

84. The same verb (באש) in 2 Samuel 10:6 is connected with acts that bring dishonor; see Stansell, "Honor and Shame," 68–69.

85. "כִּסֵּא," *HALOT* 2, 487.

of figurative meaning to it, thus representing "royal dignity, authority, power."[86] In 1 Samuel, three times (1:9; 4:13, 18) Eli the priest is described as sitting on a כסא. In her hymn of praise, Hannah also mentions the inheritance of a כסא for the poor (2:8). In this part, I will discuss the nuance of the meaning of כסא in its different occurrences.

The multiple portrayals of Eli's sitting on a כסא cannot be accidental in 1 Samuel. The determination of the nature of כסא is closely associated with the identity of the person who sits on it and the context in which it is described. If it is a king who sits on a כסא in his palace, his royal identity decides that most likely he sits on a throne (see for example, Exod 11:5; Deut 17:18; 1 Kgs 1:46). If it is a visitor who comes into an ordinary house and is welcomed by the host to sit, the כסא is an ordinary chair, as in the case of the prophet Elisha whom the Shunammite woman hosted (2 Kgs 4:10).

Though many scholars consider Eli's seat as an ordinary chair,[87] Robert Polzin is the first to challenge such a customary reading. Polzin presents Eli as a royal figure – that is, Eli, as a leader, functions like a king in Israel at this time, since kingship is not yet instituted. Thus Eli was sitting on "the throne" (1 Sam 1:9; 4:13, 18; הכסא) of rule.[88] According to Polzin, Eli's death, falling off his throne (הכסא), displays the Deuteronomist's view of all the "burden and doom" that kingship first brought to Israel.[89] In response to Polzin's proposal, Spina argues that Eli is consistently described in 1 Samuel as a "priest" who judges Israel rather than a royal figure, and thus Eli's כסא is not a royal seat.[90] It seems to me that Spina's argument is very convincing. Nevertheless, Polzin contributes something by bringing out an important element of the seat (הכסא) on which Eli sits: Eli's seat seems to go beyond the literal level of a piece of wooden furniture.

---

86. "כִּסֵּא," BDB, 491.

87. Spina, "Eli's Seat," 68. Spina helpfully gives a detailed list of scholars who favor the reading of an ordinary chair, e.g. Klein, *1 Samuel*, 37; McCarter, *1 Samuel*, 49, 110; Eslinger, *Kingship of God*, 76.

88. Polzin, *Samuel and the Deuteronomist*, 23, 62, 64; also Firth, *1 & 2 Samuel*, 56; Bodner, *1 Samuel*, 17. There is a record in the ancient Near East of a high priestess who sat on her throne of office in Emar. See Fleming, *Installation*, 118.

89. In other words, Eli is doomed from the start. See Polzin, *Samuel and the Deuteronomist*, 64.

90. Spina, "Eli's Seat," 70.

If Eli's seat (כסא) is not a royal seat (a throne) and is more than an ordinary chair, then how should it be perceived? Eli's identity may point us in a promising direction. One should note that Eli is not only portrayed as a priest in 1 Samuel but also as the leader of Israel who had judged (שפט) Israel for forty years (1 Sam 4:18).[91] Being a judge, one can presumably think of Eli's ruling as continuous from the periods of many other judges in the book of Judges. As both a priest and a judge, Eli's leadership and authority in Israel transcended all other Israelites of the time,[92] and it is not a problem to say that Eli's כסא should be seen as "symbolic of his priestly and ruling office."[93] The reference to Eli's כסא in 1 Samuel thus evinces his authority and privilege as a religious and civic leader of Israel. Such a seat embodies the rank of the person who sits on it. Eli's seat was a sign of his authority.[94] Not every ordinary person could come and sit on *the* seat (הכסא).[95] So Eli's כסא, though not a throne, should most probably be seen as "a seat of honor," reserved exclusively for such a distinguished leader as he.[96]

Having said this, Eli's כסא, the seat of honor, can be seen as a middle point between an ordinary chair and a royal throne. Such a seat of honor, not necessarily a royal seat, can be affirmed by examples of many other biblical texts. In 1 Kings 2:19, King Solomon, while sitting on his throne (כסאו), asked that a seat (כסא) be brought to Bathsheba when she came to see him. The

---

91. Spina, 70–71.

92. Spina, 71. Spina even goes so far as to say that Eli is superior to the other judges in the past.

93. Spina, 71. Having shed negative light on Eli's leadership, Spina goes on to argue that Samuel's era signals the transition from priestly to prophetic leadership, a greater kind of leadership. But even this great Samuel is not portrayed as one who occupies the כסא as Eli had (unless one reads 1 Sam 2:8 as an allusion to him), as Samuel's main role is to prepare the right king to sit on the כסא (throne). It turns out that Saul could not be and had not been seated on the royal כסא (no כסא is referenced pertaining to him), as he was in the end unworthy as king. Thus, Saul was a king without his throne (כסא). The rightful throne (כסא) belongs to God's chosen line, the Davidic family (2 Sam 7:13–16).

94. It was more usual for people of the day to sit on mats or on the earth itself; sitting above the ground level implied the possession of elevated social authority. See Bergen, *1, 2 Samuel*, 68. Similarly, Eli's chair was a sign of his office as high priest. See Steinmann, *1 Samuel*, 54.

95. Note the definite article ה even when it appears the first time in 1:9. Thus, together with the participle יֹשֵׁב, the sentence can be paraphrased as "Now Eli the priest was frequently sitting on *the* special seat which is on the doorpost of the temple of the Lord." The הכסא was a seat of special rank and honor.

96. Commenting on הכסא of 1 Samuel 1:9, Tsumura also implicitly indicates that Eli's seat was "a sign of honor" in that particular social setting. See Tsumura, *First Book of Samuel*, 116.

seat, which was put at the right side of the king, was quite likely a special seat designated for the king's wife or his high officials who sought the king's face.[97] Such a seat, embodying a special ranking, was also likely a seat of honor. In Esther 3:1, King Ahasuerus promoted Haman and set his seat (כסאו) above all other officials who were with him. The seat given to Haman signaled his power and privilege as the king's favored one; thus, it should be seen as "a seat of honor" (NIV). To sum up, we do not see a problem that, in certain circumstances, a כסא can designate a special seat of honor but not a royal seat. The meaning of a word should not be determined alone by its semantics; the context can tell us more about its nuances.

In 1 Samuel 2:8, however, the word כסא, as a "seat of honor," is obvious by the connecting absolute noun כבוד following after it: thus, וכסא כבוד. Perhaps being misguided by a nearby phrase in 2:10 where key terms such as "king" (מלך) and "anointed one" (משיח) conceivably convey a royal status, many read וכסא כבוד in 2:8 as "a throne of honor."[98] While 1 Samuel 2:10 does accord with the theme of kingship, it only apprises us of a singular king, an anointed one; the poor and needy as a group, however, are plural, as suggested by the pronominal suffix ם in ינחלם ("he makes *them* inherit"). The poor and needy are not the royal group per se; they will only sit with noble ones (נדיבים).[99] McCarter also points out the poem's connection to Psalm 113:7–8, which, in its context, also does not mention either the poor or needy inheriting a royal status but rather sitting with noble ones.[100] In Hannah's mind, the poor and needy are people from the grassroots level (people like herself) whom the Lord, nevertheless, values and honors with "a seat of honor."

---

97. Spina, "Eli's Seat," 69.

98. Polzin, *Samuel and the Deuteronomist*, 31, 38. According to his Deuteronomist framework of exilic readership, Polzin conjectures the exiled king Jehoiachin (2 Kgs 25:28) as the person who inherits the throne of honor. See also Arnold, *1 and 2 Samuel*, 65; similarly, "a glorious throne," Klein, *1 Samuel*, 12. Translations that follow this path are, for example, NIV, KJV, NKJV, AV, HCSB.

99. Though many translations render the word as "princes," the word נדיב itself does not necessarily imply royalty but nobility; see "נָדִיב," *HALOT* 2, 674.

100. McCarter, *1 Samuel*, 73. For a further comparison of the Song of Hannah and Psalm 113, see Willis, "Song of Hannah," 139–154. According to Willis, the Song of Hannah most likely originated in connection with the ark, probably at the Shiloh sanctuary. If so, kingship was not yet instituted and thus the concept of linking the poor with a throne of honor is less likely.

2.6 The Honor of a "Chief Position" in a Meal (1 Sam 9:22)[101]

Dining is an important part of any culture. Eating is not only a vital necessity for the needs of the body, but even more so, a social occasion for people to meet and associate together. The ancient Israelites also valued the etiquette of meals.

In 1 Samuel 9, the narrator brings Saul onto our horizon after the Israelites asked in chapter 8 for a king to rule them (as other nations had). Saul searched for his father's lost donkeys to no avail for three days. At the insistence of his servant, Saul went to a city in the land of Zuph to inquire from the prophet Samuel the whereabouts of the lost donkeys. Before Saul's arrival, God had revealed to Samuel that Saul was his chosen one for Israel (9:17). Accordingly, Samuel prepared a banquet in advance to host this honorable guest.

When Saul arrived in the city, Samuel brought Saul and his servant to a chamber and gave them the best reserved seats, literally "the place at the head" (1 Sam 9:22; מקום בראש). Since head (ראש) is an important organ of our body, it has the "public symbol of honour."[102] It is used here metaphorically to accentuate the guest's importance. Some translations thus reflect such nuances, "the chiefest place" (KJV, AV), "the place of honor" (NKJV), "a choice place at the table" (NCV). Samuel honors Saul with the chief seat in front of all the invited guests.[103]

The honor rendered to Saul is shown not only in the reserved chief seat in the evening meal, but also in the portion of meat which Samuel set aside for him in advance (9:23–24). Meat, in biblical times, was not a common food for daily meals and would only be eaten on special occasions, usually in the context of sacrificial worship. Samuel reserved probably the best part of the meat for Saul. The thigh was usually kept for the officiating priest (Lev 7:32–34),

---

101. As I mentioned previously in chapter 1 (section 1.7), though the title of this research is *Honor and Shame in 1 Samuel 1–7*, I do allow for an extended discussion of relevant honor and shame terms covering the whole book of 1 Samuel in this chapter (in this section as well as in the ones following).

102. Mahlangu, "Ancient Mediterranean Values," 91.

103. In East Asia today, people still carry this tradition by keeping certain seats at a meal for guests more honorable than others. Such seats are often reserved for distinguished guests.

but here Samuel yielded it to his guest of honor.[104] Such a special cut of meat is a mark of Saul's special future rank.[105]

In the ancient Near East, a guest's honor could be seen from the seat assignment and the provision of food during meals.[106] Though Saul considered himself insignificant in his origin and status (1 Sam 9:21),[107] Samuel rendered him the greatest honor in front all the guests because such honor is due God's soon-to-be anointed one (1 Sam 10:1). Saul is honored in a way befitting a king.[108]

2.7 A Monument (יד), the Proclamation of Honor (1 Sam 15:12)

Being anointed as the king of Israel, Saul proved himself as the leader of his people through his military success. He gained victory in the battles against the Ammonites (1 Sam 11:11) and the Philistines (1 Sam 14:1–23) and thus stabilized his ruling. However, Saul also had his fatal weaknesses: a concern for his own honor. In a new battle against the Amalekites, Saul was instructed by the words of the Lord through Samuel to put them to complete destruction (1 Sam 15:3, והחרמתם). In response to their mistreatment of Israelites as they came out of Egypt, the Lord had sworn that he would wipe out the memory of Amalek (Exod 17:14). The Israelites were not unfamiliar with this kind of חרם ("to exterminate") war in history (Josh 6:17; Deut 20:17). Saul did win the battle and killed all the Amalekites, but he spared the life of Agag, the king of the Amalekites, and the best part of their animals. The reason that Saul spared Agag, as a direct disobedience to God's commandment, is probably that Saul desired to do honor to his royal ruling by displaying this captured

---

104. Walton, Matthews and Chavalas, *IVP Bible Background Commentary*, 294; McCarter, *1 Samuel*, 180.

105. Tsumura, *First Book of Samuel*, 279.

106. Joseph also arranges different seats and foods for his brothers while they dine together. Benjamin is given five times as much food as his brothers, thus acquiring much more honor (Gen 43:32–34).

107. However, 9:1 reveals Saul's familial background: he seems to come from a prominent family, his father being a גבור חיל, which could be rendered "a man of wealth" (ESV, NRSV) or "a mighty man of power" (NKJV), since חיל can ambiguously imply both "wealth" or "strength." Saul's evaluation of himself may be oriental humility.

108. Brueggemann, *First and Second Samuel*, 73.

royal slave.[109] But God regretted that he had made Saul the king of Israel due to his disobedience to the Lord's words.

Saul's eagerness to proclaim his own honor is further shown from his haste to set up a monument for himself at Carmel following the battle. The man who replied to Samuel concerning the whereabouts of Saul must have been very impressed with the new monument, and thus he said: והנה מציב לו יד ("and behold, he set up for himself a monument"[110]). The "lo, and behold" (הנה) phrase may hint that this dialogue actually happened at Carmel and that the monument was visually conspicuous to any passerby. The setting up of the moment had certainly become a top item of news in the region. The significance of setting up the monument (יד) was to commemorate the victory against the Amalekites. Thus, Saul's erection of the monument was to "imprint the memory of the battle in the nation's psyche (והנה מציב לו יד) and [evidence of] his desire to be honored in the sight of Israel and the elders in v. 30."[111] Likewise, Hertzberg also suggests that Saul's pillar indicates that he intended to ascribe the glory of the victory to himself.[112]

According to ancient Near Eastern traditions, a monument usually recorded details of successful military campaigns and declared a king's sovereignty over the area.[113] Archaeological evidence shows that some stelae were set up in Israel. For instance, Sheshonq I, pharaoh of Egypt, set up an Egyptian stela in Megiddo in order to clearly demonstrate his power as the ruler of Megiddo. Similarly, an Aramean stela was found in Dan commemorating a victory against Israel and the house of David.[114] Such discoveries allow us to see the commonness of setting up monuments in the ancient Near East to assert one's victory. By doing so, the monument constantly reminded the people of the king's victorious glory. What Saul failed to acknowledge is that it was by the hand of the Lord (יד יהוה) that the Israelites gained the victory.

---

109. Keil, *Biblical Commentary*, 153.

110. Saul sets up the monument *for himself* (לו). The preposition lamed (ל) should be considered as *dativus commodi* (dative of advantage). See Joüon-Muraoka, § 133d.
Perhaps not by coincidence, later we find Absalom also put up a similar monument (יד) for himself so that the Israelites would remember his name (2 Sam 18:18; הזכיר שמי). Again, the purpose of honoring oneself is plain in this occasion.

111. Zimran, "Divine vs. Human," 404–405.

112. Hertzberg, *I and II Samuel*, 126.

113. Walton, Matthews, and Chavalas, *IVP Bible Background Commentary*, 304.

114. Dietrich, *Early Monarchy in Israel*, 146–154.

The readers should still have had the fresh memory of the awesome work of the hand of the Lord against the Philistines (1 Sam 5:6, 9; 7:13). The ironic thing is that while God rejected him as king of Israel (1 Sam 15:10), Saul tried to enhance his own honor by setting up the monument for himself.

We are not sure of the connection, but if this picture of Saul setting up a monument after the victory against the Amalekites is compared with an intertextual reading of Exodus 17:16, one may find the irony that, against the same enemy, Moses acknowledged that it was by the "hand upon the banner of the Lord" (יד על כס יה)[115] that the Israelites gained victory. Moses dared not seize God's honor for the victory against the Amalekites though he kept upholding his hands in prayer to the point of exhaustion (Exod 17:12). The difference is obvious; Saul paled in comparison to Moses for his spiritual character in giving glory to God.

Readers might be aware that after a similar victory against Israel's enemy, Samuel set up a stone between Mizpah and Shen and named it "stone of help" (1 Sam 7:12; אבן העזר) to commemorate the help of Lord in defeating the Philistines. It is quite clear that Samuel's erected stone gives honor to the Lord for his deliverance. Saul did not have the humility to learn from Samuel and other heroic ancestors' example in giving honor to God for his help and deliverance.[116]

In my findings, it seems that setting up a monument (יד) has a close relationship to the proclamation of honor. It is unfortunate that Saul's action of erecting a monument (יד) in 1 Sam 15:12 served his own interests and proclaimed his own honor.

---

115. The Samaritan Pentateuch reads כסא ("throne"). In this reading, the Amalekites challenged Yahweh's throne, namely his sovereignty, by attacking Israel. See Durham, *Exodus*, 237. Alternatively, however, and very plausibly, כֵּס is a scribal error for what was correctly נִסִּי ("my banner") in 17:15, the previous verse. Cole sees "banner" in vv. 15–16 as a possible name for an altar which Moses dedicated to YHWH, thus consequentially a title of God himself. In this way, "a hand upon the banner of YHWH" is seen as "an oath of perpetual war" wherein the right hand is placed on YHWH's altar, emphasizing God's divine power against the Amalekites. See Cole, *Exodus*, 137. Dozeman also prefers the emendation of "banner." See Dozeman, *Commentary on Exodus*, 397–398.

116. For instance, Joshua commanded the people of Israel to set up twelve stones, according to the number of the Israelite tribes, to commemorate God's mighty act of making the water of the Jordan stop flowing as they crossed over it (Josh 4:5–8, 20–24).

2.8 David's Esteemed Name (1 Sam 18:30)

People's names carry their reputation. A name represents all aspects of a person, be it honor or shame, good or bad.[117] Thus, a good name conveys honor, and a bad name entails shame. God also concerns himself with the reputation of his name. Thus, the psalmist prayed while being humiliated in the context of a Babylonian invasion, "Help us, O God of our salvation, for the sake of the glory of your name, deliver us and forgive our sins on account of your name" (Ps 79:9). It is as if the reputation of God's name was put at risk if God did nothing to deliver the disgraced Israelites, who called upon the name of YHWH.

In 1 Samuel 18:30, however, we witness the rise of David's name and reputation. David's rise was inevitable after God chose to anoint him as the new king of Israel (1 Sam 16:1–13), yet David had not actualized his power and honor as a king, remaining instead a humble shepherd. Such an imbalance soon changed when David defeated Goliath and married Michal, the daughter of Saul.[118]

The narrator, interestingly, does not bring attention to David's ascribed honor as Saul's son-in-law (an honorary relationship),[119] but to his acquired honor through his bravery and competence in wars against the Philistines. As David became more successful (שׂכל) than all Saul's servants during those wars, his name was highly esteemed (1 Sam 18:30; וייקר שמו מאד, literally, "his name was greatly valued"). Obviously, David's precious and valuable name was tied to his honor. He was honored in front of all of Saul's warriors because of his dedication and contribution in the wars. Later a similar summary note is picked up by the narrator in 2 Samuel 8:13 in a war-report context: "And David made a name" – that is, David won honor and fame.[120] David's acquired honor is particularly highlighted when it is contrasted with

---

117. Hundley, "To Be," 535–536.

118. The women of Israel gave even more honor to David than to Saul as they celebrated the victory over Goliath with singing, dancing and chanting: "Saul has struck down his thousands, and David his ten thousands" (1 Sam 18:7).

119. David actually risked his life (18:25) and acquired this title by collecting two hundred foreskins of the Philistines as a dowry presented to Saul (1 Sam 18:20–27).

120. Stansell, "Honor and Shame," 59.

his earlier position as a shepherd boy, an insignificant person with low status, no wealth and no honor (1 Sam 18:23; נקלה).[121]

Now David had the favor of Jonathan (18:3–4), the love of Michal (18:20, 28) and the support and respect of Saul's men (18:30), and his rise to the throne became inevitable. Saul, on the other hand, entered into a downward spiral of fear, suspicion and malice.[122]

2.9 The Disgrace of Nakedness (1 Sam 19:24; 20:30)

The connection between nakedness and shame can be traced back to the Eden story (Gen 3:1–13). Public nakedness was considered shameful as it exposed the most private part of the body to the gaze of others. Such an exposure indicated vulnerability or defenselessness and thus triggered shame.[123] We will select two passages (1 Sam 19:24 and 20:30) concerning nakedness and discuss their notion of shame in the context. Both texts are related to Saul and his household.

The story of Saul lying naked (ערם) on the ground all day and night (1 Sam 19:24) has to be read in the wider context of Saul's plan to capture David (19:18–24). After God rejected Saul as the king of Israel (1 Sam 15:23) and turned to anoint David instead (1 Sam 16:13), the break between Saul and David would be inevitable. When Saul sensed the rapid growth of David's reputation after he killed Goliath (1 Sam 18:7–9) and married Michal (1 Sam 18:17–30), Saul decided to have David killed. Nevertheless, Jonathan befriended David and leaked the news to him. Michal, the daughter of Saul, also protected David, allowing him enough time to escape.

David fled to meet Samuel at Ramah (1 Sam 19:18) because Samuel was the one who had anointed him and should be able to tell him what to do in

---

121. Stansell, 58.
122. Klein, *1 Samuel*, 191.
123. Daube, "Culture of Deuteronomy," 1005; Bechtel, "Shame as a Sanction," 67; Klopfenstein, *Scham and Schande*, 32. Indeed, nakedness as shame can be seen from the great humiliation (נכלמים מאד) David's servants suffered in their journey to Ammon (2 Sam 10:1–2). David sent them to express condolences to Hanun, the new king of Ammon, after the death of his father; the new king, however, misguided by his council, shaved off half their beards, cut off their garments at the hips, and sent the men back to David. David, in order to spare his servants from public shame, sent his men to escort them to Jericho until their beards had grown back and (presumably) provided them clothing to cover their bodies.

this crisis. When Saul was informed that David was staying with Samuel in Ramah, he sent his messengers to capture David. But when these men encountered a company of the prophets prophesying (1 Sam 19:20; נבאים) with Samuel, they were also overcome by the spirit of God and prophesied (1 Sam 19:21; ויתנבאו). When Saul heard the news, he sent a second delegation, which fell into the same state. The third time, Saul sent more men, but yet the same thing happened. All these men stayed there prophesying and ignored the mission given to them. Without success, Saul went there in person to Ramah to capture David. But it turned out that before even reaching Naioth in Ramah, Saul was found prophesying (1 Sam 19:23–24; ויתנבא) with his clothes stripped off. This phenomenon of prophesying and being naked is bizarre.[124] Thus the exact nature of the term "prophesy" (נבא) requires investigation.

Obviously, here the work of prophesying has a close relationship with the spirit of God. It is the Spirit who moved them to prophesy. The context suggests it was a prophetic ecstasy.[125] While the ecstatic state of the men whom Saul sent may have lasted for a short period of time, Saul's prophetic ecstasy continued for a day and night.[126] It is ironic that Saul's prophesying was accompanied by the state of lying naked on the ground. How can one prophesy and be naked simultaneously? Readers have known since chapter 15 that Saul is the rejected king. The spirit of God, thereafter, intended not goodness but torture and affliction for Saul (1 Sam 16:14; 18:10; 19:9).[127] Saul and his messengers prophesying should be seen as seemingly exhibiting the characteristics of prophetic behavior.[128] The verbs, in the *hitpael* (HtD) stem, could be potentially rendered as "behaving surprisingly like a prophet."[129] More

---

124. It is possible that Saul may have been called "naked" while still having his inner tunic next to the skin. See Driver, *Notes*, 160. However, it is argued that ערום has the basic meaning of complete nakedness unless the context suggests otherwise. For a detailed discussion, See Hanley, "Use of Nakedness," 135–141, 158. I prefer the latter reading of Saul's complete nudity.

125. For the sake of clarity, Wilson avoids the use of the term "ecstasy," describing it as "a form of uncontrolled trance." See Wilson, "Prophecy and Ecstasy," 334.

126. Arnold, *1 and 2 Samuel*, 290–291.

127. Klein, *1 Samuel*, 198.

128. Klein, 198. See also "נבא," *HALOT* 2, 659.

129. See Jenni, "Nifal und Hitpael," 195–198. Jenni suggests a fundamental distinction between the *niphal* and *hitpael* stems in that the HtD offers new and unexpected information, whereas the *niphal* presents given, normal and expected action. Putting the theory to work, Saul's prophesying in 1 Samuel 19:23–24 (as well as that of his messengers' in vv. 20–21) was

likely, the nature of their prophesying was probably different from what the prophet Samuel did in communicating God's words to the people of Israel (1 Sam 3:19–21).[130] The situation here in 19:24 is negative and ironic: Saul fell into an uncontrollable state so that he even striped off his garment and lay naked all day and night. Saul's nakedness exposed the king's shame to the public. The king's honor was degraded by the mocking eyes of others. It was God's judgment upon someone who opposed him.

One cannot help but recall 1 Samuel 10:1–12, which relates a similar event wherein Saul was touched by the spirit of God and ostensibly prophesied. The first time when people saw Saul prophesying (נבא),[131] they asked each other with an element of surprise (10:11), "What on earth has happened to the son of Kish, is Saul also among the prophets?" Here, people repeat the same old question/proverb, "Is Saul also among the prophets?" It should be noted that the context of the question is different than before. Instead of surprise, the people reinterpreted it in this new situation with a tone of contempt.[132] The spirit of God rushed through Saul for bad.[133] Saul's experience in chapter 10 was seemingly positive, but here in chapter 19, it is obviously negative. As Firth points out, the Spirit's presence in chapter 10 proves that Saul was the chosen king, whereas here the Spirit restrains him from killing. The proverb/question that once proved Saul's status as the anointed king now turns him into a laughingstock.[134]

Another text in 1 Samuel that points to the shame of nakedness is 20:30. The text states: "Saul became angry with Jonathan, and he said to him, 'Son of a perverse, rebellious woman! Have I not known that you choose the son of Jesse to your shame (לבשתך) and the shame of your mother's nakedness (לבשת ערות אמך)?'" At the beginning of this chapter, we find that David had

---

unexpected (all in the *hitpael*), contra the text-coherent (expected and usual in the flow of the text) prophesying (*niphal* participle) of a group of other prophets in 1 Samuel 19:20.

130. Saul's prophecy in 1 Samuel 19:23–24 appears to be temporary and ecstatic.

131. Here the stem is *niphal* – Saul's acquaintances perceived him to be overcome by normal prophecy (*niphal*; 1 Sam 10:11) together with the prophets – while 1 Samuel 10:6, 10 and 13 present his prophesying activity with a *hitpael*. With the use of the HtD stem in 1 Samuel 10:6, 10, 13, Saul's prophecy is considered unexpected and unusual. See Jenni, "Nifal und Hitpael," 196.

132. Tsumura, *First Book of Samuel*, 499.

133. The spirit of YHWH works for good (1 Sam 10:6, 10; 11:6; 16:3) and the evil spirit for bad in 1 Samuel (1 Sam 16:14–16, 23; 18:10; 19:9).

134. Firth, *1 & 2 Samuel*, 219.

returned from his fugitive journey to Ramah and sought to be reconciled with Saul through Jonathan the mediator. Some chronological problems are noted by scholars, since previously Saul had already tried to kill David (18:11; 19:10).[135] However, the narrator's main concern here is not chronological accuracy but foregrounding David's loyal character which stands in contrast to Saul's bad faith. By doing so, the text further explains why David had to leave the court.

When David came to Jonathan for help, Jonathan, sensing David's unavoidable rise to succession, and out of his love toward David (20:14–17), decided to help test his father's true intention toward David. Saul soon realized that Jonathan supported David instead of siding with him. Betrayal of such a family blood tie was intolerable and extremely humiliating to the father;[136] thus, Saul burst out with volcanic anger toward Jonathan. Saul saw Jonathan as a stupid traitor who spared the life of the biggest threat to the royal throne. His vulgar description of Jonathan as the "son of a perverse, rebellious (woman)" is a graphic insult.[137] The insult was directly hurled at Jonathan, not his mother. Saul's language also allocates Jonathan's birth to an inferior class, "You are son of so and so," and thus the usage is considered to be shameful.[138] As Gary Stansell rightly points out, Saul's shaming of Jonathan is a consequence of the disgrace Jonathan has brought upon Saul, who is both father and king.[139]

To continue, how should one understand Jonathan's alliance with David as his own shame and the shame of his mother's nakedness? Saul conjectured that if Jonathan continued to befriend David and waited for his opponent to take his throne (also Jonathan's future throne) without doing anything to stop him, the trend would be unstoppable. For Saul, it showed Jonathan's own weakness and lowliness before the challenger and thus triggered shame, though it seems that Jonathan did not perceive it as such. Jonathan was more concerned that David was disgraced by Saul's harsh remarks (20:34). In fact,

---

135. For example, Arnold, *1 and 2 Samuel*, 296; Hertzberg, *I & II Samuel*, 171–172; Klein, *1 Samuel*, 204–205.

136. Brueggemann, *First and Second Samuel*, 151.

137. Arnold, *1 and 2 Samuel*, 298; Tsumura, *First Book of Samuel*, 520.

138. McCarter, *1 Samuel*, 343. Saul's saying degrades Jonathan; see Hertzberg, *I & II Samuel*, 175.

139. Stansell, "Honor and Shame," 60.

Jonathan always believed that David was God's anointed one for Israel's future and willingly gave up his right to the throne (20:14–15).

The nakedness of Jonathan's mother can be understood euphemistically as the exposure of his mother's sexual organ, the genitals.[140] But why would Jonathan's bond with David have anything to do with his mother's nakedness? Saul's assumption is that if Jonathan continued to side with David, David would eventually rise to the throne and become the new king of Israel. If that ever happened, David would have the liberty to take the wife of his old master into his own arms; that is, even Saul's wife, Ahinoam (14:50), the mother of Jonathan, would be taken away by David to his own harem. Such a tradition was often practiced to demonstrate the superior power of the new king.[141] If so, Jonathan, indeed, would indirectly expose his mother's nakedness to David and bring shame to his mother and the whole family. The sexual purity of the wife of the king had to be guarded in order to defend the honor of the family. Feelings of shame can be closely related to the exposure of nakedness. Without further explanation, Bergen comments that Saul's appeal to the mother's nakedness elicits feelings of guilt as a motivator to bring Jonathan back to his side.[142] This explanation is less convincing, as the text clearly says that it is to "the *shame* (ולבשת) of the nakedness of your mother" that Saul rebuked Jonathan. In other words, the mother's potential suffering of shame should become a motivation for Jonathan to abandon David and honor his father by siding with him.[143]

Saul's accusation was to warn Jonathan that he had to think twice before making such a choice to support David. Saul's worry was perhaps understandably human. But such a concern was driven by his own jealousy, opposing YHWH's purposes in choosing the right king for Israel. Later, even Saul had to acknowledge that David was to be the king of Israel (1 Sam 24:21). Thus, it is futile to stand against the will of God.

---

140. Klein, *1 Samuel*, 209; McCarter, *1 Samuel*, 343.

141. For instance, Absalom lay with David's concubines on the palace rooftop (2 Sam 16:22) to show his legitimacy as the new king. Later, Adonijah unwisely asked for Abishag, David's virgin maid, from Solomon; seeing this as a direct challenge to his new kingship, Solomon immediately put him to death (1 Kgs 2:13–25).

142. Bergen, *1, 2 Samuel*, 218. He thinks the three powerful motivators in 20:30–31 are shame, guilt and greed.

143. Feelings of guilt could possibly be involved in the process, but the narrator does not portray it so.

Interestingly, it seems that David did accept Saul's wives into his harem (2 Sam 12:8) after he replaced Saul as the king of Israel, though we are not sure if Jonathan's mother was included as one of them.

Perhaps the following comments best summarize the relationship of the nakedness imagery in these two passages:

> In 1 Samuel 19, YHWH strips Saul naked in a manner that indicates both his humiliation and rejection as a king. . . . Saul later uses nakedness language against his own son, Jonathan, in an effort to shame him for his association with and protection of David (1 Sam 20:30). In doing so, however, Saul shames himself and Jonathan is honored as one who upholds YHWH's choice of David, consistent with his earlier act of removing his own royal attire and placing his clothing on David (1 Sam 18:4).[144]

2.10 The Face of Abigail (1 Sam 25:35)

The story of David, Nabal and his wife Abigail is bracketed with the notion of honor and shame; the two words denoting shame/shaming (כלם, *be humiliated*, 1 Sam 25:7, 15; חרפה, *reproach*, 1 Sam 25:39) reflect this inclusio. However, there is a different kind of honor term in this chapter whose semantic significance is often ignored or blurred in translations: the phrase ואשא פניך in 1 Samuel 25:35.

The story begins with David sending his men to Nabal's house to collect a free offering during the sheep-shearing harvest season. Unfortunately, Nabal foolishly turns down the polite request[145] of David's servants and even taunts David and his men, labeling them as disloyal runaway servants. Upon hearing the news, David is agitated and swears to kill Nabal's household in order to avenge the insult rendered to him and his men. In the midst of the crisis, Nabal's wife, Abigail, with wit, bravery and decisiveness, intervenes and saves Nabal's whole household from bloodshed.

When Abigail meets David and his men on their way, she makes a long speech (1 Sam 25:24–31) to explain the foolishness being done to them and

---

144. Hanley, "Use of Nakedness," 151.
145. David's young men referred to David as the "servant" and "son" of Nabal (1 Sam 25:8).

The Language of Honor and Shame in 1 Samuel

honors David with abundant gifts. In return, David responds favorably by commending Abigail as the timely mediator between Nabal and his men. If it were not for Abigail's intervention, David would have slaughtered Nabal's household. Affirming her contribution, David says to her, "Go up in peace to your house. See, I have listened to your voice and ואשא פניך" (1 Sam 25:35). The phrase ואשא פניך is often translated in English as "granted your petition" (ESV, RSV, NRSV) or "granted your request" (NIV, NASB, HCSB, LEB). The connotation of נשא פנים fails to be properly penetrated, in that few commentators discuss its ambiguous meaning, and even when they do touch upon it, they simply agree with the meaning of granting a request.[146]

But the problem is that neither the word "grant" nor "petition" nor "request" appear in the Hebrew texts. What we have here is the verb ואשא in the 1c.s. imperfect consecutive form, being used in parallel with שמעתי; it indicates a past tense perfective aspect consecutive (perhaps logical rather than a temporal sequence after the preceding verb שמעתי) with an emphasis on the present effect. The verb נשא is usually rendered as "lift, carry, take."[147] The second word פניך is a plural construct noun (from the word פנים, "face") plus a 2f.s. pronominal suffix.

But the meaning of the phrase נשא + פנים is still far from clear. It would be good to briefly go though its relevant span of occurrences in the OT in order to get a better idea of its meaning. According to my calculation, the expression, as a pregnant construction, occurs twenty-eight times in the OT.[148] There is no question נשא פנים covers various nuances in meaning. It can possibly mean "take face," that is, granting favor to someone (Gen 19:21; 32:21; Deut 28:50; 2 Kgs 3:14; Mal 1:8, 9; Job 42:8, 9; Lam 4:16)[149] or showing favor

---

146. Klein, *1 Samuel*, 251; Tsumura, *First Book of Samuel*, 592.

147. "נשא," BDB, 669–670.

148. The occurrences include Gen 4:7 (נשא פנים is possibly here by way of ellipsis from the previous verse); 19:21; 32:21; Lev 19:15; Num 6:26; Deut 10:17; 28:50; 1 Sam 25:35; 2 Sam 2:22; 2 Kgs 3:14; 2 Kgs 5:1; Isa 3:3; 9:14; Mal 1:8, 9; 2:9; Ps 82:2; Job 13:8; 13:10; 22:8; 32:21; 34:19; 42:8, 9; Prov 6:35; 18:5; Lam 4:16; and 2 Chr 19:7 (here it is a noun usage of נשא but with similar semantics). Moreover, נשא פנים also occurs in other intertestamental uses (e.g. 11Q13 2:11; 1QHa 6:30; 1QS 2:4; 1QSb 3:1; Sirach 4:22; 42:1) which I have not included in this counting.

149. Such a meaning can be inferred from its overall context. It is interesting that נשא פנים is used as a term synonymous to חנן I, "to show favor" (Deut 28:50; Lam 4:16), and רצה I, "to take pleasure in" (Mal 1:8), in the context.

to someone in the negative sense (hence showing partiality),[150] especially in a legal context (Lev 19:15; Deut 10:17; Mal 2:9; Ps 82:2; Job 13:8; 13:10; 32:21; 34:19; Prov 6:35; 18:5; 2 Chr 19:7). Alternatively, it can also mean "lift up or raise face" (Num 6:26; 2 Sam 2:22),[151] or, sometimes, נשא is used in the *qal* passive form with פנים to suggest the face being lifted up, hence (a person of) exalted honor (2 Kgs 5:1; Isa 3:3; 9:14; Job 22:8).

Both BDB and *DCH* assert the basic meaning of "lifting up or raising one's face" for נשא פנים in 1 Samuel 25:35.[152] Following this meaning, the phrase נשא + פנים probably has its origin in "oriental court etiquette."[153] It conceivably points to the context of someone lying prostrate in humility.[154] In ancient times, when a king summoned someone to meet him in the royal court, he or she was to come to the king with a sense of humility and respect. Summoned ones were to, at least,[155] bow their heads (i.e. with their faces low down) and avoid direct eye contact with the king so as not to offend his royal honor. Those summoned usually had to wait for the king's further signal to raise their heads (also their faces) before saying anything. When the king finally said "raise up your face/head," it signified that they had won the king's respect and were granted the honor of finally meeting the king face-to-face.[156] Therefore, it is possible that "raise up someone's face," in the original royal court context, had the connotation of being bestowed the king's respect and

---

150. Here נשא פנים is used as a term synonymous to הדר, "to honor" (Lev 19:15), and נכר I, "to regard preferentially" (Job 34:19).

151. In Numbers 6:26, נשא פנים signifies God bestowing favor toward his people. In 2 Samuel 2:22, it is about the embarrassment of looking up to someone on a relational basis.

152. "נשא," BDB, 670; "נשא," *DCH*, 7:284. The LXX's rendering of αἴρω πρόσωπόν, "to lift up face" (2 Sam 2:22; Num 6:26) is perhaps a witness to this semantic range. However, *HALOT* lists the definition #6a as "to receive someone in a friendly manner, be favourably disposed towards someone" (*HALOT* 2, 725). Such a meaning is close to the common rendition of the LXX (λαμβάνεις πρόσωπον, "to take one's face") which we will discuss shortly.

153. Bertram, "Θαῦμα, Θαυμάζω, Θαυμάσιος, Θαυμαστός," *TDNT*, 3:30.

154. "נשא," BDB, 670. Sometimes, in oriental greetings, one humbly turns one's face to the ground or sinks to the earth. See Lohse, "εὐπροσωπέω," *TDNT*, 6:779–780.

155. In ancient Chinese royal court etiquette, the one summoned had to kneel on the ground to show respect and reverence to the emperor. In this case, one definitely had to lower one's face before speaking to the king.

156. Such a necessity of showing supreme honor to the king is also reflected in the Persian royal court; even queen Esther was not able to see the king's face without being summoned first (Esth 4:11; 5:2).

favor.[157] Numbers 6:26, showing God's raising of his face (יִשָּׂא יהוה פָּנָיו) as a blessing to his people, should probably be understood within a similar context – with God's people having the honor and opportunity to behold the countenance of their heavenly king whose face is assumed to be concealed and inaccessible to mere mortals.

As language developed, one can assume that the phrase was also used in other ordinary circumstances in daily life. It seems that, later on, פנים + נשא (we should probably never separate the two but group them together as an idiom) was also used to mean exalted honor, not necessarily in a royal court context.[158] Naaman, commander of the army of the king of Syria, was someone great and וּנְשֻׂא פָנִים (2 Kgs 5:1); thus he was often perceived as someone held in honor.[159]

However, נשא פנים could possibly mean "take face" in 1 Samuel 25:35, as the word נשא can ambiguously imply both "take" and "lift up." The LXX renders this phrase as ἡρέτισα τὸ πρόσωπόν σου ("I have chosen your face").[160] Elsewhere a common rendition of נשא פנים in the LXX is λαμβάνω πρόσωπον ("take face").[161] Such a usage is even carried on in the NT (see λαμβάνεις πρόσωπον in Luke 20:21).[162] One can assume that Luke 20:21 echoes its counterpart נשא + פנים in the OT (e.g. Lev 19:15).[163]

---

157. Similarly, in a royal court context, "raise up one's head" (ראש + נשא) means that one has been granted the king's favor and honor; see Genesis 40:13, 20. Likewise, the granting of favor and honor is ascribed to "raise up one's head" in Psalm 3:3, though it is used for indicating a more personal relationship with a slightly different term רום + ראש.

158. For instance, see פנים + נשא in Isaiah 3:3 and 9:14.

159. "Highly regarded" (NIV, LEB, HCSB), "highly respected" (NASB), "respected" (NET), "honourable" (KJV), "honorable" (NKJV, ASV).

160. This is the only time that αἱρετίζω πρόσωπόν renders נשא פנים in the LXX.

161. λαμβάνω πρόσωπον is often used in the LXX to translate פנים + נשא (see, for example, Lev 19:15; 2 Kgs 3:14; Job 42:8; Mal 1:8–9; 2:9; Ps 82:2). Interestingly, by using λαμβάνω, the translators of the LXX seem to not adopt the most conspicuous meaning of "lift up" for נשא. Other ways the LXX translates פנים + נשא include θαυμάζει πρόσωπον, "to esteem or honor face"; αἴρω πρόσωπόν, "to lift up face" (2 Sam 2:22; Num 6:26); προσδέχομαι πρόσωπον, "to receive face" (Gen 32:21); ἀναλαμβάνω πρόσωπόν, "to take up face" (Job 11:15). The first rendition is most common, and I will discuss it later.

162. Another explicit text with such usage is Galations 2:6, πρόσωπον [ὁ] θεὸς ἀνθρώπου οὐ λαμβάνει.

163. This allusion to its counterpart of פנים + נשא in the OT has been affirmed by many prominent Lukan scholars; see Plummer, Critical and Exegetical, 465; Marshall, Gospel of Luke, 734; Fitzmyer, Gospel according to Luke, 115; Bock, Luke, 1610.

In the Old Testament נשא often occurs with other terminology to form a phrase, for example, נשא + עון ("to bear sin"; cf. Exod 28:38 and Ezek 14:10), נשא + כלמה ("to bear disgrace"; cf. Ps 69:7 and Ezek 16:54). But the meaning here is still ambiguous. Following the common rendition of the LXX, what does it mean to take someone's face? Of course, we cannot interpret that literally. Face, being the forefront part of the body, can be used to contain or represent a person's core value. Thus "face" can be the external display of honor; it and the head being the "particular loci of personal honour and respect."[164] If YHWH does not take someone's face, it means that God does not look at one person's face, treating them one way, and look at a different person's face and treat them in a different way. It implies that God does not extend special respect and honor to someone so as to avert the requirement of the law, regardless of that person's status or background (often translated as "is not partial" or "shows no partiality").[165] Putting this phrase in a legal case context is important because what matters in law, first and foremost, is justice.[166] Likewise, the scribes and the chief priests hypocritically praised Jesus as a teacher who, like YHWH in the OT, did not take or receive anyone's face (λαμβάνεις πρόσωπον); that is, he did not extend special respect and honor to anyone regardless of another's status or origin.[167]

---

164. Mahlangu, "Ancient Mediterranean Values," 91. The close relationship of face to honor and shame can also be found in Chinese culture which also considers face as the most conducive term to communicate honor and shame. A Chinese scholar makes some interesting observations about "face": "The positive value of gaining [face] is a [sic] honor – an honor of recognition of personal credit and worth. The positive value of keeping or saving [face] is the acknowledgement of affirmation of one's personal status and prestige in face of challenge or disgrace.... The negative value of losing or breaking [face] is a disgrace due to allowance and depreciation of one's social status and prestige and calls forth wrath, shamefulness, resentment and even hatred." Cheng, "Concept of Face," 334. These comments can be briefly paraphrased as honor in gaining face and shame in losing face.

165. See, for example, the ESV, NIV, NASB and NRSV's rendering of Leviticus 19:15, but such translations bury the notion of honor/shame culture in the text. "Partiality" or "favoritism" is only the extended and inferred meaning of taking someone's face (showing respect and honor to someone).

166. For נשא + פנים in the context of legal cases, see Deut 10:17; Ps 82:2; Job 13:8, 10; 32:21; 34:19; Prov 18:5.

167. Interestingly, though used as compound words (προσωπολημψίαις [Jas 2:1] and προσωπολημπτεῖτε [Jas 2:9]), taking someone's face is clearly put in a specific context pertaining to the church's different attitude in receiving the rich or poor. The consequence of taking someone's face (showing special respect and honor to the persons if they are rich and granting them good seats) was to dishonor (ἠτιμάσατε; Jas 2:6) the poor who happened to be in the same place and were given less respect and honor by the assignment of inferior seats. In this context, it shows that λαμβάνω πρόσωπον is a term saturated with honor.

The phrase is also used in non-legal contexts. In Genesis, upon Lot's plea, it is on account of God's respect and honor (Gen 19:21; נשׂאתי פניך) for Lot that the Lord decides not to destroy a small city called Zoar when Lot and his family were escaping God's judgment of fire on Sodom and Gomorrah. Lot's "face" (respect and honor), in this context, had an intermediary function. The survival of Zoar depended on the value of Lot's "face." In other words, the citizens of Zoar, without knowing it, borrowed from Lot's "face" in surviving this divine judgment. Such a distributive nature of "face" can be important for us to understand the concept of נשׂא + פנים in 1 Samuel 25:35. Thus the phrase נשׂא + פנים, when rendered as "take one's face," has the connotation of granting respect and honor to someone.[168]

Having said so, I favor the reading of נשׂא + פנים in 1 Samuel 25:35 as "taking one's face" in light of its usage in a similar context in Genesis 19:21.[169] The manifestation of respect and honor is conceivably conveyed in such an interpretation. The sense of honor is also ostensibly captured in the LXX's usual rendering of θαυμάζειν πρόσωπον (translated as "to esteem or honor face") for its corresponding counterpart נשׂא + פנים in the OT.[170] Hence, there is little doubt that ואשׂא פניך in 1 Samuel 25:35 should be read in the context of an honor culture. Here respect and honor were granted to Abigail by David because she was wise, brave, decisive and considerate. Moreover, she was one who held David in great honor,[171] and she persuaded him to stay away from unnecessary bloodguilt. As a result, David valued Abigail's face (thus granting respect and honor) and withdrew the attack against Nabal's household. The value of Abigail's "face" determined Nabal's life or death. In other words, Nabal was kept safe from David's attack because he borrowed respect and honor from his wife. Were it not for Abigail's "face" (respect and honor), Nabal would have been killed immediately. Abigail's "face" has an

---

168. See also Gen 32:21; Deut 28:50; Mal 1:8–9.

169. Both Genesis 19:21 and 1 Samuel 25:35 involve a conversation wherein a tragedy is averted because of someone else's face value. In both instances, the interaction is between a first person singular and second person singular (masculine or feminine).

170. For instance, θαυμάζειν πρόσωπον occurs to render its Hebrew counterpart פנים + נשׂא in Gen 19:21; Deut 10:17; 28:50; 2 Kgs 5:1; 2 Chr 19:7; Prov 18:5; Job 13:10; 22:8; 34:19. Or less frequently, λαμβάνω πρόσωπον, as mentioned earlier. The verb θαυμάζειν, in its first instance, can mean "to look on with astonishment." From that it derives the sense "to esteem, to admire, to honor." See Bertram, "Θαῦμα, Θαυμάζω, Θαυμάσιος, Θαυμαστός," *TDNT*, 3:28.

171. Abigail honors David as "my lord" (ten times) and she addresses herself as "your servant" (five times) in 1 Sam 25:24–31.

intermediary function in this context. Interestingly, the wife Abigail is seen as having much more honor than the husband, a man of great means.[172]

Some translations render נשא + פנים verbatim in 1 Samuel 25:35, for example, "accept thy face" (YLT), or the ancient Syriac Peshitta translation of ܘܢܣܒܬ ܒܐܦܝܟ, "and I received your face."[173] The LXX's αἱρετίζω πρόσωπόν in 1 Samuel 25:35 deviates from its usual rendering (θαυμάζειν πρόσωπον or λαμβάνω πρόσωπον). The meaning is, nevertheless, still obvious, "I have chosen your face."[174] In other words, David decided not to do anything against Nabal because he chose to accept Abigail's respect and honor. Some other translations capture a better sense of the honor culture, thus, "respected your person" (NKJV) and "respect your wish" (NJPS). A very good translation is probably the Wycliffe Bible, "I honoured thy face" (WYC) or the Vulgate "*honoravi faciem tuam*," clearly seeing ואשא פניך in the context of honoring someone. It is obvious that David granted Abigail's desire that nothing be done against Nabal for the sake of honoring her. The translation "grant your petition" or "grant your request," as discussed, makes clear that David grants Abigail's request but fails to explain honoring her as the motive and reason (which the text actively implies) for doing so.

To sum up, it is very likely one should not separate נשא פנים from the language of honor and shame. Failing to properly treat it in translations will only make the meaning more ambiguous and remote to modern readers.

2.11 Uncircumcision as a Sign of Disgrace (1 Sam 14:6; 17:26, 36; 31:4)

There is little doubt that "uncircumcised" was a contemptible term that Israelites used to address the Philistines,[175] Israel's most formidable enemies in 1 Samuel. The word is used three times as a noun (ערלים) and two times

---

172. This seems to be opposite from the observation of the Context Group which proposes a dominant masculine honor.

173. Kiraz and Bali, *Syriac Peshitta Bible*, 171.

174. One interpretative suggestion is that David honoring Abigail by choosing her face is an allusion to his later choice of her as a wife (25:39).

175. Tsumura, *First Book of Samuel*, 359; Firth, *1 & 2 Samuel*, 163.

as an adjective (ערל).¹⁷⁶ The use of "the uncircumcised" was to reflect a clear ethnic distinction between Israelites and Philistines. Interestingly, all the uses of this term are found in war contexts in which the Israelites waged war against the Philistines.

One needs to study the origin of Israel's circumcision in order to understand why uncircumcision was considered by the Israelites as a disgrace. The first clear reference to circumcision in the Hebrew Bible is found in Genesis 17:10–14 where God commanded Abraham and his male offspring after him, including his male slaves, to circumcise their foreskins as a sign of God's covenant with them. Thus, circumcision, at its core, was a symbol of God's covenant with Israel. Circumcision separated Israel from all other nations to denote God's special relationship with Israel as God's chosen people on earth.¹⁷⁷ Through this covenant, Israel was God's "treasured possession" and "a kingdom of priests and a holy nation" (Exod 19:5–6).

The succeeding generations of Israelites also kept this tradition by circumcising their males on the eighth day (Lev 12:3). During the wilderness wanderings, when the Israelites ignored the practice of circumcision (Josh 5:2–6), God solemnly reminded them of the necessity of continuing the practice before entering the promised land. The Israelites should never forget the circumcision which God commanded, not even during wars, as an outward expression of God's covenant with Israel.

Though the Egyptians, Midianites, Ammonites, Edomites, Moabites, Phoenicians and Arabs in the ancient Near East may also have practiced circumcision,¹⁷⁸ they were never endowed with the same significance as God's specially chosen people. As time passed, the Israelites later even identified circumcision as a kind of "cultural superiority,"¹⁷⁹ distinguishing Israelites among all other non-Israelites in status. Such a sense of superiority can be detected in the early stages of Israel's formation, for example, in considering intermarriage with uncircumcised ones as a "disgrace" (see Gen 34:14; חרפה)

---

176. Jonathan and Saul use it a mas. pl. noun (ערלים) to refer to the uncircumcised Philistines on two different occasions (14:6; 31:4). David uses it two times as an adjective to address Goliath, the uncircumcised Philistine (17:26, 36).

177. Israelites were not the only people in antiquity who practiced circumcision, but the biblical text presents the Philistine culture as well as at least some Canaanites living in the land (Gen 34) as not following the practice.

178. Myers, *Eerdmans Bible Dictionary*, 218; Sasson, "Circumcision," 473–476.

179. Block, "Beyond the Grave," 124.

for Israelites. Such disparagement with regard to uncircumcision is still keenly reflected in the Judges–Samuel period (e.g. Judg 14:3; 1 Sam 17:26).

Interestingly, "uncircumcised" is always used as a disparaging term in Israel's war against the Philistines in 1 Samuel.[180] This is perhaps not without reason. Compared to the enemy, the Israelites were often put in a disadvantageous position in terms of their weapons and equipment (1 Sam 13:19–22); thus, in order to alter such an unbalance in power, the Israelites often tried to put the Philistines down by shaming them for their uncircumcised (i.e. inferior) status, as can be seen in multiple Israelite speeches/conversations (1 Sam 14:6; 17:26, 36). Putting the Philistines in a lower position (shaming them) was a psychological tactic to suppress the enemy and encourage themselves in war, just as the Philistines also tried to lift up their own morale when the ark of the Lord was brought into in the camp of Israel for battle (1 Sam 4:9).

A death at the hands of the uncircumcised was extremely shameful. Saul, for instance, sensing the unavoidable defeat by the Philistines during a decisive battle, said to his armor bearer, "Draw your sword, and pierce me through with it, lest these uncircumcised (הערלים) come and pierce me through, and mistreat me" (1 Sam 31:4). Saul would rather take his own life than bear the disgrace of the king of Israel dying at the hands of the uncircumcised Philistines. Indeed, death at the hands of the uncircumcised was not only considered an insult in Israel, but also throughout the whole region of the Phoenicians.[181]

2.12 The Stigmatized Metaphors: A Dog, a Flea (1 Sam 17:43; 24:14; 26:20)

Though dogs are often esteemed for their companionship and loyalty in many parts of the world today, ancient Israelites viewed them unfavorably. Dogs, as a species of voracious scavengers (1 Kgs 21:19, 23–24), were considered as unclean animals (Exod 22:31; Prov 26:11) by the Israelites, and their presence often indicated violence (Ps 22:16, 20; 59:6, 14–15). In Deuteronomy 23:18,

---

180. Jonathan labelled the Philistines as "these uncircumcised" (14:6), and so did Saul (31:4). David addressed Goliath, his opponent, as "this uncircumcised" (17:26, 36). The avoidance of calling someone by name showed disrespect.

181. The king of Tyre was also judged by the Lord to die shamefully because of his sins. Thus, his death would be implemented by uncircumcised strangers (Ezek 28:10).

the male prostitute is likened to a "dog" (כלב), whose wages should not be brought into the house of the Lord, for such was an abomination to the Lord. Obviously, the word "dog" (כלב) expresses contempt in such contexts.

Thus it is not surprising that the Israelites often viewed dogs with scorn. If a person was likened to a dog, it signified his or her insignificance and thus implied contempt.[182] When Goliath saw David approaching him with staffs (not swords) in his hands, he said with satire (1 Sam 17:43), "Am I a dog, that you come to me with staffs?" Goliath read David's choice of weapons as a sign of disdain for his opponent and thus ridiculed the young challenger for treating him disdainfully as "a dog."[183]

Being hunted by Saul, David humbled himself by calling himself "a dead dog" (1 Sam 24:14). This is a typical self-abasing formula.[184] David diminished himself before his old master, emphasizing his insignificance so that Saul would be dissuaded from continually pursuing him. In other words, a person like David, "a dead dog," who does not pose any threat to the king, should deserve little attention from the king of Israel. In both occasions, the metaphor of treating someone as a "dog" is shameful language.[185]

As even less than a dog, David regards himself as a "flea" on a dog. A flea, as a miniature insect, is often known for its trivial and unimportant presence. When a person is described in a metaphor as "a flea," it expresses his or her insignificance. Thus the term is often used to trigger shame.[186] For instance, David debased himself as "a flea" (פרעש אחד), alongside the stigmatized term "a dead dog," in his appeal to Saul while being hunted by him (1 Sam 24:14). The same scornful term is used in a similar situation when David is later pursued (1 Sam 26:20; פרעש אחד). David's presence before Saul is as

---

182. Myers, *Eerdmans Bible Dictionary*, 290. "Dog" is a phrase of "self-abasement"; see Tsumura, *First Book of Samuel*, 571; Brueggemann, *First and Second Samuel*, 170. Similarly, McCarter sees "dog" as a term of "self-disparagement" to emphasize one's insignificance. McCarter, *1 Samuel*, 384–385.

183. The LXX's addition is more graphic and shameful in saying, Οὐχί, ἀλλ' ἢ χείρω κυνός ("no, but worse than a dog").

184. The Amarna texts also show that a person would equate him/herself as a "dog" before a king as self-abasement language. Coats, "Self-Abasement," 18.

185. Dog, as a metaphor, is also used as a shameful term in 2 Samuel 3:8, 9:8, and 16:9.

186. This is another term of "self-disparagement" along with "a dead dog" in 24:14 (McCarter, *1 Samuel*, 385). It is an expression of "self-abasement" (Tsumura, *First Book of Samuel*, 571; Brueggemann, *First and Second Samuel*, 170).

trivial as one single flea whose existence should not have bothered the king to take so much effort to pursue him.

From our observation, it is quite clear that both "dog" and "flea" are used in 1 Samuel as metaphors to denote the insignificance of a person.[187] Both are terms that express contempt and scorn, reflecting the speaker's emotional stance by the use of vivid images.[188] Interestingly, the term "flea" is used exclusively by David in 1 Samuel (24:14; 26:20); we do not find any occurrences in other parts of the Scriptures.

2.13 A Disfigured Body as a Sign of Shame (1 Sam 31:8–13)

The book of 1 Samuel ends with the unusual death of Saul and his sons. In the battle with the Philistines, Saul and his army could not withstand the troops of the Philistines. Eventually, with such a defeat, Saul took his own life with his own sword; his three sons also died with him in the battle.

The narrator gives further information regarding the Philistines' brutal treatment of the corpses of Saul and his sons. They cut off (ויכרתו) Saul's head, stripped off (ויפשיטו) his armor and placed (וישמו) it in the temple of the Ashtoreths, and fastened (תקעו) his body (as well as those of his sons) on the wall of Beth-Shan (31:9–10). All these actions demonstrate not only the Philistines' might as conquerors but also the extreme shame of Israel's royal house. In military campaigns, the defeated side is usually subjected to shame. The death of that side's king only worsened its shamed status. Note that the Philistines' humiliation of Saul's body was strategic.[189] A king's body without

---

187. For a book that discusses the features of metaphor in depth in the books of Samuel, see Weiss, *Figurative Language*.

188. Bar-Efrat, *Narrative Art*, 57.

189. The abuse of Saul's corpse was to expose him to the public humiliation of all the people in the region. In addition, the Philistines placed Saul's armor (the symbol of his position as a king) in the temple of the Ashtoreths as a trophy just as Goliath's sword was taken and placed in the temple of the Lord (1 Sam 31:9). In this way, the gods of the Philistines were honored, and the God of Israel defeated. See Walton, Matthews and Chavalas, *IVP Bible Background Commentary*, 321; Olyan, "Honor," 214–215. It is possible that the God of Israel was also susceptible to shame through Israel's defeat and the display of Saul's armor in the temple of the Ashtoreths, but it was because of Saul's disobedience to God's commandment that Israel suffered this defeat. Thus, the situation should probably be read as divine abandonment due to disobedience. See Bechtel, "Perception of Shame," 83–84. Interestingly, both the Elides and

its head,[190] naked[191] and fastened to the wall signified the defeated's failure, vulnerability and public disgrace. The Philistines' inhumane treatment of the corpses was not just an infliction of shame for Israel's royal house (Saul and his household) but also shame for the whole nation of Israel, because the king represented the nation in war.

The purpose of such a punishment was to terrify the Israelites. The Philistines implicitly communicated such a message, "If anyone dares to rebel against us, such will be the end of our enemies." These are strong characteristics of "psychological warfare" where shame is employed.[192] The Philistines' abuse of Saul and his sons' bodies triggered fear and shame among the Israelites, as it implied they could not turn against the Philistines anymore. Shame, in this situation, is used as a sanction of social control.[193]

The corpses being placed on the city wall of Beth-Shan also maximized the public scale of disgrace and shame for the victims because all citizens in the city and passersby could freely gaze at the king's helplessness even after his death. The shame also extended to the Israelites, for they did not have the capacity to arrange even a proper burial for their dead king. With Saul's dismembered corpse deteriorating hour by hour,[194] the urgency to have this problem handled was unprecedented.

Securing a proper burial for the king could, at least, save some face for the Israelites from being further humiliated by the Philistines. The residents of Jabesh-Gilead responded to such a concern. They traveled all night, took back the corpses, cremated the bodies and buried the remains (1 Sam 31:11–13). The reason the people of Jabesh-Gilead risked their lives to do so is probably

---

Saul suffer defeat in wars due to God's abandonment. Both suffer shame and are rejected and judged by God, leaving Israel to shameful treatment from its enemies.

190. Mutilation served to bring shame upon the victim and the community associated with the victim. See Lemos, "Shame and Mutilation," 226. The cutting of the head only aggravated the shamed status. Note that David also cut off Goliath's head when he defeated him (1 Sam 17:51).

191. For more information on how victors in the ancient Near East used nakedness as a tactic to humiliate conquered enemies, see Hanley, "Use of Nakedness," 73–76, 159–163. Goliath also threatened to expose David's body unburied, giving his flesh as food to the birds of the air and to the beasts of the field (1 Sam 17:44).

192. Bechtel, "Shame as a Sanction," 63.

193. Bechtel, 63–70. Later the Assyrians also ostensibly employed terror and shaming as a tactic for subjugating their enemies.

194. The Mosaic law prescribes that no corpse should be hung outside overnight (Deut 21:23) in that it causes defilement.

because Saul had delivered them earlier from the hands of the Ammonites and thus spared them the reproach of having their right eyes gouged out (1 Sam 11:2). They had experienced what it meant to be shamed. Being sensitive to the notion of shame, they showed their gratitude toward their master who had delivered them from such a predicament. By giving Saul and his sons a dignified burial, they, at least partly, restored honor to their master.

2.14 Conclusion

Summing up, this study finds that a culture of honor and shame was pervasive in biblical Israel, with its own unique manifestations in 1 Samuel. Not everything in 1 Samuel is about honor and shame; but there are many indications of where honor and shame issues rise to the forefront. This can be shown from the fact that the book contains a wide range of terms explicitly or implicitly denoting honor and shame. Honor and shame spread across all corners of life in biblical Israel, including politics, family, friendship, war, sex, meals, daily language and even death. The word כבד can possibly be considered a key term in understanding the meaning of different stages of the book's narratives, especially chapters 1–7. Having had an overview of the notion of honor and shame in 1 Samuel, we shall now turn in the next three chapters to detailed analyses of the texts of 1 Samuel 1–7, again from the perspective of honor and shame.

CHAPTER 3

Hannah – Competing for Honor, from the Ashamed to the Honored (1 Samuel 1:1–2:11, 18–21)

In the previous chapter, this study demonstrated that 1 Samuel is imbued with the connotations of honor and shame throughout. Such a lexical examination also solidifies my proposal of the thematic centrality of honor and shame in communicating the narrator's ideological point of view, thereby promoting the reading of 1 Samuel (at least chs. 1–7) from the perspective of honor and shame. The goal of this chapter, however, is to strengthen my proposal by studying the texts pertaining to the Hannah narratives, with the hope of exploring the interchange of honor and shame in these episodes.

3.1 Hannah Ashamed of Her Barrenness (1 Sam 1:1–8)

The narrative begins with an exposition (1:1–2) in which the characters are introduced with a typical story-telling undertone. We are informed of three things about the characters: their names (Elkanah, Peninnah and Hannah), their family relations (both Peninnah and Hannah are Elkanah's wives) and their current conditions (Peninnah has children, but Hannah has no children). Each of these three details is important for the narrative as it paves the ground for the development of the story.

Two notable things should be said about verse 1. First, placing ויהי (imperfect consecutive, the narrative past) at the beginning of the story, though not unusual, is significant.[1] The syntax presumes something happened before this, as ויהי has the function of moving the story along, thus "then it came to pass." That is to say, there is general agreement among scholars that the semantic contribution of ויהי normally denotes a sense of progression.[2] Bar-Efrat suggests that the letter *waw* is a connective formula that often joins a sequences of narratives for establishing an external or internal relation.[3] Thus, the presence of ויהי hints that this narrative has a substantial connection with what has been recounted beforehand, though the usage anticipates the lack of a time frame.[4] It should be noted that, according to the Jewish Tanakh, what precedes the book of Samuel is the book of Judges. Thus, the beginning of the narrative in 1 Samuel has already affirmed its close affinity to the book of Judges; namely, the narrative story in 1 Samuel should be read in continuity with the prior story accorded in the book of Judges.[5] Indeed, from a chronological framework, the first part of 1 Samuel recounts the lives of Israel's last two judges (Eli and Samuel), following after the introduction of many other judges in the book of Judges.

Second, according to the list of genealogy in 1 Chronicles 6, verses 12 and 19, Elkanah is identified as "a Levite from the line of Kohath" within Ephraim's territory.[6] Elkanah's identity as a Levite is important as it prepares

---

[1]. ויהי starts a story in Judges 1:1, Ezekiel 1:1 and Jonah 1:1. One would often assume היה (simple past) to start a story (Job 1:1), but always fronted by a grammatical subject.

[2]. Erhard Blum, "Das exilische deuteronomistische Geschichtswerk," 277; cited in Müller, "1 Samuel 1," 212. According to Müller, Blum thinks the phrase ויהי איש continues a preceding narrative, and that it is not possible to use this phrase to introduce a person with an absolute narrative beginning. Similarly, Van der Merwe emphasizes that the syntagm of ויהי + a nominal clause in 1 Samuel 1:1 introduces a new scene with new characters or circumstances that represents the setting of a new episode (i.e. a new scene within a series of narratives; the phrase itself does not imply an absolute narrative beginning). See Van der Merwe, "Elusive Biblical Hebrew," 98–100.

[3]. Bar-Efrat, *Narrative Art*, 132.

[4]. Auld, *I & II Samuel*, 26–27; Eslinger, *Kingship of God*, 67.

[5]. Jobling sees the story of Hannah as an extension of the book of Judges; see Jobling, *1 Samuel*, 171; also Fokkelman, *Vow and Desire*, 4–7.

[6]. Steinmann, *1 Samuel*, 52; McCarter, *1 Samuel*, 58; Arnold, *1 and 2 Samuel*, 54; Eslinger, *Kingship of God*, 67. However, other scholars see Samuel's priestly office in Shiloh and thus reject recognizing Samuel's role as a Levite. According to their assertion, a later redactor (i.e. the Chronicler) tried to provide Samuel with a Levite ancestry, in accordance with the later normative regulations. See, for example, Hutzli, "Role and Significance," 428. Such a reading perhaps presupposes the concept of Levi as a tribe and perhaps misreads אפרתי, often translated as "Ephraimite," as a reference to his association with the tribe of "Ephraim" in 1:1. But, according to Leuchter, being a Levite was not a matter of "tribal" affiliation but of occupying

Samuel's role as a Levite, serving the Lord in the tabernacle (1 Sam 2:18). This background is important, as the Levites were set apart among the Israelites in the service of the Lord (Num 8:18–19). The main function of a genealogy is perhaps to tell about one's familial background, accomplish legitimation and "justify the right of possession and heritage."[7] Nevertheless, according to his family genealogy, Elkanah is just an ordinary and insignificant person in the social stratum. Thus, Eslinger comments, "Paradoxically, the names in Elkanah's genealogy are important because of their unimportance. They are all names of insignificant obscure people."[8]

The structure of verse 2 should be given some attention. The first part of verse two is a nominal clause which here introduces the background. Here we are informed of a man with his two wives. The sequence of the order for the wives introduced should be noted: Hannah is first listed, followed by Peninnah.

The description of names in verse 2 forms a chiasm for its structure.[9] The names of the two wives are Hannah and Peninnah. Now Peninnah had children. But Hannah had no children. Thus, the name order in verse 2 is set forth as Hannah – Peninnah – Peninnah – Hannah.[10] The chiastic structure serves to form a contrast between these two women and their fortunes. One can presume the reason Hannah is placed first in the first part of verse 2 is perhaps that she was married to Elkanah first.[11] The sequential order in the second part of verse 2, nevertheless, is reversed as the narrator contrasts their marital status with regards to their progenies, namely, Peninnah preceding Hannah (against the prior sequence in which Hannah was placed first). This may have to do with the elevation of Peninnah in her status due to her

---

a social/sacral typology. The tradition of the Chronicler that ascribes to Samuel the status of a Levite should not be brushed off lightly. And indeed, a connection between Samuel and the Levitical priesthood should be considered as one reads the narrative texts in 1 Samuel 1–3. See Leuchter, *Samuel*, 22–40, 111.

7. After leaving Shiloh, Samuel continued to live in Ramah (7:17) and was even buried there (25:1). This reality shows Samuel's close attachment to his hereditary property. See Hutzli, "Role and Significance," 429.

8. Eslinger, *Kingship of God*, 66.

9. Tsumura, *First Book of Samuel*, 108; Eslinger, *Kingship of God*, 69.

10. Tsumura, *First Book of Samuel*, 108. It seems that Peninnah is given initial prominence as the center of the chiasm.

11. אחת in the context probably means "first." See Tsumura, *First Book of Samuel*, 108; McCarter, *1 Samuel*, 49; Klein, *1 Samuel*, 6; Auld, *I & II Samuel*, 28.

propagation of children within the family.¹² If so, the different arrangement of names in the second part of verse 2 perhaps suggests Hannah's primacy was challenged because of her barrenness. The contrasting fortunes between Hannah and Peninnah give rise to further tension in the development of the rest of the story.

This is a story about two women. Elkanah, the husband, is in the middle as the anchor point in the family; Hannah is on one side, being the focus (and central figure) of the story throughout the Samuel birth narrative;¹³ Peninnah is on the other side, as a literary foil whose name will not appear after 1:7 (although she may have won her favor pragmatically up to this point). Within a patriarchal society, it is very striking that a woman appears as a central figure in the biblical narrative.¹⁴

A woman's barrenness, as I have discussed in section 2.4.1, was considered to be a shame in the ancient Near East. Her social status was closely related to her capability of bearing children. To this Hennie J. Marsman comments:

> Being a mother was the most prestigious position for a woman in the ancient world. . . . With regard to the reproductive role of a woman, we have seen that the status of a wife could become endangered if she did not bear a child to her husband. She sometimes would be downgraded or even divorced. ¹⁵

Childlessness was often perceived as a defect in the wife.¹⁶ The resultant sense of incompleteness and inferiority thus often triggered shame. A barren woman was prone to suffer shame, for she left the family without an heir to carry on the family line.¹⁷ Being without a child, Sarai also suffered shame (קלל I, "to be insignificant," Gen 16: 4–5). Likewise, when Rachel finally gave birth to a son, she looked back at her misery and said, with a heart-wrenching release, "God has taken away my reproach" (חרפה, "reproach," Gen 30:23). The grave consequence of lacking an heir meant the termination of one's

---

12. Steinmann, *1 Samuel*, 52.

13. Tsumura, *First Book of Samuel*, 108; Campbell, *1 Samuel*, 40; Alter, *Art of Biblical Narrative*, 82.

14. Such a prominent feature dictates that Hannah's life experience will be extraordinary. The book of Ruth is perhaps another example of placing a woman as a central figure.

15. Marsman, *Women*, 191.

16. Marsman, 176.

17. Arnold, *1 and 2 Samuel*, 55.

family.[18] As such, a barren woman suffered shame both in her family and in the community in which she lived. The fate of Hannah, thus, looks very unfortunate in the opening scene.

Though the narrator only gives a summary statement at the end of verse 2, stating that Peninnah had children and Hannah had none, readers can still envisage the complications behind the scene. Since Hannah was not able to conceive a child, it explains why Elkanah resorted to marrying a second wife in an attempt to produce an heir, despite his genuine love for Hannah (v. 5).[19] Such a practice of taking a second wife if the first did not bear any children for her husband was common not only according to biblical references (Gen 16:2; 30:3–4, 9) but also according to ancient extra-biblical texts.[20] In actual fact, this attempt to produce offspring turned out to be fruitful as Peninnah had at least two sons and two daughters (1:4). The fact that Elkanah had the capacity to have children through Peninnah shows that it was not the impotence of the husband but a defect on Hannah's part that led to childlessness. As such, Hannah's agony and shame would only aggravate her situation. Rumors may have spread, speculating whether it was Hannah's physical defect or her sin against God that caused her infertility.[21]

The narrator's introduction of Peninnah having children and Hannah having none in verse 2 is reminiscent of the biblical type-scene[22] of the "agony of the barren wife" (Gen 16:1–6; 21:1–7; 29:31–30:24; 1 Samuel 1), wherein readers would presuppose the following expected elements in the scene:

1. The favored wife is barren.
2. There is a rival woman.
3. The rival woman is fertile, bears a son for the barren woman's husband.
4. The rival woman belittles the barren wife, brings about the agony (conflict, contest).

---

18. Tsumura, *First Book of Samuel*, 108.

19. McCarter, *1 Samuel*, 58; Klein, *1 Samuel*, 6.

20. Byron, "Childlessness and Ambiguity," 22–23; Van Seters, "Problem of Childlessness," 401–408.

21. Barrenness was often seen as a curse and a punishment as a result of disobedience to YHWH (Lev 20:20–21; Deut 28:18).

22. Biblical type-scene is often seen as a basic convention known to the readers of biblical narratives. For an introduction to biblical type-scene, see Alter, *Art of Biblical Narrative*, 47–62, 82.

5. The barren wife is eventually heard by God, has a son.²³

Given the basic information of a family of two wives (one with children and the other childless), the readers can glimpse a foreshadowing of this type-scene. The suspense is built up. Complications are bound to be seen.

The eye first zooms in on Elkanah, the husband. He is said to go up, year by year, to Shiloh to worship the Lord of Hosts.²⁴ The consecutive verb ועלה ("go up"), as a past tense habitual aspect consecutive, indicates that the action was repeated regularly as a custom or habit.²⁵ The action thus reflects his "religious devotion."²⁶ Although the law regulated that three times a year Israelites were to keep feasts to the Lord (Exod 23:14), it is not certain whether it was actually implemented in real life. If one keeps in mind that the story here is in continuity with the book of Judges preceding it, Elkanah's piety is particularly foregrounded, contrasting with other Israelites' godlessness, corruption and depravity as portrayed in the book of Judges.²⁷ This is a man of a different class and quality. Readers would be curious to see what will happen to him and his family.

The insertion of the two sons of Eli, Hophni and Phinehas, as priests of the Lord, though seemingly irrelevant to the current story, is nevertheless purposeful. The nominal clause, again, serves to introduce background. Readers will soon find that the narrator constantly juxtaposes the pious Samuel (son of Elkanah) and the impious Elides to bring out contrasts.²⁸ No particulars

---

23. Williams, "Beautiful and the Barren," 109. Cook adds one last point to this type-scene: The child receives a significant name. See Cook, *Hannah's Desire*, 14. Of course, it is hard to verify this last point unless one covers a long range of texts to see its development.

24. Literally speaking, "the Lord of armies." This is the first time this motif appears in the Hebrew Bible (also in 1 Sam 1:11; 4:4; 15:2; 17:45), perhaps indicating the Lord's kingship and sovereignty with a military stance. For more discussion on Shiloh as a cultic site, see Schley, *Shiloh*.

25. Bar-Efrat, *Narrative Art*, 166; McCarter, *1 Samuel*, 59; Alter, *Art of Biblical Narrative*, 82; Fokkelman, *Vow and Desire*, 9; Driver, *Notes*, 5; Eslinger, *Kingship of God*, 69.

26. Bar-Efrat, *Narrative Art*, 81.

27. A motif repeatedly occurs in the book of Judges: "In those days there was no king in Israel. Everyone used to do what was right in his own eyes" (17:6; 21:25). This brief statement perhaps summarizes the root of Israel's spiritual and moral decay.

28. Namely, the Elides in 2:12–17, Samuel in 2:18–21, the Elides in 2:22–36 and Samuel in 3:1–21. Such contrast, in general, is also noted by Steinmann; see Steinmann, *1 Samuel*, 53.

are yet given pertaining to the two sons of Eli.²⁹ At this stage, the narrator refrains from providing further information about them, and consequently their character does not stand out as being clearly negative. The suspense is kept until they are mentioned again in 2:18.

Hannah's barrenness triggers jealousy and enmity within the family. Whenever Elkanah offered a sacrifice, he would distribute some portions to his wife Peninnah and to all her sons and daughters. But to Hannah, he would give possibly "one (special) portion, (gaining) face".³⁰ The reason for showing a special honor and favor to Hannah is because of Elkanah's special love for Hannah (v. 5).³¹ Contrary to the conventional Hebrew word order (predicate + subject + object) in biblical narrative, here the predicate is preceded by the object (את חנה). Placing the object (see nota accusativi את) at the beginning of the sentence is emphatic. It shows that Elkanah's love toward Hannah is genuine and intense.

However, the Lord shut up Hannah's womb. There is no need to consider the *waw* in the last part of verse 5 as causal ("because"), as if casting a negative light on Elkanah's deep love toward Hannah. A simple contrastive *waw* ("but") would better explain the situation.³² Despite being favored by Elkanah, Hannah had her own misfortune. Barrenness, the reality of Hannah's shame, is emphasized. Surprisingly, the Lord is seen as the one who actively closed her womb. In the previous examples of the "barren wife" typescene, the Lord's closing of someone's womb is implied (Gen 30:2) but not clearly specified. Such a minor but remarkable variation from the common

---

29. According to Eslinger, the Elide priests play passive roles (they are just there in Shiloh without action), contrasting with Elkanah who actively sacrifices and worships in Shiloh. See Eslinger, *Kingship of God*, 70.

30. See section 2.4.1 for a text critical examination of מנה אחת אפים.

31. Reading מָנָה אַחַת אַפָּיִם as "one (special) portion, (gaining) face" one necessarily will read the כִּי as a causal conjunction. Alternatively, reading מָנָה אַחַת אֶפֶס כִּי as a retrojection from the LXX μερίδα μίαν . . . πλὴν ὅτι, one would read the כִּי as a concessive conjunction ("but to Hannah he would give one portion, *although* it was Hannah he loved"). Amos 9:8, as an example, contains one such use of אֶפֶס כִּי/πλὴν ὅτι. For more concessive uses of כִּי in the OT, see Exodus 13:17, Hosea 13:15 and Proverbs 6:35. As I have discussed in appendix 1, I favor the reading of "one (special) portion, (gaining) face," thus considering כִּי as causal.

32. Disjunctive *waws* include the categories of contrastive, circumstantial, explanatory and initial or terminative constructions. See Lambdin, *Introduction to Biblical Hebrew*, 162–165. And I would add concessive (see #9 under וְ in *DCH*). "Although" is another possibility here.

type-scene pattern serves to emphasize divine intervention even at the beginning of Hannah's barrenness.³³

As can be expected, a family with two wives can hardly be at peace, especially when one of them is barren (as in the case of Sarah and Hagar, Leah and Rachel).³⁴ In this case, Peninnah would provoke (וכעסתה) Hannah severely because of her barrenness. The repetition of using the cognate noun (כעס) serves to intensify the gravity of the provocation.³⁵ However, Peninnah's name is implied and is only mentioned as "her rival" (צרתה). This seems to indicate that the narrator identifies with Hannah in her misery since the term "rival" communicates an emotional hostility toward the person described.

The reason Peninnah provoked Hannah was to humiliate (רעם II; 1 Sam 1:6) her.³⁶ The narrator repeats himself by saying that "for the Lord had closed her womb" (as in v. 5), strengthening the indelible fact of Hannah's barrenness. The shame of barrenness is the nucleus that stirs up all the momentum behind the expressed actions. Interestingly, the "barren wife" type-scene also suggests that shame is most probably involved here.³⁷ In previous type-scenes, it is obvious that both Sarai and Rachel suffered shame from their rivals because of their barrenness. Both קלל I, "to be insignificant" (Gen 16:4–5), and חרפה, "reproach" (Gen 30:23), are clearly shame-related terms. This adds more evidence to the conclusion that shame is evinced here.

Peninnah's haughty and aggressive treatment of Hannah would have been unusual, given that the second wife often remained at a lower status than the first wife in the ancient Near East.³⁸ In other words, Peninnah should hold a secondary status following after Hannah. If so, it makes Peninnah's action of belittling Hannah all the more ignoble. Readers cannot help but feel empathy and compassion for Hannah.

---

33. Fokkelman, *Vow and Desire*, 23–24; Eslinger, *Kingship of God*, 71.

34. For instance, Yardney argues at length that the narratives of Rachel and Leah in Genesis 29–30 have a great impact for understanding the story of Hannah and Peninnah in 1 Samuel 1:6 (esp. the Septuagint rendering). See Yardney, "Interpretation," 50–128.

35. The use of the particle גם (though often remaining untranslated) also intensifies the idea of provocation.

36. See section 2.4.1 for my argument that it should be רעם II ("to humiliate") and not רעם I ("to rage") in the context.

37. The fourth point of Williams's type-scene list is "The rival woman *belittles* the barren wife, brings about the agon (conflict, contest)." See Williams, "The Beautiful," 109. Italics mine.

38. Byron, "Childlessness and Ambiguity," 35; Stol, *Women*, 163. According to Stol's investigation, the first wife is called "first-ranking wife" in the laws of Hammurabi.

Thus it would be done (יעשה) this way year by year.[39] It was a "perpetual burden" for Hannah, since the scar recurred each year.[40] As often as she (Hannah) went up to Shiloh, conflict between these two women would resurface. A festival season (with many relatives and tribespeople present) would probably be the best occasion for the wives to flaunt their social status and position, which perhaps explains why the spirit of competition, jealousy and enmity would soar high at this time of the year.[41]

The abundance of personal pronouns, in their ambiguity, also adds confusion to our understanding of 1 Samuel 1:7. The subject and object of the verb תַּכְעִסֶנָּה (H-stem) in 1:7, customarily translated "she would provoke her" (e.g. ESV, NRSV, NIV, NASB), however, is ambiguous. The question is: who is angry at whom? Is the subject here Peninnah or Hannah? What really requires attention are the stem semantics of the verbal root כעס, occurring in 1:6 as a *piel* and in 1:7 as a *hiphil*. A plausible reading (contra the conventional translation that "she [Peninnah] would provoke her") is that, in response to Peninnah's infliction of vexation and humiliation (v. 6), Hannah, in return, would also exhibit grievance toward Peninnah (תַּכְעִסֶנָּה, H-stem); namely, Hannah was annoyed.[42] Hannah's sorrow was deep and was expressed through weeping and abstaining from food.

The narrator appears to identify with Hannah in view of her being emotionally abused (having been made distraught). The root of all these problems is her childlessness (1:6) – a sign of shame. The sense of shame overwhelms her. Pedersen even pushes this perspective to the extreme by saying, "Hannah

---

39. Issues of textual corruption in the MT cannot be easily solved. There are three views on how to interpret the text. First, following the reading of MT (יַעֲשֶׂה), "he would do," referring to Elkanah's distributing of sacrifice meats in vv. 4–5, which would inevitably place v. 6 as a gap. See Klein, *1 Samuel*, 7. Second, following the flow of the text in v. 6 (Peninnah's action of provocation), a slight alteration of a consonant is implemented to make sense in the context; thus, תעשה, Peninnah doing so year by year. See Driver, *Notes*, 11. Third, adjust the vowel pointing and read it as an impersonal passive verb, thus, יֵעָשֶׂה, indicating that such a thing is done year by year (pointing to all preceding actions in vv. 4–6). See Tsumura, *First Book of Samuel*, 112. Many English translations also favor such a reading, for example the ESV, NIV, NASB and NRSV. Among these options, I slightly favor the last reading. The imperfective past verb יעשה also suggests repeated actions in the past. Thus, it was repeated year by year that Peninnah would customarily provoke Hannah. See GKC, § 107e; Driver, *Notes*, 6.

40. Arnold, *1 and 2 Samuel*, 55.

41. The social dynamics of honor and shame contributed to the pressure people felt.

42. See appendix 2 for details.

is so bowed down by her childlessness that she nearly dies with shame."[43] The hostility of her rival only makes her situation even worse. Time lingers in slow motion during these difficult years for Hannah.

Barrenness was considered not only shameful but also pitiable.[44] The husband (a term of relational closeness) showed his solicitous concern for Hannah by calling her by name and asking four continuous questions: Why do you not eat? Why is your heart sad? Why do you not drink? Am I not better to you than ten sons? The first two questions are posed as if Elkanah was not aware of the tension between his two wives, especially of Peninnah's role in heightening the stress and agony Hannah was being subjected to.[45] Despite Elkanah's kind and gentle words, Hannah was not comforted (1:8) because her husband could never stand in her shoes and understand all the shame and torment she had suffered as a childless woman.[46] Hannah's lack of response to Elkanah's questions also indicates that Elkanah's attempt to provide consolation did not help.[47]

The husband's insensitivity to Hannah's agony perhaps can be seen from his untimely mentioning of "ten sons" to Hannah. Such a term can only be poignant to a barren and shamed woman who does not even have one son. In fact, the fate of a woman in the ancient Near East was dependent on a male figure as her guardian.[48] In this case, Hannah's survival rested on the responsibility of her husband Elkanah. However, if a husband was to die before his wife (usually a husband was older than his wife), the responsibility would shift to his son(s).[49] Hannah's status would have been severely diminished since she did not have a son of her own to care for her. Although she was the favored wife, without a son she would have no rights of succession and thus would be categorized only as a childless widow.[50] Hannah's social and

---

43. Pedersen, *Israel*, 231.

44. Marsman, *Woman*, 224.

45. It seems that Elkanah was not able to grasp Hannah's sorrow. See Steinmann, *1 Samuel*, 53.

46. The last question "Am I not better to you than ten sons?" is very self-centered. If Elkanah had phrased it "Are you not better to me than ten sons?," it would probably have sounded much better as a caring husband.

47. Campbell, *1 Samuel*, 41.

48. Byron, "Childlessness and Ambiguity," 26.

49. Byron, 26.

50. Byron, 39.

financial status was precarious at best as a barren woman in the family, and there was not much Elkanah could do to extricate her from this predicament.

The narrator slows down the pace here by highlighting Hannah's emotional trauma as a result of Peninnah's provocation and humiliation. The vivid scenic description heightens the tension between these two women. There has to be a way out of this distressing puzzle.

3.2 God Clears Hannah's Shame by Giving Her a Child (1 Sam 1:9–20)

The agony and shame of Hannah's childlessness seemingly could not be mitigated even if her husband were to come to her support. Being weighed down by her predicament, Hannah turned to the Lord for divine aid.[51] Indeed, in the past God had listened to people's prayers for the healing of barrenness and miraculously granted them children (Gen 25:21; 30:22). Hannah's problem of childlessness was a result of divine intervention.[52] If it was YHWH who closed (סגר; vv. 5–6) Hannah's womb, then only God himself could open it up (פתח; Gen 29:31; 30:22). Thus, Hannah had at least come to the right place to seek help.

Hannah's determination to seek divine help can be seen from a chain of active and adjacent verbs associated with her: ותקם, "then she rose" (v. 9); ותתפלל, "and she prayed" (v. 10); בכה תבכה, "and she actually cried" (v. 10); ותדר, "and she vowed" (v. 11); ותאמר, "and she said" (v. 11); הרבתה להתפלל, "and she exhibited much prayer" (v. 12).

Hannah rose after the family had finished eating.[53] The partaking of the sacrifice was a joyous occasion, but one wherein she did not feel a sense of belonging.[54] Hannah wanted to avoid public attention and remained discreet

---

51. "Appeal to the gods" was probably the most common option available to childless women in the ancient Near East. Other options included turning to "medicine and magic" and "adoption." Byron, "Childlessness and Ambiguity," 28–34.

52. The husband Elkanah likely understood the closure of the womb as a divine disfavor in light of the Deuteronomic covenant.

53. See appendix 3 for more details.

54. This joyous mood contrasts with that portrayed by the tautological infinitive absolute construction בָּכֹה תִבְכֶּה in the next verse (v. 10), where the infinitive absolute likely emphasizes the mood, here the indicative – "and she actually cried." Such unusual behavior at an otherwise joyous occasion was very incongruous and out of place. According to Callaham, the tautological infinitive usually emphasizes modality. See Callaham, *Modality*.

as she drew near to the Lord. This was her personal direct encounter with God, and she would prefer to have a moment of privacy. Before further description of Hannah's subsequent actions, a circumstantial clause is inserted in the second part of verse 9 to tell about Eli: "Now Eli the priest was sitting on the seat on the doorpost of the temple of the Lord." The description of the priest simply sitting probably has a passive connotation, especially when readers later find that he misreads a woman in her prayer as one who drinks excessively (v. 14). הכסא ("*the* seat"), with an unexpected definite article ה, even though occurring here the first time, seems to suggest a distinguished special seat in accordance with Eli's rank and honor as a priest and a judge.[55] The narrator's artistic juxtaposition of different characters is not a strange thing to readers (see earlier in v. 3). Both Eli and Hannah are located spatially in the house of the Lord in Shiloh while the story of Hannah develops.

The bitterness of her soul, recalling the issue of childlessness, compels Hannah to pray to the Lord in tears. Hannah's action of weeping is emphasized by the use of an infinitive absolute that precedes the verb (ובכה תבכה). The infinitive absolute emphasizes the mood (here the indicative) – that on an otherwise joyous occasion, she is in fact weeping rather than rejoicing.[56] Hannah's action of weeping in prayer contrasts with her earlier similar action of weeping (as a response to Peninnah's provocation in v. 6), but perhaps with a different overtone. Unlike her previous signs of vulnerability, here we see a determined woman who wrestles with God in prayer.[57]

Hannah's fervent prayer indicates her total dependence on the Lord for help. The narrator, however, is selective in providing the details of her prayer to the readers. But given the circumstances, it seems very likely Hannah was praying a prayer of lament,[58] expressing the sorrow and shame of her childlessness and appealing to God for divine intervention and deliverance.

---

55. I previously discussed the nature of הכסא in section 2.5.

56. Webster, *Cambridge Introduction*, 288. Another view is that infinitive absolute lays greater stress and emphasis on the lexical meaning of the verb (GKC, § 113n; *IBHS*, § 35.3.1; Joüon-Muraoka, § 123e), thus "wept bitterly" (ESV, NASB, NRSV).

57. Hannah's dependence on divine aid contrasts with Sarai and Rachel who looked to human sources for help with the problem of their barrenness. See Williams, "Hannah," 46. Williams suggests (on p. 52) that what deviates from the common constructed type is most valuable in the foregrounding of one's character.

58. For further information on lament Psalms, see Villanueva, *Uncertainty of a Hearing*.

Nevertheless, the details of Hannah's vow are recorded. Though vow-making is not uncommon in the Tanakh (Gen 28:20; Judg 11:30; Jonah 1:16), people usually made vows to God in urgent and desperate situations. According to Tony W. Cartledge, the formula of Hannah's vow complies with the traditional form of vow-making.[59] While McCarter sees Hannah's vow as formal poetry,[60] it seems there is no need to make such a connection since the language of her speech is very direct and straightforward.[61] Hannah's vow can be paraphrased as such: "If you give your maidservant male seed, I will give him to the Lord all the days of his life." The style is like personal dialogue within a narrative.

Hannah addresses God as "the Lord of hosts," stressing his sovereignty over the world.[62] Before Hannah asks the Lord to grant her male seed, she appeals to him for three relatively parallel petitions: that the Lord would indeed look on her affliction, remember her and not forget her.[63] It is obvious Hannah earnestly seeks to draw God's attention to her plight of childlessness. Unless God will intervene in her life, she will have no hope. In the vow, Hannah addresses herself as a "maidservant" (v. 11). The threefold repetition of this title is to emphasize her humility and piety before the Lord.[64]

In order to stress the seriousness of her vow, Hannah adds that "no razor shall come upon his head." The language echoes the Nazirite vow, consecrating the person to the Lord for special service (Num 6:2). One may recall in the near past that Manaoh's barren wife gave birth to a son (Samson) who became a Nazirite (Judg 13) and delivered Israel from the oppression of neighboring

---

59. The formula of a "Vow Account" consists of (1) narrative introduction, (2) address to the deity, (3) protasis of the vow (condition) and (4) apodosis of the vow (promise). Cartledge, *Vows*, 145.

60. See McCarter, *1 Samuel*, 49, 60. The drawback of considering it poetry is the ambiguity of the language used. Was Hannah referring to a general dedication of the child or literally surrendering the child to the temple for holy service?

61. Alter, *Art of Biblical Narrative*, 84.

62. The use of such a title is perhaps purposeful, since 1 Samuel consists of many military struggles between Israel and other foreign nations. Ross emphasizes that יהוה צבאות is a royal and cultic title; see Ross, "Yahweh," 83–92.

63. Cartledge, *Vows*, 148; Klein, *1 Samuel*, 8.

64. Cartledge, *Vows*, 148. Cartledge seems to contradict himself as he states later that the character of Hannah, revealed through the vow, is flowing with both humility and brashness ("daring to bargain with Yahweh Sabaot," p. 192). In my opinion, there is no evidence to support her brashness in her prayers, as clearly stating one's terms is an essential part of any vow-making.

nations.⁶⁵ Scholars debate whether the MT describes Samuel as a Nazirite or not.⁶⁶ But a Nazirite did not need to stay in the house of the Lord all the days of his life; he was allowed to leave after the completion of his days of separation (Num 6:13). According to the Torah, every firstborn male child belonged to the Lord, yet was allowed to be redeemed later at a certain price (Num 3:46–47). A woman who had suffered prolonged barrenness usually would not willingly dedicate her first son for lifetime service once he was born.⁶⁷ Thus Hannah's vow is selfless in nature, and her religious piety is underscored here.

The granting of a son would not help her in the long run if his life would be wholly and exclusively God's, and he would serve the Lord in Shiloh all his days.⁶⁸ However, it would definitely extricate her from the label of being a shamed barren woman.

The miraculous birth of Samuel, as a fulfillment of Hannah's vow, further adds importance to his role as a great leader of Israel.⁶⁹ While the vow heightens Samuel's role as an extraordinary leader, it also subverts the role of Eli as a priest (an intercessor).⁷⁰ Hannah earnestly sought the Lord in prayer in the house of the Lord, and her overstay probably caught Eli's attention. This lonely woman silently prayed in great anguish, but Eli misjudged her as a drunken woman. Eli erred in observing with his "weak" eyes (1 Sam 3:2), rather than sensing the heart of the individual. His assessment is wrong. Eli's opening words are not of comfort but of rebuke, "How long will you stay drunk? Put away your wine from you!" As a priest, Eli should have interceded for God's

---

65. Polzin believes that Hannah has Samson in mind in her prayers (despite his struggle with weakness and failure). See Polzin, *Samuel and the Deuteronomist*, 24.

66. McCarter argues, based on LXX and 4QSamᵃ's longer text, that "and wine or strong drink he will not drink" should be added before this final phrase. See McCarter, *1 Samuel*, 53–54. The longer text, as often the case, is perhaps only secondary in nature. Scholars who also see Samuel as a Nazirite include Klein, *1 Samuel*, 2–3; Steinmann, *1 Samuel*, 55; Bodner, *1 Samuel*, 19; and Bergen, *1, 2 Samuel*, 69. Others see that no explicit reference is made to Samuel as a Nazirite; see Tsumura, *First Book of Samuel*, 118; Firth, *1 & 2 Samuel*, 56. In any case, the allusion to the Nazirite status is present.

67. Tsumura, *First Book of Samuel*, 118.

68. Arnold, *1 and 2 Samuel*, 56.

69. Bar-Efrat, *Narrative Art*, 154–155; Alter, *Art of Biblical Narrative*, 86.

70. Alter clarifies, "This oblique undermining of Eli's authority is of course essentially relevant to the story of Samuel: the house of Eli will be cut off, his iniquitous sons will be replaced in the sanctuary by Samuel himself, and it will be Samuel, not his master Eli, who will hear the voice of God distinctly addressing him in the sanctuary." Alter, *Art of Biblical Narrative*, 86.

people and been sensitive to their needs. However, he failed to notice Hannah in her great agony and rebuked her instead. As such, Eli's role stands out negatively to the readers. Though his physical eyes see, he is a person of no spiritual discernment.[71] The contrast between Hannah and Eli is very obvious.

Hannah's immediate reply denies Eli's misjudgment with an emphatic "no." She explains that she has never touched any wine or strong drink but that she is a woman of "hard spirit" (אשה קשת רוח), and she has been pouring out her soul before the Lord. Various are the suggestions on the meaning of the phrase קשת רוח.[72] The interpretive difficulty is generated by the ambiguous meaning of קשת רוח, which can possibly mean "a hard spirit" (i.e. a difficult, troubled or sorrowful spirit) or "hard-spirited" (i.e. being determined, strong-willed or persistent). Though either reading is possible, I slightly prefer the latter reading of Hannah being a woman of determined and resolute spirit. Being occupied with the sorrow and shame of childlessness, she desperately sought the Lord in prayer. Throwing herself into prayer, she totally disregarded Eli's presence since she was pouring out her soul before the Lord. How can one's soul be poured out? The metaphor is used to indicate the involvement of her whole being and full concentration in her prayers before God. What Hannah poured out were words of excruciating petitions.[73]

To continue, Hannah rushes to defend herself and insist that Eli should not regard her as a בת בליעל. The exact meaning of this phrase has to be discussed. It is obvious Hannah felt that her reputation had been tarnished

---

71. Bodner, *1 Samuel*, 20.

72. The LXX renders it as σκληρὰ ἡμέρα, "hard day," which deems it an unfortunate and difficult experience. Many translations seem to follow this path, thus "troubled in spirit" (ESV; similarly NIV, NRSV), "a sorrowful spirit" (NKJV, AV), "a heart-broken" woman (REB) and "a very unhappy" woman (NJPS, likewise Vulg. "*mulier infelix nimis*"). However, Driver sees it as "hard-spirited" in the sense of being obstinate and unyielding; see Driver, *Notes*, 14. This is also supported by Klein ("a persistent" woman; see Klein, *1 Samuel*, 9). Similarly, Muraoka thinks it refers to Hannah's determinedness in taking up the matter with her God; see Muraoka, "1 Sam," 98–99. Muraoka defends a causative transitive form; for example, קשה ערף ("stiff-necked") in Exodus 32:9 is found in a causative transitive form in 2 Kings 17:14, ויקשו את ערפם ("they hardened their neck"); thus, likewise, קשת רוח in 1 Samuel 1:15 can be related to its causative transformative form in Deuteronomy 2:30, הקשה יהוה אלהיך את רוחו ("The Lord your God hardened his spirit"). Hannah, called by the narrator a מרת נפש ("bitter soul"; 1:10), did not follow the conventional wisdom of the sages by taking strong drink (Prov 31:6) as a cure for her deep distress but rather, to the contrary, firmly took up her matter with God in prayer. As such, קשת רוח in 1 Samuel 1:15 can be understood as tough-spirited, namely, Hannah being a woman of a determined or persistent spirit.

73. Tsumura, *First Book of Samuel*, 121.

while being treated as a בת בליעל. Thus the need for clarification is necessary. The word בליעל is often used with the plural form of בן, thus בני בליעל.[74] The difference between בת and בן is only of gender distinction. What matters is how one understands בליעל. It seems it is a compound word which consists of בלי ("without") + יעל ("profit, benefit").[75] Thus it is often rendered as "worthlessness"[76] or "uselessness, wickedness."[77] The daughter of בליעל is thus a worthless woman. It is also noted that בליעל is a term characterizing someone who is not simply useless but also of dubious moral character.[78] If so, that seems to fit the context better, as Eli was not just simply scolding Hannah (for presumably being drunken) as a person of no value but rather perceiving her as a morally licentious and destructively base woman.[79] The implication is that Hannah did not come before the Lord with proper propriety (rightfully so) and thus should be regarded as reprehensible. Thus, בת בליעל is a degrading and "derogatory label"[80] (thus a term of shame) which Hannah does not accept from Eli.

The reason that she looked like a drunken person, murmuring without voice, is because she had been speaking out of her great anguish and grief in silent prayer. Placing "anguish and grief" at the forefront of the sentence is again emphatic. In other words, she came to the Lord with a great burden. This burden in her heart has driven her to the point that she has kept praying until now (עַד־הֵנָּה), which seems to suggest that Hannah had forgotten about the time in her prolonged prayers and thus lingered on. The wordplay between עַד הֵנָּה, "until now," and חַנָּה, "Hannah," should be noted. The name Hannah (חַנָּה) probably derives from the verb חנן I ("be gracious, be favorable").

---

74. See Deut 13:14; Judg 19:22, 20:13; 1 Kgs 21:10, 13; 2 Chr 13:17. Ironically, Eli's sons are described in 1 Samuel 2:12 by the narrator as that exact kind of person.

75. Another theory is that it consists of בלי ("without") + עלה ("to go up"), which would eventually be identified with "Sheol," the underworld. See Thomas, "בְּלִיַּעַל," 19. Emerton, based on a different verbal root בלע I ("to swallow, destroy"), points out that the word refers to people whose characters are destructive, harmful and evil. He treats the word as a noun with an afformative ל. According to him, G. R. Driver earlier proposed a similar theory but with a different homonymic value, namely, בלע III, "to confuse." See Emerton, "Sheol," 217. Tsumura argues that בליעל refers to the name of an underworld goddess. See Tsumura, *First Book of Samuel*, 123–124.

76. "בְּלִיַּעַל," BDB, 116.

77. "בְּלִיַּעַל," *HALOT* 1, 133–134.

78. Firth, *1 & 2 Samuel*, 52; Steinmann, *1 Samuel*, 50.

79. RSV probably captures it rightly by rendering it as "a base woman."

80. Firth, *1 & 2 Samuel*, 57.

Ironically, thus far God has not seemed to have shown favor toward her as she has suffered so much until now. Perhaps, as with the emergence of a great leader, a test of faith is always required.

Surprisingly, Eli does not even bother to ask Hannah the cause of her grief but extends a high-sounding blessing: "Go in peace! And may the God of Israel grant your petition which you asked from him" (1 Sam 1:16). In response, Hannah humbly accepts this blessing: "You are being so gracious (חֵן) to your maidservant."[81] The contrast between Hannah and Eli in terms of the difference in their character is accentuated through Hannah's prayer episode. Arnold rightly comments, "Eli represents the corrupt and apostate leadership of the priesthood and Hannah the simple faith that issues from suffering and pain."[82] Derived from such a simple faith, God would raise up a great leader (Samuel) who would supplant Eli's unfavorable leadership. Readers find Hannah to be sympathetic, enduring and full of faith in God, whereas Eli is insensitive, foolish and repulsive.

The episode concludes with the woman (האשה) going her way and eating her food. We are not given the exact reasons for what prompted the change of Hannah's attitude,[83] but Hannah was definitely different now. She resumed eating and her face was no longer downcast.

The pace of the narrative now speeds up. The family arose in the morning, worshipped the Lord and returned to their house in Ramah. Soon Elkanah knew (וידע) his wife Hannah. The verb ידע is a euphemistic term to describe their sexual intimacy (Gen 4:17, 25). God blessed their union, and Hannah conceived and bore a son (1:20). As Hannah pleaded with God for his remembrance of her (1:11), God answered by remembering her (1:19). The word "remember" (זכר) is noted as a "soteriological" verb. When used with the Lord as subject, it suggests the initiation of a major new activity by the covenant-making God.[84] It is a great joy that God has finally answered Hannah's prayer. As expected in the "barren wife" type-scene, Hannah, the barren wife, was eventually heard by God and had a son. The tension of the story has been

---

81. The subtle pun between the word favor (חן) and the name Hannah (חנה) is noted. See Klein, *1 Samuel*, 9; Bergen, *1, 2 Samuel*, 70; Steinmann, *1 Samuel*, 56; Bodner, *1 Samuel*, 21.

82. Arnold, *1 and 2 Samuel*, 56.

83. Perhaps she just simply accepted the words of Eli by faith as an assurance of God answering her prayers.

84. Bergen, *1, 2 Samuel*, 70.

resolved. The readers are also relieved that the oppressed and shamed Hannah received her due portion from the Lord.

It should be noted that God did not instantly answer Hannah's prayer. It took time (לתקפות הימים, "toward the circuit of days," 1 Sam 1:19) as she waited for God. Patience was still required in the process. The waiting period of time was also a test of faith for Hannah. Behind a great leader, there is a great mother.

The birth of Hannah's son is obviously a miracle from above. Hannah names her son Samuel, saying, "Because (it was) from the Lord I have requested him." The name Samuel (שמואל) has different possible interpretations, but, following S. R. Driver's analysis, it seems that the most natural and suggested reading should be "Name of God."[85] That is to say, Samuel would bear the name of God, emphasizing his divine origin as a God-given child (1 Sam 1:11; זרע אנשים . . . ונתת) despite having been conceived by Hannah's human husband.[86] The phrase "from the Lord" (מיהוה), being placed before the verb, stands in the emphatic position. The child given to Hannah is a divine grace, and Hannah wants to acknowledge such grace by exhibiting obvious features in the name of the child.

---

85. Driver, *Notes*, 16–19; Hertzberg, *I and II Samuel*, 25; Tsumura, *First Book of Samuel*, 128. The earliest scholar to present this interpretation seems to be Gesenius in his *Geschichte der hebräischen Sprache und Schrift* (Leipzig: Vogel, 1815), 11. Budde says that "der Name Gottes" maybe means "*der, über dem der Name Gottes genannt ist*, d. h. *der Gotte gehört*" ("the one over whom the name of Gott is called, that is, the one who belongs to God"). Budde, *Die Bücher Samuel erklärt*, 11. *HALOT* 4, 1554–1555 offers three possible readings for this term: first, reading *Su-mu* (the name of the deity) as the subject and *'ēl* as the predicate, i.e. *Sumu*/שׁם is god (so-called "a theophoric element"); see also Noth, *Die israelitischen Personennamen*, 123, 140. Second, the name is a construct chain with the first element as a common noun, meaning "descendant, son" (similarly, Ges[18] listing "descendant," p. 1376). Third, שׁם is a verbal element from a root שׂמה, meaning "to be high, exalted" (also Ges[18], 1376). Driver also lists three less likely options in his commentary. First, the name derives from the root שׁאל ("to ask") for its etymology. Thus, שְׁאוּל מֵאֵל, signifying "Asked of God." But such a contraction is "alien to the genius of the Hebrew language." What the narrator means to express is an assonance rather than an etymology, namely, שמואל only recalls the word שׁאול ("asked"). Second, similarly, it is suggested that the word is from שמועאל, indicating "heard of God." But there are more serious problems with this conjecture. The letter ע is not one which typically elides. We should have expected the verb שמע in the narrative if this reading was intended. Third, treating the *waw* as a suffix pronoun; thus "his name is God" – שְׁמוֹ אֵל; but the meaning of such a name, insinuating a lack of respect and veneration toward שׁם by equating himself with God, is less likely in the context.

86. Tsumura, *First Book of Samuel*, 128.

Since the verbal root שאל occurs multiple times (1 Sam 1:17, 20, 27–28; 2:20) in Hannah's episode, some historical critics claim that the name of Samuel is not original and only echoes a tradition about the birth of Saul, whose name שָׁאוּל seems to explain Hannah's frequent use of this root (a passive participle שָׁאוּל is even used in 1:28).[87] By doing so, this claim tries to justify Saul's legitimacy, valuing his kingship. However, though the name Samuel displays various archaic and ambiguous features, for a variety of reasons it is unlikely that the narrator used materials written about Saul to describe Samuel's birth.[88] After all, Saul stands out overall as a negative character in the book of 1 Samuel, especially if we perceive him through the narrator's presumed ideological point of view of honor and shame. Thus it is less likely that Hannah (or the narrator) would want this God-given child (a great future leader of Israel) to foreshadow someone whose reputation was tarnished (i.e. by dishonoring God). Having said so, it is still plausible to see that the birth of Samuel, with its sociopolitical overtones, as introducing and foreshadowing the birth of kingship in Israel (i.e. Saul).[89]

By granting Hannah a son, God removed Hannah's shame of childlessness. She was no longer branded as a disgraced "barren woman" in the midst of Israel. God turned Hannah's tears into laughter and sorrow into joy. The birth of Samuel marks the dawning of a new day and is a turning point in Israel's history.[90] This God-given child will prepare the future kings of Israel (i.e. Saul and David).

3.3 Hannah Honors God by Offering Samuel to the Lord (1 Sam 1:21–28)

Once again Elkanah and his family went up to Shiloh to offer the annual animal sacrifice to the Lord (as in v. 3). The text also mentions Elkanah's vow. Nevertheless, the only vow that was previously known to the readers was

---

87. Dietrich, *Early Monarchy in Israel*, 318; McCarter, *1 Samuel*, 62, 65; Miscall, *1 Samuel*, 14; Bodner, *1 Samuel*, 22; Brettler, "Composition," 602. Another intriguing theory is that the root שאל is a name etymology on Shiloh; see Na'aman, "Samuel's Birth Legend," 51–61.

88. Gordon, "Who Made the Kingmaker?," 263–269; Gordon, *1 and 2 Samuel*, 23–24; Arnold, *1 and 2 Samuel*, 57.

89. Polzin, *Samuel and the Deuteronomist*, 25–26. Similarly, Auld suggests that the people's asking for a king had been anticipated by Hannah's asking for a child. See Auld, *I & II Samuel*, 34.

90. Arnold, *1 and 2 Samuel*, 57.

Hannah's (v. 11). It is possible that Elkanah had taken Hannah's vow as his own.[91] According to Numbers 30:6–15, if a married woman makes a vow and her husband is aware of it, the husband has the right to annul or accept the vow. It seems their following conversation (vv. 22–23) suggests that Elkanah approved of Hannah's vow. Thus, Elkanah, as the head of the family, also took responsibility for Hannah's vow.[92]

However, Hannah does not join the pilgrimage this time, even though Elkanah assumed she would.[93] She says to her husband, "Until (עַד) the child goes off breast feeding, then I will bring him, and he shall appear before the Lord and stay there forever." Tsumura also notes that the device of aposiopesis ("*I will not go* until . . .) seems to indicate an unwillingness to continue.[94] Women in ancient Israel usually breastfed their babies for as long as three years.[95] This long waiting period creates some tension and suspense for the readers.[96] Questions are thus raised: Was Hannah really serious about her vow to God? What was the purpose of this delay? Would she honor her own words? Was she unwilling to dedicate Samuel to the Lord after the child was born?

Once a person made a vow to God, it was important to fulfill it (Ps 76:12); otherwise, the person would be regarded as a fool (Eccl 5:3–4). Failure in fulfilling a vow, as a breach of faith, would bring dishonor to God and was often cursed (Mal 1:14). Thus Jephthah controversially fulfilled his vow even to his own harm – that is, the cost of the life of his own daughter (Judg 11:29–40).[97]

It is also interesting that the verb used is a *niphal* (יִגָּמֵל) in 1:22; the *niphal* (here as an anti-causative middle voice) presents the action not as a transitive event.[98] In other words, Hannah did not say, "until I have weaned the child,"

---

91. Hertzberg, *I and II Samuel*, 28.
92. Steinmann, *1 Samuel*, 62; Firth, *1 & 2 Samuel*, 58.
93. The first *waw* in v. 22 should be taken as contrastive, thus "but."
94. Tsumura, *First Book of Samuel*, 128.
95. Marsman, *Woman*, 533; also 2 Macc 7:27.
96. There is evidence that women in ancient Israel were often the vulnerable group in fulfilling their vows because of their lack of financial means. See Van der Toorn, "Female Prostitution," 197.
97. Alternatively, there are scholars who do not believe it was a literal fulfillment of the vow (i.e. offering her up as a burnt offering), rather arguing that Jephthah's vow involved dedicating his daughter to YHWH as a perpetual virgin. For a good summary of the history of interpretation, see Marcus, *Jephthah and His Vow*, 8–9.
98. Van Wolde, "Niphal as Middle Voice," 472–473.

as her husband says in verse 23, "until you have weaned him" (גמלך, as a *qal*, a transitive construction), referring to Hannah as the subject. Rather, she says, "until the child [as the subject] goes off breast feeding." The subtle difference signifies a mother's care and keenness that the child himself decides when it is the best time to come off his mother's breast. In other words, as long as the child continues to willingly suckle his mother's breast (without giving a specific time frame), he should stay with Hannah within the family. The event is described from the perspective of the child without the influence of an external agent, thus reducing the sense that it is Hannah deciding the period of time she will keep the boy with her. Interestingly, the LXX's rendering seems to insert more suspense into the present story by adding "until the child goes up" (Ἕως τοῦ ἀναβῆναι τὸ παιδάριον) before ἐὰν ἀπογαλακτίσω αὐτό ("if I wean him"),[99] insinuating that the child's going up to Shiloh depended on whether Hannah would actually wean him. Hannah's true intention, unknown to the readers for the time being, engenders curiosity about the development of the story.

4QSam[a] adds an additional line [ונת]תיהו נזיר עד עולם כול ימי [חייו] which McCarter translates as "[for I shall dedi]cate him as a Nazirite for[ever]."[100] Though its presence would emphasize Hannah's determination to dedicate this boy to the Lord, the surplus text is most likely a secondary gloss.

The husband's response to Hannah shows his sense of understanding and approval: "Do what is good in your eyes! Stay until you have weaned him! Only (אך) may the Lord establish his (own) words!" Elkanah's saying, stressing the Lord's sovereignty, seems to indicate that he has confidence in Hannah's words, namely, the vow she made. However, the LXX (along with the direct object alternative היוצא מפיך of 4QSam[a]) seems to show that the husband still reserves a shred of doubt and suspicion toward his wife's credibility: ἀλλὰ στήσαι κύριος τὸ ἐξελθὸν ἐκ τοῦ στόματός σου ("But may the Lord establish *what has come out of your mouth*"). However, as Elkanah's beloved wife (v. 5), there is no reason to see why the husband would not believe her. Hence, Tsumura's comments are appropriate: "What Elkanah is saying is that

---

99. Muraoka suggests that ἐὰν should be read as a conditional particle when it is used in the protasis A (aor. subj.) + apodosis B (fut.) syntagm. See Muraoka, *Greek-English Lexicon*, 183.

100. McCarter, *1 Samuel*, 56.

his wife may do whatever she thinks best, as long as God does his own will (lit. 'his word')."[101]

Indeed, the narrator also picks up the pace by describing Hannah's unhesitating actions with a series of *wayyiqtol* verbs (narrative past): ותשב, "and she remained" (v. 23); ותינק, "and she nursed" (v. 23); ותעלהו, "and she brought him up" (v. 24); ותבאהו, "and she brought him in" (v. 24); וישחטו, "and they slaughtered" (v. 25); ויביאו, "and they brought (him) in" (v. 25). Even though the time span of the event could have spread over a period of three years, such a description of smooth, swift and sequential actions (with Hannah as, or part of, the subject) within a few verses suggests that Hannah did not delay but faithfully fulfilled her promise by dedicating the child to the Lord as soon as she had weaned him. Eslinger also agrees that Hannah is not stalling because of maternal instincts although doubts were created by her earlier hesitation.[102] Clouds of suspicion concerning Hannah's sincerity can be cleared away.

Moreover, not only did Hannah dedicate her son to the Lord in his due time, but she, together with her husband, also willingly brought a large sum of offerings to show her gratitude to the Lord. It is said that Hannah brought with her "three bulls" (as per the MT, שלשה בפרים),[103] one ephah of flour and a container of wine.

It is unclear if Hannah brought three bulls or a three-year-old bull to Shiloh. Proponents of the reading "three-year-old bull" often think that three bulls would have been an "excessive offering,"[104] thus too expensive for an ordinary family to bear. Plus, verse 25 seems to indicate that only a single bull (הפר, with the definite article ה) is sacrificed. Others, however, favor the MT's reading of "three bulls." Tsumura, for example, argues for Hannah's extreme

---

101. Tsumura, *First Book of Samuel*, 129. Hornkohl also plausibly argues for the superiority of the Masoretic testimony; see Hornkohl. "Her Word," 465–477.

102. Eslinger, *Kingship of God*, 88–89.

103. But the LXX (ἐν μόσχῳ τριετίζοντι καὶ ἄρτοις) and 4QSam[a] (בפר בן] בקר משלש ולחם[) have a different reading: "with a three-year-old bull and bread." Likewise, many other English translations (ESV, NIV, NASB, NRSV, RSV) follow suit by describing a three-year-old bull, but without the additional "bread."

104. Steinmann, *1 Samuel*, 60. Other scholars who favor the reading of a "three-year-old bull" include Klein, *1 Samuel*, 10; McCarter, *1 Samuel*, 63; Hertzberg, *I and II Samuel*, 26.

generosity to the Lord through the lifelong consecration of her son.[105] If the MT reading of "three bulls" can be accepted, it profoundly demonstrates the deep love Hannah has for her son and ultimately the sincerity of her vow before the Lord. As Hannah dedicates her son to the Lord with an extraordinarily large offering, she honors God by fulfilling her promise, although it is not an easy promise to fulfill.[106]

The nominal clause added at the end of verse 24, "The boy was young," indicates Samuel's extreme youth.[107] This is an additional piece of information which supports that Hannah did not hold back her son at Ramah for her own interests. As per her foregoing vow, she did not selfishly keep her only son to herself.

Furthermore, Hannah's willingness to dedicate her son to the Lord can also be seen from the mood of her speech (as they bring the boy to the priest Eli) and her words of acknowledgement. Hannah approaches Eli and says (1 Sam 1:26): בי אדני חי נפשך אדני אני האשה הנצבת עמכה בזה להתפלל אל יהוה. This can be translated as, "Please, my lord! By the life of your soul, my lord, I am the woman, who was standing with you in this (place) to pray to the Lord." The two-fold use of אדני here shows Hannah's courtesy toward Eli the priest. Meanwhile, readers cannot fail to notice that her speech is fast paced and contains interruptions.[108] Such a style of language perhaps suggests a joyous mood. Hannah's dedication of her son is voluntary and not out of reluctance.

---

105. According to Tsumura, the generous offering of three פרים (possibly "younglings") matches an ephah offering of flour (the priestly regulation often specifies 3/10 of an ephah of grain offering for each bull offered, cf. Num 15:9; 28:12, 20, 28). See Tsumura, *First Book of Samuel*, 129–132; also Bergen, *1, 2 Samuel*, 73. Ratner also defends the MT reading by explaining that הפר in v. 25 is a collective term. Thus, though ostensibly seen as singular, it should be rendered as plural in context (i.e. "the bulls"). He also cites Genesis 15:10 and 2 Samuel 6:18 as examples of collective singular nouns which clearly suggest a plural in context. It is perhaps conceivable to conjecture that the LXX translators and the 4QSamᵃ scribe reconstructed the version of a "three-year-old bull" in order to alleviate the contradiction (only בקר is extant, for בפר בן] בקר] is reconstructed from the MT), as they were baffled by the apparent "discrepancy" between verses 24 and 25 with regard to the number of animals described. See Ratner, "Three Bulls or One," 101–102. It should be noted that Hannah's original vow (1:11) only consists of dedicating her future-to-be son to the Lord; it does not specify the number (value) of sacrifices to be offered.

106. One can relate Hannah's dedication of her only son Samuel to Abraham's offering of his only son Isaac in Genesis 22:1–14.

107. Tsumura, *First Book of Samuel*, 132.

108. The second use of אדני actually interrupts the flow of the sentence.

She continues by saying, "It is this boy I prayed for, and the Lord granted me my request (שְׁאֵלָתִי) which I asked (שָׁאַלְתִּי) from him. Thus I also have lent him (הִשְׁאִלְתִּהוּ) to the Lord; as long as he lives, he shall be lent (שָׁאוּל) to the Lord." This summary statement reminds Eli of her prayer to the Lord at Shiloh and states the logical reason she now dedicates Samuel to the Lord.[109] The artful wordplay of the root שאל is obvious in her remarks. The Lord granted her request and fulfilled her petition, thus Hannah sees it as her part of the responsibility to dedicate her son to the Lord, just as she had vowed. Moreover, this is an expression of Hannah's faith in God.[110] Hannah gave back Samuel to God just as she had promised. Again, there is no need to connect the root שאל here to Saul's birth account.

The Lord's granting of Samuel brought joy and comfort to the once shamed and childless woman. It should be said that, by lending her son to the Lord, Hannah still considered Samuel to be her son by name. By fulfilling her vow, Hannah honored the Lord by dedicating her only son to the Lord at Shiloh, rather than selfishly keeping her son for herself. The loss experienced by this faithful woman proved to be a gain for the whole nation of Israel.

The episode concludes by stating that Hannah and her husband Elkanah worshipped the Lord in Shiloh after they joyfully dedicated Samuel to the Lord. The piety of the couple is highlighted. The narrative ends with their yielding, grateful, trustful worship rather than with a conclusion concerning Samuel's birth. Such an ending is perhaps unusual since the problem of barrenness is mentioned in the beginning (1:1–2). Such a crafting of the narrative suggests that the narrator wants the readers to see more than the reality of a miraculous birth.[111] Indeed, the devout parents prepared Samuel to emerge as a godly and important leader of Israel, as can be seen from the later narratives. From a broader framework, the narrative of Hannah's barrenness (ch. 1), placed in the narratives of the books of Samuel, is only "a sense of a beginning" for the later narratives concerning the rise of David's monarchy.[112]

---

109. Steinmann, *1 Samuel*, 63.
110. Bergen, *1, 2 Samuel*, 73.
111. Brueggemann, "I Samuel 1," 39.
112. Brueggemann, 43.

3.4 Hannah's Thanksgiving Song: The Lord Who Oversees Men's Honor and Shame (1 Sam 2:1–10)

The context of worship in Shiloh at the end of the last episode prepares one for Hannah's song of thanksgiving. In my second chapter (section 2.2), I briefly discussed that terms denoting honor and shame are conspicuous in Hannah's song (2:1–10) in the exchange of high and lowly status and the contrast between the gaining and losing of wealth. The purpose of this part of the study is to explicate the changes in honor and shame shown in this song.

It should be noted that this song, as a psalm of thanksgiving, is poetic in nature.[113] It is not surprising that a poetic song was embedded (as is the Song of Moses in Exodus 15) in the midst of the narrative, namely, the couple's worship in Shiloh (1:28) and their return to Ramah (2:11). It is also appropriate that people were filled with hearts of praise and thanksgiving after witnessing God's miraculous work of deliverance in their lives. Instead of treating the Song of Hannah as merely the later insertion of an already existing psalm,[114] we should take note of the many signs of thematic connection with the story of Hannah and the rest of the book of 1 Samuel.[115] As many have noticed, the Song of Hannah corresponds to the Song of David in 2 Samuel 22, and the two bracket the entire narrative of the books of Samuel.[116] Thus, Brevard Childs concludes that the Song of Hannah, together with 2 Samuel 22, serves as "an interpretive key" for what follows.[117] Similarly, McCarter says that the Song of Hannah "sounds a clear keynote" for the rest of the narratives.[118]

---

113. McCarter notes its obvious poetic symmetry and parallelism; see McCarter, *1 Samuel*, 74–75.

114. For proponents of the later insertion of the Song of Hannah, see, for example, Hertzberg, *I and II Samuel*, 29; Polzin, *Samuel and the Deuteronomist*, 30; Klein, *1 Samuel*, 15.

115. For example, the word "barren" in 2:5 can easily recall Hannah's previous status; God's judgment against enemies is expressed through the thundering in heaven (cf. 2:10; 7:10); and the mentioning of the "anointed" one (2:10) forecasts the inauguration of Israel's kingship. Fokkelman offers numerical data to support the song's thematic importance in the book of Samuel; see Fokkelman, "Desire Divine," 14–24.

116. See Arnold, *1 and 2 Samuel*, 69; Polzin, *Samuel and the Deuteronomist*, 31.

117. Childs, *Introduction*, 273.

118. Namely, the story of Samuel, of Saul, of David; see McCarter, *1 Samuel*, 76; also Steinmann, *1 Samuel*, 70; Gilmour, *Representing the Past*, 105.

Of special interest are the multiple voices expressed in this song.[119] Not only does the psalm aptly allude to the life situation of Hannah as a barren woman in verse 5,[120] but more importantly, the universality of the language also potentially echoes the lives of other main characters in 1 Samuel.[121] Fokkelman says the high level of abstraction and the universal themes in the poem refuse to be pinned down to one individual or the unique event of one historical setting,[122] and Gordon suggests that the song proactively outlines the history of the early monarchy recounted in the books of Samuel.[123] Similarly, Arnold says that "Hannah's song is the harbinger of things to come."[124] Indeed, the Song of Hannah seems to set a tone for the unfolding of the rest of the book. On the one hand, the upward trajectory of Hannah's life moves her from oppression and lowliness to victory (over Peninnah) and exaltation as she totally depends on God in prayer. Likewise, Samuel and David also ascend from humble backgrounds as God exalts both of them as they honor God. On the other hand, Peninnah and her "high" position of bearing children could parallel the high statuses of Eli and Saul in the sight of men, both of whom are humbled for lightly esteeming God. The role reversal comes in both directions.

Furthermore, it is important to note that the Song of Hannah lays great emphasis on God's sovereignty. It is hard to imagine Hannah speaking of God's support of his king (the anointed one) when such an office was not established yet in Israel. Possibly the unexpected reference to the "king" is prophetic in nature, speaking from God's perspective.[125] Thus, Childs says

---

119. Polzin identifies a trio of voices: (1) Hannah, (2) a persona of the exultant king, and (3) the Deuteronomist, the "author" of the song. See Polzin, *Samuel and the Deuteronomist*, 30. However, my understanding of the voices expressed in this song is different and more complex (see my following discussion for details).

120. But this is not without problems, since Hannah eventually has six (including Samuel; 2:21) instead of seven children as alluded to in v. 5. See Klein, *1 Samuel*, 14.

121. Tsumura, *First Book of Samuel*, 68, 136.

122. Fokkelman, *Vow and Desire*, 101, 110. Hannah's concern for the national interest in asking God's support for the king (2:10) also suggests a high level of awareness of the actual history of her own people.

123. Gordon, *1 and 2 Samuel*, 78.

124. Arnold, *1 and 2 Samuel*, 70.

125. The need for a good king (an Israelite monarch) to lead Israel permeates the recurring lament (17:6; 21:25) in the book of Judges: "In those days there was no king in Israel; every man did what was right in his own eyes," though one can also conceivably argue God (as the

the Song of Hannah has to be understood from "a theocentric perspective."[126] The voice of God (as well as the author) can thus be discerned through the mouth of a woman.

The Song of Hannah assures the readers that the Lord God is the sovereign one behind the historical narratives of Israel. Of particular note here is that God's sovereignty is also closely related to the changes of honor and shame highlighted in this song, especially in verses 4–8. On this Jumper comments:

> Section B (i.e., vv. 4–8) significantly focuses on how YHWH exerts his dominion over the world social order to give ascendency to the lowly. This is set out in terms of military supremacy (v. 4), economic privilege (v. 5ab; 7ab), and familial status (v. 5cd). The familiar themes of honor–shame as life–death also appear (v. 6) alongside the notion of sitting with rulers.[127]

YHWH is seen clearly as the one who has dominion over honor and shame in the social order. Interpreters have noted the frequent exchanges of honor between those in high positions and those in low positions.[128] The Lord gives victory to some but allows others to suffer defeat. The Lord makes some rich but makes others suffer want. The Lord gives life to some but takes life from others. The Lord raises up and exalts some but humbles and brings down others. From the Deuteronomistic perspective of honor and shame expressed in Deuteronomy 28, each of these contrasting pairs of statements can be considered as broader honor-versus-shame related terms.[129] Ascending and descending in social position can be viewed as the gain of honor and the loss of honor (i.e. the increase of shame), respectively. Thus, the Song of Hannah communicates a clear message that YHWH is the sovereign one who oversees one's honor and shame in the social sphere. No one can go beyond God's plan.

---

king) is the one being implied. For a further discussion on the assessment of kingship, see Dumbrell, "In Those Days," 23–33.

126. Childs, *Introduction*, 273.
127. Jumper, "Shame and Honor," 183.
128. Jumper, 183–186.
129. Jumper, 183.

The structure of this song can plausibly be divided into three sections:[130] the first stanza (vv. 1–3), the second (vv. 4–8) and the third (vv. 9–10).[131] The first stanza is an exaltation of praise to YHWH. The focus pertains to beholding the glory (honor) of YHWH through his unparalleled holiness, protection, knowledge and judgment. The second stanza tells about God's sovereignty in the human world as he paradoxically reverses the fate of those of lowly and high status. Some gain their honor; others lose their honor. But it is the sovereign Lord who oversees men's honor and the loss of it (i.e. their shame). The last stanza presents the conclusion to exalt the anointed king. My following discussion of the Song of Hannah will thus follow such an outline:

- The first stanza (vv. 1–3): Give glory to YHWH.
- The second stanza (vv. 4–8): The sovereign Lord who oversees men's honor and shame.
- The third stanza (vv. 9–10): YHWH will honor the God-assisted king.

In the first stanza, the song opens with Hannah's prayer. Hannah bursts out to express herself as the person who has personally experienced God's salvation, thus "*my* heart" (לבי), "*my* horn" (קרני), "*my* mouth" (פי) and "*I* rejoice" (שמחתי).[132] Hannah confesses that her heart has rejoiced in the Lord and that the Lord had exalted her horn. The metaphor of lifting up a "horn" compares her to a bull who "carries his head high and is proudly conscious of its strength."[133] However, the raising up of one's horn seems to go beyond the ostensible meaning of a demonstration of strength or the language of triumph. For ancient readers, the image also captures a sense of boastful pride (Ps 75:5). It symbolizes her "dignity" or "visible distinction or exaltation."[134] The term thus evokes Hannah's elevation in honor. Later the Lord would also lift the horn of his anointed one (2:10).

---

130. For terminology concerning Hebrew poetry (such as "stanza," "strophe," etc.), I consult Watson, *Classical Hebrew Poetry*.

131. Klein, *1 Samuel*, 14; Steinmann, *1 Samuel*, 78–80.

132. The first person references also indicate Hannah's intimate relationship with God. See Tsumura, *First Book of Samuel*, 142.

133. Klein, *1 Samuel*, 15; thus NRSV and LEB render it, "my strength is exalted."

134. Tsumura, *First Book of Samuel*, 142. Arnold, *1 and 2 Samuel*, 69.

The meaning of the next line, "my mouth opens wide (רחב) over my enemies," is ambiguous. There are two main interpretations: (1) It refers to "swallowing enemies" (see Isa 5:14), thus figuratively describing triumphing over one's enemies. (2) It is an expression of contempt (Ps 35:21; Isa 57:4), thus "derides" (ESV, NRSV), "boasts over" (NIV, HCSB) or "gloat over" (NJPS). Being placed in synonymous parallelism with the previous line,[135] namely, "my horn is exalted in the Lord" (Hannah's elevation in honor), it is doubtful that the first interpretation rightly expresses the relationship between the two. The second seems to best fit the context.[136] Readers may recall that Hannah has previously suffered taunting from Peninnah (1:6); now the fortune is reversed. As Hannah's enemies are abased, she, on the contrary, is elevated and honored by implication.

The last line explains the reason Hannah should be boastful: because (כי) she has experienced the salvation of the Lord. The word "salvation" is an ambiguous term which may be seen as victory wrought by Yahweh for his people. In this case, Hannah's victory over Peninnah through the birth of her son.

Jack M. Sasson's following rendering of this verse is a good example which reflects the nuances of honor and shame in the original context:[137]

> My heart glories in the Lord
> My pride soars because of the Lord
> I boast widely over my enemies;
> for I delight in your deliverance.

Since Hannah had received so much favor and blessing from the Lord, it is very natural that she was motivated to sing praises to God (2:2): "There is no one holy like the LORD, for there is none besides you; and there is no rock like our God." Hannah affirms several attributes about YHWH: his holiness, uniqueness and incomparability. With אין fronting each clause, it

---

135. McCarter considers the first three lines as straightforward parallelisms; see McCarter, *1 Samuel*, 74. Fokkelman, however, regards the first four lines as a chiastic structure (AB–BA). This is supported by the semantics of the word pair "exult–rejoice" and the alliteration between רחב-רמה. See Fokkelman, *Vow and Desire*, 83. It seems Fokkelman's division is preferred. But, at any rate, lines two and three are parallel.

136. For scholars who endorse this interpretation, see Omanson and Ellington, *Handbook*, 52; Firth, *1 & 2 Samuel*, 50; Arnold, *1 and 2 Samuel*, 69; Bergen, *1, 2 Samuel*, 75; Polzin, *Samuel and the Deuteronomist*, 31; Klein, *1 Samuel*, 12.

137. Sasson, *Jonah*, 165; also noted by Fokkelman, *Vow and Desire*, 84–85.

is very interesting that the exaltation of YHWH starts with three negations. Such a formula of "there is no . . . like . . ." has been noted by Labuschagne as "comparative negation."[138] The basic idea is that YHWH is incomparable, and his divine attributes are without equal. YHWH's holiness is first emphasized. The holiness of the Lord can be revealed through "his intervention in human history as the redeeming God."[139] But sometimes his holiness is also expressed through his awesomeness (6:20). Such holiness is rooted in his singleness. There is no other God but the Lord alone. The Lord is not only transcendent in his moral character, but he is also mighty in power. No other rock can compare with YHWH. The image of "rock" often evokes the idea of God as the source of protection and security (Ps 18:3; 31:3; 62:7) for his people.[140] The Lord God has the strength and power to save. The switch from the second person singular to first person plural suggests that Hannah invites her listeners to identify with her and join in this hymn of praise.

While praising God, Hannah also admonishes (2:3) those who have opposed God: "Do not speak so much with such incredible haughtiness! Let not arrogance come out of your mouth! For the Lord is a God of knowledge, and for[141] him deeds are weighed." The first and the second lines are parallels (similarly, lines three and four). It is uncertain whom Hannah is addressing here, but it can be conjectured that, among other enemies of God (2 m.pl. verbs), Hannah's opponent, Peninnah, is being included here.[142] Pride and arrogance are demonstrated through the boastful speeches of these opponents. The repetition of the adjective גבהה ("high") should not be regarded as a dittographic error.[143] Rather, it is the author's emphatic purpose to tell about the gravity of their haughtiness, thus "incredible haughtiness" (גבהה גבהה).

---

138. Labuschagne, *Incomparability of Yahweh*, 11; see also Tsumura, *First Book of Samuel*, 143.

139. Labuschagne, 99.

140. Omanson and Ellington, *Handbook*, 54; Tsumura, *First Book of Samuel*, 143.

141. There is a textual issue here – *qere* reads לו while the *Ketib* is לא. Since both terms sound the same, it could have been confused in oral transmission by copyists. The LXX seems to favor לו, but with the inclusion of θεὸς, *niphal* medio-passives almost universally do not have a stated agent; see Van Wolde, "Niphal as Middle Voice," 460. When the ל is present with a *niphal* passive (specifically a medio-passive), it should likely be read as "for" or "with." I am indebted to Dr. Tim Undheim for offering this insight.

142. Peninnah is described as Hannah's rival (1:6).

143. Klein, *1 Samuel*, 13.

The boastful wicked need to learn the lesson of humility because (כי) the Lord is an all-knowing and judging God. The knowledge (in the plural form) of God speaks of its quality, not its quantity.[144] Thus the Lord is an "all-knowing God" (NJPS) and nothing can be hidden from his scrutiny. More importantly, "for him (i.e. the Lord) deeds are weighed." The text does not state explicitly whose actions are meant. Although there is a suggestion to read it as God's deeds,[145] it is more likely that this is an evaluation of the deeds of all humans who have to be brought before God's judgment.[146] It is contradictory in reasoning to suggest that divine actions would be subject to divine judgment. However, the general gist is still clear: the Lord is a God who judges.

To recap, in the first stanza (vv. 1–3), Hannah exalts God for his salvation, his holiness, his protection, his knowledge and his judgment. The focus is on amplifying God's honor and proclaiming his glory. Hannah's exaltation of the Lord is motivated by her personal experience of a gracious God who has brought radical change (from ashamed to honored) in her life through the birth of her son Samuel.

In the second stanza (vv. 4–8), Hannah affirms God's sovereignty in the human world: God repeatedly reverses human fortunes, thus bringing dramatic changes in their honor-rating systems. Thus, Fokkelman even calls this song "the song of the great reverser."[147] The Lord God overturns the stratum of human society. The dramatic change of their statuses can be seen from the following table:

---

144. Tsumura, *First Book of Samuel*, 144.
145. Tsumura, 144.
146. Fokkelman, *Vow and Desire*, 87.
147. Many cases of reversal can be found in the book of Samuel on the individual story level. The dynamic alternations of the fates of Samuel and the Elides, David and Saul are prefigured in this song. See Fokkelman, *Vow and Desire*, 110.

Terms Denoting High Status ⤊	Terms Denoting Status Reversal ↓	Terms Denoting Lowly Status ⤋	Terms Denoting Status Reversal ↑
Warriors v. 4	Shattered v. 4	Stumbling ones v. 4	Girded (with strength) v. 4
Well-fed ones v. 5	Were hired for bread v. 5	Hungry ones v. 5	Ceased (being hungry) v. 5
(One who has) many sons v. 5	Languished v. 5	Barren one v. 5	Gave birth to seven ones v. 5

I consider the second stanza as forming three different strophes: strophe 1 (vv. 4–5); strophe 2 (vv. 6–7); strophe 3 (v. 8).

In the first strophe, as can be seen, the author lists three pairs of contrasting groups (warriors vs. stumbling ones; well fed ones vs. hungry ones; one who has many sons vs. the barren one). All of their fortunes are reversed.[148]

"The bows of the warriors are shattered; but the stumbling ones are girded with strength." Many terms in this line (v. 4) evoke military imagery.[149] Goliath, though seen as a mighty warrior in the eyes of men, was struck down by a shepherd boy with a slung stone (17:51). Victory in battle does not depend on human strength but on the Lord (7:10).

Those who are well fed are found with lack of supply, thus they have to earn a wage for bread. But those who were hungry have ceased hungering. Readers will soon find out that the descendants of Eli, as priests who used to be well fed, are accursed and will have to bow before other priests to implore them for an opportunity to work (2:36) in exchange for a loaf of bread, or even, in their own words, "a scrap of bread" (פת לחם).

The contrast is further intensified by the use of עד to suggest a higher degree, thus "even a barren woman bears seven children, but the one who has many sons withers away." A woman who has no child is a barren one (Gen 11:30; 25:21). Certainly, Hannah would identify herself as a barren woman. The mention of the birth of seven children suggests the ideal number

---

148. Tsumura, *First Book of Samuel*, 145.

149. Israel and its neighboring nations were often in conflicts and wars in 1 Samuel (4:1; 7:7; 11:11; 14:31; 15:8; 17:2; 23:5, 27; 28:1; 29:1; 31:1). This may explain why Hannah employed such ideas in this song.

of children a family could have in the ancient Near East.[150] Hannah would later have five more children, bringing the total number to six (2:21). Though not ideal, it is still a good number. Nothing more is said about Peninnah's children in 1 Samuel. The narrator's lack of reference to them suggests their insignificance despite Peninnah's family being introduced as important in the introduction. The sons of Eli, Hophni and Phinehas, died for their sins as a result of God's judgment (1 Sam 2:34; 4:17). All descendants of Saul except Mephibosheth would be executed by the Gibeonites (2 Sam 21:7–9). No human eye can penetrate the intrinsic cause of such changes in fortune and honor.

It should be noted that as fortunes are reversed, status in the eyes of people also alters dramatically. That is to say, those who were originally of high status (warriors, well-fed ones, the one who has many sons) are abased, but those who were originally of lowly status (stumbling ones, hungry ones, the barren one) are elevated. In other words, those of high status are lowered in their significance and shamed, but those of lowly status are elevated in their positions and honored.

What Hannah notes are dramatic changes in people's lives, for good or bad. But the driving force behind such abnormal reversals is worthy of investigation. To this Tsumura rightly comments: "Though the agent of this reversal is not explicitly mentioned, it is clear that it is the holy and sovereign God, who holds everyone's fate in his mighty hand and can certainly reverse human fortune according to his own will."[151] The Lord God, who is sovereign over all human activities, is in control. God's invisible hand monitors and governs the course of human events.

In the next strophe, God's sovereign will and power are explicitly communicated through a series of reversals of fate. Such reversals also bring significant change to the experience of honor and shame in the social stratum (see the following table):

---

150. Tsumura, *First Book of Samuel*, 145; Bergen, *1, 2 Samuel*, 76. שְׂבֵעִים ("satiated") in the beginning of the verse certainly resonates with a sound similar to שִׁבְעָה ("seven"), also part of the verse – both have similar letters but different sibilants. It adds to the rhetoric of the passage. I am indebted to Dr. Tim Undheim for offering this insight.

151. Tsumura, *First Book of Samuel*, 146.

Terms Denoting Abasement ↘	Terms Denoting Elevation ↗	Terms Denoting Abasement ↘	Terms Denoting Elevation ↗
The Lord brings death v. 6	The Lord makes alive v. 6	The Lord brings down to Sheol v. 6	The Lord raises up v. 6
The Lord makes poor v. 7	The Lord makes rich v. 7	The Lord brings low v. 7	The Lord exalts v. 7
	The Lord raises up the poor from the dust v. 8 To make them sit with the noble ones v. 8		The Lord lifts the needy from the ash heap v. 8 To make them inherit a seat of honor v. 8

As can be seen, in stylistic structure, verses 6–7 form four symmetrical pairs of fate reversals but verse 8 only mentions the groups who are elevated. The dramatic changes lead to obvious abasement or elevation with regard to their honor-rating system.[152] It is interesting that most of the verbal terms (mostly participles) in verses 6–8, with the Lord as the explicit subject, are *hiphil* stems (as causative agency). As such, they further affirm the Lord's sovereignty. With the dramatic reversal of abasement or elevation in people's lives, the sovereign Lord oversees their honor and shame.

In the first pair, the Lord is seen as the one who "brings death and makes alive" (2:6). The Lord is the one who has authority over one's life and death, alluding to the words of Deuteronomy 32:39. The Lord is described as the causative factor of death (ממית, *hiphil*), which seems to imply an unnatural death; thus, many translations render it as "the Lord kills" (ESV, NASB, NRSV, NET). It is peculiar מחיה ("make alive") is *piel* when all other verbal terms in this verse are in the *hiphil* stem (i.e. ממית, מוריד, ויעל). Steinmann explains that the *piel* of חָיָה can have the meaning "to restore the dead to life."[153] Indeed, the

---

152. Tsumura, 141. Tsumura notes that abasement and elevation occur throughout this song except in vv. 2–3.

153. Steinmann, *1 Samuel*, 72. The subject-object relationships can be close between *hiphils* and *piels*, particularly if they are stative verbs wherein the *hiphil* is indeed causative rather than exhibitive. As with the earlier discussion on the verb בעס, the *piel* signifies turning an object into the state described by this stative verb. The *hiphil* (if causative), signifies the subject acting upon the object in such a way that its object functions as a second subject, acting out the state of the verbal root (i.e. to cause an event). So the H-stem of חיה would mean the subject causes

next pair – "bring down to Sheol" and "raise up" – seems to parallel the first pair in meaning. Thus, מחיה corresponds to ויעל in this parallelism.

While it is certain that "Sheol" is associated with "grave," the term often implies a broader concept for biblical authors, meaning "underworld" – the place reserved for evildoers and miserable ones.[154] The term thus has a negative connotation of a "bad death" in mind.[155] Thus being brought down to "Sheol" denotes the notion of God's judgment. Hannah is confident that the Lord has sovereignty to judge some with an unusual (bad) death, but God also has the free will to bring some to life, or, to be more exact, to restore or raise up to life.[156] Fokkelman says, "Death and life are the most inclusive terms in human reality."[157] The sons of Eli, Hophni and Phinehas, unfortunately, died prematurely (4:17). Saul and his sons also died in a brutal and decisive battle with the Philistines (31:1–7). Life and death are in the firm hands of God.

Furthermore, the Lord is portrayed as the one who "makes poor (רוש) and makes rich (עשר I)."[158] This means that God has control over the social welfare of people and their economic status. From a Deuteronomistic perspective, material blessings are contingent on obedience to YHWH and dependent on God's favor (Deut 6:10–15; 8:1–9). Change of one's wealth would significantly affect one's honor in the eyes of others.[159]

The next colon speaks of God as the one who "brings low (שפל) and exalts (רום)."[160] This speaks to God's sovereignty in the event of both human abasement and elevation. "He demotes the socially prominent to insignificance and promotes the socially insignificant to high prominence (v. 7b)."[161] The fluctuating lives of Hannah, Samuel, Eli, Saul and David all testify to such a truth.

---

the object to act out as a second subject the process of staying alive (the majority of uses) or coming back to life (2 Kgs 8:5). The D-stem, so close to the H-stem, would signify conveying life to an object without the object acting out the state. See *IBHS*, § 21.2.2, 24.2, 27.1d. There is perhaps virtually no difference in actual usage, except for in Genesis 19:32, 34, where life is portrayed as being conveyed to an object not yet living. I am indebted to Dr. Tim Undheim for offering this insight.

154. Bar, "Grave Matters," 145–153.
155. Bar, 145–153.
156. The seed of resurrection and immortality may be implied.
157. Fokkelman, *Vow and Desire*, 92.
158. These two terms are discussed previously in section 2.2.2.
159. As would be the case for Job (cf. Job 30:15; 42:10–12).
160. Both terms are discussed previously in section 2.2.1.
161. Tsumura, *First Book of Samuel*, 147.

The four pairs of fate reversals in the second strophe (vv. 6–7) infer God's sovereignty in human lives; he has the capacity to elevate or abase the lives of humans, bringing honor or shame. Though not explicitly, the text seems to imply a certain moral principle underlying God's treatment of humans.[162] As Bergen rightly says, "Yet the Lord does not perform these actions indiscriminately."[163] The differentiation of the "faithful ones" and the "wicked ones" in verse 9 will perhaps provide further insight.

In the last strophe, the author transitions from the broader topics (2:6–7) of life and death, wealth and poverty, humility and exaltation to a more concrete form of fate reversal, for "the essential changes in the life of a person are, in the final analysis, made possible and ordained by Yahweh."[164] The rhyme of the derived stems of the verbal roots רום (in the end of verse 7) and קום (occurring twice in verse 8) perhaps also points to the close connection between these two. The Lord raises up (מקים) the poor from the dust; he lifts up (ירים) the needy from the ash heap. Both "dust" and "ash heap" denote a diminished or demeaned status.[165] The repetition of the verbal root רום is notable in this bicolon. The setting on high is not the lifting up of a spatial relationship but the exaltation of a social status.[166] The two images of honor are clearly indicated.[167] In verse 8, the author slows down the pace to describe the exaltation of a group of lowly, insignificant, marginal and vulnerable people. The purpose, as shown by the next two subordinate clauses, is "to make them sit with noble ones and make them inherit a seat of honor."[168] These subordinate clauses, as a chiastic unit, further strengthen the idea that the poor and the needy were granted a highly honored position. The motion of elevation is visually noted

---

162. Thus, I cannot agree with Fokkelman that "God at last takes sides socially and politically" in v. 8 and not before. Fokkelman, *Vow and Desire*, 94.

163. Bergen, *1, 2 Samuel*, 76.

164. Fokkelman, *Vow and Desire*, 95.

165. Muenchow, "Dust and Dirt," 609. Though only עפר and אפר are mentioned in Job 42:6, a similar socio-cultural overtone denoting "insignificance" for עפר and אשפת should be expected in 1 Samuel 2:8. Driver suggests that אשפת (often translated as "ash heap" in English) was actually the mound of dung accumulated outside an ancient Eastern town. Driver, *Notes*, 26. As such, it would only heighten the degree of "insignificance" attached to the term.

166. Previously, Hannah used the same verb root to speak about her elevation in honor (2:1).

167. Fokkelman, *Vow and Desire*, 93.

168. I discussed in section 2.5 that it is perhaps better to translate it as a "seat of honor" instead of a "throne of honor" in 2:8.

in verse 8. The trajectory moves from a lowly position on the bare ground to a higher position of being seated with honor.

The last line accentuates God's sovereignty over the course of human fate by pointing out that he is a God of creation. The clause fronted by כי explains that the pillars of the earth belong to the Lord and that he has set the world on them.[169] Since the Lord created this world, "he has the right to intervene in the social order."[170] That the Lord oversees the fate of humans should not surprise the readers.

Given the identity of the speaker, the description of a "poor" and "needy" person can definitely allude to Hannah herself. She was a person of insignificance, coming from the town of Ramah. She suffered shame and humiliation for years because of her barrenness. Out of her misery and desperation, she made a vow to God who graciously granted her request. The stigma of being a barren woman came to an end through the birth of her son, whom she dedicated to the Lord for all his life. Indeed, Samuel, the son she bore, would be elevated and greatly honored in the sight of Israel.

To recap, the reversals of fate in the second stanza (vv. 4–8) implicitly or explicitly indicate the Lord's sovereignty over the human social world. God has a decisive influence over the development of historical events. The reversal of the abasement or elevation of status shows that the Lord oversees human honor and shame. Therefore, the implication is that "obedience to God's word is of prime importance in human life."[171]

The last stanza focuses on the exaltation of the anointed one. However, before that, the author touches upon an important moral principle which underlies God's judgment of human events. Hannah proclaims that the Lord will guard the feet of his faithful ones (חסידו), but the wicked (רשעים) ones shall perish in darkness (2:9). The bicolon stands out clearly as an antithetic parallelism. The Hebrew word translated as "faithful ones" derives from the root חסד II, an important term in the Hebrew Bible which indicates the covenantal love/obedience of God's people to YHWH.[172] Those who obey the Lord will have his favor and blessings. On the contrary, the wicked, those who

---

169. Portrayed in their cosmology, ancient Israelites believed the earth was established upon foundations supported by pillars (Job 9:6; 38:4; Ps 18:15, 75:3).

170. Gordon, *1 and 2 Samuel*, 80.

171. Tsumura, *First Book of Samuel*, 72.

172. Glueck, *Hesed in the Bible*, 66–68.

disobey the Lord, will suffer his divine judgment. In view of the preceding discussion, it is natural to surmise that the faithful are those elevated and the wicked are those abased.

The last subordinate causal clause supports that it is not by human strength that one prevails. God exerts determinative influence on human success or failure. The theme of God's sovereignty has been repeatedly shown in the previous stanza.

In verse 10, the wicked have turned into the enemies of the Lord and thus shall be shattered.[173] Being placed at the head of the sentence in the MT, יהוה should be understood as a *casus pendens*, thus "As for Yahweh, his adversaries[174] are shattered."[175] Against them[176] the Lord thunders in heaven. God turns against them in a frightening and fearsome way (7:10).

Finally, in view of YHWH's sovereignty, Hannah declares God's judgment to the entire world and his exaltation of his anointed king. As Hannah was rejoicing that her horn was exalted in the Lord (2:1), she now looks forward to the exaltation of God's anointed one (משיח), namely, God's anointed king.[177] As I have discussed previously, the mention of the "anointed one" (i.e. a king) should not be taken as a later insertion but as prophetic in nature[178]; that is, she prophesied about the coming of the anointed king before the actual institution of kingship was established in Israel. The verb יָרֵם, as a *hiphil* jussive in form, should probably be seen with the force of a regular imperfect, thus "he lifts up."[179] This makes more sense if one notices that וְיָרֵם parallels וְיִתֶּן (a *qal* jussive with *waw* in form). It is Hannah's expectation that YHWH will do

---

173. The LXX has a long insertion of Jeremiah 9:23 which is likely secondary.

174. The *BHS* textual note indicates that many Hebrew manuscripts and *qere* are plural.

175. Lewis, "Textual History," 40–41. Another probability is 4QSam^a, "יהוה יחת מר[י]בו]," which, possibly siding with the LXX's transitive reading, reads "Yahweh shatters his adv[e]rsary." Such a reading would require a *hiphil* stem (pointed as יָחֵת) for the verb. But 4QSam^a, following the LXX with its long insertion possibly derived from Jeremiah 9:22–23, is more likely a secondary gloss.

176. The *BHS* textual note indicates that many Hebrew manuscripts and *qere* are plural.

177. The theme verb רום constitutes an *inclusio* for this song. See Tsumura, *First Book of Samuel*, 72; Arnold, *1 and 2 Samuel*, 70.

178. Another option is that an already existing psalm was used by the author and put into Hannah's mouth because it fit the context. Or that the psalm was composed by the author based on preexisting materials.

179. Steinmann, *1 Samuel*, 75; also GKC, § 109 k.

this for the king without specifying a time frame.[180] The topic of the "anointed one" runs through all the poems in the books of Samuel, thus suggesting an important theme throughout the book.[181]

As can be seen in the later development of the story, Samuel first anointed Saul as the king of Israel (10:1). Thus, he was the first one in the Scriptures to be called "anointed one" (מְשִׁיחוֹ, "his [Yahweh's] anointed one," 12:3). Saul was later rejected by God due to his disobedience. Consequently, Samuel was told to anoint David to replace Saul (16:12). Hence, Samuel became the kingmaker of Israel, installing both Saul and David in their kingly roles. Hannah's prayer thus not only focuses on thanksgiving for her own son, and on his welfare,[182] but also prepares for the coming of God's "anointed one," who is bound to make a great impact on the people of Israel.[183]

The exaltation of God's anointed one, in this context, implies that he is the one favored by YHWH. The rejection of Saul and the selection of David suggests that the latter is the true "anointed one" from YHWH. The moral principle seems to apply also to God's "anointed one." The Israelite monarchy only exists in a subordinate role determined by YHWH.[184] The king of Israel, unlike the kings of the surrounding nations, has to understand that real authority ultimately comes from YHWH.[185] By yielding to YHWH as the source of all honor, the divinely-assisted king will also be elevated in honor. The author prepares the readers to embrace this topic by introducing kingship at the threshold of his message.

---

180. Hertzberg, *I and II Samuel*, 31.

181. Steinmann, *1 Samuel*, 77.

182. Hannah is certainly concerned about the destiny of her son Samuel whom she has dedicated for lifelong service of God. The setting of the song is her official handing over of Samuel to the temple. See Fokkelman, *Vow and Desire*, 111.

183. For further study of the Messiah in the OT, see Satterthwaite, Hess, and Wenham, *Lord's Anointed*. Even Mary's Magnificat in Luke 1:46–55 echoes Hannah's words as Israelites were expecting the coming of their Messiah (i.e. χριστός in Greek) while under the suppression of the Romans.

184. Eslinger, *Kingship of God*, 111.

185. Firth, *1 & 2 Samuel*, 62–63.

3.5 The Lord Honors Hannah by Giving Her Many Other Children (1 Sam 2:18–21)

In contrast to the two sons of Eli who served their own bellies, the boy Samuel served before the presence of the Lord. Two things are mentioned pertaining to Samuel's clothing: first, he was clothed with "a linen ephod" (2:18). The linen material suggests its preciousness (Isa 3:23). The ephod was worn primarily by Israelite priests (Exod 28:4; 29:5).[186] Second, his mother used to make for him "a little robe" every year she went up with her husband to offer the yearly sacrifice (2:19). The "robe" (מעיל) may have been the formal vestment of priests, worn for cultic purposes (Exod 28:4, 31). Samuel's distinctive uniform probably anticipates a priestly role under the training guidance of the priest Eli.[187]

The devout couple was favored by Eli, who blessed Elkanah and his wife, "May the Lord give you offspring by this woman in place of the loan which she made to the Lord!" Hannah has unquestionably remained Elkanah's wife, though Peninnah may still have been the second wife and come with her husband for the annual sacrifice in Shiloh (1:4). The fact that only Hannah is mentioned as Elkanah's wife at this point signifies her high status. Peninnah and her children are nowhere to be found; they are insignificant at this point in the eyes of the narrator.

As soon as they return home, the Lord takes note of (פקד) Hannah (2:21), as the Lord had taken noted of the barren Sarah (Gen 21:1). Hannah too conceives and bears three more sons and two daughters. If the birth of Samuel eliminated the disgrace and taunting Hannah suffered as a barren and defective woman, then the birth of five more children was a further honor the Lord granted to his faithful maidservant. Hannah could now boast before all of her enemies that she was also a blessed "fruitful vine" (Ps 128:3). If seven children was the ideal number for Hannah to expect (2:5), her life (with six children) now came close to the perfect ideal.

But, of course, of Hannah's many children, Samuel remained unique. He is singled out by the narrator. We are told he grew up (ויגדל) with the Lord (2:21).

---

186. King David also wore a linen ephod (2 Sam 6:14) as he celebrated the entry of the ark into Jerusalem.

187. Auld, *I & II Samuel*, 49; Eslinger, *Kingship of God*, 120; Fokkelman, *Vow and Desire*, 123; Polzin, *Samuel and the Deuteronomist*, 42; Tsumura, *First Book of Samuel*, 160; Hertzberg, *I and II Samuel*, 35; Klein, *1 Samuel*, 25; Arnold, *1 and 2 Samuel*, 71.

Samuel certainly had God's favor. Later he would grow up to become the prophet of Israel (3:20). Both Samuel and the sons of Eli are characterized by the same root גדל. Samuel was becoming a great man of God, but the sons of Eli were becoming great sinners before the Lord (2:17).[188]

3.6 Conclusion

Various characters (Elkanah, Hannah, Peninnah, Eli) present different voices within the story. There is no doubt that Hannah remains the central figure in every scene.[189] But it is the voice of the narrator, from the ideological perspective of honor and shame, that shapes the development of the story. The narrator not only notices that the cause of Hannah's problem is her barrenness (which further complicates the story) but also portrays shame, as a result of her childlessness, as being the root of her inner struggles and social embarrassment. In fact, the narrator recounts the whole event through the lens of honor and shame. With the fluctuation of Hannah's fate, her status and reputation also change dramatically in the public eye (from lowly to exalted). As readers, if we are sensitive enough to embrace the narrated perspective of honor and shame, then we will be able to gain a greater appreciation for the story and its features.

The Song of Hannah functions as a significant interpretative tool for understanding the whole narrative of 1 Samuel. The perspective of honor and shame, being richly reflected in the song, is also an important implicit standard by which readers can evaluate God's response to those who serve him and those who reject him. The sovereign Lord reverses the fate of those of lowly and high statuses. He oversees human honor and shame. Hannah's personal fate, as well as that of Israel's anointed, rests on God's ultimate exaltation.

---

188. Brueggemann, *First and Second Samuel*, 22–23; Arnold, *1 and 2 Samuel*, 72.
189. Bar-Efrat, *Narrative Art*, 101.

CHAPTER 4

The Elides and Samuel – Honoring Selves versus Honoring God (1 Samuel 2:12–17; 2:22–4:18; 7:2–17)

In chapter 3, I demonstrated that the world of the life of Hannah is replete with honor and shame. The change of her fate, from a barren woman to a fruitful one, also communicates a trajectory from shamed to honored in the public eye. The competition for honor is a driving force that often motivates one's mind and actions. In this chapter, guided by the narrator's ideological point of view, I will continue reading the stories of 1 Samuel from the perspective of honor and shame. Particular focus will be given to the contrasting lives of the Elides and Samuel. In my argument, they each represent a totally different character and lifestyle: honoring the self versus honoring God. The difference of their attitudes in honoring God also triggers opposite consequences in their lives, whether for good or for bad.

4.1 Eli Honors His Sons More than the Lord (1 Sam 2:12–17, 22–25, 27–36)

The two sons of Eli, Hophni and Phinehas, are reported as being priests of the Lord (1:3), but the narrator refrains from making any comments about their character until 2:12. It is indeed shocking that the two sons of Eli, as priests of Lord, are described as "worthless men" (2:12; בני בליעל). Their actions of robbing the worshippers' sacrificed meat and their illicit sexual relationships with women who were serving at the tent of meeting were horrific sights in

Israel. The sons of Eli, as priests of the Lord, defiled and profaned God's holy name; thus, God would hold them accountable for their sins. In this section, we will study 1 Samuel 2:12–17, 2:22–25 and 2:27–36 in order to investigate the deeper reason for the fall of the Elides.

In contrast to the child (2:11; הנער) Samuel who was serving the Lord in Shiloh, the two sons of Eli, as "young lads" (2:17; הנערים), served their own bellies and sinned against the Lord. Juxtaposed contrasting descriptions are also frequent in subsequent episodes (2:21 vs. 2:22–25; 2:26 vs. 2:27–36). The stigma of the sons of Eli being labelled as "worthless men," echoing Eli's earlier improper description of Hannah as the "daughter of בליעל" in 1:16, determines that whatever is said about them hereafter will be negative. Indeed, Eli's sons did not know the Lord. It is ironic that the priests of the Lord did not know the God whom they served (cf. Jer 2:8). The knowledge they acquired was only for show, as they lacked an intimate relationship with YHWH and failed to obey God's obvious commandments.[1]

When the Israelites came to offer sacrifices in Shiloh, the servant of the priest (נער הכהן, i.e. he who served the interests of the priest) would come with a three-pronged fork in his hand and forcefully take the choicest parts of the sacrificed meat from the cooking vessels of the worshippers. Such a blasphemy had become משפט הכהנים, "the custom of the priests" (ESV, RSV). Though the Mosaic law decreed that the priests could have their due portion of the sacrificial meat as a reward for their service, it seemed to be restricted to the waved breast and right thigh of the sacrifice (Lev 7:28–36).[2] The rest of the peace offering meat was reserved for the worshippers to enjoy with their family and friends (Lev 7:11–16). But here the priests would take any meat they grabbed, as if they were faint with hunger.

Scholars are divided as to whether one should see such a hideous practice as the abuse of Eli's sons or as supplying background information on the accepted practice (albeit degenerate) of the time.[3] Following after the narrator's disparaging condemnation of the sons of Eli (2:12), it is more likely these despicable deeds point to the abuse of Hophni and Phinehas and are not a

---

1. Tsumura, *First Book of Samuel*, 154–155.

2. A varied description is given in Deuteronomy 18:3, where it is said that the shoulder and the two cheeks and the stomach should be given to the priest.

3. Tsumura, *First Book of Samuel*, 155.

mere description of the custom of the time. The narrator "is engaged, without delay, in furnishing proof against them."[4] The Israelites who came to Shiloh did not accept the coercion of the priests as a custom (משפט, "an ordinary thing"). They were forced to succumb to such an unreasonable demand. The summary statement in 2:14 – "thus they used to do to all Israel who came there in Shiloh" – again echoes the evil nature of the משפט. The sons of Eli, as priests of the Lord, made their abominations into the convention of the day. The description only makes the sins of the sons of Eli more intolerable.

The fact that the servant of the priests robbed the meat just as it boiled and before the fat was even sent up in smoke further shows the greed of the sons of Eli. The use of גם is for the purpose of intensification, thus *"even before they had burned the fat."*[5] The burning of the fat was to produce an aroma pleasing to YHWH (Lev 1:9, 13, 17), as would fit the recurring use of the *hiphil* verb קטר in Leviticus.[6] The sons of Eli dared to grab the raw meat before God received his portion in the form of smoke from the burned fat. They put their own needs first before YHWH. Even when the worshippers offered them any meat they desired after the burning of the fat, the priestly attendant refused to make any concession but threatened to take it by force if they continued to tarry. It is ironic that ordinary worshippers had to teach the priests about the proper order and value of cultic sacrifice. The sons of Eli wanted a different taste – roasted meat rather than boiled. What they insisted on was a clear "now and here" gratification. Tsumura's rendering of the sentence, "Now! You must give it to me! Or I will take it by force!" is a good suggestion of the mood of the servant's speech.[7] The short lines indicate the lack of patience and growing irritation toward the protests of the worshipper. Putting עתה (Now!) at the front, preceding the predicate, emphasizes the "immediateness" of the demand.[8] Such a blasphemous attitude against the sacrifice of the Lord was indeed shocking. Thus, Eslinger comments: "Sacrifice in their eyes is only a means to their own ends, which are pursued with total disregard for the sacrificer or Yahweh."[9]

---

4. Fokkelman, *Vow and Desire*, 117.
5. Firth, *1 & 2 Samuel*, 68; GKC, § 153. Alternatively, one can possibly also read it as "also."
6. Steinmann, *1 Samuel*, 85.
7. Tsumura, *First Book of Samuel*, 156.
8. Tsumura, 156; Fokkelman, *Vow and Desire*, 121.
9. Eslinger, *Kingship of God*, 118.

The summary statement in 2:17 allows the readers to see the direct characterization voiced by the narrator: "The sin of the young men was very great before the Lord." The narrator's emotional stance against the sons of Eli is clear in this statement and should be accepted without question. It should be noted that the singular young servant of the priest (נער הכהן) has now shifted to the plural "young lads" (הנערים). The plural הנערים most likely points to Hophni and Phinehas, though Fokkelman suggests it does not need to be restricted to the sons of Eli but could extend to all the temple servants.[10]

The description of Eli's sons as נערים is of great significance in this context. The term נער can possibly cover a wide range of age.[11] Generally speaking, a נער was a dependent youth (regardless of his age, but usually before reaching his maturity) who was still considered to be under the supervision of his parents within the circle of family. A נער was often seen as someone who was still under the authority of the parents and thus was inadequate in making independent decisions. Though we are not sure of the exact ages of the sons of Eli, one can assume they were of marriageable age, since later Phinehas is about to have a son (4:20). The narrator, however, purposely names the sons of Eli as "young lads" (הנערים), despite them possibly being mature physically, because he sees Eli's negligence of duty in overseeing his own children. As a father, the priest Eli was partly responsible for his sons' moral corruption and had failed to guide his children to walk in the commandments of the Lord.

There are also reasons to believe that Eli was not unaware to his sons' evil practices, although his name is not explicitly mentioned in the episode. At the very least, Eli was a beneficiary of the robbed sacrificial meat since he is included with his sons in the accusation of fattening themselves (להבריאכם)[12] on the choicest part of the offering (2:29). His obesity, perhaps due to the consumption of too much meat and fat, was also part of the reason that caused

---

10. Fokkelman, *Vow and Desire*, 122.

11. The three-month-old baby Moses was called a נער (Exod 2:6). The boy Samuel, probably about three years old, was also called a נער (1 Sam 1:25; 2:11). Isaac, a teenage boy who had enough strength to carry the wood of the burnt offering, was also called a נער (Gen 22:5, 12). Jonathan's bodyguard, a mighty warrior who carried his armor, was also called a נער (1 Sam 14:1, 6). The adolescent David who challenged Goliath was called a נער (1 Sam 17:33, 42, 55, 58). Even Absalom, after his failed attempt to usurp the throne, was still a נער in the eyes of the father (2 Sam 18:32). In the last example, David's purpose was probably to play down his rebellion and treat it as a foolish escapade of youth. See Fuhs, "נַעַר," *TDOT* 9:481.

12. However, 4QSam[a] reads לְהַבְרִיֽךָ מֵרֹאשׁ כֹּל מִנְחוֹת ("... by giving a blessing from the best of all the offerings"). I will discuss this textual problem shortly in this section.

his death (4:18). Thus, Eli was held accountable for the sins of his two sons whom the narrator calls "young lads" (הנערים). McCarter, however, thinks that there is no suggestion that Eli himself is portrayed as wicked and that Eli had no direct responsibility for the corruption of his sons. He says, "As in c[hapter] 1 he is depicted as well intentioned, if clumsy and ineffectual, while direct responsibility for the corruption at Shiloh is attached to his sons."[13] However, as I have explained, the fact that the narrator views Eli as being culpable for the sins of his sons is an important observation. While Auld declares, "We are given no reason to suspect that the priest is as bad as his 'lads' make him out to be," the very implication that he is not "as bad" as his sons' behavior indicates that he is, at the very least, not guiltless.[14] Tsumura also comments plainly, "Despite God's provision for the priests, Eli has closed his eyes to his sons' devices, and Eli is responsible."[15] God's judgment, through the mouth of the man of God, also reveals that Eli's fundamental problem is that he honored his sons more than the Lord (2:29). His spoiled love for his two sons prompted him not to take any disciplinary actions against them for their sins.

The sins of Eli's two sons were very great before the Lord because they treated the offering of Yahweh with contempt (נאצו).[16] The priests themselves treated the offerings with disrespect. Instead of bringing God's people closer to the Lord, the sons of Eli pushed them further away. As Fokkelman rightly says, "The covenant relationship between the deity and his chosen people is now completely subverted. The men whose holy office is to mediate, now bring about a fatal separation of all things, between the Lord and his inheritance."[17] Eli, as the high priest and the father, was blamed for tolerating the guilt of his sons.

The wicked sons of Eli are contrasted with the boy Samuel who was serving the Lord and growing in maturity (2:11, 21). As time progressed, Eli became very old. The narrator concludes with an overt summary that evokes the previous scandal pertaining to what the sons of Eli were constantly doing to

---

13. McCarter, *1 Samuel*, 84.
14. Auld, *I & II Samuel*, 47.
15. Tsumura, *First Book of Samuel*, 166–167.
16. I briefly discussed this term נאץ in section 2.4.2.
17. Fokkelman, *Vow and Desire*, 122.

all Israel. The use of the verb יַעֲשׂוּן as a *qal* imperfect form (2:22) indicates its iterative effect: they never stopped abusing God's people as time passed by.

Eli heard that his sons were sleeping with the women who served at the entrance to the tent of meeting (2:22). It is difficult to identify the nature of the service these women were performing, since they could possibly have been involved in different tasks, "From menial tasks to priestly duties, from celibacy to prostitution, from short-term periods as a result of vows to lifelong dedication – examples of all sorts are available."[18] It seems likely that the women were involved in some work of piety which provided them access to the entrance of the tent of meeting. The tent of meeting was supposed to be the holy place where God met with his people. But the sons of Eli were constantly sleeping (יִשְׁכְּבוּן, again the *qal* imperfect indicates the frequentative aspect) with these women who served at the entrance of the tent of meeting. Though the exact place where they had sexual relations is not mentioned, it is very likely that such an outrageous thing happened in the tent of meeting itself, as it was where the priests presumably had most of their close contact with these women. The priests even committed adultery right before God! Such a sacrilege is unthinkable in view of the sanctity of the tent of meeting in the eyes of Israel. Fokkelman also points out that it is possible that the text presents the priests as abusing their power and taking advantage of these women who had a mind to serve God.[19] In other words, what is of concern here may be abuse of their position of authority. Likewise, Hertzberg suggests that these women should be counted among the "sacral personnel" by virtue of their tasks.[20] If so, it would only make the sins of the priests all the more horrific.

Starting with a rhetorical question, Eli's long response to the evil deeds of his sons is rather weak and impotent: "Why do you do such things – (namely) your evil deeds which I am hearing from all these people. Don't, my sons! For the report is not good I am hearing the people of the Lord spread around. If a man sins against a man, God will mediate for him[21] [or more likely, 'they

---

18. Walton, Matthews, and Chavalas, *IVP Bible Background Commentary*, 284.
19. Fokkelman, *Vow and Desire*, 128; also Kasle, "Analysis," 126.
20. Hertzberg, *I and II Samuel*, 36.
21. This reading is suggested by the MT וּפִלְלוֹ אֱלֹהִים.

shall pray for him']²²; but if against the Lord a man sins, who can intercede for him?" It is important to note that Eli happened to hear this news after his sons must have practiced such evil things for a period of time, since the scandal about his sons had already been a topic of gossip among all people (כל העם). The use of the participle שֹׁמֵעַ also implies Eli may have been hearing such news at various occasions. It is ridiculous that Eli had to hear about the report about his sons through other people when his blindness is not yet introduced until 3:2.²³ His "sharp" eyes were able to detect the abnormal behavior of Hannah (1:12–14) but not the debauchery of his evil sons. The late arrival of Eli's first recorded rebuke here suggests that he "neglected his parental responsibilities earlier in life (cf. Deut 6:7; 21:18–21)."²⁴

Eli's long statement against his sons can be shortly summarized as, "Don't, my sons! For the report is not good!"²⁵ The next verse (v. 25) can be seen as a further explanation that clarifies why the report is not good. What strikes the reader is the light tone of Eli's rebuke against the grave sins of his sons, as if the consequence of such serious sins could be bypassed easily. Firth correctly points out that Eli never directly rebukes his sons, only posing a pair of questions and expressing his disappointment. Even in verse 24, Eli's disappointment is expressed; still it is not a direct rebuke. Firth goes on to say, "Rather, in a classic understatement, he observes the spreading report is not good."²⁶ Furthermore, with the repeated use of "if" (אם) clauses in verse 25, Eli's speech signals wrong information to his sons, as if their crime were

---

22. The LXX reads καὶ προσεύξονται ὑπὲρ αὐτοῦ πρὸς Κύριον ("and they shall pray for him toward the Lord"). Likewise, the 4QSamᵃ [ופללו] ל[ו] אל יהוה also supports such a reading although the first part is reconstructed from the MT. Given the reliable information conveyed by the latter part אל יהוה ("toward YHWH"), it is more likely that ופללו should be read as a plural verb, thus "and they shall pray." Auld suggests 'lyhwh in the 4QSamᵃ may have been corrupted into 'lhym in the MT. The MT reading is less likely with its signs of corruption as informed by the LXX and 4QSamᵃ. See Auld, *I & II Samuel*, 46. It also makes more sense in the context that others would intercede for him to God (rather than God praying for him as portrayed by the MT) at his offense against his fellow. For a good book serving as an introduction to the use of the LXX in text critical issues of the Hebrew Bible, see Tov, *Text-Critical*.

23. Firth, *1 & 2 Samuel*, 69.

24. Bergen, *1, 2 Samuel*, 80.

25. The LXX μὴ ποιεῖτε οὕτως has the addition of an imperative in v. 24: "Do not do thus!" 4QSamᵃ, not being extant, presumably accords with the LXX in the sentence. For an extensive discussion of textual comparisons of 1 Samuel 2:24, see Trebolle, "Textual Criticism," 280–282. But the expanded reading of the LXX and possibly 4QSamᵃ is more likely a secondary gloss.

26. Firth, *1 & 2 Samuel*, 69.

a mere misunderstanding that could be downplayed. The corruption of Eli's sons is not the hypothetical possibility of sin – "*if* a man sins (יחטא) against the Lord" – but the tangible actuality of sin. They *are* sinning against the Lord with their illicit sexual relationships.[27] Eli's response gives readers the impression that he either has no intention of immediately disciplining his sons or has simply lost control of restraining them.

Indeed, we see no response from Eli's sons following Eli's speeches. They do not bother answering their aged father. Only the narrator concludes that they would not listen to the voice of their father. Eli's attempt to warn them had no effect on his stubborn sons who had no ears to listen. As Pharaoh hardened his heart, rejecting Moses's offer to let the people of Israel go out of Egypt (Exod 8:28), the sons of Eli also willfully reject their father's words.[28] From a theological perspective, it is God who delights to put them to death (2:25). It may come as a shock to readers that it was YHWH's pleasure to put them to death, but that was the response to the way they had stubbornly chosen to be. Hannah was right in saying, "The Lord brings death" (2:6). The Lord God determines the destiny of all humans; the wicked shall be cut off in darkness (2:9). Eli's sons had provoked God's wrath; thus, no human intercession could be effective when they refused to listen to their father's warning.

Again, it is important to recognize that it was Eli's negligence in overseeing his sons and his failure in disciplining them that brought them to such a degree of sacrilege. It was probably too late for Eli to express his criticism at that moment, since, being "very old," he had lost the opportunity to take any tough or physical measures against his sons.[29] As a father who had failed in his parental responsibility,[30] Eli should be at least partly blamed for having loved and honored his sons more than God. A father's spoiled love is a chronic poison for the children. Eli's consistent inaction and inability to rectify the corruption of his sons would eventually bring about their death. Likewise,

---

27. The same root חטא ("to sin") is found in v. 17.

28. Some believe that the cause of the downfall of Hophni and Phinehas was their own willful rejection of God. See, for example, Gordon, *1 and 2 Samuel*, 84; Arnold, *1 and 2 Samuel*, 72.

29. Fokkelman, *Vow and Desire*, 132.

30. Sweeney correctly characterizes Eli as an "incompetent priest and father." Sweeney, "Eli," 59–75.

Arnold says, "Eli is either unwilling or unable to control his wayward sons."[31] In a similar tone, Mark Leuchter makes the following comments:

> The "manner of the priests" related in 1 Samuel 2:13–17 may reveal the sins of the sons, but Eli's lack of punitive action (vv. 22–5) lays bare the sins of the father: he is quick to castigate the commoner Hannah (1 Sam 1:12–14), but his permissiveness regarding his sons suggests elitist entitlement.[32]

Eli's complacency about his sons' wrongdoings eventually brings about their downfall. Eli's own words condemn himself as he knows full well that such evil deeds as his sons' would bring disastrous things for the priestly family but he does nothing earnest and substantial to stop them from their evil ways.

The depravity of Hophni and Phinehas has now been fully revealed. Of course, Eli, their father, was held accountable for the fall of his sons due to his lack of parental discipline and responsibility. Again, the corruption of the Elides is accentuated by the contrast with the good example of the young Samuel, who continued to grow and was in favor both with the Lord and with people (2:26).

Any readers who have understood the wickedness of Eli's sons will foresee that divine judgment is inevitable, as is in line with the moral principle demonstrated in the Song of Hannah (2:9). God's punishment of the Elides was finally announced in the form of a judgment oracle through an unnamed man of God (i.e. a prophet; see 2 Kgs 1:9; 5:8). It is important that, just as Eli was depicted as being primarily responsible for the corruption of his sons, the judgment oracle was also issued directly against him.[33] Note that the prophet "came to him and said to him" (i.e. Eli), carrying the authoritative words of God in the typical prophetic formula "Thus says the Lord" (כה אמר יהוה).

The long speech of the man of God basically contains three important messages: (1) A review of God's election of the Elide priesthood (the history reviewed, vv. 27–28).[34] (2) Eli's honoring of his sons more than God

---

31. Arnold, *1 and 2 Samuel*, 72.

32. Leuchter, *Samuel*, 32.

33. The judgment oracle was not issued directly against his sons in 2:27, though judgment concerning his sons will be included eventually in 2:34.

34. The MT in verse 27 poses it as a question (with the interrogative particle הֲ), "Did I actually appear . . . ?" Here the expected answer in this context would be "yes," although the answer

(the current problem, v. 29). (3) God's judgment of the Elides in detail (the future judgment, vv. 30–36). We will look at each point respectively in the following discussion.

The privilege God gave to the Elide priesthood can be seen in the fact that God appeared openly and chose their fathers from all the tribes of Israel to be his priests while they were still subject to the house of Pharaoh in Egypt.[35] The sense is that the Elide forefathers, as slaves of Pharaoh, did not deserve the right of being called priests of God, but it was God's divine grace that freely gave them such a prerogative. As priests of God, they were honored to go up to God's altar, to burn incense and to wear an ephod (2:28).[36] No ordinary Israelite (not even the king of Israel; see 2 Chr 26:16–21) was allowed to participate in such sacral duties. It was exclusively reserved for the priests of God. As a reward for their service to God, God also gave them the offerings by fire from the people of Israel. The Torah prescribes that a portion of the "fire offering" (Lev 2:10; 6:18 [HB 6:11]; 7:35) be given to the priests.[37] Thus, as priests of the Lord, they were ensured of receiving enough food to eat. In other words, when God called them to be priests, he also cared about their daily necessities.

However, the Elide priests certainly did not value the priesthood which God graciously gave them. The rebuke of the prophet starts with a rhetorical question, "why" (למה), which suggests their abnormality and unreasonableness. The accusation is "Why then have you looked at my sacrifices and my

---

can possibly be "no" in the Hebrew syntax. The LXX reads it as a statement "I appeared. . . ." It is often considered as a case of dittography, as the previous word ends with the same letter ה.

35. Both the LXX and 4QSam^a state that they were "slaves" of Pharaoh. The repetition of בית אביך ("the house of your father") in 2:27–28 perhaps points to an emphasis on the concept of lineage through which the Israelite social order was structured. The text, however, is not explicit in identifying this ancestor. The Scripture does not list Eli's genealogical account (1 Chr 6:4–10, 49–53) probably due to his ill reputation. According to Leuchter, the ancestor appears to be Moses. See Leuchter, "Samuel," 155. However, with Eli as a priest, the text would emphasize this ancestor in his priestly status and function. The best candidate would be the chief priest Aaron and his sons. See Tsumura, *First Book of Samuel*, 166; Firth, *1 & 2 Samuel*, 70; Hertzberg, *I and II Samuel*, 37. An extra-biblical source also indicates that Eli came from Ithamar, a son of Aaron. See Josephus, *Antiquities*, 215.

36. Tsumura suggests that this high priest's ephod, which included the jeweled breastplate and the Urim and Thummim, was different from Samuel's linen ephod (2:18). See Tsumura, *First Book of Samuel*, 166. If so, such an ephod would look more magnificent and noble.

37. Steinmann, *1 Samuel*, 99.

offerings that I commanded, speculating (on them) . . . ?"[38] Despite God's provision for the Elide priests, they have despised God's sacrifice and offering by overturning the sacrificial system and coveting what was not rightfully theirs. It is interesting that here the Elides were not criticized for their specific misbehaviors, but for coveting the divinely ordained sacrifices. God looks at the heart of a person. The corruption of the Elides springs first from their despicable disposition toward God deep inside their souls. As priests of God, they had departed far from serving God on behalf of the people.

In contrast to this contemptible attitude toward the Lord, Eli honors his sons by participating in their fattening of themselves (להבריאכם)[39] from the choicest part of every offering in Israel. The verb כבד obviously contrasts with the previous term נבט. The use of the *wayyiqtol* syntagm (ותכבד) can possibly be contrastive or sequential. Eli had honored his sons more than God, for he had despised the sacrificial system. The rather positive term כבד is used here with a negative connotation. As a priest of God, it was a common understanding to Eli that only God himself deserved glory (כבוד). The glory of the Lord (כבוד יהוה) is even a token for God's personified presence among his people (see Exod 24:16; Lev 9:6; Num 16:19). The first commandment of the Decalogue also says that Israel shall have no other gods before the Lord (Exod 20:2). However, it seems that Eli had placed his sons above God. To put it uncompromisingly, Eli's sons became his idol whom he loved and valued most. It is a true statement that he tolerated the evil practices of his sons (2:12–17; 22–25) by breaking God's obvious laws. As I explained earlier, Eli is at least partly responsible for the corruption of his sons. The root of Eli's problem is that he had reversed his priority of devotion, moving it from the Lord to his sons.[40]

---

38. See appendix 4 for more details.

39. 4QSamᵃ reads להבריך מראש כול מנחות (". . . by giving a blessing from the best of all the offerings"). It also accords lexically with the LXX's ἐνευλογεῖσθαι ἀπαρχῆς πάσης θυσίας Ισραηλ ("to bless themselves from the first fruit of every sacrifice of Israel"). A problem with 4QSamᵃ, להבריך, is that the *hiphil* of ברך II only occurs in 1QS 6:5 (post-classical), not in classical Hebrew. McCarter amends it to לְהַבְרֹתָם ("letting them eat [from the first fruits of . . .]"), thus from the verbal root ברה I. He questions the MT reading of לְהַבְרִיאֲכֶם in that Eli is included with his sons in the eating, when the prophet's question is presented in the singular. See McCarter, *1 Samuel*, 87–88. McCarter's emendation does not seem to be convincing to me, as the prophecy also concerns the destiny of Eli's sons (2:34).

40. Tsumura, *First Book of Samuel*, 167.

It is important to note that the prophet's criticism of the Elides is framed in the shame/honor perspective, which, as I have argued in section 1.1, is important to the narrator's ideological point of view. It is perhaps also not a strange thing to readers that God's subsequent judgments against the Elides (2:30) are also consistently presented in the category of a shame/honor perspective, to which I shall now turn.

As can be expected, every sin has its ramification before a holy and just God. The great wickedness of the sons of Eli is no exception. God's immediate judgment, following the accusation, is direct and straightforward. The inferential particle construction לכן ("therefore") again implies the causal relationship between the Elides' sins and their judgment. The prophet conveyed a solemn "oracle of the Lord" (נאם יהוה), quoting from the very word of the God of Israel. As descendants of Aaron, God had indeed said to their fathers that they and their sons would be priests of the Lord forever (Exod 29:9). However, since the Elides have broken God's covenant, he has decided to forfeit their right to remain in the service of the Lord. It used to be that the Elides could walk back and forth (i.e. go about freely, יתהלכו) before the Lord; but now God regrets his promise. The formula "far be it from me!" (חלילה לי), as an adversative exclamation, shows God's disappointment and firm determination to revoke his previous statement.[41] Indeed, the following repetition of the "oracle of the Lord" (נאם יהוה) only strengthens the solemnity of such an announcement.

God's judgment of the Elides would also be calculated according to the perspective of honor/shame: "For those who honor me I will honor (אכבד), but those who despise me shall be insignificant (יקלו)" (1 Sam 2:30b). The statement (only five words in the Hebrew) indicates that the Lord is just and impartial. If one obtains the impression that Eli was not able to do anything about his sons in verses 22–25 because of his old age and their rebellion, the narrator makes it clear here to portray Eli as "an appeaser of his wicked sons" and "culpable before God."[42] It is also noted that God is the subject, turning those who honor him into the state of being honored, that is, giving them a place of honor. But those despising God shall simply be insignificant, without

---

41. Fokkelman, *Vow and Desire*, 142; Tsumura, *First Book of Samuel*, 168.
42. Klein, *1 Samuel*, 27.

any mention of God's involvement. It is common sense that God cannot be dealt with lightly.

The priest Eli clearly understood that his family fell into the category of despising the Lord. According to how the Elides treated the Lord, so they would be dealt with.[43] It is obvious that here in verse 30 the verb "to honor" (כבד) is contrasted with "to be insignificant" (קלל I). As antonymous terms, they point to the world of honor and shame.[44] Thus Fokkelman makes a similar-sounding statement, "Here the rule on honour and shame is applied for the first time by God regarding the question as to whether people hold *him* in high or in low esteem."[45] God would honor those who honor him but those who despise him shall be put to shame. God's pronounced judgment is sovereign and absolute. The narrator, fully agreeing with such a divine value, incorporates this ideological concept and adopts it into his own values and principles to guide the development of the narration in 1 Samuel 1–7.

The verb "to be insignificant" (קלל I) is an abstract term that needs further explanation. As such, the following passage (2:31–36) further clarifies "how" the Elides will be shamed.

God's judgment of the Elides starts with the use of הנה (behold!). Together with the clear reference to the future ("The days are coming"), it serves to introduce "a solemn and important declaration."[46] What is about to happen should be heeded with extreme caution. The day of judgment is about to come wherein the Lord will cut off the strength (lit. "arm") of Eli and his priestly household, so that there will be no old man in the house (2:31). The males of the family will die young in the prime of their lives. The Elides will become a family without any old men among them. Any Israelites who witnessed such an oddness and abnormality would understand that such a family had been

---

43. Note that the same root כבד also appears in the previous verse (v. 29). Likewise, בזה and קלל I denote shame in v. 30. בזה is also a term synonymous to נאץ in 2:17.

44. I have discussed these two terms in sections 2.3 and 2.4.3. One can define the literal/physical meaning of כבד as "to be heavy" and קלל I "to be light." The wordplay on the heavy/light theme is deliberate. From such literal meaning evolves the figurative sense of "to honor/consider weighty (in value)" and "to be lightly esteemed/consider light (in value)." It is obvious that the use here is figurative, pointing to the ideological perspective.

45. Fokkelman, *Vow and Desire*, 143.

46. "הִנֵּה," BDB, 243. הִנֵּה with a participle often denotes action which is imminent or near at hand. See GKC, § 116p. The days are about to come; that is, they are almost here.

accursed by God.⁴⁷ The dignity of the Elides will deteriorate. Thus Hertzberg notices the presence of shame in this judgment: "The 'shame' announced here seems to consist in the future absence of those persons, the old, who by nature are owed the reverence of the community."⁴⁸ Shame is expressed through the unusual shortness of the life span of the Elide descendants.

The priest Eli himself is judged by YHWH and God will cut off his strength and that of his father's house (2:31a).⁴⁹ The following indictment that there shall be "no old man" among the Elides better explains God's judgement (2:32b). In fact, the similar idea that the descendants of Eli will die as men (אנשים)⁵⁰ who are in the prime of their years will be repeated again in 2:33.

Nevertheless, God will not completely eliminate Eli's descendants. He shall not totally cut off (כרת) his offspring from God's altar, that is, the position of priest.⁵¹ Even so, anyone from the line of Eli whom God spares shall exhaust

---

47. According to the Deuteronomistic covenant, long life is a blessing and honor from the Lord as a reward for those who faithfully observe his commandments (Exod 20:12; Ps 91:16; 1 Kgs 3:14). Short life, on the contrary, is generally conceived of as a cursed consequence of disobedience (Deut 28:20–24).

48. Hertzberg, *I and II Samuel*, 38.

49. The MT has a long addition of vv. 31b (מְהִיֹת זָקֵן בְּבֵיתֶךָ) and 32a (וְהִבַּטְתָּ צַר מָעוֹן בְּכֹל אֲשֶׁר־יֵיטִיב אֶת־יִשְׂרָאֵל). The MT וְהִבַּטְתָּ צַר מָעוֹן, suggesting looking in distress/at the distress of dwelling, is rather odd. Alternatively, as I discuss in the use of מָעוֹן in v. 29 (see appendix 4), the word is possibly emended to מְעַיֵּן ("gazing at . . ."; the *piel* participle from the root עין "eye"). Thus, Eli would look in distress (alternatively, צַר could be the direct object complement to the verb, meaning "enemy"; i.e. Eli would look at an enemy), eying the ways God exhibits goodness toward Israel. However, both the LXX and 4QSamª simply omit 31b and 32a. McCarter, following Wellhausen, suggests that the MT, with signs of conflation (the idea of Eli not having an old man in his house reappearing in 32b), as well as a potential conflict in meaning (the MT of v. 32a presumes that Eli will see the actual demise of the Elide house – when in fact he will only see the sign of it as suggested in v. 34), is less likely the original text. See McCarter, *1 Samuel*, 88–89. Thus, the Vorlage of the LXX (and 4QSamª) is more likely the primitive text.

50. The rendering of 4QSamª and LXX, "by the sword of men," is another possibility.

51. Tsevat thinks כרת means premature death as a result of divine punishment. In the Torah, כרת is also the consequence of committing the sin of "בזה (despising) the word of God" (Num 15:30–31) and slighting (קלל I) God (Lev 24:15–16). The Elides were accused of both sins of בזה and קלל I God (2:30; 3:13). Thus, כרת is the penalty of the Elides. See Tsevat, "Interpretation," 191–216. The premature death punishment is more pronounced in 2:34.

(wear out) his[52] eyes and grieve his[53] soul, bringing sadness to the family. The use of the language strongly evokes "the curse formula" of Deuteronomy 28:65.[54] As Jumper has noted, such curses are expressions of shame in the Deuteronomistic covenant.[55] By extension, the tragedy will inevitably bring with it the loss of the family's reputation. It is suggested that an allusion to Abiathar, who escapes the slaughter Saul brings about among the sons of Eli (22:18–20), may be the person implied here in verse 33.[56] If so, though Eli would not witness such a tragedy in his living days, he would, nevertheless, lament over the decline of the Elide priestly line.

To ensure the reliability of God's word of judgment, Eli will receive a sign (אות) through which he will come to realize the full and irrevocable accomplishment of God's own words. The sign is that his two sons, Hophni and Phinehas, will die on the same day (2:34). When the sign is fulfilled (4:11), the certainty of the rest of the threat to the Elides will be assured. The forthcoming death of Eli's two sons is another specific expression of the house of Eli "being insignificant" (קלל I) in 2:30. Such an unnatural and unexpected death represents a dramatic decrease of the Elide honor and prestige among the people.[57] In other words, the death of Hophni and Phinehas is another concrete demonstration of the Elides being shamed. Thus, Fokkelman says the life/death motif can be placed with ease alongside honor and dishonor.[58]

To continue God's indictment of the Elides, the prophet declares that God will replace the Elide priesthood with a "faithful priest" (כהן נאמן) because

---

52. The DSS 4QSam[a] and the LXX each read a third person singular (his), while the MT has a 2ms suffix (your). The third person singular reading is more probable. The context refers to the one (a third person) whom God would spare from being cut off among the Elide line. Eli could not have lived to witness this prophecy coming to its fulfillment. The rhetoric of Deuteronomy 28:65 also suggests that it is the people themselves that God sends into captivity to suffer; i.e. it is the survivor himself who suffers – not Eli the priest who would soon be deceased (4:18).

53. Again, the MT has a 2ms suffix (your). Likewise, the LXX is third person singular. The DSS is not extant here, but presumably it is third person singular to accord with the previous 3ms suffix in the sentence. See the above note.

54. Gordon, *1 and 2 Samuel*, 87.

55. Jumper, "Shame and Honor," 141–144.

56. Hertzberg, *I and II Samuel*, 38; McCarter, *1 Samuel*, 91; Klein, *1 Samuel*, 27; Tsumura, *First Book of Samuel*, 169; Driver, *Notes*, 39. Abiathar's future banishment (1 Kgs 2:26) is also an example of an event that brings weeping and grief in Abiathar's life.

57. Premature death in the ancient Near East was often seen as a punishment of God upon an individual. See Tsevat, "Interpretation," 195.

58. Fokkelman, *Vow and Desire*, 142.

of their unfaithfulness. Unlike the replaced Elides, the faithful priest will do God's bidding, following after his heart and his soul. God promises to build a "sure house" (בית נאמן) for this priest, and he will have the privilege of walking back and forth (והתהלך)[59] before the "anointed one" (משיח, i.e. the king) for all time.

The oracle indicates that an unspecified faithful priest will replace the Elide priesthood. A question that has to be answered is concerning the identity of this faithful priest. Scholars are divided over this identity. Some commentators suggest that Zadok, who served before David as priest, was the direct and exclusive fulfillment of the faithful priest.[60] However, such a reading encounters many interpretative challenges.

First, the pattern set up in 1 Samuel 1–7 is not the contrast between Eli and Zadok but between Eli and Samuel. As I argued previously in section 1.3.3.3, frequent contrasts between the Elides and Samuel in 1 Samuel 1–3 are very obvious. The narrator has often put Samuel and the Elides in juxtaposition to highlight obvious contrasts in their character. Thus, the immediate context suggests that such a faithful priest points to Samuel, who follows after God's own heart and soul.[61] Such a reading would be more natural from both the narrator and readers' point of view. The reason for regarding Samuel as a כהן נאמן, when his name is more often associated with his role as a prophet, is because of the need here to compare him with Eli, the priest. By doing so, the narrator hopes to demonstrate that Samuel was the priest par excellence (though much more than a priest). One also needs to know that priests and prophets were not necessarily distinct types in early Israelite religion.[62]

---

59. The HtD-stem conveys the pluralitive-repetitive aspect in this context; i.e. the faithful priest can go about freely ("go in and out," ESV, NRSV) before the king. The usage here brings contrast to the Elide line who used to go about freely (יתהלכו, also in HtD-stem) before God in v. 30.

60. See, for example, McCarter, *I Samuel*, 91–92; Klein, *1 Samuel*, 27; Tsumura, *First Book of Samuel*, 170; Hertzberg, *I and II Samuel*, 38–39; Bergen, *1, 2 Samuel*, 84; Vannoy, *1 and 2 Samuel*, 60; Evans, *Message of Samuel*, 37; Caquot and Robert, *Les Livres de Samuel*, 55.

61. Eslinger, *Kingship of God*, 138–140; Peterson, *First and Second Samuel*, 36; Ackerman, "Who Can Stand," 5–6; Murphy, *1 Samuel*, 26. Gilmour also notes that Samuel's succession to Eli is conspicuous in the ongoing narrative in 1 Samuel. See Gilmour, *Representing the Past*, 54. As I will argue in the last section of this chapter, Samuel's identity as a prophet is most prominent (as 1 Sam 3:20 portrays it) among his multifaceted roles. His priestly role is assumed despite him never being titled as a priest. He performed the responsibilities of a priest throughout his life.

62. See Leuchter, *Samuel*, 117. Indeed, there is no necessary conflict between these roles. See Steussy and Crenshaw, *Samuel*, 47.

Besides, the anointed one (מָשִׁיחַ) in the book of Samuel refers to kings Saul and David (1 Sam 12:3, 5; 16:6; 2 Sam 22:51). It should be noted that Samuel is the one who anoints both of them (1 Sam 10:1; 16:13) and walks before them all his days, suggesting a special relationship with both kings.[63]

Second, if one exclusively reads Zadok, as the one who would displace Abiathar, as the faithful priest, such a remote reading may leave the meaning of the oracle unclear to the reader. The problem would be further enhanced if 1 Kings 2:27–46 is not taken as from the same source as this part of Samuel (i.e. if they both have different authorship).[64] The immediate concern, which is critical to the reader, is that if the Elides are the unfaithful priests and are abandoned by God (Eli and his two sons soon dying as a result of the divine judgment), who will succeed them to take over the priestly role and duty? The constant contrasts in 1 Samuel 1–7 between Samuel and the Elides would suggest Samuel as the prime candidate for the faithful priest.

Third, Samuel is obviously recognized as a prophet and a judge throughout Israel, especially as the former. Both the text (3:20) and the people (9:20) underscore his identity as a prophet. However, while Samuel is mostly known as a prophet, this does not mean that his identity as a priest should be ignored or denied. In fact, Samuel's priestly role could be visually shown in his donning a linen ephod (2:18) while he was under Eli's priestly apprenticeship. His priestly role also appears to be prevalent in Israel after Eli's passing away, particularly with regard to his exclusive right to offer sacrifices on behalf of the people (7:9; 13:8–15; 16:2). Thus, Samuel is uniquely recognized as a person with multifaceted roles: he is a priest, a prophet and a judge. Thus Bruce says, "In this time of confusion and dissolution it may have been possible and necessary for Samuel to exercise authority in roles that would normally not converge in a single individual (priest, prophet, judge)."[65]

In fact, Mark Leuchter thinks 1 Samuel 2:35 echoes Numbers 12:7,[66] equating Samuel with Moses in parallel: both characters are considered to be

---

63. Admittedly, those who favor the allusion to Zadok can also argue that Zadok also qualifies here in connection to David (walking before the anointed one), as well as his descendants for the later kings (see 2 Sam 19:11; 1 Kgs 1:32; 1 Chr 15:11; 24:3, 31; 29:22).

64. Firth, *1 & 2 Samuel*, 71.

65. Bruce, "Samuel," 1162.

66. Numbers 12:7 describes Moses in summary: "Not so with my servant Moses. He is faithful (נֶאֱמָן) in all my house."

faithful (נאמן) and both are remembered in biblical tradition as "liminal and thus capable of occupying many roles."[67] In another article, Leuchter points out that Moses functioned as a prophet, a priest (citing Psalm 99:6 as support) and a judge – the multifarious roles that Samuel also held. While Numbers 12:6-7 does refer to Moses as a prophet, this does not deny the existence of his priestly role as well.[68] 1 Samuel 2:35 thus identifies a priestly figure who was about to replace Eli, but one with distinctively Mosaic characteristics – unlike the corrupted Elides, this one would be faithful (נאמן).[69] This Moses/Samuel parallel is also supported by Eslinger who thinks that Samuel was born to be a new Moses, and much information in 1 Samuel could allude to the Exodus material.[70] If so, Samuel, the faithful priest who replaces the Elides, is seen as a Mosaic figure in typology, a quality that is not applied to Zadok in the Tanakh.[71] Interestingly, the multiple roles held by the person of Samuel, as a priest, a prophet and a judge, do not contradict but cohere in a multifarious mission of teaching the divine Torah and praying on behalf of the people of God, acting as an intercessor between Israel and YHWH and conducting judicial proceedings.

Thus, reading Samuel rather than Zadok as the faithful priest in 1 Samuel 2:35 is more plausible in the immediate context. Nevertheless, Keil suggests multiple fulfillments.[72] That is to say, in each generation, beginning with

---

67. Leuchter, *Samuel*, 31, 33–34. According to Leuchter, the Moses/Samuel parallel is also recognized in other biblical sources (Jer 15:1; Ps 99:6). It is not as prophets but as priests (כהנים) that Samuel and Moses are put in parallel in Psalm 99:6. According to Leuchter, it is a witness to early predated Deuteronomistic material.

68. Leuchter, "Something Old." One cannot downplay Moses' priestly role in the Pentateuch – he was already performing priestly functions, such as building up altars and sprinkling the blood of covenant (Exod 24:3–7), before Aaron and his sons were actually commissioned as the priests of the Lord (Exod 29:1–9). In Exodus 40:1–33, Moses was the one who set up the tabernacle, burnt incense and even consecrated Aaron and his sons as priests. He was the "priest" before the officiating of the Aaronic priests. Most important of all, Moses, not Aaron, was the one who passed on the high-priesthood from Aaron to Eleazar on Mount Hor (Num 20:22–29). In other words, Moses had only delegated the office of priesthood to Aaron and his sons. See Ellison, *Centrality*, 17; also Milgrom, *Leviticus 1–16*, 555–558.

69. Leuchter, "Something Old."

70. Eslinger, *Kingship of God*, 77–78. For example, the same description of "affliction" (ענה) in 1 Samuel 1:11 and Exodus 3:17 indicates that Samuel will be the answer to Hannah's affliction as Moses was to the Israelite's affliction in Egypt. For others who support the Moses/Samuel parallel, see Steussy and Crenshaw, *Samuel*, 47; Sweeney, "Eli," 61; Page, "Establishment," 210–212.

71. Leuchter, *Samuel*, 34.

72. Keil, *Biblical Commentary*, 38–48.

Samuel, God would raise up "a faithful priest" who would obey him and do his will. Such an indefinite reading would leave more space for imagination.[73] Firth also favors such a view by pointing to the establishment of "a succession of priests," beginning with Samuel and reaching the climax with Zadok.[74] Such a reading accords with the grammar of the text as well as the intertextual connections between this verse and 2 Samuel 7:1–16.[75]

Though Samuel is plausibly seen as the direct and immediate fulfillment of the role of כהן נאמן, as I have argued, one also needs to bear in mind that among his multifarious roles (as a priest, a prophet and a judge), his prophetic role and function is accentuated overall in view of the ministries of his entire life. Thus, Samuel's priestly role may have been transitional, with him being the liminal figure of the critical period he was born into. That being said, the suggestion of multiple fulfillments in which God raises up a כהן נאמן in each generation (with Zadok being included as one such in the line of faithful priests)[76] is the most satisfactory way of reading this text.

---

73. For instance, Van Rooy, after evaluating the views of different scholars on this prophecy, argues that it is not the interest of the narrator to explain clearly the exact identity of the faithful priest in this pericope. This prophetic utterance can be considered an example of a narrative with "blanks." In his opinion, the endorsement of the Zadokite priesthood as the exclusive fulfillment of the faithful priest of verse 35 is strongly influenced by the point of view of the Deuteronomistic redaction. See Van Rooy, "Prophetic Utterances," 203–218.

74. Firth, *1 & 2 Samuel*, 71.

75. Some key terms appear in both places: the HtD-stem of הלך, the H-stem of קום, the N-stem of אמן, the use of בית with reference to the N-stem of אמן, the use of בנה with בית as object, as well as the adverbial synonyms כל הימים and עד עולם. In 2 Samuel 7:1–16, it is the house of David that would be built and be secure forever. In 1 Samuel 2:35, the burden of proof is to demonstrate that it is the individual – the כהן נאמן – rather than the house of the כהן נאמן that will act as priest before the Lord's anointed for כל הימים (the synonym being עד עולם in 2 Sam 7). בית in both places arguably refers to a dynasty. What might be contended to be a singular person in והתהלך לפני משיחי כל הימים is better seen as an entire secure dynasty of priests as represented in a person. I am indebted to my mentor Dr. Tim Undheim for sharing this insight.

76. Zadok remained prominent as a priest of the Lord during the reigns of King David and King Solomon. The Zadokites eventually assumed the priestly roles for the nation. The Zadokite priesthood is even accentuated in the anticipation of the post exilic temple (Ezek 40:46; 43:19; 44:15; 48:11). They continued as the authorized Israelite priesthood well into the Second Temple period (see, for example, 1 Chr 5:29–41; Ezra 2:2; Hag 1:1; Zech 6:11; Neh 12:22; 1 Macc 12:7–2 Macc 4:7; Josephus, *Ant.* 11.302–15.41; Elephantine Papyri 30:18 and 31:17; CD 4:1, 3; 1QS 5:2, 9). יֵשׁוּעַ of Ezra 2:2, the יְהוֹשֻׁעַ of Haggai 1:1 and Zechariah 6:11, can be traced back to Zadok (1 Chr 5:29–41) through the connection with Jehozadak, father of Jehoshua in Haggai 1:1 and Zechariah 6:11. The Zadokite priesthood was prominent in the Persian period (Neh 12:22) and most likely remained in position until the succeeding Greek period after the notorious Antiochus Epiphanes IV became ruler over the Seleucid Empire in 175 BCE (Elephantine Papyri 30:18 and 31:17; Josephus, *Ant.* 11.302–15.41; 1 Macc 12:7–2 Macc 4:7). The expressed high regard for the Zadokite priesthood by the later Dead Sea Scrolls community – CD 4:1, 3;

The Elide priests being replaced due to their disqualified service is another specific expression of the house of Eli "being insignificant" (קלל I). Being displaced from the priestly position due to their failure is a clear demonstration of the Elides being shamed. The Elides would be diminished in their position and power and excluded from the privileges of priestly service.

As for the surviving Elides, they would also be judged with a scarcity of food (2:36). They shall come and bow down before the faithful priest for a piece of silver or a loaf of bread, and shall say, "Please, assign me to one of the priestly duties, that I may have a morsel of bread to eat." They shall desire the priestly role they were once entitled to. The scarcity of food is another form of the curse formula (Deut 28:16–24), which comes as a result of disobedience. The motif of food echoes Hannah's song in 2:5, "those who were full earn a wage for bread." The once fattened Elides now shall suffer hunger and a low status.[77] The lack of sustenance exposes their inability and vulnerability and thus triggers shame. Thus, Leuchter also says, "The surviving Elides shall be demoted to a client status."[78] The scarcity of food for the remaining Elides is one more specific demonstration of the house of Eli "being insignificant" (קלל I). With the ensuing curse of hunger, they shall be humiliated in the sight of Israel.

In summary, the message by a man of God (2:27–36) concludes the fate of the Elides. The demise of the house of Eli will be unavoidable, for Eli honored his sons above God. The Elides have not honored YHWH to whom all honor is due but have despised him instead. God's resounding response is the clear declaration: "Those who honor me I will honor, but those who despise me shall be insignificant." According to this criterion, the Elides shall be judged accordingly with shame. They are to be removed from the prestige and honor entitled to the priestly roles. To be more specific, the cost of dishonoring the

---

1QS 5:2, 9 – is likely a response to the demise of this long-lived dynasty due to the usurping Hasmonean hierarchy with the formal installation of Simeon Thassi as both leader and high priest (1 Macc 2:1–5; Josephus, *Life* 4; Josephus, *Ant.* 12.265–66) in 142 BCE (1 Macc 13:1–9; 14:41). It was this radical unseating which probably gave rise to the Dead Sea Sect, an order profoundly disturbed by various trends of this era, particularly in the priesthood. However, there is still controversy pertaining to Zadok's origin. 1 Chronicles 5:34, 38, and 2 Samuel 8:17 record him as the son of Ahitub, yet Ahitub is presented in 1 Samuel 14:3 as being from the line of Eli – a problematic view when 1 Samuel 2:35 is taken into account (the house of Eli being supplanted). Again, I am grateful to Dr. Tim Undheim for sharing this insight.

77. Fokkelman, *Vow and Desire*, 152.
78. Leuchter, *Samuel*, 34.

Lord includes the withdrawal of God's promise to sustain the Elide priestly line; the premature death of their descendants (with the deaths of Hophni and Phinehas on the same day as a sign); their displacement from priestly leadership; and their abasement with a scarcity of food.

4.2 Samuel Honors the Lord by His Faithful Service (1 Sam 3:1–10)

In contrast to Eli who has honored his sons more than the Lord, Samuel is a person of different quality. In fact, the narrator has purposely placed Samuel as the counterpoint (2:11, 18, 26; 3:1) to the increasing crimes of the Elides (2:12–17, 22–25, 27–36). In contrast to the waywardness of the Elides, Samuel remains the one who serves the Lord (2:11, 18; 3:1) throughout the course of time. Such a literary device of contrastive comparing brings an inevitable conclusion to the rejection of the Elides and the confirmation of Samuel.[79] Placing Samuel's call immediately after the prophecy (2:27–36) naturally leads the readers to see events in chapter 3 as the fulfillment of chapter 2.[80] Unlike the Elides who brought shame to God's holy name, Samuel, as we shall see, honors the Lord by his faithful service. In this section, we shall investigate 3:1–10 concerning Samuel's ministries which serve as an expression of honoring God.

The passage of 1 Samuel 3:1–10 is often considered form-critically as "a prophetic call narrative."[81] Gnuse, however, describes it as a "dream theophany" due to the lack of prophetic commission for Samuel.[82] However, it is important to note that Samuel remains awake during each of the call experiences.[83]

The indictment against the Elides in the previous chapter (1 Samuel 2) has made them obviously unsuitable for continuous service before the Lord. At

---

79. Campbell, *1 Samuel*, 48–49.

80. That is to say, it encourages the readers to entertain the reading that Samuel is the promised new priest who will replace Eli and his sons (3:11–14). See Eslinger, *Kingship of God*, 145. This chapter also prepares for the transition of Samuel from being a priestly adept to a prophet.

81. Tsumura, *First Book of Samuel*, 172.

82. Gnuse, "Reconsideration," 386.

83. Verbs denoting Samuel's dynamic actions (וירץ, "then he ran"; ויאמר, "then he said"; וילך, "then he went"; וישכב, "then he lay down"; ויקם, "then he arose") also support that Samuel was not dreaming.

this important juncture, it is important that someone like Samuel is still "serving the Lord" (1 Sam 3:1; משרת את יהוה).[84] God has preserved his own faithful servant to succeed the Elide leadership. But, of course, this will take some time. For the moment, Samuel is still serving the Lord before Eli (לפני עלי), suggesting that Samuel is still subject to his authority, even though Eli has lost his rank and title as "priest" after the judgment oracle (2:27–36). However, the real focus of Samuel's service and dedication is God himself.[85]

Following the introduction of Samuel, it is reported that "And the word of the Lord was rare in those days; there was no widespread vision." Such was the environment in which Samuel served. According to Sasson, these two clauses are not redundant but complement each other (describing the aural and visual aspects) to tell about "the dearth of communication from God."[86] It was a period of spiritual famine. Indeed, given the deteriorated Elide priestly leadership and the two sons of Eli who do not even know the Lord (2:12), it could hardly be expected that God would speak through them via visions or words. In fact, the only time when God speaks before chapter 3 is through a man of God (2:27) to condemn and judge the Elides for their crimes. However, the theophany accorded Samuel will bring a reversal of the scarcity of God's revelation. The Lord will reveal the word of God to Samuel the prophet (3:21).

The next temporal clause[87] introduces Eli the priest lying down in his place (3:2). It is interesting that Eli is sitting (יֹשֵׁב) on his honorable seat in two other scenes, one beside the doorpost of God's temple (1:9) and the other following this narrative by the road of the city (4:13). The frequent portrayal of Eli being attached to a particular place may suggest his passive role, whereas Samuel is actively ministering before the Lord.[88]

The text states that Eli's eyes have begun to be dull so that he could not see. The description of the deterioration of his eyesight at this juncture can be both literal as well as metaphoric. The aged Eli fails to see diagnostically

---

84. Sasson notices that the same phrase appears in 2:11 and 2:18 (with a slight difference in the Hebrew text of 2:18). See Sasson, "Eyes of Eli," 172; also Campbell, *1 Samuel*, 47–48.

85. Fokkelman, *Vow and Desire*, 157.

86. Sasson, "Eyes of Eli," 174–175.

87. For an introduction to temporal clauses, see Lambdin, *Introduction to Biblical Hebrew*, 123.

88. Eslinger, *Kingship of God*, 76.

but he also has become dull in a spiritual sense. In the past, even when his eyesight was excellent, he still could not see through things (a lack of spiritual vision).[89] As a priest of the Lord, he is not even aware of the coming calamity that the ark of the Lord would be soon captured by the Philistines (4:17–18). Readers may note that the attention to Eli's lack of eyesight will be repeated again during the disaster (4:15). The references to Eli's loss of eyesight during these crucial junctures can be hardly accidental. Thus, Eli's lack of vision will prepare the development of the next plot and accentuate the importance of Samuel receiving a special "vision" (3:15; מראה) from the Lord.[90]

The next setting is introduced with the statement that the lamp of God had not yet gone out (3:3). The lamp of God is a symbol of God's presence in Israel. Though the situation is dim and gloomy, there is still hope because the Lord has not totally cut off his relationship with Israel.[91] The diminution of sight and light – dim eyesight and a lamp about to be extinguished – is full of symbolic imagery that communicates divine displeasure and a lack of spiritual insight under the Elide leadership.[92] The lamp of God was attended to by the priest (Exod 30:7–8) to illuminate the sanctuary from evening until morning. The fact that the oil had not yet gone out may also suggest that the present event took place before the dawning of the day.[93] Obviously, the nearly blind Eli could not attend to God's lamp. The responsibility of tending God's lamp fell to the young Samuel, who has seemingly replaced the high priest Eli for such priestly duties.[94] With Samuel sleeping in the temple where the ark of God resides,[95] he was readily available to serve YHWH in times of

---

89. With his sharp eyes, he observed Hannah moving her lips but without her voice being heard. He misjudged Hannah as a worthless woman (a drunkard) when she was in fact devoting herself in prayers. Eli's eyes were also blind to the corruption of his two sons that eventually led to God's rejection of the Elide priesthood.

90. Sasson, "Eyes of Eli," 178.

91. Samuel would light up the hope for Israel, as God had chosen him and would speak to the Israelites through him. See Eslinger, *Kingship of God*, 148–149; Van Wijk-Bos, *Reading Samuel*, 44.

92. Polzin, *Samuel and the Deuteronomist*, 49; Bergen, *1, 2 Samuel*, 86.

93. Tsumura, *First Book of Samuel*, 175; McCarter, *1 Samuel*, 98; Klein, *1 Samuel*, 32.

94. Steinmann, *1 Samuel*, 113.

95. Driver suggests that Samuel was sleeping in a chamber contiguous to the היכל. See Driver, *Notes*, 42. This is the first time the ark of God is mentioned in 1 Samuel; it will capture more attention in 1 Samuel 4–6.

need. The temple of the Lord was also an ideal place to prepare Samuel for his encounter with the divine.

After the background introduction, the narrator zooms in to foreground Samuel's experience of being called by God. The first three times Samuel assumes it is Eli who called him. It is not until the fourth time that Samuel directly responds to God's call. The fact that the narrator records each of the occurrences in detail indicates that he intends to underscore Samuel's character in contrast to the Elides.[96] The rise of Samuel and the decline of the Elides is inevitable. The following table gives a concise summary of Samuel's experience of God's call:

The First Call (vv. 4–5)	The Second Call (vv. 6–7)	The Third Call (vv. 8–9)	The Fourth Call (vv. 10–14)
The Lord called Samuel	The Lord called Samuel	The Lord called Samuel	The Lord called Samuel
Samuel ran to Eli and responded with הנני ("Here I am")	Samuel arose and went to Eli and responded with הנני ("Here I am")	Samuel arose and went to Eli and responded with הנני ("Here I am")	Samuel responded with "Speak, for your servant is listening."
Eli denied the call	Eli denied the call	Eli realized God's call to Samuel	God revealed his words to Samuel concerning the fate of Eli's family
Samuel went back and lay down	A comment from the narrator about Samuel (v. 7)	Eli instructed Samuel to respond properly if God called again. Samuel went back and lay down	

---

96. Alternatively, the narrator could just have summarized these occurrences with succinct statements: "The Lord called Samuel three times; it was not until the fourth time that Samuel realized and responded...."

The Lord first intervenes in the age of spiritual darkness,[97] calling Samuel by his name (3:4). Samuel's immediate response is הנני ("Here I am"). Assuming it to be Eli's call, he runs to Eli and says, "Here I am; for you called me." Eli denies the call, saying, "I didn't call you. Go back and lie down." Following Eli's instruction, Samuel goes back and lies down.

Some observations can be made with regard to this first call. It is clear that Samuel responded with הנני ("Here I am") twice, the first time before he went to Eli and the second time after he ran to the priest. This is a term that will be repeated in this episode (3:6, 8, 16), and it is thus important to note its significance. The word הנני is actually a compound term consisting of the interjection הנה and the first person singular suffix. It introduces one's announced presence when being summoned.[98] In this context, it indicates Samuel's availability to serve despite the inconvenience of the hour. Thus, Arnold rightly comments on this term: הנני is "the expression of those who volunteer themselves for service. He is placing himself at the disposal, at the beck and call, of his master."[99] Interestingly, הנני is also used elsewhere in the Scriptures (Gen 22:1; Exod 3:4; Isa 6:8) to suggest one's availability to obey the divine call. Samuel was ready, responsive and willing to serve, but he did not realize it was the Lord who had called him. Believing that Eli had called, Samuel ran to him. The urgency of "ran" in the middle of night also shows Samuel's humility and diligence in his daily routine service. With no further confirmation from Eli, Samuel goes back to his own place and lies down.

The second time the Lord calls Samuel, he comes to Eli saying הנני and assures him of his availability for service. The recurrent use of הנני is an obvious sign of Samuel's patience and humility in service. Samuel could have come to Eli this time without using הנני and simply saying, קראת לי ("You called me").[100] The repetitive use of הנני, thus, is the narrator's tactic to emphasize Samuel's humble and faithful service. It is a key word that ties together the

---

97. Important to the setting is that the Lord appeared to Samuel in deep darkness; the physical darkness is perhaps a symbol of the spiritual darkness Israel went through under the Elides' corrupt leadership. See Fokkelman, *Vow and Desire*, 160.

98. "הִנֵּה," *HALOT* 1, 252.

99. Arnold, *1 and 2 Samuel*, 81.

100. Alternatively, the whole second call could be summarized with a few words, since it repeats a scene and actions similar to the first.

different stages of the call experience.[101] Samuel's eager attitude in service may have aroused Eli's sympathy for Samuel who had walked back and forth to attend to his need, although he had not summoned him. The added term בני ("my son") in verse 6 may reflect Eli's emotional endearment and support for this boy. Indeed, great patience is required of one while being awakened in the midst of sleep. The inconvenience and strain could have irritated many, but Samuel, as a faithful servant of the Lord, behaves in a respectable and humble manner.

The narrator's editorial comments at the end of the second call indicate that Samuel does not yet know (ידע) the Lord. As one starting out in his ministry, the word of God has not yet been revealed (יגלה) to him (3:7). That also explains why Samuel did not know it was the Lord who had called him. One recalls that Eli's sons also did not know the Lord. Though the same verb root ידע is used in both assessments, Samuel's lack of knowledge of the Lord is obviously different in nature from that of Eli's sons. Here, Samuel not knowing the Lord implies his lack of experience and relationship with YHWH.[102] The double use of טרם ("not yet") suggests that it is inevitable that in the future he will become one who does know YHWH. What it will take is only a matter of time. But the sons of Eli were different in not knowing the Lord: "For them not to know Yahweh meant they did not acknowledge Yahweh as Lord, or they did not obey him, or they had no relationship to him. None of these seems relevant for the situation of Samuel."[103] Samuel and the sons of Eli share no part of their character.

Samuel's willingness to serve prepares him to receive God's revelation. What distinguishes the Elide priests from members of the other tribes of Israel is that God truly was revealed (2:27; הנגלה נגליתי) to their forefathers. Now the Lord has rejected them because of their reversed priorities in honoring people above God, and God has prepared his own faithful servant to whom he will reveal (יגלה) his own word. The wordplay on the verb root גלה ("to reveal") is apparent in both places. Samuel is about to receive the same direct divine revelation from the Lord as the forefathers of the Elides did.

---

101. For the repetition of words as a stylistic feature in biblical narrative, see Bar-Efrat, *Narrative Art*, 211–215; Alter, *Art of Biblical Narrative*, 88–113.

102. Firth, *1 & 2 Samuel*, 77; Arnold, *1 and 2 Samuel*, 82; Tsumura, *First Book of Samuel*, 177; McCarter, *I Samuel*, 98; Fokkelman, *Vow and Desire*, 167–68; Eslinger, *Kingship of God*, 151.

103. Klein, *1 Samuel*, 32.

Samuel's encounter with the divine is an important and necessary step to authenticate his sacred leadership and prepare him to supersede the Elides.[104] Thus Robert Alter concurs:

> The idea of revelation, in other words, is paramount to the story of Samuel, whose authority will derive neither from cultic function, like the priests before him, nor from military power, like the judges before him and the kings after him, but from prophetic experience, from an immediate, morally directive call from God.[105]

The recurring verb root קרא ("called"; 3:4, 6, 8, 10) in the call narrative is another obvious sign of God's direct revelation to Samuel. Indeed, God persistently calls Samuel and insists on speaking to him, not just one time, but four times.

The Lord calls Samuel a third time. Samuel repeats the same action of rising up and going to Eli, suggesting that there was an interval in between each call. Samuel offers the same humble statement, "Here I am (הנני); you called me." Samuel comes with the same assured availability to serve despite Eli's repeated denial that he had called Samuel. There is no sign of Samuel murmuring or complaining against his master despite the inconvenience. In every circumstance, Samuel's attitude toward service does not waver. He is always ready and willing to carry out any duty immediately.

If there is a chance one may mishear a voice twice, it is very unlikely that this would continue a third time. It is at this juncture that Eli begins to understand that the Lord is calling Samuel. It is a tragedy that God had rejected the high priest Eli and now is choosing to reveal himself to a young boy instead.

God insists on speaking to Samuel; this also accentuates the importance of God's message. Eli then tells Samuel to go back to sleep but instructs him to respond with proper courtesy ("Speak, Lord, for your servant hears!") if God were to call him again. Following Eli's instruction, Samuel goes back to his own place and lies down again. The boy is now ready for his encounter with God.

---

104. Leuchter, *Samuel*, 34.
105. Alter, *Art of Biblical Narrative*, 86.

The fourth time the Lord calls, he reveals himself to Samuel. The Lord comes and stands,[106] calling Samuel by his name ("Samuel! Samuel!") just as previously. This repetition of the name Samuel allows the readers to infer that the Lord actually summoned his name twice during each of the calls. The Lord has chosen Samuel to be his instrument of communication and thus calls him by his personal name (also Gen 22:11; Exod 3:4). Samuel responds properly with what Eli had taught him, "Speak, for your servant hears!" The ellipsis of God's name ("YHWH") may support the narrator's previous evaluative statement in verse 7 that "Samuel did not know YHWH."[107] The term "servant" (עבד) is a very appropriate title for Samuel who has been faithfully serving the Lord in front of Eli.

Thus, in each of the call experiences, Samuel is portrayed as a humble, obedient, vigilant and faithful servant of the Lord. It is important that, ideologically, Samuel was serving the Lord (3:1; משרת את יהוה) rather than Eli. Nevertheless, he willingly and humbly subjected himself to Eli's authority despite his master's severe spiritual defect. His love for God motivated him to serve before Eli with great care and effort.

Though going beyond the delimitation of our discussion, 12:3–5 is another text in 1 Samuel that shows clearly how Samuel has been faithful in his ministry to the Lord. He is described as blameless and free from any accusation before the people. Throughout his life, he defended justice; he never defrauded or oppressed any of the people; and he never took advantage of his position to fulfill his personal gain. He is depicted as a person with true integrity, and even God can be a witness of it.

Unlike the ungodly Elides who put the Lord to shame through their corrupt and immoral deeds, Samuel, by contrast, is presented as a faithful servant of the Lord who humbly offers himself for service. He is a man of integrity and character. His ministry brings honor and glory to the Lord.

---

106. The Lord visually appeared at a close distance. What Samuel received was not only a word but also a vision. See Arnold, *1 and 2 Samuel*, 82; McCarter, *1 Samuel*, 98; Tsumura, *First Book of Samuel*, 178–179; Fokkelman, *Vow and Desire*, 169; Eslinger, *Kingship of God*, 144. Apparently, Samuel's encounter with God in a vision is against the assertion which describes 1 Samuel 3 as an example of "dream theophany."

107. Fokkelman, *Vow and Desire*, 171.

4.3 Eli's Family Judged with Shame (1 Sam 3:11–18; 4:12–18)

Every sin will bring its own consequence. Though sometimes God does not immediately intervene to judge, this does not mean he overlooks iniquity (2:25). The moral principle reflected in the Song of Hannah is still effective: the faithful ones God will keep but the wicked shall perish in darkness (2:9). In due time, God will judge the Elides. In as much as they despised the Lord, they shall be insignificant (2:30; i.e. they shall be put to shame).

God's revelation to Samuel (3:11–14) is basically an affirmation of God's judgment and punishment against the Elides. Just as the anonymous "man of God" prophesied about the end of the Elide priesthood (2:27–36), the Lord is about to execute a great disaster against the Elides so that anyone who hears of it will be horrified (their ears will tingle). God will fulfill all the words that he had spoken through the unnamed prophet, and now confirms his judgement again through Samuel. The description of "from the beginning to the end" (3:12) further confirms its ultimate fulfillment.

God is about to judge the Elides. The reason is that Eli knew that his sons blasphemed (מקללים) God but did not rebuke (כהה II) them to stop it.[108] The participle מקללים shows that they had low regard and light esteem for God himself and such sacrilege was ongoing.[109] The account is related somewhat differently in 2:29 where it is reported that the Elides looked at God's sacrifices and offerings with greedy eyes and that Eli honored his sons above God. In other words, the action of coveting God's sacrifices and offerings (to the extreme of theft; 2:16) is understood as blaspheming (מקללים, *piel*) God (esteeming God lightly; making God contemptible; i.e. putting God to shame).[110] The indictment of not rebuking his sons is also a confirmation that Eli had not done his part as a godly father when his children departed from

---

108. Interestingly, the verb "rebuke" (כהה II) forms a wordplay with the earlier verb "to become dim" (כהה I) in 3:2. The same root foreshadows Eli's spiritual fallout. The MT text מקללים להם is often recognized as "emendations of the scribes" of the more likely reading מקללים אלהים. The LXX ὅτι κακολογοῦντες Θεὸν probably preserves the true reading, thus favoring מקללים אלהים. See Driver, *Notes*, 44; McCarter, *I Samuel*, 96; Steinmann, *1 Samuel*, 111; Klein, *1 Samuel*, 30; Tsumura, *First Book of Samuel*, 180; Adair, *Inductive Method*, 222.

109. Fokkelman, *Vow and Desire*, 177.

110. Note the same root קלל I appears in 2:30.

God's commandments in the previous episodes (2:12–17, 22–25).[111] Eli's top priority was never to honor God above all else in his life. For this reason, God solemnly swears that the iniquity of the sons of the Elides shall not be forgiven even through the medium of sacrifices and offerings. The impossibility of atonement for the sins of the Elides shows God's profound aversion toward their crimes. Expiation for priestly offenses, possible according to Leviticus 4:3–12, cannot avail to clear those guilty of "the high-handed kinds of sins" which Hophni and Phinehas committed.[112] Such willful and offensive sins, cutting to God's heart, shall never be forgiven even at the cost of sacrifices and intercession.

As a faithful servant of the Lord, Samuel still opens the door of the house of the Lord the next morning despite a disturbing night. On the one hand, such an action of continually fulfilling his duty shows his humility despite the revelation of God;[113] on the other hand, Samuel fills the dark temple with the light of day, prevailing over darkness and ushering in a new era of spiritual consciousness in Israel.[114] However, Samuel, as a student of Eli, is afraid to tell him of the vision concerning the doom of his family.

After the Lord called him four times, in this last episode it is Eli who calls (ויקרא) Samuel again and asks him to tell him everything about God's revelation (3:16). The address of "Samuel, my son" is a form of courtesy in order to form a special affinity in their relationship. As usual, Samuel responds again with "Here I am" (3:16; הנני), indicating his persistent deference and availability. As I said before, this is a key term that appears in the call narrative. The repetition of הנני serves to foreground Samuel's humble and faithful service.

Eli was certain that Samuel had received the word of God. From his own perspective, he was not sure if it was related to the bad news about himself. Fearing that Samuel would be reluctant to tell him everything about the message, Eli evokes a prophetic announcement ("God will do so to you and

---

111. One may argue that it is not true that Eli did not rebuke his sons (2:23–25), but it is obvious that he was not genuine in correcting their evil deeds.

112. Klein, *1 Samuel*, 33.

113. Bar-Efrat, *Narrative Art*, 79. Such a minute detail – opening the door in the early morning – is an important way of characterizing Samuel's humility.

114. Bergen, *1, 2 Samuel*, 87; Eslinger, *Kingship of God*, 153. For more information concerning the symbolic nature of this action, see Janzen, "Samuel Opened the Doors," 89–96.

more, if you hide anything from me of all the words that he told you")[115] to coerce him to speak it out. The impending threat is that if Samuel withholds anything from him, curses (כה, "so and so," an accompanying gesture indicating what the curse might be), as a result of the breaking of the oath, would be inflicted on the transgressor. In this short statement, Eli utters the root דבר ("word") five times in different forms.[116] What Eli stresses here is the right to know the full word of God that has been communicated to Samuel.[117] Of course, Samuel humbly obeys this request and tells him everything about it.

Interestingly, what Samuel received was the divine word (דבר) from the Lord, but the sons of Eli were the evildoers, doing evil "things" (2:23; דברים) in the sight of Israel. Thus, the play of words on the root דבר shows that it is seemingly inevitable that the leadership in Israel is about to pass from the Elide priesthood to Samuel. In the beginning of the chapter, the description of the situation is prefaced with the rarity of the word of God and the lack of widespread vision (3:1). Now Samuel has received both the word of God and the vision (3:15–18). Eli, as the head of the Elide priesthood, has to acknowledge the trend of this change. Eli's embarrassed response, "He is Lord. He will do what is good in his eyes," reflects his impotence and despair in altering the situation.[118] After all, this is the second time he has received such a message of judgment and thus has no means to resist it.

Following the prophecy of God's judgment of the Elides, conveyed through "a man of God" and Samuel, the decline and demise of the Elide priesthood is irrevocable. As their ascribed prestige and honor as priests of the Lord diminish, the Elides will definitely suffer shame. To be more exact, the most obvious way the Elides will be shamed is in the arrival of their fate, namely, the ending of their lives – both for the sons of Eli and for Eli himself. Thus we now turn to 4:12–22 for a closer portrayal of their unusual and shameful deaths.

Although the end of 1 Samuel 3 does not provide an explicit description of the termination of the Elides, their devastating fates are sealed with God's

---

115. See also 1 Samuel 14:44. Alternatively, many translations (e.g., ESV, NIV, NASB, NRSV) render the verbs יַעֲשֶׂה and יוֹסִיף as jussives, albeit being full imperfects in form, thus "May God do so to you and more, if you hide. . . ."

116. Klein, *1 Samuel*, 33.

117. Fokkelman even thinks the chapter revolves around the word of God. See Fokkelman, *Vow and Desire*, 172.

118. Eslinger, *Kingship of God*, 154–155. Eli's response here should be read as "culpably passive." See Cook, "Pious Eli?," 166.

repeated oracles of judgment against them. The capture of the ark of God (implying God's departure from Israel), which we will discuss more in the next chapter, leads to the demise of the army, along with the two sons of Eli, Hophni and Phinehas. The narrator does not simply report their deaths but relates at length and in detail how the messenger transmits the news and how Eli reacts to it.

As the Israelites went out with the ark of the Lord to fight with the Philistines, Eli waited anxiously for news from the battlefield. A messenger, a man of Benjamin, ran from the battlefield and came to Shiloh the same day, with his clothes torn and earth upon his head (4:12). His outward appearance, the tearing of his clothes and the sprinkling of his head with dust, suggests that he brought with him news of grief and mourning (see also 2 Sam 1:2).[119] The calamity of the defeat was so shocking that it led him to cover the eighteen-mile distance from Ebenezer, the camp of the Israelites (1 Sam 4:1; 5:1), to Shiloh on the same day.[120] The following circumstantial clause in 4:13 tells that Eli was sitting on his seat by the road "watching expectantly [for an answer]" (מצפה). The messenger came to Shiloh with the sad news and the whole city cried out with a loud voice in response to it. As Eli puzzled over this commotion, the man hastened and came to report to him concerning the battle. The pace of the narrative is held back, however. The messenger does not directly inform Eli of the situation but speaks with some hesitation: "I am he who has come from the battle and from the battle I fled today." Eli responds to him with some encouragement, "How did things go, my son?" The relational term "my son" enables the man to have the courage to continue to speak about this dreadful disaster.[121] The messenger's delay in reporting the news, however, is to heighten tension in the story.

The messenger reports to Eli the bad news of the defeat. "Israel has fled during the battle." The conjunctive particle combination וגם ("and also") which follows implies the close relationship between the joined clauses. "And there has been also a great slaughter among the people, and your two sons also, Hophni and Phinehas, are dead, and the ark of God has been captured."

---

119. McCarter, *I Samuel*, 114; Steinmann, *1 Samuel*, 131; Tsumura, *First Book of Samuel*, 197–198; Firth, *1 & 2 Samuel*, 87; Hertzberg, *I and II Samuel*, 49.

120. Klein, *1 Samuel*, 43; Hertzberg, *I and II Samuel*, 49.

121. Bar-Efrat, *Narrative Art*, 66.

To paraphrase his statement: "There has been a great defeat for Israel, and in the midst of the battle, your two sons were killed and the ark captured." Commentators have indicated that the climax of the news is the last part of the sentence – the ark captured.[122] Indeed, Eli's tragic death is triggered by his hearing of the capture of the ark. "As soon as he mentioned the ark of God, Eli fell backward from his chair beside the gate. His neck broke and he died." It seems that the defeat of Israel and even the deaths of his two sons did not surprise Eli. What concerned Eli most was the fate of the ark of God. Israel had hoped to win the battle by bringing the ark of God into the battlefield, but now they have to suffer the humiliation of their defeat, even ostensibly, the defeat of their God. With regards to this tragedy and the significance of the capture of the ark of God, we will save it for the next chapter for further discussion.

The narrator also reveals an item of information that contains an explanation or comment about Eli's death: "for the man was old and heavy (וכבד)." Eli's old age has been noted earlier (2:22; 4:15), and thus his oldness is not surprising to the readers. But the comment on his heavy weight suggests a satirical nuance which has to be seen within the semantics of the Hebrew language. While it is true that Eli's heavy body weight (possibly fattened up by the choicest sacrificial meat; 2:29)[123] contributed to the imbalance of his movement and thus caused his backward fall and death, readers can also readily entertain the ambiguity that his whole life had been one that honored his personal agenda rather than God's.[124] The use of כבד is ironic as his family is insignificant (קלל I).[125] As a failed father, he was held accountable for the sins of his two sons and failed to train them in times of need. Thus, the satirical use of כבד in this context serves to give prominence to Eli's culpability.[126] The description of the unusual means of his death is a caution to anyone who does not honor God in his or her life.

---

122. McCarter, *I Samuel*, 114; Firth, *1 & 2 Samuel*, 87–88; Tsumura, *First Book of Samuel*, 199; Klein, *1 Samuel*, 44.

123. Alternatively, however, 4QSam^a reads להבריך מראש כול מנחות ("by giving a blessing from the best of all the offerings"). Similarly, the LXX reads ἐνευλογεῖσθαι ἀπαρχῆς πάσης θυσίας Ισραηλ ("by blessing themselves with the first-fruits of every sacrifice of Israel"). I have addressed this problem earlier in section 4.1.

124. As a homonym, כבד can possibly cover the meaning of "to be heavy" or "to honor."

125. Fokkelman, *Vow and Desire*, 226.

126. See also section 2.3 for my discussion of כבד.

Thus far, Eli's two sons, as well as Eli himself, have suffered abnormal deaths as a result of God's judgment against them. In Deuteronomistic theology, the life/death motif can be framed easily in honor/shame language.[127] A brutal and premature death, as one of the expressions of God's curses in the covenant, seals the diminishment of the Elides' social status (i.e. their shame) in the eyes of others. In Deuteronomy 30:19–20, God places life and death, blessing and curse before Israel. It is a choice the Israelites have to make to love the Lord and obey his words so that they might live. In that perspective, the Elides persistently choose death through their disobedience. Thus, the suffering of their shame and dishonor is inescapable.

The devastating fate of the Elides echoes the resounding voice in the previous chapter: "Those who despise me shall be insignificant (יקלו)" (2:30). The Elides are put to shame because they held the Lord in light esteem and had no regard for God's house. The Lord is righteous in his dealings with them.

4.4 Samuel Honors the Lord by Establishing a Stone Monument (1 Sam 7:2–12)

In the previous section (4.2), we have seen how Samuel honored the Lord by his faithful and humble service. However, more good things can be said about Samuel. It is he who first leads the Israelites to erect a stone monument (7:12) to remember God's deliverance after victory against the Philistines. The purpose was to give God the honor that was due to him so that all Israel might learn the lesson that victory belongs to God alone. We shall take at a closer look at it now.

The war with the Philistines was placed in the context of Israel's renewal of their covenant with the Lord (7:3–4).[128] After a gap of twenty years in which the Israelites struggled with idolatry as the ark of God sat in cold storage, they began to turn[129] after the Lord (7:2). Samuel, as a prophet, prompted

---

127. Jumper, "Shame and Honor," 135–146.
128. Eslinger, *Kingship of God*, 236.
129. BDB, with no other homonymic number for נהה, takes the meaning of "lament," as do other conventional translations (ESV, NRSV, NASB, NKJV). But the problem with the syntax of reading אחרי with נהה I ("lament after") is that a different preposition על (e.g. Ezek 32:18) would have more properly been used with נהה I ("lament over") to form the same lexical semantic. *HALOT* 2, 675 reads it as נהה II, thus "to stick to" (similarly, "long for" in NET; "yearn" in NJPS). Alternatively, I am referring to the *DCH* for its homonym #3, נהה III ("to

such a spiritual renewal. In response to his call, the Israelites determined to turn away from their idolatry and reclaim their allegiance to the Lord (7:3). The national repentance, as well as the succeeding military victory over the Philistines, was the crowning achievement of Samuel's career.[130] To further implement Israel's return to the Lord, Samuel called a gathering in Mizpah for a ceremony of community purification. As the people of Israel gathered for confession and fasting (7:5–6), the Philistines received the news and advanced their attack against Israel (7:7). In fear of the Philistines, the Israelites turned to Samuel and pleaded for his intercession to the Lord for their deliverance (7:8). In the midst of the crisis, Samuel offered a burnt offering and cried out to the Lord for help (7:9). In reply, the Lord answered Samuel's prayer and thwarted the Philistines' attack with loud thunder.[131] While the Philistines were thrown into confusion and panic, Israel took advantage of the situation and won a great battle. This sweeping victory was so significant that the Philistines dared not bother Israel's territory all the days of Samuel, and the cities that they had taken were restored to Israel (7:13–14).

After the defeat of the Philistines, Samuel takes a stone and sets it up between Mizpah and Shen and calls its name "Ebenezer" (אבן העזר), literally "Stone of Help." The erection of the stone is to commemorate the divine help accorded to Israel in the battle against the Philistines. Thus Eslinger says plainly, "The stone set up by Samuel is a tribute to the renewed aid given by Yahweh to his people."[132] Likewise, Tsumura comments that "Ebenezer" is not a usual place-name, but it is a reminder of God's powerful intervention in the history of Israel.[133] Samuel also states explicitly, "Until now the Lord has helped us." The phrase "until now" (עד הנה) which is placed in the forefront has an emphatic function. Israel has long lived treacherously against the Lord in idolatry. They have failed to abide in the covenant of the Lord and have

---

turn"), in this occasion for two reasons. First, נהנ here might be cognate to Akkadian nê'u/ne'û, meaning "to turn back" (see *CAD*, 11.2:198–199). Second, "returning" would fit the lexical semantic of שוב in the next verse – אם בכל לבבכם אתם שבים אל יהוה. The Lord has already returned to Israel in the presence of the ark. Now is the preparation for the returning of the heart of the house of Israel to the Lord.

130. Frolov, "1 Samuel 1–8," 83.

131. Thundering on high as the supernatural means of God's victory against his adversaries is mentioned in the Song of Hannah (2:10).

132. Eslinger, *Kingship of God*, 242.

133. Tsumura, *First Book of Samuel*, 238.

turned to foreign gods for many years. The aid which the Lord granted Israel was not something they deserved. Rather, it was undeserved grace given to Israel as they returned to the Lord in confession. Thus R. P. Gordon rightly explains the sentence, "until this point in Israel's history Yahweh has been her helper."[134]

Samuel publicly acknowledges the importance of this divine aid. The victory of the battle was hardly fortuitous; even the thundering on high was in God's sovereign control (Exod 9:23, 29, 33). In other words, Samuel renders the glory to God for such a decisive battle. Unlike other forms of worship, the erection of a stone has a lasting influence on the people due to its visual impact. Whenever people see it, it will remind them of God's special help in this place. Even the next generation of Israelites would also be able to learn from it. Thus Samuel is intentional in setting up the stone to pay tribute to YHWH. Hence, Bill Arnold says that this stone monument is "a benchmark on the ground" which acknowledges that this decisive victory was not dependent on Israel's own strength or military strategy.[135]

While it is uncertain if this "Stone of Help" (Ebenezer) is the same as the one mentioned in 4:1 and 5:1, it is more likely that this is a different "authoritative and authentic replacement."[136] It is ironic that the Israelites were not able to receive divine help in the place called "Stone of Help" in 4:1. Now Samuel gives this place a name that illustrates its meaning – "Stone of Help." The Lord has helped Israel again and has reversed the misfortune of the

---

134. Gordon, *1 and 2 Samuel*, 108.

135. Arnold, *1 and 2 Samuel*, 143. However, not everyone would have such spiritual discernment. Following the victory against the Amalekites, Saul set up a monument for himself (1 Sam 15:12; מציב לו יד) to proclaim and boost his own honor in the sight of Israel (see previous discussion in section 2.7). The notable contrast is that Samuel ascribed the glory of the victory to the Lord while Saul ascribed it to himself.

136. Fokkelman, *Vow and Desire*, 306. One can argue that the site in 7:12 is the same as in 4:1 and 5:1 due to Samuel determining to set up a visual reminder that the defeat of twenty years earlier had been reversed and traveling north to do so. Unlike in chapter 4 where they relied on a physical object (the ark) to save them, here they made a pact with the Lord, putting away their foreign gods and Ashtoreth images and agreeing to follow him only. However, the stone that Samuel erected in 7:12 was close to Mizpah, implying it is a new site (while the Ebenezer of 4:1 and 5:1 was close to the Aphek of the coastal plain). Thus it served to recall the previous battle against the Philistines, which ended in defeat, alongside this later victory, which reversed their past failure. A site different from 4:1 and 5:1 is more likely in 7:12. Scholars who propose that this is a new Ebenezer include Arnold, *1 and 2 Samuel*, 143; Klein, *1 Samuel*, 68; Tsumura, *First Book of Samuel*, 238; Hertzberg, *I and II Samuel*, 69; Baldwin, *1 and 2 Samuel*, 80; Vannoy, *1–2 Samuel*, 81–83.

previous disaster.¹³⁷ Thus, Hertzberg notes that the theological significance of this "Stone of Help" is more important than the historical.¹³⁸

In short, Samuel's setting up a stone monument in honor of YHWH for his deliverance is significant for the Israelites who have newly returned to the Lord after a period of apostasy. It is an important symbol that could strengthen Israel's faith to serve YHWH only and that could constantly remind them of God's mighty works in history and in their own lives.

4.5 God Honors Samuel by Establishing Him as a Prophet (1 Sam 3:19–21)

Earlier in this chapter, we briefly discussed Samuel's multiple roles in 1 Samuel, namely, as priest, prophet and judge. The purpose of this section is to examine further these roles and functions in Samuel's life. However, it is interesting to note that Samuel is mostly known as a prophet both in the books of Samuel (1 Sam 9:9) and outside the books of Samuel (1 Chr 9:22; 26:28; 29:29; 2 Chr 35:18; Acts 3:24; 13:20). That the honor entitled to a prophet is greater than that of priest and judge may explain this.¹³⁹

There is hardly any doubt that Samuel functioned as a dedicated priest while he was under Eli's priestly apprenticeship, especially in 1 Samuel 1–3. Samuel's background as a Levite from the line of Kohath (1 Chr 6:22–27), the clan that used to tend the holy things of God's tabernacle (Num 10:21), prepared him to become eligible to be the priest of the Lord.¹⁴⁰ His godly parents showed their devotion by going to Shiloh year by year to offer sacrifices and worship the Lord. Such a pious family background had a great influence on

---

137. Eslinger, *Kingship of God*, 243; Baldwin, *1 and 2 Samuel*, 80.

138. Hertzberg, *I and II Samuel*, 69.

139. Samuel is quite akin to Moses in that both assumed multiple roles in ancient Israel. Interestingly, Moses is only commended as a paradigmatic prophet (his most honorable role) whom the Lord knew face to face (Deut 34:10).

140. It is still possible that Levites could become full-blown priests as circumstances allowed in the early period when no other priestly family was dominant in a particular area. In Samuel's case, however, he displaces an existing priestly family. See Leuchter, *Samuel*, 40. Ackerman also explains that Samuel could be allowed to join the ranks of Shiloh's priests even though he did not come from the Levitical lineage which the biblical tradition required of priestly authorities. See Ackerman, "Who Is Sacrificing," 25. On another occasion, Leuchter explains more clearly that the Elide priestly clans accepted new devotees from the kinship groups involved in priestly service at their sanctuary in order to reinforce their influence over the populations from whence these priestly adepts were drawn. See Leuchter, "Samuel," 152.

Samuel's life. The description of Samuel's clothing as "a linen ephod," as well as a "little robe" prepared yearly by his dear mother, is a distinct feature to suggest that Samuel was trained to become a priest to serve the Lord (2:18). Though implicit, the fact that it is repeatedly mentioned (2:11, 18; 3:1) that Samuel was serving the Lord (before Eli) also evinces his priestly role and function.[141] With the failure of the Elide priesthood, God promised to replace it with a faithful priest (2:35) to serve in God's house. As I have argued, Samuel is the best candidate for this faithful priest in the context. Samuel's priestly role is more conspicuous after the passing of the Elide leadership (7:9; 13:8–15; 16:2). His priestly duty of offering sacrifices on behalf of the people could not even be replaced by king Saul (13:8–15).

Certainly, serving as a priest of the Lord was a great honor and privilege. No ordinary person could perform such a holy duty. However, the right of being a priest was very much determined by one's family origin. To put it forthrightly, being priests of the Lord was hereditary among the circles of the Levites. Perhaps for this reason, the narrator does not accentuate Samuel's identity as a priest of the Lord.

Chapter 3 of 1 Samuel is a transitional juncture introducing the rise of Samuel from a priest to a prophet (נביא); it begins with Samuel as a priestly servant and ends with him as a prophet (3:20).[142] Unlike being a priest, being a prophet was not restrained by any genealogical credit. Traditionally, to become a prophet, one had to have a direct encounter with the Lord and receive his holy words.[143] A prophet then carried the special word of God and conveyed it to the people.[144] The prophets were the spokespeople for God. Israel had their priests with them all the time, but not every generation would

---

141. For instance, it is often assumed that Samuel is the one who attended the lamp of God (a priestly duty) in the temple of God when Eli's eyes had become dull (3:2–3). His lying down beside the ark of God also availed him of the opportunity to serve in the temple (as per Eli's instruction).

142. Arnold, *1 and 2 Samuel*, 82–83; Eslinger, *Kingship of God*, 143.

143. A prophet's status of having a direct encounter with God could be expressed by one being recognized and endorsed by the community. 1 Samuel 3:19–20 would seemingly serve to set that paradigm.

144. Samuel's role as a prophet seems to be different from other groups of prophets described in 1 Samuel 10:5, 10, and 19:20a, not to mention the seemingly prophetic and ecstatic behavior of Saul and his servants (1 Sam 19: 20b–24). For more information about the role and function of prophets, see Petersen, *Roles of Israel's Prophets*; Coggins, Phillips, and Knibb, *Israel's Prophetic Tradition*; Day, *Prophecy and Prophets*; Gordon, *Place Is Too Small*; Kratz, *Prophets of Israel*.

have the privilege of having a prophet of God in their midst.[145] A prophet was called and ordained by God alone. The office of prophet was not established by human institution and hence the works of the prophets were often not restrained by human power. Prophets were often called to encounter the sins of the people, and many of them even had to confront and criticize the wrongdoing of kings and priests.[146] Such a unique responsibility granted a special honor to the office of prophet. In general, the honor of being a prophet of God was greater than the honor of being a priest of God.

It is obvious that Samuel was called directly by God. In fact, the Lord called (קרא) him four times (3:4, 6, 8, 10) in order to speak to him; God did not give up until Samuel was ready to receive the word of God. It was soon well known in Israel that Samuel had become a prophet of God (3:20). The fact that God conveyed the judgment message concerning the doom of the Elides through Samuel adds special weight to his status as a prophet. Samuel would be honored in Israel and the Elides put to shame. Samuel had surpassed the Elides and would take over their priestly leadership, and indeed, much more than that, he had become a prophet of God among the people. The honor accorded Samuel was not just the new priestly leadership, but even more importantly, he received the status of a prophet who communicated God's words to his people.

Samuel continued to grow, both physically and spiritually. As a prophet of God, God confirmed Samuel's prophetic identity by fulfilling all the words that he delivered to him. The fulfillment of God's words through Samuel was a confirmation that he had indeed established Samuel as a prophet.[147] The reality of Samuel as a prophet is further accentuated by the fact that God continued to appear (ראה) and became visible (גלה) to him through his word (3:21).[148] Samuel's privilege of receiving God's special revelation was continuous even

---

145. The last occurrence of the term נביא ("a prophet"), before Samuel, is found in Judges 6:8. When Samuel is publicly recognized as a prophet (3:20), a gap of a few hundred years had passed between the two occurrences.

146. For example, Nathan rebuked king David for his sexual affair with Bathsheba, the wife of Uriah (2 Sam 12:7).

147. The verb נאמן ("trustworthy") echoes the description of the "faithful priest" (כהן נאמן) in 2:25 as the root אמן appears in both places. Samuel was a faithful prophet as well as a faithful priest. See Firth, *1 & 2 Samuel*, 79.

148. A prophet sees what others usually do not see and has a special vision from God. The narrator explains in 9:9 that a prophet was formerly called "the seer" (הראה). The seer turns out to be Samuel.

after the night-call experience. Samuel's encounter with God was not a one-time exceptional event but rather "the first of a series."[149] His reputation as a prophet spread from Dan in the north to Beersheba in the south (3:20).[150] Thus, the narrator has emphasized Samuel's prophetic role in various ways by the end of 1 Samuel 3. As the one who received and proclaimed the word of God (contra the scarceness of the word of God during the Elide leadership; 3:1), Samuel was honored as a prophet of God (not just as a priest of God) in all Israel because of his faithfulness in serving the Lord.

The people also remembered Samuel as a prophet. His reputation as a prophet was so widespread that even a servant of Saul could recognize Samuel as a "man of God" (i.e. a prophet; 9:9) who was held in honor (9:6; נכבד). The additional comment, "all that he says surely comes true," is a rephrasing of 3:19 wherein the narrator states that God let none of his words fall to the ground. The words of Saul's servant reflect Samuel's high esteem as a prophet among the people.

Samuel was not just honored as a prophet in Israel, but a leader who judged Israel all the days of his life (7:15-16), which was an additional honor. The office of judge often involved both the leadership role of a political leader and the civic duty of dispensing justice, punishing the evildoer and vindicating the righteous.[151] Eli judged Israel forty years (4:18), but it is not certain whether he could execute justice in disputes, at least not pertaining to the corruption of his two wayward sons. However, it is obvious that Samuel's tenure as a judge was welcomed and embraced by the people, so much so that he had to make a yearly circuit to Bethel, Gilgal and Mizpah in order to perform his duty of jurisdiction.[152] Fokkelman also notes that the repeated use of "all" (כל) in verse 15 and verse 16 indicates his expanded influence in time and space.[153] In addition, Samuel's declaration of his own innocence in 12:3-4 is also a sensitive reflection on his role as a judge in Israel.

---

149. Arnold, *1 and 2 Samuel*, 84.

150. Hertzberg, *I and II Samuel*, 42; Fokkelman, *Vow and Desire*, 190. Of course, it took a certain interval of time for the whole nation to gradually understand and acknowledge that Samuel was a true prophet.

151. Manley and Wiseman, "Judges," 627.

152. Samuel as a judge is regarded as paradigmatic among many other judges in pre-monarchic Israel. See Spronk, "Samuel," 129-140.

153. Fokkelman, *Vow and Desire*, 308-309.

Thus, Samuel assumed the roles of prophet, priest and judge. Such a profusion of different functions coalescing in one person is closely related to the special needs of the time, as Israel made a transition from the system of judges to kingship.[154]

Of all the offices assigned to Samuel – priest, prophet and judge – his role as prophet is accentuated (9:6, 9).[155] To this Arnold comments, "His role as a prophet makes him, like Moses before him, a leader par excellence."[156] Even after Samuel's death, the helpless Saul tries to consult the deceased Samuel through a medium (28:3-19), as turning to prophecy was one of the available methods of acquiring the will of the gods in the ancient Near East.[157] Thus it is obvious Samuel's prophetic role was primary even though it was set up after his original priestly function.[158] Even the LXX Sirach (46:13) commemorates Samuel's prophetic role first, along with his other roles as judge and priest:

---

154. Arnold, *1 and 2 Samuel*, 84; Gilmour, *Representing the Past*, 56; Briscoe, "Implications," 139-141; Hare, "Literary Portrait of Samuel," 2. Textual critics, however, often see Samuel's manifold roles due to a process of textual growth. See Nissinen, "Prophets and Prophecy," 121.

155. It has to be noted that the narrator only identifies Samuel as a prophet (3:20) and never directly labels him as a priest and a judge, though he clearly performed the functions of a priest and a judge. As a prophet of God, Samuel consulted YHWH concerning the people's request for a king and reported all of YHWH's words to the people (8:7-18). Samuel carried the prophetic messenger formula כה אמר יהוה צבאות ("Thus says the Lord of Hosts"; 15:2) against Amalek; he also delivered a prophetic word of God against Saul in 13:13-14. Samuel was also able to foretell the fate of the kings of Israel (which are two of the most important events in the books of Samuel that govern the rest of the narrative development), both the forfeiture of Saul (15:26-29) and the establishment of David (16:12-13).

156. Arnold, *1 and 2 Samuel*, 84.

157. Nissinen, "Prophets and Prophecy," 104.

158. I am aware of other scholars who try to explain his different roles in different ways. Dietrich's interest is in searching for the historical Samuel. In his point of view, Samuel should be mainly seen as a religious-political leader – a savior and the last judge of Israel. See Dietrich, "Samuel," 1-17. Sweeney thinks Samuel originally represented a model of priest in northern Israel. Later the Deuteronomistic writer turned him into a prophet for his own benefit. See Sweeney, "Samuel's Institutional Identity," 165-174. Likewise, Leuchter argues that the Deuteronomists reworked a tradition which initially emphasized Samuel's priestly stature and turned it to a prophetic career for their own needs. See Leuchter, "Samuel," 147-168. Thus, all of the above writers see Samuel's prophetic role as the result of a later literary development. However, their main interests are not in how the Scripture as it is portrays Samuel's identity (primarily as a prophet). Polzin, in view of his disfavor of Samuel in the call narrative, while acknowledging Samuel's primary prophetic role over his identity as priest and judge, describes him as "an imperceptive and mostly passive prophet" who wants nothing more than to sleep and whom God can hardly wake up in order to tell him important things. See Polzin, *Samuel and the Deuteronomist*, 50. Frolov proposes a theory that the prophet Samuel is introduced as an agent provocateur, misleading the people into a disaster upon themselves. See Frolov, "1 Samuel 1-8," 77-85. Such a reading of the prophet Samuel has its problem, as the text never indicates

Ἠγαπημένος ὑπὸ κυρίου αὐτοῦ
Σαμουηλ προφήτης κυρίου κατέστησεν βασιλείαν
καὶ ἔχρισεν ἄρχοντας ἐπὶ τὸν λαὸν αὐτοῦ·

"Beloved by his Lord, Samuel the prophet of the Lord established a kingdom and anointed rulers over his people."

Indeed, being a prophet of God was the most honorable recognition God bestowed upon Samuel, his faithful servant. The narrator was fully aware of Samuel's multiple roles, but it was his prophetic role that mattered most, and perhaps to other biblical writers as well (1 Chr 9:22; 26:28; 29:29; 2 Chr 35:18; Acts 3:24; 13:20). Hence, "Samuel the prophet" is the most common epithet rendering respect to this great servant of God.

Though going beyond the delimitation of our discussion, it is perhaps worthy to mention briefly that the prophet Samuel was given the honor of anointing the first two kings of Israel, Saul and David (10:1; 16:12–13). He would be the kingmaker for Israel.

Samuel was honored as prophet, but he was much more than a prophet.

4.6 Conclusion

The ideological perspective of honor/shame guides the way the narrator portrays the fates of the Elides and Samuel. This study has found that the Elides and Samuel exhibited distinctly different character in their service to God. Unlike the Elides who honored their own personal agenda, Samuel wholeheartedly honored God through his humble and faithful service. God is also just in his treatment of his servants, for with the same measure they ascribe honor or dishonor to God, so it will be measured back to them. Namely, God will honor those who honor him, but those who despise him shall be insignificant (2:30). Accordingly, the Elides were judged with shame through their unusual deaths, but Samuel was honored as a prophet of God throughout all Israel.

(even implicitly) that Samuel encouraged the people to go to war against the Philistines. It is more likely that Israel's ambition, which tried to put an end to the long period of Philistine oppression, stirred up the war and thus brought the casualty upon themselves.

CHAPTER 5

The Ark Narrative – YHWH Defends His Own Glory (1 Samuel 4:1–7:1)

In the previous two chapters (chs. 3 and 4), I have shown how the narrator's ideological perspective of honor and shame can be offered as a guide to our reading of the texts in 1 Samuel 1–7. Indeed, the life of Hannah can be summarized as a reversal of her fate from the ashamed to the honored in the public eye. Likewise, the contrasting lives of the Elides and Samuel can be perceptively portrayed as those who honor themselves versus the one who honors God. According to the extent one honors or dishonors God, by that same measure God will also hold the person in esteem or shame (2:30). Thus, the Elides (the ones who dishonored God) were shamed and Samuel (the one who honored God) was honored. With a retrospective glance, one finds that the perspective of honor and shame is employed by the narrator as a standard of judgment for God's election of Samuel and his rejection of the Elides.

In view of the foregoing discussion, in this chapter we will read the so-called "Ark Narrative" (chs. 4–6)[1] from the perspective of honor and shame.

---

1. Critical scholars typically see it (i.e. 1 Sam 4:1b–7:1) as an independent narrative. See Rost, *Die Überlieferung*, 119–253; Miller and Roberts, *Hand of the Lord*, 30–36; McCarter, *1 Samuel*, 26; Campbell, *Ark Narrative*, 165–178. Such an isolation of the text is really not necessary. Gitay, for instance, in his article, "Reflections on the Poetics of the Samuel Narrative," 221–230, argues that the ark narrative is inseparable from the rest of Samuel; likewise, see Willis, "Anti-Elide Narrative," 288–308. The sins of the Elides are presupposed in the earlier chapters and their deaths as a consequence of their sins is also forecasted in the earlier episode (2:27–36; 3:11–14). Thus, some choose to add other materials (e.g. 1 Sam 2:12–17, 22–25 is added by McCarter, *1 Samuel*, 26; additionally 2:27–36 is added by Miller and Roberts, *Hand of the Lord*, 30–31) as part of this "independent" composition. For clarification, the term "ark narrative" is used in this dissertation to refer to the narratives of 4:1a–7:1.

I will demonstrate that the narrator's ideological point of view can offer us a fresh lens for reading this remarkable story in Israel's history. It should be remembered, as I have explained earlier in section 1.7, that the reason this part of the story is placed at the end of our examination is due to my conviction that the ark narrative is the conclusion of the story in chapters 1–7 and is of greatest theological significance.[2]

The construction of the scenes of the ark narrative can be briefly expressed in the following manner.[3]

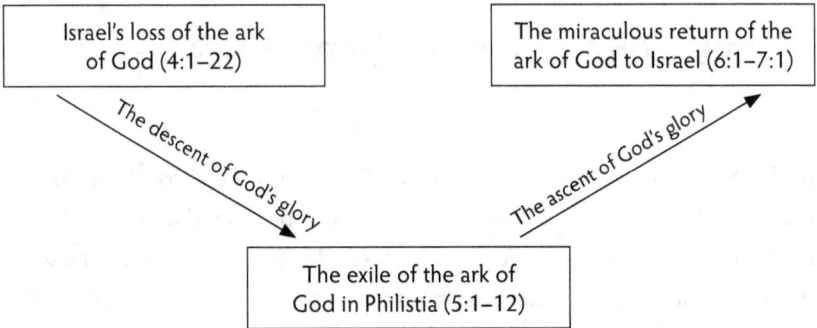

According to this chart, chapter 4 concerns the departure/exile of God's glory (4:21-22) and chapter 6 portrays the acknowledgement, restoration and exaltation of God's glory (6:5). Chapter 5 stands in-between as a transition in which God proves himself to be a superior deity by defeating both Dagon and the Philistines.

---

2. The ark narrative is often seen as a piece of theological narrative. See Campbell, "Yahweh and the Ark," 31–33. McCarter argues that the theological purpose of the ark narrative as a whole is to deal with this problem: "How can the Philistines have defied the power of Yahweh and prevailed?" While affirming YHWH's sovereignty, he thinks the purpose is to expose the corruption of the Elide priesthood. The capture of the ark shows that God chose to abandon Israel on account of the wickedness of the Elides. See McCarter, 1 Samuel, 109. Without denying the truthfulness of his statement, I would argue the theological purpose of the ark narrative, from the ideological perspective of honor and shame, is to show God defending his glory while he allows the ark to be captured by the Philistines due to the sins of Israel.

3. This chart is adapted from Brueggemann, First and Second Samuel, 44.

5.1 The Glory of the God of Israel Is Not Present at the Capture of the Ark of the Lord (1 Sam 4:1–22)

Although some scholars align 4:1a ("and the word of Samuel came to all Israel") with the ark narrative story, others suggest the real beginning of the ark narrative should start with 4:1b.[4] The caution against placing 4:1a as part of the ark narrative is that it gives one the impression that Samuel's word was "a call to arms" to all Israel to rally against the Philistines.[5] Tsumura, however, argues that it would be strange to place 4:1a as the end of a section when 3:19–21 is already treated as the terminus. Instead, he proposes that it can be treated as a temporal clause, an example of "transitional technique," to offer background information to the whole ark narrative: "Around the time when the word of Samuel came toward all Israel."[6] Read this way, Tsumura proposes that while the story of the ark narrative develops, Samuel still functioned as a prophet of God. But this *wayyiqtol* syntagm can be arguably seen as a simple summary of 3:19–21 (not a new event in the temporal flow):[7] "And ['so' or 'thus'] the word of Samuel came/occurred to all Israel."

---

4. For scholars who propose 4:1a as the beginning of the ark narrative, see Tsumura, *First Book of Samuel*, 185; Auld, *I & II Samuel*, 62; Steinmann, *1 Samuel*, 118. For others who prefer 4:1b for the start, see Campbell, *1 Samuel*, 63; McCarter, *1 Samuel*, 105; Klein, *1 Samuel*, 36; Hertzberg, *I and II Samuel*, 47; Firth, *1 & 2 Samuel*, 84; Miller and Roberts, *Hand of the Lord*, 43; Arnold, *1 and 2 Samuel*, 91; Driver, *Notes*, 45; Polzin, *Samuel and the Deuteronomist*, 55; Gordon, *I & II Samuel*, 89; Bergen, *1, 2 Samuel*, 89; Brueggemann, *First and Second Samuel*, 29; Fokkelman, *Vow and Desire*, 190.

5. Campbell, *1 Samuel*, 63. Similarly, Frolov suggests that the prophet Samuel is introduced as an agent provocateur, inciting the people to war against the Philistines. See Frolov, "1 Samuel 1–8," 77–85. Such a view parallels that of David Qimḥi (a medieval Jewish Hebrew grammarian and commentator) who thinks that Samuel commanded the Israelites to go out to war by the word of the Lord, see https://www.sefaria.org/Radak_on_I_Samuel.4.1.1?lang=bi&with=all&lang2=en.

6. Tsumura, *First Book of Samuel*, 185–188. He suggests that such a setting is particularly important as it was considered reprehensible for the people of Israel to go to war without even inquiring of the prophet of God in their midst. Similarly, Spina also supports the use of the *wayhî* clause as a temporal expression; see Spina, "Prophet's 'Pregnant Pause,'" 66.

7. The *wayhî* clause in 4:1a can be read as the summation (GKC, § 111k; Joüon-Muraoka, § 118i; *IBHS*, § 33.2a) of the previous narrative or as an epexegetical statement (*IBHS*, § 33.2.2). Reading it as a summation, it is simply a recapping of the earlier statement in 3:20 that all Israel from Dan to Beersheba knew that Samuel was trustworthy as a prophet. Buttressing this summary idea is the presence of כל ישראל in both 3:20 and 4:1a. The repeat in 4:1a alludes to a summary of what goes back to 3:19. However, 4:1a has been lost in the rendering of the LXX's Καὶ ἐγενήθη ἐν ταῖς ἡμέραις ἐκείναις ("And it came to pass in those days"), which seems to reflect a different Hebrew *Vorlage*, וַיְהִי בַּיָּמִים הָהֵם. The translation "in those days" is endorsed by Klein; see Klein, *1 Samuel*, 36. The phrase ויהי דבר שמואל ל (or ויהי דבר with any other human agent) occurs only once here in the entire OT. A more common formula would be ויהי דבר יהוה אל,

One obvious phenomenon in the ark narrative is Samuel's absence. Why is he not part of this important event? A simple explanation could be that Samuel is not a direct participant in this tragic incident. Firth suggests the ark narrative should be read as a "bifurcated narrative" wherein the narrator leaves one part of the story aside until the completion of the other.[8] Indeed, after the completion of the ark narrative, Samuel, whose role is ignored in the narrative itself, has grown into a mature prophet (having advanced beyond the description נער in 1 Samuel 3) who leads a national revival of repentance in Israel (7:3–6). The fact that the Israelites go to war without first consulting the prophet in their midst may suggest they do not value his prophecy on this occasion.[9] Likewise, Spina argues Samuel's absence in the ark narrative indicates that Israel ignored the prophetic voice (shown in 4:1a) which had been so badly needed in such a critical time.[10] In other words, Samuel's role is trifled with by the leaders of Israel. Thus his absence in the ark narrative does not mean his disappearance from the story. From the narrator's ideological point of view, the ark narrative is a shameful tragedy in Israel which points the blaming finger at the sins of the Elide priests and the corruption of the Israelite leadership. The narrator seemingly would not want Samuel (a prophet to be honored) to be a part of this disgraceful scandal and have his reputation tarnished.

The ark story starts with a battle between Israel and the Philistines, Israel's long-known foe in the period of the judges (see Judges 13–16), without giving any details about the reason for this hostile engagement.[11] It seems that this was likely a conflict caused by border interests wherein the Philistines

---

occurring eighty-eight times in the Bible. The use of such a rare phrase (with less chance of being invented and introduced at a later date) suggests that the MT is more likely the original; see Pisano, *Additions or Omissions*, 33–34.

8. Firth, *1 & 2 Samuel*, 83.

9. Steinmann, *1 Samuel*, 123; also Tsumura, *First Book of Samuel*, 187.

10. Spina, "Prophet's 'Pregnant Pause,'" 66.

11. The LXX starts with 4:1b and introduces the section by insinuating a period when the Philistines gathered against Israel for war (Καὶ ἐγενήθη ἐν ταῖς ἡμέραις ἐκείναις καὶ συναθροίζονται ἀλλόφυλοι εἰς πόλεμον ἐπὶ Ισραηλ, "And it came to pass in those days that the Philistines were gathering themselves against Israel to war"). This reading seems to offer a better transition between the ending section of chapter 3 and the current ark narrative. Indeed, the starting point of MT (if one starts the narrative with 4:1b) is very abrupt, without giving any explanation on the nature of the following לקראת (i.e. the question of who started the war). See Driver, *Notes*, 45.

were the aggressors.[12] Both sides prepared for a battle, with Israel encamping at Ebenezer[13] and the Philistines at Aphek on the opposite side (4:1b). The Philistines drew up battle lines with their troops to fight against Israel. Israel suffered a defeat in the battle, but not a decisive one, since the troops of Israel were still able to form their battle line on the field despite this defeat.[14] The Israelite casualties from this battle were about four thousand men (4:2).[15]

In response to this defeat, the elders of Israel complained before the people: "Why did the Lord smite us (נגפנו)[16] this day before the Philistines? Let us take to ourselves the ark of the covenant of the Lord from Shiloh, that it might come in our midst and save us from the hand of our enemies" (4:3). Obviously, the elders of Israel, consisting of seventy members in Numbers 11:16–17, were a group of influential senior tribal leaders and were entrusted with important decision making.[17] Though Eli was still officially the judge for Israel, he was too old (4:15) to function in his duty in such a circumstance of war. The elders assumed that the Lord himself was the one who smote them and was the reason for their defeat before the Philistines. The elders of Israel posed a rhetorical question ("why did the Lord smite us?") without expecting an answer. If they were genuine enough to enquire of God, they would have turned to him (most likely through Samuel the prophet) and waited for his answer before proceeding (as in the defeat of Ai; Josh 7:6–15). They put the

---

12. The Philistines, a more civilized people and being advanced in the use of iron technology (1 Sam 13:19–21), were part of the migrated "sea peoples" and were settled in the southwestern coastal plains, occupying the main cities in the area; Israel was neighbored in the central hill region of Canaan. The Philistines' desire to expand into Israelite territory had probably resulted in this battle in chapter 4. See Arnold, *1 and 2 Samuel*, 93.

13. As I have explained earlier in section 4.4, this Ebenezer should likely be distinguished from the new Ebenezer ("Stone of Help") in 7:12. See Driver, *Notes*, 45; Klein, *1 Samuel*, 41. It is ironic that Israel suffered defeat in a place of "help."

14. Firth, *1 & 2 Samuel*, 85; Klein, *1 Samuel*, 41.

15. Such a number is often thought to be hyperbolic. Following Wenham's suggestion of military units known as "thousands" rather than a literal number (see Wenham, "Large Numbers," 19–53), a number of scholars have accepted such a view, which would make the number of casualties significantly smaller. See Firth, *1 & 2 Samuel*, 85; Klein, *1 Samuel*, 41; Campbell, *1 Samuel*, 64; Fouts, "Defense of the Hyperbolic," 377–387; McCarter, *1 Samuel*, 105. MacCarter even suggests that the number "four thousands" was equivalent to about twenty to fifty-six men. However, I am inclined to take the number literally. If one questions the literal number here, then all the numbers associated with אלף II ("thousand") elsewhere in the books of Samuel should also be possibly questioned.

16. The verb וַיִּנָּגֶף in v. 2 (as a *niphal*) suggests Israel experienced defeat before the Philistines with YHWH as the ultimate agent of defeat.

17. Tsumura, *First Book of Samuel*, 190.

blame on God instead of repenting of their own sins. Rather than turning to the true God, they turned to the ark of God, a cultic object that symbolized the presence of God. Their hubris prompted them to coercively take the ark of the God in their midst, hoping for God to act on their behalf.[18] The elders did not just mention the ark of God, but *the ark of the covenant of the Lord*.[19] They forced the Lord, the God of Israel, to mind his covenant relationship with Israel while they themselves failed to abide in such a covenant relationship. They thought the presence of the ark of God would guarantee them victory.

The people acted quickly to take the ark of the covenant of the Lord of Hosts, who sits between the cherubim.[20] The speed of their action also confirms they were only asking a rhetorical question earlier.[21] The term "hosts" (צבאות) echoes military imagery wherein the Lord would act as a mighty warrior for his people. The people sought to make it a holy war of YHWH even though the Lord did not initiate it.[22] The elders presumed that God could be compelled to fight for them as they brought the ark into their midst. The ominous atmosphere is enhanced by the presence of the two sons of Eli, Hophni and Phinehas,[23] with the ark of the covenant of God. The corruption of Eli's two sons (2:12–17; 22–25) is already known to the readers, and their crimes were offensive to the Lord. Would God really be with these sinful priests? Suspense hangs in the air.

As soon as the ark of God arrived into the camp, all the Israelites raised such a loud shout (תרועה) that even the inhabitants of the land shook (4:5). The loud shout was a battle cry[24] that expressed the people's confidence in the ark of God. In the battle against Jericho, the people of Israel were instructed to raise such a loud shout (Josh 6:5, 20) after circling the city seven times with the

---

18. According to Tsumura, the collocation *take* (לקח) + *the ark* suggests a loss of the sense of awesomeness toward God's holy presence, and the Israelites treated this sacred object without respect. See Tsumura, 190–91.

19. The ark is said to contain two tablets of the covenant (Exod 25:16; Deut 10:5).

20. The expanded title emphasizes the majesty, power and authority of YHWH. See Stirrup, "Why Has Yahweh," 89.

21. Firth, *1 & 2 Samuel*, 85.

22. Firth, *1 & 2 Samuel*, 85; Miller and Roberts, *Hand of the Lord*, 45; Arnold, *1 and 2 Samuel*, 95. Arnold notes that the ark served an important military function as part of Israel's holy war against the Canaanites as they entered the promised land.

23. The narrator even ignores their title as "priests of the Lord" (cf. 1 Sam 1:3). His disfavor toward Eli's two sons is obvious.

24. The battle cry is typical of holy war contexts. See Klein, *1 Samuel*, 42.

ark of the Lord, and were then decisively victorious. Ironically, here the people of Israel trusted in the ark of God rather than the true God whom the object symbolized. The Philistines who heard such an unusually loud cry responded with concern: "What is this loud cry in the camp of the Hebrews?" They were curious to know the reason that prompted this unusual phenomenon. The term "Hebrews" (עברים) is possibly used here with disrespect and contempt.[25]

The Philistines soon discover that the shout was caused by the arrival of the ark of the Lord in the camp of Israel. They are frightened by this news, for they think they are fighting not against mortal strength but a deity, a god[26] having come into Israel's camp (4:7). The chance for prevailing in such a fight is doomed from the beginning. The Philistines, as the Israelites, assume that the coming of the Lord will ensure victory for Israel.[27] Thus, the Philistines lament with two "woe" cries: "Woe to us! For nothing like this has happened before. Woe to us! Who can deliver us from the hand of these mighty gods? These are the gods who struck the Egyptians with every kind of smiting (בכל מכה) and pestilence."[28] The Philistines face the battle with a bleak prospect. They probably interpret the deity of Israel from a polytheist point of view, as would be the prevailing culture of most people in the ancient

---

25. Thus a "pejorative" term (Tsumura, *First Book of Samuel*, 193) or a "disparaging" name that was understood as an "outlaw" category (see Klein, *1 Samuel*, 125–26 for his discussion of this term in 1 Sam 13:3) or a term of "derision" (Sturhahn, "Investigation," 192). "Hebrews" is an ethnic term distinct from religio-political designations such as "Israel" and "sons of Israel." For more information on the background and origin of this term, see McCarter, *1 Samuel*, 240–241; Tsumura, *First Book of Samuel*, 193.

26. The LXX reads plural οἱ θεοὶ ("gods"). This is probably a secondary reading modified to accord with the plural description of gods (האלהים האדירים) in the following verse (v. 8).

27. Firth, *1 & 2 Samuel*, 86; Miller and Roberts, *Hand of the Lord*, 45. It serves to underscore the unexpected and devastating report in v. 10 that the coming of the deity did not bring victory for Israel.

28. However, the MT has בַּמִּדְבָּר ("in the wilderness"). Likewise, the LXX reads καὶ ἐν τῇ ἐρήμῳ ("and in the wilderness"). But it contradicts biblical tradition wherein the ten "plagues" (if מכה is understood as such) occurred in Egypt and not in the wilderness. A better suggestion is that καὶ ἐν τῇ ἐρήμῳ alludes not to "desert" but "plague" – וּבְמוֹ־דָבָר ("and with plague") – במו being a long archaic and poetic form of the preposition ב, and καὶ (וּ) signaling that what follows is an extension of כָּל־מַכָּה. See McCarter, *1 Samuel*, 104; also Klein, *1 Samuel*, 36. Steinmann plausibly suggests that the noun מכה, from the root נכה, "to strike," can possibly be translated as "plague" (4:8), "blow" (6:19), "slaughter" (4:10), "attack" (14:14) or "defeat" (14:30) depending on the context. See Steinmann, *1 Samuel*, 121. Likewise, Driver suggests that בכל מכה should be translated as "with every manner of smiting"; see Driver, *Notes on the Hebrew Text*, 47. Polzin, however, solves this puzzle by arguing that the Philistines had "misheard or misread their opponent's sacred traditions." See Polzin, *Samuel and the Deuteronomist*, 58.

Near East.²⁹ Ironically, it is the Philistines who note the mighty deeds of the God of Israel in striking the Egyptians with a great blow.

Mentioning the exodus event brings back the memory of God's awesome power in delivering the Israelites from Pharaoh's tyranny. But the Philistines do not give up easily and surrender themselves. They exhort each other: "Be strong and be men!" They brace themselves for this fight lest they become slaves to the Hebrews, just as the latter had been to them. The Hebrews' subordination to the Philistines likely led to the latter's cultural and military superiority (13:5–6, 19–20).³⁰

Paradoxically, to the surprise of the Philistines (perhaps also of the Israelites), Israel is defeated (וַיִּנָּגֶף) badly. The defeat is much worse than that of the first battle – every man flees and scatters for home (lit. "each to his tents") instead of holding their ranks in the field as in the first battle.³¹ Israel suffers a great slaughter (המכה גדולה).³² Some 30,000 men of the infantry are killed.³³ Not only does the ark fail to bring victory for Israel, but this symbol of God's very presence is taken (נלקח)³⁴ by the Philistines, and the two evil sons of Eli, Hophni and Phinehas, who are attendants of the ark of God, also die during the battle (4:11). When the ark of God came to the camp of Israel, both the Israelites and the Philistines assumed that it would ensure Israel's victory. But, unexpectedly, Israel is defeated. Brueggemann says accurately, "The defeat with the ark is even more devastating than the defeat without the ark."³⁵ The defeat of Israel was willed by YHWH. The God of Israel was not present even though Israel coercively attempted to bring his presence through the instrumentality of the ark.

---

29. A monotheistic Israelite viewpoint can be possibly seen in the 3m.s. verb ויבא ("that he [i.e. YHWH] might come") in v. 3, although one can also argue alternatively that the subject of the verb is the ark of the covenant of YHWH as a cultic object.

30. Klein also notes the wordplay between "serve" (עבד) and "Hebrew" (עבר) in v. 9 may insinuate Israel's low status in the eyes of the Philistines. See Klein, *1 Samuel*, 42–43. However, Baldwin suggests the term עברים can possibly entail a wider racial connotation. See Baldwin, *1 and 2 Samuel*, 75.

31. Baldwin, 43.

32. The same word מכה is used in v. 8 to describe God's smiting of the Egyptians.

33. Again, there are others who see it as hyperbolic expression.

34. It was Israel's self-initiative to "take" (נקחה, v. 3) the ark to the battlefield and now the ark "was taken" (נלקח, v. 11) by the Philistines. Tsumura notes the wordplay on the active and passive connotation of לקח. See Tsumura, *First Book of Samuel*, 190.

35. Brueggemann, *First and Second Samuel*, 29.

Indeed, the corruption of the two sons of Eli (2:12–17, 22–25) made it abhorrent for God to dwell in their midst. How could God continue to be with them after all the offensive crimes they committed in the sight of Israel? They had driven God away by their sins. Thus, as prophesied (2:34), Hophni and Phinehas die on the same day.

However, the capture of the ark of God brings a profound theological crisis to Israel.[36] The tragedy of Israel's defeat proves the absence of the God of Israel despite the presence of the ark of God. In other words, the presence of God is not tantamount to a cultic object. YHWH is not bound to the ark. The wife of Phinehas has it right that God is gone, and the glory has gone into exile (vv. 21–22). The God of Israel cannot be manipulated and kidnapped according to Israel's own selfish desires. Meanwhile, the defeat of Israel also exposes Israel's moral and spiritual decay. For this reason, the Israelites are abandoned by the Lord despite the presence of the ark of the covenant.

The notions of honor and shame offer a slightly different perspective. It is obvious that the Israelites suffered shame in this terrible defeat.[37] One may raise the objection that YHWH should have the obligation in the covenant relationship to protect Israel from being shamed.[38] The problem is that covenant honor is reciprocal.[39] Namely, YHWH is to honor Israel if they also honor him. However, both the crimes of Eli's two evil sons and the corruption of disrespectful elders have shown that the leadership in Israel has violated the covenant relationship. Thus, YHWH would be unjust if he continued to grant them victory in such circumstances. It is thus fair to say that the defeat of Israel is an opportunity for God to chasten his people for their violation of the covenant.[40] The question is whether the God of Israel is also susceptible to Israel's shame. Brueggemann comments openly, "It is YHWH who has been

---

36. Arnold, *1 and 2 Samuel*, 97; Brueggemann, *First and Second Samuel*, 32. The God of Israel was either too weak, which did not match his reputation of doing great works (even the Philistines were familiar with YHWH's mighty deeds in Egypt), or he simply chose not to stay with Israel.

37. Shame is experienced through the inferiority of their military strength and power.

38. For more information on the honor/shame dynamics in the covenant relationship, see Olyan, "Honor," 201–218; Bechtel, "Perception of Shame," 84–85.

39. Olyan, "Honor," 205. In ancient vassal-suzerain treaties, a suzerain was expected to confer honor to the vassal should he remain loyal to the covenant relationship.

40. Arnold, *1 and 2 Samuel*, 97. Brueggemann, however, does not see sin as the issue attributing to the second defeat when he says, "the loss was no longer aligned with Israel's guilt." Brueggemann, *Ichabod toward Home*, 10.

shamed and humiliated, and who has lost credence."[41] Likewise, Bechtel also endorses that YHWH too "was vulnerable to shame," especially in the risk of Israel's defeat before enemies.[42] Indeed, the fortune of the people of Israel is closely tied to their God. However, the God of Israel remains silent to such inquiry until he acts against Dagon, the god of the Philistines, in 5:1–5, which we will discuss more in section 5.2.

The next two episodes (4:12–18, 19–22) will continue to elaborate on the consequences of the ark's loss to Eli's family. The human response to the sad news is granted greater emphasis than the factual event.[43] Since I have examined 4:12–18 in section 4.3, in speaking of the Elides' unusual and shameful deaths, I will only briefly review the passage here and move to discuss the consequences more in my comments on verses 19–22.

Eli's reaction to the news of defeat is portrayed in verses 12–18. The old priest's extraordinary anxiety (4:13) discloses his sense of impending disaster. To some extent, Eli may have foreseen Israel's defeat in the battle or even the death of his two evil sons due to the prophecy of the man of God and the revelation to the young lad, Samuel (2:34; 3:11–14), but the capture of the ark was unthinkable and unbearable (4:18). The sad news brings a wave of shock and Eli loses his balance, falls backward off his seat, breaks his neck and dies. With the ark, a symbol of God's presence, taken away, Israel would become a nation without its god. Without its own deity, Israel would be at a total loss, losing guidance and protection. Israel had often believed in a god who was powerful and assertive and triumphant. The ark's capture subverts Israel's faith in an endlessly triumphant God.[44] The God of Israel is "defeated." The theological crisis and its aftermath are even more challenging for Israel than the calamity itself.

Eli's daughter-in-law, the wife of Phinehas, also responds to such a concern (4:19–22). The shocking news of the loss of the ark of God and the deaths of

---

41. Brueggemann, 9.

42. Bechtel, "Perception of Shame," 87. One example of YHWH's vulnerability to shame is demonstrated in Sennacherib's humiliation of Judah in 701 BCE when he taunted YHWH's inability to save Israel from being conquered by his military might, just as he had conquered other nations (2 Kgs 18:28–35; 19:3–4).

43. Bar-Efrat, *Narrative Art*, 152. The battle is briefly recorded in vv. 10–11. The narrator gives more attention in 4:12–22 to matters pertaining to the human mind, its motives, decisions and attitudes.

44. Brueggemann, *Ichabod toward Home*, 120.

her father-in-law and her husband overcome her with such magnitude that she is forced to give premature birth (4:19). Right before her death, the women attending her try to comfort her (as the midwife comforted Rachel in labor in Genesis 35:17) with the news of a newborn son, which would otherwise be the highest joy and honor for women in ancient Israel.[45] But the wife of Phinehas takes no comfort in delivering a son: "She did not respond or pay any attention" (4:20). In face of the calamity, she pays no regard to her motherhood and her own impending death. The fact that this unnamed woman is recorded here is unusual, since she only plays a minor role (being referred to in the narrative through her relationships with other major figures). This has to do with the noteworthy and interpretative comments she gives to the name of her child.

She names the child Ichabod (אי־כבוד). The exact meaning of the name of this child has to be examined further for better clarity. One possibility is it means "Where is the glory?"[46] Others suggest reading it as "no glory,"[47] "Woe, Barchabod"[48] or "Woe, the Glory."[49] I slightly favor the first reading in view of an instructive comparison with Ugaritic and other biblical Hebrew names.[50] By all means, the sense of a negative connotation is clearly implied in all these possible readings. The joy and honor of being a mother are tarnished in the face of "the stigma of national shame,"[51] namely, the Philistines' capture of the ark. This pitiful woman dies in sadness, overwhelmed with shame.

---

45. Marsman, *Woman*, 192; Arnold, *1 and 2 Samuel*, 108.

46. Brueggemann, *Ichabod toward Home*, 8; Tsumura, *First Book of Samuel*, 201; Steinmann, *1 Samuel*, 130; McCarter, *I Samuel*, 115–116.

47. Fokkelman, *Vow and Desire*, 232; Miller and Roberts, *Hand of the Lord*, 52; Arnold, *1 and 2 Samuel*, 108.

48. The LXX renders it Οὐαὶ βαρχαβωθ. βαρχαβωθ is probably two words from a transliteration of בַּר כָּבוֹד – "son of glory" – a sarcastic name giving definition to the son who was born (the situation was anything but glorious). Another possibility is that βαρ refers to βάρος ("oppressiveness, weight, load"), pairing it with the second term χαβωθ appositionally, thus meaning perhaps "heaviness, glory." Among these two options, I favor the first reading.

49. Codex Alexandrinus has Οὐαὶ χαβωθ.

50. Steinmann, *1 Samuel*, 130; McCarter, *I Samuel*, 115–16. The Hebrew interrogative particle אַי ("where?") is likely a cognate of the Ugaritic *'iy* which has the most basic meaning "where is?" Similar is the biblical name Jezebel (אִיזֶבֶל), meaning "Where is (the) Prince?" (or "Alas, the prince"), and Ithamar (אִיתָמָר), "Where is the palm tree?" (or "Alas, the palm tree"; Exod 6:23).

51. Fokkelman, *Vow and Desire*, 232.

The implication of this name is clearly stated in her repetition in verses 21–22 of גלה כבוד מישראל, "The glory has gone into exile from Israel." For this woman, the glory has gone into exile from Israel because the ark was taken away (לקח),[52] though verse 21 also includes the deaths of her father-in-law and her husband. But the ark's loss, being the most serious problem, is placed first in verse 21 (contra its climactic position in verse 17). The additional explanation (כי) in verse 22 also makes it perfectly clear to readers that the loss of the ark is her foremost concern. Despite the fact that she bore a son, the gravity of the national catastrophe is so intense that it overshadows her joy. The assumption is that her boy will tragically grow up in a world without hope or a future.

It is interesting that the wife of Phinehas links the ark with the glory of YHWH. In Moses's time, God's glory filled the tabernacle (משכן, "the dwelling place"), in which the ark resided in the midst of God's people (Exod 40:34–36). God's glory was the essence of God's being and presence.[53] If God was to "gain glory" through the exodus deliverance (Exod 14:4, 17), Israel's encounter here is ironically a reversal of that memory – the "glory" has departed from Israel.[54] From a theological perspective, the absence of the glory of the Lord is the reason that Israel is routed before the Philistines. The name of the child thus expresses the problem of the absent God.[55] Now, with the ark of God captured, Shiloh is only an empty tabernacle.[56] Thus the glory of God (i.e. God himself) will no longer be in their midst. It is a shame and lament that Israel now has an empty temple without God dwelling in it.

---

52. The verb is repeated as many as five times (4:11, 17, 19, 21, 22) to emphasize the fact that "the ark was taken."

53. Brueggemann thinks the glory refers to God in all his sovereign splendor and power (cf. 1 Sam 15:29). See Brueggemann, *First and Second Samuel*, 33. Ezekiel beheld the glory of God while he was exiled in Babylon (Ezekiel 1). It is interesting that the glory of God was movable and not constrained to the tabernacle or the temple (Ezekiel 10). But that was perhaps a more developed theological understanding of the glory of God in post-exilic times.

54. Birch, "1 and 2 Samuel," 1011.

55. Klein, *1 Samuel*, 45; Brueggemann, *First and Second Samuel*, 33.

56. It is often assumed that Shiloh was also desolated (Ps 78:60; Jer 7:12) by the Philistines following this defeat. See Driver, *Notes*, 50; Steinmann, *1 Samuel*, 132–133; Arnold, *1 and 2 Samuel*, 109.

The significance of the exile of the glory of God, or the loss of the ark of the covenant,[57] should not be underestimated. Since the ark is "the most visible and powerful symbol of Israel's covenant relationship with Yahweh," its loss implies the loss of Israel's unique covenant relationship with YHWH.[58] Israel falls into unprecedented shame and despair with the loss of the ark, thus "we reach a point in Israelite history lower than any since the captivity in Egypt. The author resists the temptation to depict the horror of the situation in any deeper colours."[59] With the forfeiture of YHWH's covenant relationship with Israel, Israel has been abandoned by its God.[60] Though the sins of the sons of Eli are not explicitly mentioned here, it is still noticeable that Israel is no longer worthy of the presence of the Lord.[61] In other words, the problem is not YHWH being unmindful of his covenantal duty but his required justice in punishment for sins. YHWH's allegiance to his covenant with his people, as shall be unfolded in 1 Samuel 4–6, is still unwavering.

The wife of Phinehas rightly stated that the glory of the Lord was not present with Israel in this crisis (YHWH is not acting for the interests of Israel). However, the nature of גלה ("go into exile")[62] seems to imply that the God of Israel is not gone forever. The ark is only on a "temporary exile" because the God of Israel cannot be subjugated even if the ark is captured and in the hands of the enemy.[63] The insinuation could be that someday the glory of the Lord may make an unexpected return to Israel according to his free will, as will be exhibited in 1 Samuel 6.

---

57. The term "covenant" is mentioned four times in vv. 3–4 to emphasize YHWH's commitment to Israel.

58. Arnold, *1 and 2 Samuel*, 108–109.

59. Hertzberg, *I and II Samuel*, 50.

60. Eslinger, *Kingship of God*, 173.

61. Hertzberg, *I and II Samuel*, 50–51. The train of thought is explained in more detail in Psalm 78:56–64.

62. The use of this term does not necessarily presume the Babylonian exile, meaning Israel's later exile to Babylon. See Tsumura, *First Book of Samuel*, 201. Fokkelman also notes the wordplay on גלה in 3:21 and 4:21–22 in highlighting the Samuel/Eli contrast: Samuel becoming the recipient of divine revelation in 3:21, whereas the Elide line suffers destruction in 4:21–22. See Fokkelman, *Vow and Desire*, 151–152.

63. Gordon, *1 and 2 Samuel*, 36.

5.2 The God of the Philistines Shamed Before the God of Israel (1 Sam 5:1–5)

The discussion of the above section culminates in the glory of the Lord going into exile and the divine presence leaving Israel. Now, with the ark of God fallen into the hands of the enemy, the focus of attention is diverted to the land of the Philistines, where the ark was taken. The ark of God, however, cannot be submissively restrained in an alien land. It refuses to be manipulated in the hands of the foe.

After the battle, the Philistines capture (לקח) the ark of God and take it from Ebenezer to Ashdod. Then they bring the ark into the house of Dagon (i.e. the main god of the Philistines)[64] and set it up beside (אצל) Dagon (5:2).[65] Such actions need to be explained in order for readers to better understand their significance. As discussed, the God of Israel is susceptible to suffering shame in Israel's defeat. What makes it worse is that the Philistines captured the ark of God and triumphantly presented it as a war trophy before Dagon, paying respect and honor to their own deity.

One has to note that ancient human battles were often considered as contests for superiority between the deities of the two opposite sides. According to Bechtel, the hanging question in the constant struggle for superiority was "who is the high God?" The victorious god received honor and the defeated god (being inferior) was shamed.[66] Thus the action of bringing the ark of God into the temple of Dagon is emblematic – it enhances the honor of Dagon and humiliates the God of Israel (the ark being the most visible symbol of

---

64. Dagon (alias "Dagan") was perhaps seen by the Philistines as the god of grain; the deity was certainly adopted from the ancient Mesopotamian region. See J. F. Healey, "Dagon," in *DDD*, 216–219. For more information on Philistine culture and religion in its different forms and its relationship with Israel's religion, see Albright, *Yahweh and the Gods*; Day, *Yahweh and the Gods*.

65. It is interesting that the ark of God was placed alongside Dagon. Such a move plausibly indicates that the Philistines may have adopted the captured god to be their own god as an object of worship, despite the fact that Dagon had been proven to be "superior" to YHWH. The ark was probably seen as a minor god honoring the might of Dagon. After all, the Philistines had seen the god(s) of the Israelites as threatening. See Miller and Roberts, *Hand of the Lord*, 57. Similarly, the handling suggests the ark's "equality" to Dagon. See Bechtel, "Perception of Shame," 91. The *hiphil* verbs used in vv. 1–2 suggest the Philistines' freedom and initiative in directing and deciding the pace of the movement; their quest was to humble the God of Israel by taking his ark as a trophy to Dagon. See Fokkelman, *Vow and Desire*, 252.

66. Contests for superiority among the deities were clearly seen in the Assyrian practice of capture and spoliation of the images of defeated gods. See Bechtel, "Perception of Shame," 89–90.

his presence).[67] Dagon had been the superior god in battle and YHWH appeared to be the inferior one. Thus, a symbol of the "inferior" god – the ark of YHWH – has to be taken as a war captive in order to publicly demonstrate its inferiority. Simultaneously, the superiority of Dagon is assured and proclaimed.

Though the gods of the Philistines are not even mentioned in 1 Samuel 4, the Philistines obviously give the credit of the decisive victory to their own gods. As shown in their own woe laments (4:7–8), they thought their fight against Israel was doomed with the presence of the ark in the camp of Israel. Emotionally speaking, it was a fight they were not prepared for. Unlike Israel, the Philistines did not have any tangible symbol of their gods with them. Despite their call to a courageous fight, it seemed the chance for them to win was slim. In the eyes of the Philistines, it was a fight between human strength and divine strength. However, the outcome of the battle turned out to be quite unexpected: the Philistines won. It was a miracle for the Philistines. Thus it was very natural for them to uplift the gods who energized them and turned around the tide of the war, because they saw this victory as divinely driven. The Philistines and their god defeated Israel and its god.[68] Brueggemann vividly portrays the envisaged scene as the ark of God was being transported to the house of Dagon in a triumphal procession:[69]

> The Philistines move the evidence of victory to Ashdod, core habitat of Dagon. The Philistines form a victory parade that features all the captured booty of war. YHWH is a prisoner of war put on exhibit. One can imagine the Philistines on the sidewalks of Ashdod cheering; YHWH on YHWH's ark caged, looking through the bars of the cage, utterly humiliated, now in Ashdod, far from home, far from governance, failed. . . . The parade winds its way to the temple where the priests of Dagon wait to receive the victory, engaging in prayers of thanksgiving, escalating the victory from military combat to cosmic significance.

---

67. So, for example, the vessels of the house of the Lord were carried away from Jerusalem and placed in the house of the Babylonian gods during the reign of Nebuchadnezzar (Ezra 1:7). By doing so, the Babylonian gods were ostensibly honored and YHWH humiliated.
68. Miller and Roberts, *Hand of the Lord*, 46.
69. Brueggemann, *Ichabod toward Home*, 26–27.

The priests at the door of the temple receive the parade, accept the booty, and carefully bring the booty to the icon of Dagon, who may not be the "Divine Warrior," but who is good enough to prevail over Israel. Perhaps in their version, the priests and people uttered the victory liturgy:

Lift up your heads, O gates!
and be lifted up, O ancient doors!
that the King of glory may come in.
Who is the King of Glory?
Dagon, strong and mighty,
Dagon mighty in battle . . .
he is the King of glory. (see Ps. 24:7–10)

These creative and even humorous comments helpfully accentuate the perception of the struggle for status and significance involving Dagon and YHWH. Dagon, supposedly the victorious god, is honored and YHWH, the God of Israel, is shamed. However, the contest proper between Dagon and YHWH is just about to begin.

The next day, when the people of Ashdod rise early in the morning, lo and behold (הנה adds the element of surprise), there is Dagon, fallen with his face on the ground before the ark of YHWH (5:3). It is a mysterious night. During the night YHWH had defeated Dagon and knocked him down on the ground.[70] The position of putting one's face down was used to "humiliate captive kings or warriors by making them feel helpless and defenseless, a way of lowering their status, literally a way of 'putting them down.' If bowing the head demonstrated submission and often humiliation, then lying facedown on the ground represented ultimate submission and shame."[71] In a striking reversal of roles, YHWH shames Dagon. Dagon's face, the body organ

---

70. The lack of description of any action from YHWH in the narrative has made Eslinger infer that Dagon's submission before YHWH, or the presence of the ark, was the willing submission of an inferior god quite naturally showing deference in the presence of a superior. See Eslinger, *Kingship of God*, 191. However, the *qal* passive participle כְּרֻתוֹת ("being cut off") in 5:4 (i.e. the second fall of Dagon) seems to suggest a passive and forceful submission. Firth also suggests that the implication is that YHWH cut off the head and hands of Dagon; see Firth, "Parallelismus Memborum," 652–654.

71. Bechtel, "Perception of Shame," 91.

embodying one's respect and honor, is fallen on the ground.⁷² Dagon utterly loses his face before the ark of YHWH.

To their embarrassment, the people of Ashdod took (לקח) the image of Dagon and returned him to his place.⁷³ It is ironic that Dagon, the god of the Philistines, required human aid to get back to its original place.

On the second morning, the people of Ashdod rose up and found Dagon again fallen with his face on the ground before the ark of YHWH.⁷⁴ But it was even worse. This time Dagon's head and the two palms of his hand had been cut off (כְּרֻתוֹת)⁷⁵ on the threshold; only the trunk of Dagon remained intact (5:4). Since the head was a symbol of superiority and the palms of the hands a symbol of physical power,⁷⁶ a god without his head and his palms demonstrated its weakness and impotence. In this contest for superiority, Dagon was proven to be an inferior god before YHWH. Dagon was further shamed.

The victory of YHWH over Dagon also indicates that it was not due to the impotence of YHWH that the Israelites had lost their earlier battles against the Philistines (4:2, 10). As known to the readers, Israel was to be blamed for their own sins and the defeat was thus intended by YHWH himself.

It is also interesting to note that Dagon was subdued before the ark of YHWH (ארון יהוה). The name for the God of Israel mentioned in verses 3-4 (by the voice of the narrator) is the covenant-making God (Exod 3:15), namely, YHWH.⁷⁷ The more generic description of God – ארון אלהים (the ark of God [of Israel]) – is applied when it is associated with the Philistine foes who do not know YHWH (5:1-2, 7, 8 [3x], 10 [2x], 11; 6:3) or the disfavored

---

72. For a discussion of "face" (פנים) with its relationship to honor/shame, see section 2.10.

73. The wordplay of לקח is noted. Previously, the Philistines took (לקח; occurring twice in vv. 1-2) the ark of the God as captive. Its repeated occurrences in 4:3, 11, 17, 19, 21, 22 are also significant.

74. The repeated fall proves Dagon's collapses were not accidental. Wiggins even argues that the use of *npl* points to Dagon's death; see Wiggins, "Old Testament Dagan," 268-274.

75. The *qal* passive participle suggests that it was an outside force that cut them off.

76. Wolff, *Anthropology*, 67-69.

77. The elders of Israel stressed that it was the ark of the covenant of YHWH they wanted to bring to the battlefield (4:3-4). The description of the ark of YHWH in 4:6 is the narrator's voice instead of that of the Philistines. The use of the "ark of YHWH" is dominant in the rest of the ark narrative (6:1, 2, 8, 11, 15, 18, 19, 21; 7:1[x2]). Even the Philistines use the "ark of YHWH" in 6:2 and 6:8. Perhaps the Philistines have begun to recognize YHWH as the national God of Israel and to acknowledge his unique power. See Tsumura, *First Book of Samuel*, 213; Fokkelman, *Vow and Desire*, 262. What was restored was the honor of the covenant-making God.

Elide line (4:11, 17, 18, 19, 21).[78] But it seems here that the God of Israel did not act for the sake of his commitment to the Israelites because the sinful leadership was the reason he abandoned his people. It is probably fair to say that YHWH, who was concerned about the name of his own reputation, acted for his own glory and honor. The God of Israel was not to be trifled with in the sight of the foreign gods.

With a reversal of fortune, the contest for superiority between Dagon and YHWH concludes with the defeat of Dagon and the victory of YHWH. The narrator's additional comment explains why the priests of Dagon and all who enter the house of Dagon do not tread on the threshold of Dagon in Ashdod "until this day" (5:5).[79] The threshold became a taboo because it was on this place Dagon exposed his weakness and humiliation with his severed head and hands. It portrayed such a tradition of shame that it left a lasting and indelible influence on the psyche of the Ashdodites.

5.3 The Hand of the Lord Is "Heavy" upon the Cities of the Philistines (1 Sam 5:6–12)

YHWH demonstrated his awesome power and superiority against Dagon, the god of the Philistines. But the occasion on which YHWH overthrew the Philistine god was the darkness of night and the privacy of the temple, and thus unseen by any. The ark of God, however, had been captured and brought in openly in humiliation. Thus YHWH will also openly direct his judgment against the Philistines, defending his own honor. The ark of God wrings such havoc throughout the land of the Philistines that the people there beg to return it to its proper place. Previously, the wife of Phinehas lamented that the כבוד had gone into exile from Israel (4:21), but when the Lord appeared in the land of the Philistines, the burden was too "heavy" (כבד) for them to bear.

---

78. An obvious example is in 4:4, where the narrator uses the "ark of the covenant of YHWH of hosts" (ארון ברית יהוה צבאות) to describe the ark being carried but switches to use the "ark of God" (ארון אלהים) when pointing to the evil sons of Eli. Firth has also noted the stylistic differences between the different terminologies concerning the ark, but it seems he fails to see the possible reason behind the stylistic changes. See Firth, *1 & 2 Samuel*, 93. Campbell, however, simply sees it as different traditions of growth in the text. See Campbell, *1 Samuel*, 72.

79. The narrator's insertion, "until this day," is a historical note that shows the time gap between this event and the time of the composition of the narrative, adding credibility to the witness.

The Philistines were aware that the Lord had struck the Egyptians with plagues in previous generations (4:8). Now they themselves were suffering this terrible fate. Ashdod and its territory were inflicted with "hemorrhoids" (5:6).[80] Though the LXX suggests mice as the host and transport of the disease, the narrator has attributed the deeper cause of the plague to the works of YHWH. The "hand of the Lord" was seen as the prime force. In contrast to Dagon, the palms of whose hands were chopped off and thus powerless, the hand of the Lord was heavy (כבד) on the Ashdodites, relentlessly destroying and smiting them (5:6).[81] People in the ancient Near East often perceived of plagues as the ominous judgments of the "hand" of a god. Thus, in the Philistine mind, there was no doubt that the disaster was due to the hand of the Lord.[82] When the Ashdodites realized the situation, they decided that "the ark of the God

---

80. There is a textual issue here – the *qere* reads טחרים while the *ketib* has עפלים. The term עפלים, originally "hills, mounds," may be a euphemism for referring to general "swellings" (being a coarse word) without pronouncing the actual name of the disease (Tsumura, *First Book of Samuel*, 208). The term טחרים is used interchangeably with עפלים in the MT (see also Deut 28:27) to perhaps clarify the nature of עפלים. A majority of lexica explains טחרים as "haemorrhoids" (see *DCH*, 3:363; *HALOT* 2, 374; "Hämorrhoiden" in Ges[18], 423), thus it is not surprising that עפלים is also interpreted as hemorrhoids in these lexica (see *DCH*, 6:514; *HALOT* 2, 861; Ges[18], 995;). Only BDB is implicit by glossing טחרים as "tumours" (p. 377) while giving three different medical diagnoses (i.e. eject; strain at stool; dysentery) to this term, but it still equates the meaning of טחרים in the ark narrative (1 Sam 5:6, 9, 12; 6:4–5) with that of עפלים, "hemorrhoids." Again, BDB lists עפלים (see p. 779) under the definition "hemorrhoids," marking its multiple occurrences in the ark narrative. The LXX also takes עפלים as an infection of the anus (cf. 5:12; ἐπλήγησαν εἰς τὰς ἕδρας, "were smitten upon the seats"). The LXX in 5:6 has connected the plague with infected rats, first in the ships and then in the land (καὶ ἐξέζεσεν αὐτοῖς εἰς τὰς ναῦς, καὶ μέσον τῆς χώρας αὐτῆς ἀνεφύησαν μύες, "and it burst forth upon them into the ships, and mice sprang up in the midst of its country"), but the MT does not mention the "golden mice" image until 6:4–5, perhaps implying the mice as an element in the plague. Geyer, "Mice and Rites," 293–304, cites Caird (G. B. Caird, *IB* 2 (New York and Nashville, 1953)) on p. 295 as reading that the mice were the carrier of the plague (a view which I favor), and cites Thenius (O. Thenius, *Kurzgefasstes exegetisches Handbuch zum AT*[2] (Leipzig, 1864)), Klostermann (A. Klostermann, *Kurzgefasster Kommentar* (Nordlingen, 1887)) and Stoebe's (H. J. Stoebe, *KAT* (Gütersloh, 1973)) composite reading that the tumors affected the cities and the mice plagued the rural areas (a combination of the LXX and the MT). Geyer appears to read the golden mice as a symbol of ancient ritual practice for the removal of the plague. By all means, the plague was caused by divine judgment as a result of disobedience (Deut 28:27). The relationship with "mice" has led some to identify the disease as a bubonic plague. See Driver, "Plague of the Philistines," 50–52; Wilkinson, "Philistine Epidemic," 137–141.

81. The "hand of the Lord" is noted with its association for bringing a plague against the Egyptians in Exodus 9:3. See Tsumura, *First Book of Samuel*, 207. Miller and Roberts see the "hand" of YHWH (4:8; 5:6, 7, 9, 11; 6:3, 5, 9) as an important thematic motif in the ark narrative that demonstrates the power of YHWH through the phenomenon of the plague. See Miller and Roberts, *Hand of the Lord*, 64.

82. Arnold, *1 and 2 Samuel*, 119.

of Israel must not remain" with them (5:7). They also acknowledged that the hand of the God of Israel was "severe" (קשתה) against them and against Dagon their God.[83] The God of Israel who fought against the Egyptians was now fighting against the Philistines and their gods.

The Ashdodites convened an urgent meeting with other lords of the Philistines to discuss the problem asking, "What shall we do with the ark of the God of Israel?" The decision from the meeting was to let the ark to be moved to Gath. As suggested, the moving plan was immediately executed (5:8). The expectation was that a plague could be avoided if the ark of God was moved to the next place. The Philistines presumed that the disaster in Ashdod could have happened only by chance. They refused to submit to the might and power of the God of Israel as they continued to retain the ark and exhibit their "unrepentant will."[84]

The LXX presents the Gittites as taking the initiative to care for the ark of God.[85] It appears that the Philistines were still "sitting on their high horse."[86] But the high spirit of the Gittites soon came to an end as soon as the ark of God was brought into the city. Again the hand of the Lord was against the Philistines, and it struck all humans in the city of Gath with the same "hemorrhoids" that occurred previously in the city of Ashdod. The same pattern of plague is established, and no one is exempted from the disaster, both young and old. Thus there was a great panic in Gath (5:9). The situation was probably too urgent for the Gittites to summon another meeting as in Ashdod; rather, they simply sent the ark of God straightaway to Ekron even without the city's consent. They just wanted to get rid of this "holy object" as quickly as possible.

As soon as the ark of God came to Ekron, people in the city, who must have heard about God's prior awesome works in the cities of Ashdod and Gath, cried out (ויזעקו) in lament, "They have moved to me the ark of the God of Israel to kill me and my people" (5:10).[87] The Ekronites did not understand

---

83. The verb קשה, being used also in the exodus account (Exod 7:3; 13:15), is used synonymously with כבד in the previous verse (v. 6).

84. Eslinger, *Kingship of God*, 195.

85. The LXX of 1 Samuel 5:8b reads: καὶ λέγουσιν οἱ Γεθθαῖοι μετελθέτω κιβωτὸς τοῦ θεοῦ πρὸς ἡμᾶς ("And the Gittites said, "Let the ark of God come over to us").

86. Hertzberg, *I and II Samuel*, 55.

87. The LXX contains plural pronouns, πρὸς ἡμᾶς . . . θανατῶσαι ἡμᾶς καὶ τὸν λαὸν ἡμῶν ("to us . . . to kill us and our people"). The LXX probably attempted to smoothen the more difficult singular wording of the Hebrew text. Similar plural changes are made in 5:11.

why this plague-bringing object was brought in their midst. Thus, as did the Ashdodites, they immediately gathered another urgent meeting with all the lords of the Philistines to discuss the crisis brought about by the ark of God. With no other alternative, the Ekronites demanded that the lords must send away the ark of the God of Israel[88] and let it return to its place (i.e. its original place in Israel).[89] The purpose was that it might not "kill me and my people."[90] Indeed, the panic of death pervaded the whole city and the people who were spared from death were struck with the same "hemorrhoids." The situation was even worse than before, for death is clearly mentioned (vv. 11–12). The narrator once again explains that the hand of the Lord was too heavy (כבדה) there (5:11b), pointing to divine wrath as the cause of the plague. Thus Fokkelman says, "All destruction must be understood as a manifestation of God's 'weight.'"[91] The power of YHWH proved his "weight"; thus the expression "the heavy hand" is used repeatedly.

Despite the cry of the city (שועת העיר) going up to heaven, none of their gods could heed it and come to their aid. It is ironic that, in the exodus account, when the Israelites' cry (שועתם) came up to God in the midst of their slavery, the God of Israel heard their cry and remembered his covenant (Exod 2:23).[92] While the hand of the Lord brought severe affliction upon the land of the Philistines, the handless Dagon could do nothing about it.[93]

Thus far YHWH has demonstrated his might and power both before Dagon and the Philistines. The Philistines now learn the hard lesson that the God of Israel was not to be offended, and his honor had to be acknowledged. The ark of God refused to be manipulated as a demeaned object – a trophy of their victory.[94] The "glory" (כבוד) from Israel (4:21) was now in charge, and

---

88. The term "the ark of the God of Israel," occurring in 5:7, 8 (x3), 10, 11; 6:3, reflects a Philistine view of the close relationship between Israel and its God.

89. The Philistines were forced to respectfully return the ark of God to its (own) place. Dagon, however, must receive human support to return it to its place (5:3; למקומו) after being knocked down by the God of Israel. The contrast of power is obvious.

90. Driver attributes the first-person pronouns in 5:10–11 to a person speaking in the name of the people as a whole. See Driver, *Notes*, 53.

91. Fokkelman, *Vow and Desire*, 259.

92. Also in 1 Samuel 9:16, this "cry," paralleling the exodus account, is likewise noted by Klein, *1 Samuel*, 51–52; Driver, *Notes*, 53; Eslinger, *Kingship of God*, 197–198. The same contrasting parallel can be found with the verb זעק in Exodus 2:23 and 1 Samuel 5:10.

93. Arnold, *1 and 2 Samuel*, 119.

94. Arnold, 117.

it proved to be too burdensome (כבד) for the Philistines to take. The *kabod*, occurring multiple times in 1 Samuel 5, also indicates that the God of Israel has "indeed 'gotten glory' over the Philistines and over Dagon," as he had gained glory previously in the smiting of Pharaoh and his army (Exod 14:4, 17).[95] The God of Israel is exalted. Thus Eslinger comments, "The keynote of Yahweh's Philistine adventure is glorification amongst the nations (6:5–6)."[96] The Philistines, like the Egyptians, are defeated and humiliated by the powerful hand of the Lord.

5.4 The Unusual Return of the Ark of the Lord (1 Sam 6:1–18)

The God of Israel was glorified as Dagon was defeated in his own temple, and the Philistines who humiliated the ark of God were heavily inflicted with the plague of "hemorrhoids." The demand the Ekronites insisted on was that the Philistines must immediately send back the ark of the God of Israel to its own place in Israel (5:11). In this section, the main concern is how the ark of the Lord could be properly returned to Israel and the implication of such an action.

The time the ark remained in the land of the Philistines was about seven months (6:1). It is surprising that they allowed the ark to stay there for such a long period given the presence of a severe plague in their midst.[97] It perhaps portrays the stubbornness of their hearts in resisting God's awesome work. Thus the length of seven months implies that the Philistines had reached the "maximum limit" of their suffering.[98] This time the Philistines convened a special meeting with the priests and the diviners[99] to discuss the matter. They

---

95. Brueggemann, *First and Second Samuel*, 39. Fokkelman also notes the heavy/light polarity (כבד vs. קלל I) characterizing the catastrophes of chapter 5 and the reverent strategy for atonement in chapter 6. Both terms have positive and negative implementation in these chapters; see Fokkelman, *Vow and Desire*, 250. The semantic opposition between these two terms often suggests the realm of honor and shame.

96. Eslinger, *Kingship of God*, 189.

97. The LXX 6:1 adds the presence of the infected mice in the land.

98. Tsumura, *First Book of Samuel*, 213.

99. The LXX adds τοὺς ἐπαοιδοὺς αὐτῶν ("and their enchanters"). 4QSam[a] adds a fourth category, ולמעונ[ני]ם ("and to the soothsayers"). All these people were religious professionals skilled in eliciting communications from the divine realm. See McCarter, *1 Samuel*, 132.

turned to their own religious specialists for consultation, since the handling of the ark of YHWH was considered a spiritually sensitive case that endangered the lives of many. The question of concern was how they should properly return the ark of YHWH: "What shall we do to the ark of YHWH? Tell us with what we shall send it off to its place?" The Philistine rulers already knew the presence of the ark was the probable cause of the plague. The pressing question was how to send it back to Israel without further offending the God of Israel. In the eyes of the Philistines, the God whom the ark represented was offended, since the ark was taken by force and was presented humiliatingly as a trophy to their gods. The offended God had become angry and that was why the plague occurred. Any improper treatment of this crisis might further deteriorate the situation, and thus the situation needed special attention from their religious leaders. Meanwhile, sending back the ark was an acknowledgement of "religio-political defeat" on the side of the Philistines[100] which would further inflict shame on themselves. Thus they exercised extreme caution in dealing with this matter.

The Philistine priests and diviners responded to the inquiry, "If you are sending away the ark of the God of Israel, you must not send it away empty (ריקם). You must surely return a guilt offering (אשם) to him" (6:3a). The warning was that when the Philistines returned the ark of God, they must not send it away empty-handed.[101] The reason for doing so was self-explanatory: a proper compensation gift had to be made to appease this God, since they had done him wrong earlier. Otherwise, it would constitute a serious offense to the honor of the God of Israel. It is important to note that the Philistines began to differentiate between YHWH and the ark. They now knew what really mattered was the invisible God who stood behind the ark.[102]

The exact meaning of אשם requires discussion here. The term is mostly used as a sacrificial term in the Priestly Code as atonement for transgressions against a deity with an emphasis on the requirement of restitution for the offender.[103] The use of this term in 1 Samuel 6 should be seen from such a

---

100. Tsumura, *First Book of Samuel*, 214.

101. See the parallel with the exodus account in Exodus 3:21–22. See Tsumura, *First Book of Samuel*, 214–215; McCarter, *1 Samuel*, 132; Eslinger, *Kingship of God*, 205.

102. Fokkelman, *Vow and Desire*, 265–266.

103. Kellermann, "אָשָׁם," *TDOT*, 1:431–432. See, for example, the use of אָשָׁם in Lev 5; 6:7, 10, 14; 19:21, 22; Num 6:12; 18:9.

background to mean "propitiatory sacrifice, compensation, indemnification."[104] According to Milgrom's investigation, the אשם sacrifice "expiates for sacrilege."[105] He explains further, it "expiates for the *desecration* of the sanctuary and its sancta (including God's personal sanctum – his name)."[106] In other words, the Philistines may have thought they had committed sacrilege against YHWH by coercively bringing the ark of God and humiliatingly putting it on parade. It was a sacrilege against YHWH because they had mockingly degraded the great God of Israel as a "minor" deity when he was in fact the greatest God of all gods (Ps 95:3; 96:4–5; 97:9; 135:5; 136:2–3), whose name should be honored (Ps 96:6–7; 104:1; 145:5) and revered (Ps 96:4; 102:15) above the whole earth.

Now to remove the offense and the disaster brought by this angry God, a compensation gift ("indemnity," NJPS), as a form of a "reparation offering,"[107] must be paid as "protection against further suffering."[108] The offering was thus "an appeal for divine forgiveness and a halt to punishment" which assumed a posture of submission.[109] The chance was that the Philistines could be healed from these catastrophes by obeying the words of the religious leaders. As the Philistines came to seek knowledge (6:2), the priests now emphasize the importance of such common knowledge (6:3) as it being none other than YHWH who had brought about the catastrophes.[110] The word that "his hand does not turn away from you" is a euphemistic way of addressing the divine disaster. If the Philistines could acknowledge the source of their problems, it would be easier to handle the crisis. The God of Israel could only possibly be placated if they gave him honor and, to this end, offered him highly

---

104. Kellermann, "אָשָׁם," *TDOT*, 1:431.

105. Milgrom, "Further," 511.

106. Milgrom, 514. The emphasis is his.

107. Milgrom, 511; Klein, *1 Samuel*, 56. Similarly, Fokkelman sees it as a "peace offering" (expiatory gift) for compensation; see Fokkelman, *Vow and Desire*, 264.

108. McCarter, *1 Samuel*, 133; likewise Miller and Roberts, *Hand of the Lord*, 69.

109. Eslinger, *Kingship of God*, 205.

110. The key word "know" (ידע) appears both in v. 2 and v. 3. Fokkelman, *Vow and Desire*, 264. But 4QSam[a] reads נכפר לכם[ו], "[and] it shall be ransomed for [you]" which is supported by the LXX καὶ ἐξιλασθήσεται ὑμῖν instead of the verb "know" (ונודע) in v. 3. It is hard to rule out such a possible reading. See Miller and Roberts, *Hand of the Lord*, 70; McCarter, *1 Samuel*, 133. McCarter explains that the term *kippēr* refers primarily to purgation from ritual impurity.

valuable offerings as compensation.[111] Likewise, Campbell comments that the reparation made for the given offense was not simply the return of the ark, but the concern for "the honor of its god."[112] God would be glorified at the submission of the Philistines.

The Philistines ask a second, practical, question: "What should be the guilt offering that we shall return to him?" The answer the priests and diviners give is "five golden hemorrhoids and five golden mice, according to the number of the lords of the Philistines,[113] since the same [lit. 'one'] plague was on all of you and your lords" (6:4). Why the mentioning of "one plague" when the offerings were the hemorrhoids and the mice? It is suggested that the hemorrhoids were the symptoms of the plague, and the mice were carriers of the disease (the ones destroying the land, v. 5).[114] The more intriguing question is why YHWH would even be interested in the ugly (disgusting) hemorrhoids and the unclean mice as offerings? Firth responds to this question by asserting that the giver's attitude is more important than the gift.[115] Tsumura suggests that the golden mice (or alternatively tumors) was "sympathetic magic" with the purpose of getting rid of the disease.[116] The answers provided do not seem satisfactory. My suggestion is that these golden objects not only point to the reality of the plague, but, more importantly, they bring to mind the previous arrogance of the Philistines and accentuate the sense of their own shame. After all, it would be extremely humiliating for the Philistines (as the defeated ones) to prepare these very unpleasant and repulsive golden objects.[117] Thus Fokkelman notes, the offerings were seen as "a gift to God, a

---

111. Fokkelman, *Vow and Desire*, 264. The plague prayers of Mursilis in a Hittite document also suggest restitution through compensational offerings as means of appeasing the Hattian storm-god. See Miller and Roberts, *Hand of the Lord*, 70–71.

112. Campbell, *1 Samuel*, 83.

113. It is suggested that the five main cities of the Philistines were inflicted with the plague (6:17–18), although 1 Samuel 5 only mentions three of them. The golden objects can be understood as "a kind of booty or plunder that the victorious God takes on his return home" (cf. Exod 3:22 and 12:36). See Miller and Roberts, *Hand of the Lord*, 73.

114. Firth, *1 & 2 Samuel*, 98. The LXX 5:6 and 6:1 also suggest mice as the transport of the plague. However, some think the LXX supports two independent plagues, namely, one of hemorrhoids and one of mice. See, for example, Hertzberg, *I and II Samuel*, 58.

115. Hertzberg, 99.

116. Tsumura, *First Book of Samuel*, 216.

117. These were not just golden images of hemorrhoids and mice, but *your* hemorrhoids and *your* mice (v. 5). Again, *their* hemorrhoids in v. 11. The deficiency of the Philistines is stressed.

sort of votive gift in the negative and honour him as victor."[118] The reason for making such ugly and dirty objects in gold was to recognize YHWH's honor in an astonishingly tangible and permanent form.[119] Thus, on the one hand, the golden hemorrhoids and mice are presented to YHWH as the offering of compensation gifts; on the other hand, it reminds the Philistines of the reality of their guilt and shame due to the grave offense they had committed against YHWH. The God of Israel has played a trick on the Philistines.[120]

The note on making the images of hemorrhoids and mice is reiterated for emphasis in verse 5. Together with the images, the Philistines are urged to give glory (כבוד) to the God of Israel; that is, they must honor him and acknowledge his glory. The concern for the glory of the God of Israel is the core message delivered here with imperative force. Thus Fokkelman says that the honor of YHWH was viewed as a "beacon" for the Philistines, Israel and the narrator.[121] It is true that the Philistines had offended God's honor by violently and humiliatingly treating the ark of God; now they have to make appropriate proceedings and valuable golden offerings to make up for this offense and restore his due honor.

Only under the condition of the Philistines' obedience would the God of Israel perhaps lighten (קלל I) his hand (i.e. relieve this plague)[122] over them and their gods and their lands. The religious leaders who should supposedly serve the interests of the Philistines seem to stand on the side of the Israelites. This is especially so in the following verse (v. 6): "Why would you make your hearts insensitive (תכבדו את לבבכם) as the Egyptians and Pharaoh made their hearts insensitive (כבדו)?[123] When God treated them harshly, did they not send the people away, and they departed?" Gordon makes an amusing observation that the Philistine priests were made to "speak like Hebrew prophets."[124]

---

118. Fokkelman, *Vow and Desire*, 278.

119. Fokkelman, 278.

120. NJPS (6:6) suggests that God "made a mockery" of the Egyptians and they had to let Israel go.

121. Fokkelman, *Vow and Desire*, 266.

122. Contra the heavy (כבד) hand of God in 5:6, 11.

123. The play of the key root כבד occurs here in the form of a new word, "to make (heavy) insensitive." Any refusal to give glory to the God of Israel suggests the implication of making one's heart insensitive (i.e. the unwillingness to let the ark go), which, according to the exodus experience, would lead to great suffering.

124. Gordon, *1 and 2 Samuel*, 36.

The allusion to the exodus memory is obvious in this speech. The Egyptians were obstinate in keeping the Israelites as their slaves and refused to let them go when YHWH called them out of Egypt. It was only when God dealt with them harshly through severe plagues that Pharaoh released them. The God of Israel received glory (כבוד) despite Pharaoh exhibiting insensitivity in his heart (Exod 8:11, 28; 9:34). The implication is that the Philistines did not have to learn the lesson the hard way, as did the Egyptians. Resistance to YHWH is in vain and obedience to this God of Israel is the easiest approach.

Despite saying all this, the Philistine priests are still skeptical about the works of YHWH in their midst.[125] They ask for a sign as proof of YHWH's involvement, even as they recommend the Philistines return the ark. The test is to use two new unyoked milking cows (with their young calves shut up at home) to deliver the ark of God and the guilt offerings on a new cart. The newness of the cart and the draught animals suggests an act of reverence and recognition of the God of Israel.[126] That is to say, they must acknowledge the honor of the God of Israel, expressing etiquette appropriate for such an occasion (contra the hostility of carrying the ark off as a trophy in 5:1–2).

If these cows go straight toward Beth-Shemesh, then it was he (i.e. YHWH, the God of Israel) who brought this disaster upon the land. If not, it would mean it only happened to them by coincidence (6:9). The Philistines crafted several barriers into this task. First, unyoked cows, as young beasts, would usually be impatient with the yoke constraint and go wherever they pleased since they would not have been trained properly.[127] As Gordon notes, the Philistines hoped for a complete absence of "human interference in their movements."[128] Second, milking cows would be emotionally attached to their young ones due to their maternal instinct and thus unsuitable for pulling the cart if their young calves were shut up at home.[129] Thus it was a test that, from a human perspective, was bound to fail. What the Philistine priests required

---

125. The consideration was if YHWH was not responsible for this plague, then some other deities were. The Philistines needed to search out the correct deity who was behind the plague. See Miller and Roberts, *Hand of the Lord*, 74.

126. Fokkelman, *Vow and Desire*, 272. The Philistines must strictly follow the cultic regulations and implement them with precision, as such would befit the service of the sacred.

127. Tsumura, *First Book of Samuel*, 217.

128. Gordon, *I & II Samuel*, 102.

129. Arnold, *1 and 2 Samuel*, 119; Hertzberg, *I and II Samuel*, 59; Steinmann, *1 Samuel*, 151. The cows would usually moan anxiously for their young ones and continuously search for

was next to impossible. Only a divine supernatural force would lead these cows to deliver the ark straight to Beth-Shemesh.

The Philistines follow the advice of their priests. The repetition in verses 10–11 serves to emphasize that the procedure is carried out as suggested: the cows are gathered, their calves separated from them, and the ark of YHWH and the golden offerings are placed on the cart.[130] The golden vessels are placed on the cart with true weight. The lament that "the כבוד has gone into exile from Israel" is over and the journey of "giving כבוד ['glory,' lit. weight] back to the God of Israel" has begun.[131] Now that the cows are ready to go, readers hold their breath to see what might happen to this journey.

Against normal expectations, the cows go straight ahead to Beth-Shemesh, without turning aside to the right or to the left (6:12).[132] It is as if an invisible divine hand is leading the two cows as they go along the one highway. As Arnold notes, the cows acted "against nature" and were "under divine compulsion."[133] These animals submitted to God's will and purpose despite their discomfort.[134] Even the cows served the interests of the God of Israel. The Philistine rulers, who went after the cows, were able to witness and monitor the whole event. It had been proved that what happened in the Philistine land was not by chance (מקרה). It was YHWH's honor they had offended, and thus the God of Israel brought the plague into their midst. The Philistines would have been relieved that they had made a right choice in following their priests' suggestions. As they returned the ark of God with these offerings as compensation gifts, they attempted to restore the honor to YHWH.

---

them during their absence. Having their full attention in pulling a cart was almost impossible in such a situation.

130. Firth, *1 & 2 Samuel*, 99.

131. The wordplay of the root כבד (glory/heavy) in the ark narrative is also noted by Miscall in various locations; see Miscall, *1 Samuel*, 29–32.

132. A threefold parallelism in v. 12 is noted by Fokkelman to emphasize the straightness of the route: 12a (the duplication of *drk*) and 12b (the duplication of *hlk*) positively repeating the straightness of the movement, with the left/right metric pair in 12c negatively describing what "not deviating" means; see Fokkelman, *Vow and Desire*, 281–282.

133. Arnold, *1 and 2 Samuel*, 121.

134. The action of their "lowing" was understood as the "reluctance of the animals." See Hertzberg, *I and II Samuel*, 59. I would see it as the cows' continuous summons to their young ones. The infinitive absolute can possibly function as a participle or as an action accompanying the main verb. See *IBHS*, § 35.5.3; GKC, § 113s; Joüon-Muraoka, § 123m.

The men of Beth-Shemesh[135] were reaping the wheat harvest in the valley and were surprised to find the ark unexpectedly returning. When they saw the ark, they rejoiced at the sight (6:13). Israel's rejoicing mood is set in contrast to the anxiety of the Philistines.[136] The Philistine rulers, perhaps motived by curiosity, stood aside to observe Israel's reception of the ark after being severely inflicted by its presence.

The cart came to a halt at the field of Joshua in Beth-Shemesh, where there was a large stone. The Levites took down the ark of YHWH, together with the chest containing the gold objects, and placed them on the large stone. The people immediately cut up the wood of the cart and offered the cows as a burnt offering and made sacrifices on that day to the Lord (6:14–15). The repetition of offering burnt offerings in verses 14–15 is sometimes explained by taking verse 15 as a later addition.[137] However, the repetition can arguably be treated as a supplemental detail within the narrative – adding the presence of Levites in verse 15 avoids any misunderstanding about the mishandling of the ark and the sacrifices.[138] Unlike the havoc brought upon the Philistine land, the presence of the ark of YHWH promotes a harmonious divine-human relationship in Israel. The ark's peaceful reunion with the Israelites further solidifies the evidence that it was YHWH who caused the smiting of the plague upon the land of the Philistines. Having watched the celebration ritual in Beth-Shemesh, the Philistine rulers know that the test was successful and thus return to Ekron that same day (6:16) with a sense of relief.

Verses 17–18 are the endnote for this section. They list the guilt offerings that the Philistines returned to YHWH. These were the five golden hemorrhoids: one for Ashdod, one for Gaza, one for Ashkelon, one for Gath, one for Ekron. Likewise, the number of the golden mice also corresponded to the number of Philistine cities that belonged to the five lords. Both fortified towns and unwalled villages are mentioned, thus describing the widespread influence of the mice in Philistia. The plague was the same in each Philistine town (6:4); none of them was exempted. The narrator recapitulates these

---

135. It was a Levitical city in Israel (Josh 21:16) that bordered Philistia. The name of the city, "house of the sun" (בית שמש), obviously retained its Canaanite flavor. According to Judges 1:33, Canaanites inhabited the city before Israel's arrival.

136. Tsumura, *First Book of Samuel*, 220.

137. McCarter, *1 Samuel*, 136; Klein, *1 Samuel*, 59.

138. Firth, *1 & 2 Samuel*, 100.

offering details even though they were mentioned previously in verse 5. This may have to do with the triumphant and boastful sentiment the Israelites felt after the Philistines' return of the ark of YHWH. The great stone,[139] which was still in the field of Joshua of Beth-Shemesh "until this day," bore silent witness to God's marvelous works against the Philistines.

To sum up, the Philistines' compulsory return of the ark of YHWH is significant in its theological implications. It was YHWH's honor they had offended in the capture of the ark of God. The divine direction of the ark's return to Israel not only convinced the Philistines to realize YHWH as the source of their plague but also compelled them to acknowledge and restore the honor of YHWH as they returned valuable guilt offerings to YHWH as compensation gifts.

5.5 God's Glory Is Not to Be Offended (1 Sam 6:19–7:1)

When readers think the ark's reunion with the Israelites will be the happy ending of the narrative, a turning point appears again. Without giving much information, it is said that he (presumably God) struck the men of Beth-Shemesh, because they looked at the ark of YHWH (6:19a). An immediate question is raised concerning this abrupt change of attitude. Why did YHWH strike his own people when he had accepted their offerings earlier? What was the exact offense of this "looking"? Nothing is said or explained in the text.

The LXX provides an alternative inserted reading at the beginning of verse 19: Καὶ οὐκ ἠσμένισαν οἱ υἱοὶ Ιεχονιου ἐν τοῖς ἀνδράσιν Βαιθσαμυς ("And the sons of Jechonias were not pleased with the men of Beth-shemesh. . . .").[140]

---

139. Thus the MT אבל הגדולה is emended to אבן הגדולה (following the LXX), which is mentioned earlier in vv. 14–15. Wellhausen revocalizes the MT וְעַד ("and as far as") to וְעֵד (וְעֵד הָאֶבֶן הַגְּדוֹלָה, "and a witness [is] the great stone") and thus offers a different interpretation; see Wellhausen, Der Text, 65.

140. McCarter, however, based on the syntax of Job 3:6 (the syntagm חדה ב meaning "to join in celebration"), following Klostermann, retroverts this into Hebrew וְלֹא חָדוּ בְנֵי יְכָנְיָהוּ בְּאַנְשֵׁי בֵית שֶׁמֶשׁ, thus translating it differently: "But the sons of Jeconiah did not join in the celebration with the men of Beth-Shemesh." Still, he considers that בְּנֵי יְכָנְיָהוּ is a corruption of בְּנֵי הַכֹּהֲנִים, thus suggesting it was the lack of the presence of the members of the priesthood that caused this casualty. Such a reading may accord with the testimony of Josephus (Ant. 6.16) where the smiting of the men of Beth-Shemesh was because they were not priests. See McCarter, I Samuel, 131; likewise, Miller and Roberts, Hand of the Lord, 77.

The insertion, which tries to make sense of the situation by supplementing more detail, however, is most likely a secondary gloss. The number of casualties in this smiting is another thing that complicates the problem. The MT reads שבעים איש חמשים אלף איש, "seventy men, fifty thousand men," namely 50,070 men (NET, NASB).[141] Modern scholars often think this huge number is an exaggeration for such a small town in ancient Israel due to its conflict with modern demographical/archaeological studies on ancient Palestine. Thus, many have conceded to accept a smaller number, namely, "seventy men among the people fifty thousand" (NJPS; *Ant.* 6.16).[142] If so, the preposition מן (or the enclitic מ) would have been omitted before חמשים by way of haplography.

A weakness of reading the number of "seventy" men is the description of the destruction as a "great smiting" (מכה גדולה). When the Israelites suffered their first defeat, they lost some four thousand men (4:2). The number was just reported. But when they were defeated in the second decisive battle, the casualties were much higher – thirty thousand infantrymen were killed (4:10).[143] This time, the grave defeat was described as a "great smiting" (מכה גדולה).

---

141. The word איש is absent in a few manuscripts. Some manuscripts add *waw* (ו) before חמשים. The LXX ἑβδομήκοντα ἄνδρας καὶ πεντήκοντα χιλιάδας ἀνδρῶν, adding καὶ in between ἑβδομήκοντα ("seventy") and πεντήκοντα χιλιάδας ("fifty thousand"), also clearly supports this reading. The variant readings, however, bring no significant change to the total listing of the number.

142. For scholars who support the reading of "seventy" men, see McCarter, *I Samuel*, 128; Klein, *1 Samuel*, 54; Firth, *1 & 2 Samuel*, 101; Arnold, *1 and 2 Samuel*, 121; Steinmann, *1 Samuel*, 152; Miller and Roberts, *Hand of the Lord*, 77; Fouts, "Added Support," 394. Tsumura, however, proposes a new interpretation of the terms חמשים (מ not as plural form but as an enclitic *mem*) and אלף (possibly "clan" or "thousand") and comes to the conclusion of 350 or 14,000 for the population of the clan (city). For details, see Tsumura, *First Book of Samuel*, 227. Tur-Sinai proposes the intended number is "one thousand," arguing that what precedes אלף איש should be read as a summary of the categories of persons smitten, שָׁב עִם אִישׁ חָמָשִׁם, "old men and warrior." See Tur-Sinai, "Ark of God," 280–282. But such a number is still considered high by historical estimates for the general demographic data of the time. Though "seventy" might be a more realistic number from the perspective of current historical research on ancient Palestine, it should be noted that what we have here is not an accurate historical record by modern standard but a story that portrays the general socio-political landscape of the pre-monarchic period of Israel. The narrator has his freedom to shape the story in accordance with his own concerns. A high number would accentuate the tragedy of Israel without the presence of its God.

143. Some would question these figures as well, given the likely population of the entire area at the time. But it is important that the narrator portrays it through such large numbers in his telling of the story. His motivation is not the pursuit of historical numerical accuracy but his theological concerns.

The exact phrase מכה גדולה also occurs here in 6:19. Can the loss of seventy men be considered a "great smiting"? I am less convinced to read it that way.

Now we are perhaps in a better position to respond to the question raised earlier at the beginning of this section: Why did God strike his people (and such a great number of people if one accepts the number as 50,070) for merely looking at the ark? The ancient Jewish historian Josephus, favoring seventy persons, claimed the Beth-Shemeshites who were not priests and were thus unworthy, had approached the ark (*Ant.* 6.16). McCarter agrees with such a view, saying that "Yahweh would not permit his ark to be approached with unclean hands."[144] The problem is that a lack of priests is not even implied in the text. As a Levitical city, it is likely that there were some priests in the city.[145]

Others have tried to explain it with other approaches. Bergen sees the problem as connected to the earlier "female animal offering" (vv. 14–15), which does not accord with the requirement of Torah (Lev 1:3) for the necessity of male animals being used in burnt offerings.[146] Arnold explains the loss as a continuous spread of the plague from the earlier contacts with the Philistines or perhaps a lack of proper care of the sacred ark.[147] The answers provided do not seem convincing or satisfactory.

The cause of this divine judgment, according to the MT, is that some Beth-Shemeshites looked at (ראה ב) the ark of God.[148] The conjecture is that some people may have been curious to see what happened with the ark after having been exiled in the land of the Philistines. Certainly, the chest which contained the offerings of five golden hemorrhoids and five golden mice was scrutinized. But was the ark of God the same after having passed through the hands of the Philistines?[149] It is possible that some people may have entertained such

---

144. McCarter, *I Samuel*, 131. McCarter believes that the mention of Levities in v. 15 is a late insertion.

145. Beth-Shemesh was a designated home for the descendants of Aaron (Josh 21:13–16). See Bergen, *1, 2 Samuel*, 102.

146. Bergen, 102. However, it seems that God was pleased with the earlier offering. No trespass was committed against the ark.

147. Arnold, *1 and 2 Samuel*, 121; likewise McCarter, *I Samuel*, 139. McCarter suggests there was a lack of priests in Beth-Shemesh.

148. Many translations render it as "look into" (NIV, NASB, RSV, NKJV, LEB, NET, NJPS), depending on how one reads the proposition ב. Driver argues that ראה + ב does not mean "to look into" (which would be rather ראה אל תוך), but "to look on or at." He cites Psalm 27:13, Genesis 34:1, Ezekiel 21:26 and Judges 16:27 as examples. See Driver, *Notes*, 58.

149. The ark contained the tablets of testimony (Exod 25:21; Deut 10:5).

curiosity. If so, it would be shocking since the action would imply the opening of the ark.[150] In other words, people may have wanted to look at[151] the ark and observe its details – a disregard for the ark's sanctity. Though the exact manner of "look" remains uncertain, such a general gesture was understood as desecration against the honor of YHWH, and thus it is understandable why God struck the Israelites so badly. Thus Brueggemann notes, "The holiness of the ark and the restless glory of Yahweh permit none to draw too close, either Philistine or Israelite."[152]

The Beth-Shemeshites were obviously overwhelmed with terror at God's smiting of their fellow citizens. They mourned for their dead ones and said, "Who can stand before YHWH, this holy God?"[153] In this rhetorical question, the holiness of God, on an experiential level, is emphasized. Eslinger sees the phrase "this holy God" as a sarcastic remark on "Yahweh's unapproachability and incomprehensibility."[154] But it was God's glory and holiness they offended as they possibly tried to peek into the ark (or performed any looking with offense). The great smiting indicates that there had been some "gross affront to Yahweh's honor."[155] Thus the punishment was a divine retribution for their lack of respect for YHWH. Hertzberg is right in saying that the people did not show "due respect to the high God"[156] as they came before him. Firth treats the problem from a broader perspective. The ark narrative as a whole "emphasizes Yahweh's glory and holiness, emphasized through the ark."[157] The Israelites did not seem to learn the lesson well from their previous defeats and the exile of the ark. They still treated the ark of God lightly. From the larger narrative of chapters 1–7, it is easy to see that Israel still had problems in their loyalty to YHWH (7:3–4). It is perhaps fitting to say that the actions

---

150. Tsumura, *First Book of Samuel*, 226.

151. The nature of the verb "look at" here is different from the same verb used in v. 13 (the Israelites noticed the ark's arrival) and in v. 16 (the Philistines observed Israel's welcome of the ark), since ראה with ב expresses a durative and intentional activity. See Malessa, *Untersuchungen*, 122–123.

152. Brueggemann, *First and Second Samuel*, 43.

153. 4QSam^a reads יהוה הקדוש הזה, "this holy YHWH." This is supported by the LXX (κυρίου τοῦ ἁγίου τούτου).

154. Eslinger, *Kingship of God*, 225. The problem was with YHWH who could hardly be approached. He was totally "other."

155. Stirrup, "Why Has Yahweh," 99.

156. Hertzberg, *I and II Samuel*, 61.

157. Firth, *1 & 2 Samuel*, 100.

of "Israel after the ark's exodus were not significantly different from what they were before."[158] They still understood YHWH and the ark in their own terms. The loss of the ark of God, as a great theological crisis, did not seem to bring much transformation in the people's relationship with YHWH.

Eslinger explains the situation from the dimensions of time and space in the narrative:

> The defeated Israelites in the story are not allowed any insight into the reasons for the return of the ark in 6:12, nor do they know what Yahweh or the ark have been doing during the time of the ark's stay amongst the Philistines. By limiting access to these events the narrator illuminates the meaning of Israel's defeat for his reader, while leaving Israel in the dark.[159]

The Beth-Shemeshites had perhaps never heard of YHWH's great deeds in the land of Philistia, nor did they know why the Philistines had suddenly returned the ark of God with their compensation gifts after forcefully taking it away. Or perhaps it was not so much in their interests to know what had transpired.

YHWH refused to succumb to their own terms when Israel was unwilling to operate on his terms. Thus Fokkelman observes keenly, "The Beth-Shemesh incident includes the lesson that the ark is the property of nobody but God, and is not, therefore, that of the covenant people, and this lesson is a repetition of what the people could have learned twice already in chapter 4 on the battlefield."[160] It is clear that YHWH was not on the side of the Philistines. But neither was he on the side of the Israelites when his people did not come to him in an appropriate and respectful manner.[161] YHWH belonged to no one. He did marvelous things for his own sake.

If YHWH himself defended his own honor in the land of the Philistines, the people of Israel would have needed to ensure that his honor and his holiness were not offended even before his own people. Indeed, Israel should and must respect YHWH more than the Philistines.

---

158. Firth, 101.
159. Eslinger, *Kingship of God*, 187.
160. Fokkelman, *Vow and Desire*, 249.
161. This story was not told to the Philistines but to the Israelites. See Brueggemann, *First and Second Samuel*, 46. Thus it is the Israelites who were meant to learn this lesson.

Obviously, the Beth-Shemeshites were not ready to digest such profound theological truth. They too insisted on the ark's removal: "And to whom shall he go up from us?"[162] As with the pagan Philistines, it is ironic that God's own people did not welcome the presence of the ark of God. Their urgency in having the ark removed is vividly described in the series of verbs: וישלחו ("and they sent"), רדו ("come down"), העלו ("take up"). The latter two record their words in the imperative mood. It appears they still showed no respect for the ark of God after going through all these crises. The ark was banished again, this time by his own people.[163]

The Beth-Shemeshites obviously concealed the fact of God's destructive smiting from the people of Kiriath-Jearim. They simply informed them of the ark's return and indicated their desire to have them guard it (6:21). It is uncertain why the Beth-Shemeshites sent their messengers to Kiriath-Jearim, assuming they would take over this responsibility. It is likely that Shiloh, the original place that hosted the ark, may have been destroyed.[164] The idea of putting the ark into "cold-storage" because of the dishonor of having been "taken" by the Philistines is less likely. The ark, in actuality, returned triumphantly in honor, even with the Philistine guilt offerings as precious compensation gifts.[165] Some believe that the Philistines still exercised some sort of influence over Kiriath-Jearim, and it may have led the Beth-Shemeshites to pick this place to host the ark, making it less offensive to the Philistines.[166] The city's cultic history in housing a sanctuary (perhaps a previous connection with Baal worship), as indicated in its previous name קרית בעל (Kiriath-Baal; Josh 15:60; 18:14), may be another explanation.[167] Still, the ark being seen as a "dangerous burden," may be the natural reason why it was not sent to other important and well-known sanctuaries.[168]

---

162. Most other Israelite ancient sites would be much higher in elevation. For instance, Kiriath-Jearim was at 2,385 ft (with Beth-Shemesh at 917 ft) above the sea. See Driver, *Notes*, 59; Klein, *1 Samuel*, 60.

163. That is the equivalent of abandonment. See Campbell, *1 Samuel*, 81–82.

164. Hertzberg, *I and II Samuel*, 61.

165. Hertzberg, 62.

166. Klein, *1 Samuel*, 60; Hertzberg, *I and II Samuel*, 62. David's defeat of the Philistines took place in the valley of Rephaim (2 Sam 5:18–25), which was southeast of Kiriath-Jearim.

167. Klein, *1 Samuel*, 60; Tsumura, *First Book of Samuel*, 228; Gordon, *I & II Samuel*, 103–104; Arnold, *1 and 2 Samuel*, 121; Blenkinsopp, "Kiriath-Jearim," 143–156.

168. Eslinger, *Kingship of God*, 227.

The people of Kiriath-Jearim responded positively to the news of the ark's return. They came and took up the ark of YHWH and brought it to the house of Abinadab on the hill (7:1). Unlike the Beth-Shemeshites, the men of Kiriath-Jearim acknowledged YHWH's holiness. They consecrated (קדשׁו) Abinadab's son Eleazar to "guard" (לשׁמר) the ark,[169] most likely doing some kind of priestly holy service.[170] The ark of God was removed from public attention, silently residing in an individual's house, because the people of Israel, as a whole, had not prepared their hearts to give due respect and honor to their covenantal God.[171] The God of Israel would rather be all alone until the time of his chosen anointed servant David and the chosen city, Jerusalem (2 Sam 6:17).[172] The self-glorying God of Israel did not beg for the respect and honor of his people.

5.6 Conclusion

This study finds that the ark narrative is a captivating story imbued with a strong presence of honor and shame. The ark is at the center of the narrative which reveals the glory of YHWH. The God of Israel could not be manipulated according to the selfish desire of his people. The glory (כבוד) of the God of Israel was not present even when the Israelites were compelled to bring the ark to fight the battle against the Philistines. However, YHWH defended his own honor and glory when his name was threatened with shame. YHWH proved to be a great and superior God, as he shamed Dagon, the Philistine god, and inflicted the Philistines with plague in their cities through his "heavy" (כבדה) hand. With no other choice, the Philistines had to return the ark of YHWH to Israel with their guilt offerings as compensation gifts. The ark's miraculous return acknowledged and restored the honor (כבוד) of the God of Israel. The same root כבד, as a key term in the ark narrative, occurs repeatedly in 1 Samuel 4–6.

---

169. Eleazar is introduced as the father of Ahio and Uzzah (2 Sam 6:3). Josephus described him favorably as a "righteous man" (*Ant.* 6.16).

170. Hertberg, *I and II Samuel*, 62; Klein, *1 Samuel*, 60; Firth, *1 & 2 Samuel*, 101; Tsumura, *First Book of Samuel*, 229; Miller and Roberts, *Hand of the Lord*, 78.

171. The worship of foreign gods and the Ashtaroth (7:3–4) for twenty years was a clear sign of it. See also Tsumura, *First Book of Samuel*, 229.

172. Arnold, *1 and 2 Samuel*, 122.

The God of Israel, however, did not make it easy for his people. Israel's offense against the ark of God also brought great destruction upon themselves, just as great destruction had been brought upon the Philistines. God's glory and holiness were not to be offended even by his own people. The glory of God was theocentric and self-initiating, refusing to be subjected to human terms. In the end, both the Philistines and the Israelites had to learn the hard way to give glory (כבוד) to the God of Israel (6:5).

CHAPTER 6

Conclusion and Implications

6.1 Conclusion

There is little doubt that honor and shame were important social-cultural values in the ancient Near East. Though the concern about honor and shame in 1 Samuel surfaces in various journal articles, books, commentaries and dissertations in past scholarship, it has never been treated as a lens through which to read 1 Samuel 1–7 as a whole. In this book, I have argued that, from beginning to end, the narrator develops an ideological perspective of honor and shame in these chapters, which highlights the thematic centrality of honor and shame. It has been my contention that such a finding is significant for understanding the message of the whole book of 1 Samuel: the attitude of one honoring or dishonoring God, as a reflection of one's spiritual character, determines the rise and fall, the election and rejection, of God's chosen leadership in 1 Samuel (esp. chs. 1–7). Coming to this conclusion, it would be good to step back and review the research.

In the first chapter, I proposed that honor and shame are central to the narrator's ideological point of view in 1 Samuel. To this end, I demonstrated how the ideological perspective of honor and shame can be located in the texts and how such a value scale is employed by the narrator as a guide in composing the narrated stories. In the meantime, it can also greatly enhance the reading of the biblical story if readers can readily grasp such important social and cultural values.

To justify this study, I first reviewed the past research concerning honor and shame in OT studies, particularly literature related to honor and shame in the Deuteronomistic History and the book of First Samuel. The works of Jumper and Brueggemann,[1] which highlight the importance of honor and shame in the study of 1 Samuel (esp. chs. 1–7), have triggered interest in this study. The limitation and different emphases of their works provide the space for my further quest on this topic.

Scholars in the last few decades have been drawing more attention to the application of the cultural values of honor and shame to the interpretation of texts. However, compared with the predominant historical-critical and literary-critical methods in the study of 1 Samuel, the social-cultural (honor and shame) reading is still like a tottering infant in the circles of biblical scholarship. This dissertation endeavors to make some contribution to the honor-shame aspect of the text and its message.

On the part of methodology, I have also made extra effort to clarify what I meant regarding socio-literary criticism, a combination of social-scientific criticism and literary-narrative analysis, to reduce the chance of misunderstanding. This is not without reason, as many practitioners of social-scientific criticism have employed the field research of modern cultural anthropologists in their studies. By doing so, they greatly risk modernizing an ancient text. Thus, I submit the need for caution and discernment in employing this method in a way that is not anachronistic.

In the second chapter, I investigated the semantics of the vocabulary of honor and shame in 1 Samuel. Contrary to the traditional thematic/systematic approach which usually covers the scope of the whole Hebrew Bible, this study has taken an inductive approach wherein terms of honor and shame are examined within their own texts and contexts in 1 Samuel. As such, the discussion of honor and shame in 1 Samuel as a social-cultural value can be built on a solid grounding. The lexical information itself suggests when the text explicitly or implicitly deals with honor-shame issues. This is an important preparatory step that facilitates further analyses of 1 Samuel 1–7 from the perspective of honor and shame. I do not press to say that everything is about honor and shame in 1 Samuel. Instead, there are lexical indications of where honor and shame issues rise to the forefront.

The study finds that an honor-shame culture is pervasive, yet with its own unique manifestations in 1 Samuel. Honor and shame permeate all areas of life

---

1. See section 1.3.3.2 and 1.3.3.3 for details.

in biblical Israel, including politics, family, friendship, war, sex, meals, daily language and even death. Thus, the notion of honor and shame appears to be an important aspect of social culture that governs the thoughts, words and deeds of the people in biblical Israel. As far as 1 Samuel is concerned, honor and shame appear to be pivotal social-cultural values in ancient Israel. The root כבד is arguably a key term for understanding the meaning of different narrative stages in the book, especially chapters 1–7. This study has also discovered that honor and shame in 1 Samuel are not elucidated by the patterns of the anthropological honor/shame model claimed by the Mediterraneanists, especially the gender distinction concerning honor and shame.

In the third chapter, I portrayed the life of Hannah (the mother of Samuel) through the ideological perspective of honor and shame. Hannah's barrenness was the source of her shame. She was tormented and humiliated as a result of her childlessness, especially when her rival Peninnah continually mocked her for her infertility. Hannah turned to God with vowed prayers in her despair, and God graciously heard her prayers and miraculously granted her a son, thus clearing away her shame. As the fulfillment of her vows, Hannah honored the Lord by offering up her only son Samuel for dedicated holy service in Shiloh. As a result, the Lord continued to honor Hannah by giving her many other children. With the fluctuation of Hannah's fate, her status and reputation also changed dramatically in the public eye (from lowly to exalted). She was no longer a shamed, barren woman but an honored mother of many children, one of them even being the prophet of God in Israel.

The Song of Hannah (2:1–10), though alluding to the life situation of Hannah, functions, nevertheless, as a significant interpretative tool for understanding the whole narrative of 1 Samuel (e.g. the life of Samuel and the Elides). The perspective of honor and shame, being richly reflected in the song, is also an important and implicit standard by which God evaluates those who serve him and those who reject him. The sovereign Lord reverses the fate of those of lowly and high statuses. He oversees human honor and shame. Hannah's personal fate, as well as that of Israel's anointed one, rests on God's ultimate exaltation.

In the fourth chapter, I argued that the ideological perspective of honor and shame guides the way the narrator portrays the fates of the Elides and Samuel. This study found that the Elides and Samuel exhibited distinctly different character in their services to God. Unlike the Elides, who had honored their personal agenda, Samuel wholeheartedly honored God through his humble and faithful service. In my argument, they represent totally different lifestyles and character: honoring the self versus honoring God. Thus, with the same measure they ascribed to God, it would be measured back to them. Namely, God will honor those who honor him, but those who despise him shall be insignificant (2:30). Accordingly, the Elides were judged with shame by way of their unusual deaths, but Samuel was honored as a prophet of God throughout all Israel. Their differing attitudes in honoring God triggered opposite consequences in their lives.

The narrator's ideological perspective of honor and shame is thus employed as a standard of judgment for God's election of Samuel and the rejection of the Elides. Though one may continue to rally support for Eli as a "dedicated priest,"[2] the perspective of honor and shame sheds some fresh light and offers a different perception of his character. The honor/shame judgment standard in the Elides/Samuel episode can be even considered as a paradigmatic overture to the following Saul/David stories, foreshadowing the coming conflict and outcome. Thus, the notion of honor and shame works behind the scenes and serves as a driving force in forging the narrative.

In the fifth chapter, I continued to show how the narrator's ideological perspective of honor and shame can be offered as a guide for the reading of the ark narrative. The study has found that the ark narrative is a captivating story replete with a strong sense of honor and shame. The ark is at the center of the ark narrative, which reveals the glory of YHWH. The God of Israel could not be manipulated according to the selfish desire of his people. The glory (כבוד) of the God of Israel was not present even when the Israelites brought the ark to battle against the Philistines. Israel's unthinkable defeat was a clear message that YHWH was not willing to subject himself to their disrespectful manipulation. However, as the ark of God was captured and humiliatingly brought into the house of Dagon as a war trophy, YHWH defended his own honor and glory when his name was threatened with shame. YHWH proved to be a great and superior God as he shamed Dagon and inflicted the Philistines with plague in their cities through his "heavy" (כבדה) hand. Israel's כבוד was too weighty for the Philistines to bear. With no other choice, the Philistines had to return the ark of YHWH to Israel with their

---

2. Steinmann, *1 Samuel*, 115.

guilt offerings as compensation gifts. Ultimately, the ark's miraculous return acknowledged and restored the honor (כבוד) of the God of Israel. The ark narrative is bracketed with the descent and the ascent of God's glory.

The God of Israel, however, showed no favor toward his people after the ark's return. Israel's offense against the ark brought great destruction upon themselves just as had been brought upon the Philistines. God's glory and holiness were not to be offended even by his own people. The glory of God was theocentric and self-initiating, refusing to be subjected to human terms. In the end, both the Philistines and the Israelites had to learn to give glory (כבוד) to the God of Israel (6:5) the hard way.

The ark narrative could have held special significance for the exiled Israelites if we are to believe that the final compilation of the books of Samuel, as part of the Deuteronomistic history, took place during the exilic period.[3] The exiled Israelites had to face the crisis of worshipping YHWH without the temple or the ark of God in their midst. God's glory remained intact despite the failure of God's people.

The current chapter (ch. 6) reviews the study and concludes that 1 Samuel 1–7 can be plausibly read through the narrator's ideological perspective of honor and shame. Such a lens with a social-cultural emphasis brings a fresh reading to our interpretation of the text. Some wider implications of this study are considered with an Asian setting in mind.

In this study I have chosen to examine honor and shame in 1 Samuel 1–7 as my focus. As I have demonstrated in chapter 2, lexical information suggesting honor and shame is pervasive and conspicuous throughout 1 Samuel. Meanwhile, as I have argued, the Elides/Samuel section can arguably be considered as setting up an honor/shame paradigm for the Saul/David stories which follow. One's honoring or dishonoring of God is employed as a standard of judgment in the divine election of leadership in Israel. The rejection of the Elides and the acceptance of Samuel in 1 Samuel 1–7, illustrated from the perspective of honor and shame, foreshadows the coming fate of Saul and David. Thus, it would be meaningful for future study to continue to pursue the topic of honor and shame in the rest of the book of 1 Samuel (and 2 Samuel

---

3. For instance, the use of הֵיכָל ("temple") in 1 Samuel 1:9 and 3:3 is arguably a later term (the Solomonic temple was not yet built). One wonders if the books of Samuel are a later writing incorporating what was a later development into its terminology.

by extension). From a broader perspective, future study of honor and shame in the Deuteronomistic History sounds promising, given the contribution other biblical scholars have already made in this arena.

6.2 Implications of This Study

"Honor-and-Shame" has been considered merely a "Heuristic or Hermeneutical Tool" in biblical scholarship.[4] However, given its importance as a social concern in ancient Israel, such an approach for reading the biblical text should be taken seriously. Nevertheless, a word of caution should also be said about this approach. In some biblical texts, the concern over honor and shame is important and even overriding. But this does not support forcefully bringing an honor and shame lens to every text, with the assumption that such a concept is "pervasive and dominant."[5] As a faithful exegete, it is the text and the author's perceived intention that should always govern our interpretation. It is not that everything somehow *must* and *can* be interpreted in accord with this "Honor-and-Shame" pattern.[6] A good suggestion is that we apply this method in the understanding of texts when the concern for honor and shame comes to the fore.[7]

There is no doubt that honor and shame are important social binary contrasts enabling us to understand more adequately the biblical texts. But how people can best understand such a concept in their own contexts is an important question that biblical scholars will have to wrestle with, notwithstanding the challenge.[8] Speaking of the interface of contexts, Langdon Gilkey says, "The primary task of the theologians is the revision of the Christian message

---

4. Downing, "'Honor' among Exegetes," 55. Downing argues that the concept of honor and shame in some passages could be secondary, trivial or even not relevant at all. But it is probably safer to say that the idea of honor and shame never goes away – it is always in the back of the author's mind, if not at the front.

5. Downing, 57–61.

6. Downing, 59.

7. Moon, "Honor and Shame," 338–339.

8. If my above study of 1 Samuel 1–7 is a presentation of the cultural dynamics of "the world within the text," then the understanding of one's own cultural context can be considered "the world in front of the text." Such an "in-front-of-the-text" self-awareness intentionally addresses the need to reach today's Christian readers, who, as said by Moberly, "see their identity as standing in continuity with that of biblical Israel and are open to being shaped in certain ways by the text received as authoritative." Moberly, *Old Testament Theology*, 18.

in *contemporary terms*, a message addressed, of course, first of all to the community of the church which seeks to live by that message."⁹ Similarly, Philip Chia describes an urgent need for the text and context to "intersect,"¹⁰ by which he means that biblical scholars should best present their research to their people, those outside of the academic circle, with a strong sense of relevancy that reflects their "glocal concerns."¹¹ Given the presence of the large number of Christians in Asia, much more should be done indeed for a contextualized biblical theology to help the Asian churches root the Christian faith in their own soil.¹² Though the concepts of honor and shame are not alien to Asians, it is indispensable to see how such concepts are expressed in Asia's distinct cultures.¹³ Thus, I propose "face" (面子, *mianzi*)¹⁴ as a most

---

9. Gilkey, "Interpretation of Faith," 97. The italics in the quotation are mine.

10. See Chia, "Biblical Studies," 55.

11. Chia, 55–57. Chia proposes six significant dimensions of glocal reality (i.e. reflecting both local and global concerns) to consider for future Asian biblical scholarship: ethical, spiritual, economic, environmental, cultural and political.

12. For a good guide to the developments of contextualized theology in Asia, see Kim, *Christian Theology in Asia*; Gener and Pardue, *Asian Christian Theology*. For a commentary that reads 1 Samuel from an Asian context, see Kim, *1 Samuel*. In this work, Kim dialogues extensively with the Chinese historical novel, *Romance of the Three Kingdoms*, which has been influential in forming the worldview of people in East Asia since the fourteenth century. For a journal volume that introduces several scholars from Asia who treat honor and shame from an Asian perspective (Amanda Shao-Tan, Marlene Yap, Im Seok David Kang and Balu Savarikannu), see Johnson, "Biblical Reflections," 1–3, wherein he summarizes their works. Minschke's book is also an attempt to contextualize the gospel of Christ through the dynamics of honor and shame. See Minschke, *Global Gospel*.

13. See Villanueva, "Calling," 1–10. Villanueva stresses the importance of doing biblical research and not distancing it from one's social location and culture. For an example of his own contextualized work on lament Psalms, see Villanueva, *It's OK*. Compared to Asian Christians, Africans would certainly understand honor and shame differently in terms of family, wealth and death. See Mahlangu, "Ancient Mediterranean Values," 85–100. Even within Asia, people are still bound to their own distinct cultures in perceiving honor and shame. For example, the word *hiya* has a significant shame connotation for Filipinos; see Santos, *Transformation*.

14. Sometimes, *mianzi* can be shortened to *mian*. Another word to render "face" is *lian* in Chinese. Terms aligning with *lian* to denote honor and shame are also pervasive, such as *diulian* ("losing face"), *buyaolian* ("no need face," a scolding as a result of someone breaking some social-ethical values) and *meiyoulian* ("not having face," the most serious term for condemnation). Though both *lian* and *mian* can literally mean "face" as an important organ of the body or, by extension, a figurative understanding of personal respect, subtle differences exist between the two. For example, *mian* is probably a more archaic term, which can be traced back to the fourth century BCE, while *lian* is a more modern term that first appears in literature of the Yuan Dynasty (1227–1367 CE). Meanwhile, in comparison with *lian*, the nature of *mian* is more flexible; it can be borrowed, earned, added or even muddled. See Hu, "Chinese Concepts of 'Face,'" 41–59. This dissertation chooses not to discuss *lian* any further, since many concepts of *lian* and *mian* overlap. Admittedly, there are many other terms that may evoke honor

conducive term to communicate honor and shame in the Chinese culture. Following after a discussion of *mianzi*, I will briefly talk about wealth and status as expressions of honor and the perils of this conception (the prosperity gospel and the caste system) in Asia.[15]

Speaking of *mianzi*, the obvious question to ask is what exactly is it? To clearly define it is not an easy task. Hsien-Chin Hu, a prominent Chinese anthropologist, is probably the first one to define *mianzi*, doing so in 1944. According to Hu, "'*Mianzi*' stands for a highly valued social reputation within Chinese society; it is good names earned by personal achievement and prestige in life experiences. Such an accumulative reputation is established by intentional labors and efforts."[16] In addition to that, Jackson Wu also investigates a number of definitions in his dissertation *Saving God's Face*; he seems to endorse the proposition that "face" denotes recognition of one's social standing and identity.[17] Such a definition is in close proximity to our earlier discussion of "honor" in the first chapter. Looking back, all these definitions connect *mianzi* to social reputation, standing and identity, which many consider to be the core concepts of what honor is about.

Mianzi is a term that Chinese can hardly avoid when one talks about honor and shame. Indeed, according to Jackson Wu, the concern for *mianzi* is the most direct indication of one's honor and shame within a Chinese context.[18] The variability of *mianzi* also motivates people to strive for honor and avoid shame.

---

and shame in Chinese, but that is beyond the scope of discussion for this dissertation. For an overview of multiple terms denoting shame and guilt in Mandarin, see Bedford and Kwang, "Guilt and Shame," 127–144.

15. Ministries in honor and shame cultures encounter various aspects of Christian life: spirituality, relationships, evangelism, conversion, ethics and community. See Georges and Baker, *Ministering*, 117–246. I will touch mostly on aspects of spirituality, relationships and community.

16. English translation mine. See Huang, "Face in Chinese Society," 64.

17. Wu, *Saving God's Face*, 152–153. This book is a comprehensive work on honor and shame with contextualization in regards to Chinese culture. Wu, as an applied theologian, also endeavors to communicate the gospel through the perspective of honor and shame in Chinese culture. "The Promises of God," a gospel tract, is the fruit of such an attempt; details of it may be accessed on his personal website https://www.patheos.com/blogs/jacksonwu/the-promises-of-god/.

18. Wu, *Saving God's Face*, 151–154.

Conclusion and Implications

To further substantiate the statement that honor and shame can be communicated by *mianzi* in Chinese culture, I list the following terms closely associated with *mianzi* as highlights:[19]

Terms Associated with *Mianzi*	Meaning
Yǒu miànzi	Have reputation
Méi miànzi	Have no reputation
Gù miànzi	Concern for reputation
Zhēng miànzi	To strive for reputation in competition, especially by generously treating others with dinners, showing off wealth or excelling over others
Gěi miànzi	To give someone recognition, for good or for bad
Liú miànzi	To save reputation for someone, usually to avoid direct confrontation
Diū miànzi	To lose reputation, usually for something bad or immoral
Yào miànzi	To covet reputation by showing off or cheating
Kàn miànzi	To look up to someone's reputation (especially an elderly mediator who would step out to help defuse the tension between two parties)
Jiè miànzi	To borrow someone's reputation and relationship for one's own advantage
Jiǎng miànzi	To look for additional favor due to a special relationship, usually to circumvent laws and regulations

A glimpse of these terms related to *mianzi* at least shows that *mianzi* is arguably a valid term to communicate honor and shame in Chinese culture.[20] "Face," as an expression of honor, is not unique to the Chinese; its pervasiveness can be felt across Asia.[21] To varying degrees, Westerners also inhabit

---

19. Some terms are adapted and revised from Hu, "Chinese Concepts of 'Face,'" 51–58. This is by no means an exhaustive list, but it indicates how *mianzi* significantly impacts the culture of honor and shame in China.

20. Such a discovery may contribute to mission opportunities in such a culture wherein *mianzi* is so prominent a term to express honor and shame.

21. For instance, "face" (i.e. keeping face) is considered a central concern in Japan and Korea. See Boiger et al., "Defending Honour," 1255–1269; Choi and Rynkiewich, "Face."

"face" cultures, though there is a tendency to overlook it. Thus, we may say that "face" is a "human phenomenon."[22]

What is more interesting is that "face" is not only an indigenous term but also a biblical one to describe honor.[23] In the OT, for instance, being "face-to-face" with God was a rare privilege God rendered to his faithful servant (Exod 33:10). When Moses asked God to show his glory (כבוד) to verify his presence with his people (Exod 33:18), God revealed it by allowing Moses to behold his back but not his face (Exod 33:23). In this context, the presence of God's face (פנים) is synonymous to God's full glory (כבוד). Likewise, when the Lord shines his face (יאר . . . פניו) on his people, it is a token of God's favor and grace (Num 6:25). In contrast, when God hides his face (אסתיר פני; Deut 31:18) from his people, it is a sign of their abandonment, rejection and humiliation. The use of פָּנִים in different biblical texts often implies the expression of honor or shame.

The biblical world which existed in the wider context of the ancient Near East was known to be Eastern in both its geography and culture. Thus, it should not surprise us that the culture of the ancient biblical world embedded in antiquity would also uphold an honor and shame culture of "face," which originated in the East. Through this lens, "face" (*mianzi*), as an expression of honor and shame, is perhaps not only Chinese or Asian, but also accords with the culture of "face" in biblical literature.

The culture of Asia is more about honor and shame than guilt.[24] Honor is expressed in various ways. One obvious way to display honor in Asia (perhaps similarly to other parts of the world) is through external wealth and status. Wealth and status in general denote honor. Thus, a person with great possessions is granted honor. Likewise, a person of status (e.g. an old man, a leader, and, if in India, someone belonging to a high caste) is likely to gain more esteem from the community.

Such a social culture of honor has obviously impacted the Christian churches in various ways, the prosperity gospel being one of them.[25] When

---

22. Wu, "Biblical Theology," 7.

23. See section 2.1 for details. I list more terms associated with פָּנִים to denote honor and shame in my ThM thesis. See Kang, "Rhetoric," 113–114.

24. An "honor-shame culture" refers to a context where the honor-shame dynamic is dominant. See Georges and Baker, *Ministering*, 35.

25. For an introduction to the prosperity gospel, see Salinas, *Prosperity Theology*.

material gain, wealth and success are measured as outward expressions of God's favor on a person, the line is sometimes blurred as to whether someone is following after personal wealth or God. This is especially so for the Asian Christian community which is often marked by its poverty, suffering and persecution.[26] The desire for and pursuit of personal wealth and honor can easily become temptations for Christians in this part of world to bypass the way of the cross and choose to walk the easy path.[27]

The Scriptures, however, seem to emphasize a different outlook on honor for followers of Christ: Christians are instructed to take up their cross (Matt 16:24–26), despise material wealth (Heb 10:32–36) and suffer for Christ (2 Cor 11:23–28; Heb 11:36–38). Thus honor, in its biblical sense, is not measured according to the accumulation of wealth but is often associated with suffering for Christ, which often implies the sacrifice of giving up possessions for the sake of the gospel (Mark 10:29–30).[28] Indeed, true and eternal honor comes from obedience to Christ and suffering for his sake, just as Christ himself walked the path of the cross and was exalted in glory (Phil 2:5–11). Villanueva is right in saying that it is not the prosperity gospel but the theology of suffering that best represents the theological landscape in Asia.[29] Thus Christians in Asia should be girded with biblical principles for a correct perception of true honor and shame. True honor, as a reward from above, comes from a life of honoring God (1 Sam 2:30). God knows those who honor him and those who honor their personal ambitions and interests, as in the case of Samuel and the Elides. If anyone suffers for Christ (e.g. facing mockery, poverty or

---

26. For instance, the Philippines, due to its long period under colonial oppression, is known for its sufferings and struggles. Christians, as part of the body in the country, are also caught up in such problems. See Fernandez, *Toward a Theology*, 20–22. Many Filipino pastors still receive about USD 200 (or even lower in rural areas) for their monthly salaries.

27. For instance, David Yonggi Cho, the founder of the world's largest Pentecostal congregation in Korea, was sentenced to three years in prison with a five-year probation in 2014 for embezzling $12 million and other related financial crimes. See Ruth Moon, "Founder of World's Largest Megachurch Convicted of Embezzling $12 Million," News and Reporting, *Christianity Today*, 24 February 2014, https://www.christianitytoday.com/news/2014/february/founder-of-worlds-largest-megachurch-convicted-cho-yoido.html.

28. For instance, Christians devoted to full-time ministry often earn much lower salaries than they would have in other occupations. The Christian community in many parts of Asia, as a marginal group, is often threatened with being cut off from social services (e.g. the chance to go to the best university, the grant of subsistence allowance, the chance for a promotion in a job or the right to vote) if they continue to hold on to their Christian faith. A friend of mine was even deposed from his teaching position in his university because he was active in sharing his faith.

29. Villanueva, "Challenge," 17.

imprisonment), the Christian community should not consider it a disgrace but an opportunity to honor God (1 Pet 4:13–16).

Another thing pertaining to the honor and shame culture in Asia is social stratification. In James 2:1–7, the stratified division between the poor and rich – where the poor were shamed by being given seats of lowly position and the rich were honored with the best seats in the synagogues – was censured. Such prejudice and discrimination against poor Christians was against the honorable name of the God who created all humans equal.

One systematic social stratification in Asia today is the disputed hierarchical caste system in India.[30] The upper caste people are given great prestige and honor. Low caste people, however, are despised, assigned undesirable jobs and excluded from many civil rights and opportunities.[31] The contrast between people of high and low caste is seen in the disparity of status that is associated with dramatic honor variation in Indian society – namely, honor and prestige for high caste people contra inferiority and disgrace for those of the low castes.[32] Within this system, inter-caste marriage is strongly prohibited, as one marrying a person of a lower caste tarnishes the honor of the family of a higher caste. What makes it worse is the hereditary nature of the caste system, suggesting that, barring intervention, the exploitation of the lower castes is doomed to carry on from generation to generation.

---

30. The origin of the caste system in India can possibly be traced back to the invasion of the Aryans (around 1500 BCE) who first introduced the hierarchy of human stratification as a means of controlling the local populations. See Sharma, "Dr. B. R. Ambedkar," 843–70. The term "caste" derives from the early Portuguese tongue to mean "a pure blood-line or species." See Guha, *Beyond Caste*, 22. The term itself has already shown its sense of superiority. In the caste system, people were divided into different layers of castes. Those who were of prestigious status were the priests, leaders and warriors. Under them were traders, farmers and laborers. In the lowest social level were the "untouchables." See Rogala, "Hinduism," 40.

31. For a book that introduces the present status of Dalits ("untouchables," low caste people) in India, see Thorat, *Dalits in India*. In a typical traditional Indian town, the priests, as the high caste, lived in the center area connected to the temple; outside it were other citizens (the middle caste) who resided within the parameter of the city (circling the temple); the Dalits, as social outcasts (the low caste), dwelled outside of the city. The geographical division of the city exemplifies the role that the caste system plays in today's society. There is no doubt that the Dalits are the marginally despised group in the society. Being seen as unclean and profane, the Dalits are not allowed entry into the temples. I am grateful to my fellow student Rufus Samuel who has shared this insight with me.

32. This is affirmed by several Indian biblical scholars who also see the problem of the caste system as a variation on honor. See Savarikannu, "Expressions," 89; Guha, *Beyond Caste*, 9. Similarly, the concern of honor and shame, as a value system, is central to the caste system. See Still, *Dalit Women*, 28.

It is a disgrace that the caste system, as a defect of modernity, is even defended by the Hindu nationalist government despite the Indian constitution having officially abolished it. There seems to be no desire for them to change the status quo. Thus, India is going to live with such a hierarchical caste system for a long time to come, and social conflict is bound to rise.[33]

Given this background, it is very crucial for the Indian church to face such a challenge of social injustice. In India, Dalits ("untouchables," people of low caste) are born in dishonor, and that shame accompanies them until they die. In 1 Samuel, Hannah suffered shame and humiliation due to her barrenness, but God exalted her as she trusted in him. The voice in the song of Hannah (1 Sam 2:1–10) is also an outcry from humiliation to exaltation. In my view, any possible transformation of the caste system that uplifts the welfare and status of the Dalits should start from within the Indian church.[34] Unfortunately, prejudice still persists within the church. Dalits who convert to Christianity still face caste discrimination of various forms.[35]

Among many of the church's problems, leadership and inter-caste marriage are noted here. One obvious phenomenon in the Indian church is the insufficient representation of Dalit Christians in leadership despite there being a large number of Dalit Christian communities in the country.[36] The Dalit Christians are largely overridden vis-à-vis upper caste Christians in the granting of leadership positions. Marriage is another problem. Inter-caste marriages among Christians are still rare in the face of the outside pressure of caste discrimination. Sometimes, Christians even prefer to marry high caste Hindus than low caste Christians, as it ostensibly brings greater honor

---

33. Engineer, "Politics of Identity," 187.

34. The early church posed itself as an example (Acts 10:9–48, 11:1–18; Gal 2:11–14) of breaking the barrier of social stratifications and racial discrimination, namely, dismantling the distinction between the Jews as God's elected people (the high "caste") and the "untouchable" Gentiles (the low "caste").

35. See Borooah et al., *Caste*. While the book introduces general discriminations against various ethnic groups in India, the discrimination against the Dalits (including the Dalit Christians) is obviously in the mind of the authors.

36. As of 2000, just six of the 156 Catholic bishops in India were Dalits, the rest of them being from the upper caste community. Out of 12,500 Catholic priests, only 600 were Dalits. The data is more surprising given that 75% members of the Indian Christian community are from the Dalit community. See "Archbishop Arulappa Condemns Vatican for Promoting a Dalit Bishop as His Successor in Hyderabad, India," Dalit Christians: Promoting Rights and Freedom for the Dalit People in India, accessed 24 August 2022, http://www.dalitchristians.com/Html/arulappa.htm.

to the family. It is a regret that Dalit Christians are discriminated against and oppressed by their fellow Christians who address the same God as Father. The way to remove the wall of hostility has to be through the power of the Spirit in Christ (Eph 2:14–18). The Indian church will have to face this challenge, albeit rather painfully. The work of unity and reconciliation has to come with intentional effort.

As much as possible, people seek honor and avoid shame. But the honor/shame values should not be evaluated by the principles of this world, but rather by God's own words. Churches in Asia, in general, are still very much immersed in the culture of honor and shame. The examples of the Elides and Samuel, seen through the perspective of honor and shame, should drive one toward a proper relationship with God, orienting the people of God to desire a life that honors God, and away from the promotion of self. The honor/shame value can thus be particularly beneficial to the church in Asia in building our spiritual and moral lives.

We encounter honor and shame both in the texts *and* contexts. We need to understand the world we live in, so that we, as biblical scholars, teachers and pastors, can address the challenge of our own context in the most comprehensive way.

APPENDIX 1

Notes on אפים in 1 Samuel 1:5

The meaning of אפים is obscure. The noun אַפַּיִם is the dual form of אַף II, which is a nose (or the greater area surrounding the nose, i.e. the face). Some modern translators have read מנה אחת אפים as "only one portion" (RSV) or "one portion only" (NJPS), following the influence of the LXX πλὴν ὅτι. Others interpret it as "a double portion" (ESV, NIV, NASB, NRSV, NET, NKJV), which appears to follow the path of the Syriac: ܘܠܚܢܐ ܝܗܒ ܡܢܬܐ ܚܕܐ ܐܥܦܐ, (in Aramaic square script: ולחנא יהב מנתא חדא אעפא, "and to Hannah he gave one portion, a double amount (ʾaʿpā)."[1] Yet others render "one choice portion" (NLT, 2nd ed.) or "a worthy portion" (KJV, AV, Geneva Bible, Webster Bible), following the Targum חולק חד בחיר ("one choice portion"), or "one portion with sorrow" (Douay Rheims Bible), following the Vulgate "Annae autem dedit partem unam tristis" ("But to Hannah he gave one portion with sorrow").

The LXX renders the MT אפים כי as πλὴν ὅτι ("except that," a phrase corresponding to MT אֶפֶס כִּי in 2 Samuel 12:14 and Amos 9:8 and elsewhere to אַךְ כִּי [1 Sam 8:9]; רַק [Deut 2:8]; וְאוּלָם [1 Sam 25:34]; אַף I [Job 6:27]; and עֵקֶב כִּי [Amos 4:12]). One might argue that with the similarity of *samek* and *mem* in the Hasmonean to Herodian eras, an original אפס was misread accidentally as אפם and corrected on the spot to אפים in order to adjust it to contemporary spelling conventions. Pertaining to the possibility of reading אפס כי as the text behind the LXX, 2 Samuel 12:14 and Amos 9:8, both of

---

1. Reading אפים as the literal numerical dual meaning "two," for reasons which I will explain shortly, is problematic; the more likely rendering of "double" would be כִּפְלַיִם (Isa 40:2; Job 11:6; 41:5).

which translate πλὴν ὅτι from אפס כי, are especially relevant pertaining to our discussion here. In both places, the Hebrew אפס כי could be used as an adversative phrase, just as could be its usage in 1 Samuel 1:5, if one follows the rendition of the LXX. Alternatively, one could argue that the semantics of Amos 9:8 allow for a concessive, "although." Read as an adversative, the problem with adopting the reading אֶפֶס כִּי as based upon the LXX πλὴν ὅτι is that it would highlight Elkanah's unnatural behavior in giving Hannah only one portion despite the fact that he loved her. Such an oddness would leave Peninnah's resentfulness unexplained.² On the other hand, reading אפס כי as introducing a concessive subordinate clause would arguably elevate the oddity of Elkanah's giving a mere portion to his favorite wife, with Peninnah's taunting being based either on Hannah's childlessness or on her tacit questioning of whether her rival wife should be given anything as a barren woman. Furthermore, the LXX's additional clause ὅτι οὐκ ἦν αὐτῇ παιδίον ("because she had no child"), which really finds no equivalent in the MT and is thus likely an expanded text, suggests that the LXX might bear witness to an early text differing from the archetype the MT derives from. Thus, it is unlikely the LXX is the source of the MT here.³

Driver cites a possible meaning for אפים: "heavily," "two faces" (i.e. a double portion) or "a worthy portion." However, Driver himself favors the reading אפס כי.⁴ Many have engaged in various possible explanations of this phrase. For instance, Aberbach assumes a prosthetic א and reads מנה אחת אפים as "one portion worth a pim"; that is, Elkanah gave Hannah a considerable portion of meat, one silver pim (פים) in value.⁵ In my view, why, in the same book, the author would use פים (*pîm*) in 1 Samuel 13:21 but אפים in 1 Samuel 1:5 – words that differ in form but presumably have the same meaning – is problematic. A further problem with Aberbach's proposal is that classical Hebrew nouns with prosthetic *alephs* derive from three letter roots, meaning the middle *yod* of אפים would need to be a consonantal letter with the

---

2. See McCarter, *I Samuel*, 52.

3. Reading אפים as the literal numerical dual meaning "two," for reasons which I will explain shortly, is problematic; the more likely rendering of "double" would be כִּפְלַיִם (Isa 40:2; Job 11:6; 41:5).

4. See Driver, *Notes*, 7–8.

5. See Aberbach, "מנה אחת אפים," 350-353.

formation ʾap-yim or ʾep-yim.⁶ Such is likely not the case in the argued biform פִּים of 1 Samuel 13:21, since other MT three grapheme middle *yod* nouns such as מִין ("kind"), עִיר I ("city") and אִישׁ ("man") are written with two letters in Ugaritic (respectively *mn* and *ʿr*) and אשׁ for אִישׁ in the Siloam Inscription, suggesting the *yod* of פִּים is a *mater lectionis* rather than a consonant.

Deist emends the text to *mānâ ʾaḥat ʾăbūsā*, meaning "a portion (of) fattened (meat)."⁷ His theory of a textual corruption from *ʾăbūsā* to *ʾappayim* of the MT (using current transliteration conventions), would require making two consonantal changes to the MT אפים – namely, פ to ב and ם to ס. One perhaps cannot entirely rule out the possibility of such script confusion of *bet* and *pe*, and *samek* and *mem*, in Hebrew writings as early as the eighth century BCE and on to the Hasmonean and Herodian periods. However, given the presence of the ה *mater lectionis* in all 167 *qal* passive feminine singular absolute state participles in the MT, a defective *ā* vowel as Deist proposes, is unlikely. One would expect *ʾăbūsâ*, containing an additional grapheme.

McCarter conjectures that it should be read as "(a single portion) equal to theirs," namely emending אפים to כְּאפִים (presumably the archaic construction *kəpîmō*, the MT *kəpîmô*, but modernized to *kəpîhem*), which contains three lexical entries: כ (assuming an early confusion of כ and א), then פֶּה, plus the 3mp suffix pronoun. McCarter's emendation, an attractive one, would mean Elkanah responded to Peninnah's harassment by giving Hannah a single portion equivalent to all of the rest of Peninnah's clan put together (i.e. even larger than a double portion). This is attested in McCarter's own words in seeing preferential treatment of Hannah: "Her single portion is equivalent to the several portions of her rival's family."⁸

As Tsumura says, the semantic of אפים cannot be resolved satisfactorily.⁹ It seems best to treat אפים as an appositive of מנה אחת, namely with מנה אחת אפים

---

6. See Deist, "*APPAYIM*," 205–206.
7. Deist, 205–209.
8. See McCarter, *I Samuel*, 51–52.
9. See Tsumura, *First Book of Samuel*, 113. Tsumura himself takes אפים as "a technical term of the ritual sacrifice," favoring the literal meaning "two noses" (i.e. two heads of sheep) as reflective of the practice in ancient Canaan wherein animals were often sacrificed in pairs. Alternatively, Elkanah gave "one of two noses" to Hannah as a share. However, Tsumura's rendition of אַפַּיִם (with the meaning "two noses") as a dual noun seems to be problematic. Whereas אַף II could potentially mean nostril, nostrils in the dual, one would expect nose (which is not symmetrical – a person and animal have only one nose) to be singular in number (cf. Gen 24:47; Isa 2:22; Ps 115:6). His reference to animals being offered in pairs (the numeral *tn* followed by

signifying, "one portion, (a portion gaining) face."[10] Hertzberg suggests "portion of the face" implies a particularly large piece, a portion of honor.[11] Similarly, the Targum paraphrases אפים as בחיר ("choice"), thus rendering חולק חד בחיר as "one choice portion." Likewise, David Qimḥi (a medieval rabbi) glosses אפים as נכבדת ("honorable"), most likely reading the term figuratively. Augmenting such a reading is the argument that the Hebrew word אחת can be interpreted as one that is unique (cf. 2 Sam 7:23; Song 6:9), thus "very special, dear."[12] It is "une unique part d'honneur" ("one unique part of honor").[13] The food given to Hannah was perhaps significantly abundant and eyecatching. The context also strongly suggests Elkanah's favor toward Hannah (the verb אהב connotes Hannah's special value in Elkanah's eyes). Elkanah giving a portion of special size to Hannah may suggest the particular honor he rendered to her. The semantic overlap of אַף II in the dual and פָּנִים (different terms, but both having an overlapping usage signifying "face" or the facial area) should draw our attention. One can imagine that, with Elkanah giving Hannah a portion of the sacrificial meat which was special in quality and size (choice and large), it may insinuate her gaining of face (אפים as a paronomasia), that is, Hannah being granted honor and esteem in front of the family. Thus, מנה אחת אפים can be translated dynamically as "one (special) portion, (gaining) face." Interestingly, such a reading seems to be entertained by David Qimḥi when he says that the purpose of מנה אחת נכבדת ("one honorable portion") is להשיב אפיה וכעסה ("to restore her face and her grief"), followed by a deictic adverbial phrase וכן ארך אפים ארך כעס ("and thus long face, long grief"), insinuating that the special portion of food given

---

the animal) does not necessitate the same for the body parts. In fact, his reference to the Ugaritic sacrificial text only lists singular body members: *ap* II "a nose" and *nph* "a lung" (alternatively, *npš* "a throat") being offered to Anat. For "two noses," אפים in 1 Samuel 1:5 would need to be written as שְׁנֵי אַפַּיִם (cf. Judg 16:28; 1 Sam 3:11; Amos 3:12 for the similar expression of other body parts). The meaning of face (morphologically a dual but singular in lexical semantics) is perhaps preferred. I thank Dr. Tim Undheim for this input.

10. I will support this reading in the following paragraphs.

11. See Hertzberg, *I and II Samuel*, 24.

12. See Van Staalduine-Sulman, *Targum of Samuel*, 190; *DCH*, 1:180–181 also refers to it as "unique, singular," referencing qualify.

13. Caquot and Robert, *Les Livres de Samuel*, 33.

to Hannah is to help restore her face (i.e. honor) and alleviate her from the deep grief caused by the debasing treatment of Peninnah and her associates.[14]

A question one might immediately raise is why Elkanah did not do anything about Peninnah's persistent taunting year after year when he could have intervened to make life easier for Hannah. A good guess is that Peninnah's taunting of Hannah likely happened "under the table" (avoiding the presence of the husband) so that the husband could not ostensibly notice it. Even when Elkanah noticed it, he could hardly do much about it, because Peninnah's promoted status as a mother of many children within the family may also have made him hesitate from confronting her directly.

---

14. "Radaq's commentary on Former Prophets," Bar Ilan University, https://www.mgketer.org/tanach/8/1/5.

APPENDIX 2

Notes on תַּכְעִסֶנָּה in 1 Samuel 1:7

An important point is noting that the verbal root כעס is stative, meaning that, as with the Akkadian D-stem verbs derived from adjectives, in the corresponding West Semitic D-stem stative verb classification, the grammatical object is transformed independently of itself into a new state or condition by the grammatical subject, a function known as the factitive.[1] As such, Peninnah transposes Hannah into a state of being irritated. Treating the *hiphil* תַּכְעִסֶנָּה in verse 7 as a causative (commonly so with dynamic verbs), the object (conventionally read also as Hannah) participates as a second subject in the condition expressed by the verbal root.[2] Rendered as such, Peninnah, year after year, would cause her rival wife to become her own actor, behaving in and of herself with fits of anger. Although there is arguably a slight nuance of difference between the *piel* stative semantic and the causative agency of a *hiphil* stative, the distinction is so minimal that one can wonder why both verbs were not simply pointed with the same stem, either *piel* or *hiphil*.

A second interpretative option, and one which is semantically close to the above in the rhetoric of the narrative, but more clearly reflects a difference in stem semantics, is to read the *hiphil* of verse 7 not as a causative but as an exhibitive. Among several propositions in Goetze's seminal article, "The So-Called Intensive of the Semitic Languages," his observations on the role of the D-stem point to an important corollary to the factitive-only function of the Akkadian D-stem stative derived from adjectives (i.e. the West Semitic stative verb classification) and what he calls the "effect of the action" (i.e.

---

1. See Goetze, "So-Called Intensive," 1–8; Jenni, *Das hebräische Piel*, 20–122; and *IBHS*, § 24.2 for a description of the function itself.
2. *IBHS*, § 27.1a–e.

resultative) function of D-stem Akkadian verbs with a G-stem action verb counterpart (i.e. the West Semitic fientive or dynamic verb classification) – namely that in ancient Semitic languages, the semantic lexical modification imparted by stem variation differs for dynamic and stative verbs. Putting this assumption to work, we can expect *hiphil* statives to behave differently from the typical causative agency of *hiphil* dynamic verbs. Although not as behaviorally uniform as *piel* statives, *hiphil* statives arguably gravitate more toward the exhibitive than the causative, wherein the grammatical subject acts out the lexical semantic of the root rather than being it (*qal* stem) or causing an object to act it out.

When compared with the almost exclusively causative expression of *hiphil* dynamic verbs, unless otherwise required by context, the exhibitive should be regarded as the default function of the stative verb classification, especially in 1 Samuel 1:6–7 where an otherwise causative rendition of תַּכְעִסֶנָּה would yield virtually the same verb to object semantics as וְכִעֲסַתָּה. Were the subject and object meant to be identical in each, the same stem for both would more clearly serve this equation. Hannah is plausibly the subject rather than the object of the *hiphil* of 1:7, with Peninnah being an adjunct, the adverbially functioning object, much like the syntax of Deuteronomy 28:63a (כַּאֲשֶׁר־שָׂשׂ יְהוָה עֲלֵיכֶם לְהֵיטִיב אֶתְכֶם . . .); "just as the Lord delighted over you **by exhibiting good toward you**. . . ").[3] This use also arguably accords, albeit not syntactically, with at least one other occurrence of the *hiphil* of כעס in Nehemiah 3:37:

וְאַל־תְּכַס עַל־עֲוֺנָם וְחַטָּאתָם מִלְּפָנֶיךָ אַל־תִּמָּחֶה כִּי הִכְעִיסוּ לְנֶגֶד הַבּוֹנִים׃

"And do not cover over their iniquity or let their sin be blotted out before you, since **they have expressed rage** before the builders."

Reading תַּכְעִסֶנָּה of verse 7 as Hannah's agitated behavior toward Peninnah and her eventual pregnancy following the yearly trip to Shiloh could be seen as consonant intertextually with barren wife conflicts elsewhere in the Old Testament. Particularly in Genesis 30:8, where upon being granted a child through her maidservant Bilhah, Rachel characterizes her relationship with her sister Leah as a competitive struggle: "'With divine struggles I have wrestled with my sister. Indeed I have won.' So she called his name Naphtali."

---

3. And we can add 1 Sam 2:32, Jer 32:41 and Zech 8:15.

APPENDIX 3

Notes on אַחֲרֵי אָכְלָה בְשִׁלֹה וְאַחֲרֵי שָׁתֹה in 1 Samuel 1:9

The MT's reading, וַתָּקָם חַנָּה אַחֲרֵי אָכְלָה בְשִׁלֹה וְאַחֲרֵי שָׁתֹה, ostensibly indicating that Hannah rose after she had eaten and drunk, shows signs of corruption. Incongruities in the existing letters and their vowel pointing are apparent in the inconsistent forms following and in construct relation with the two prepositions אַחֲרֵי. Additionally, the word order of the sentence is unbalanced. Assuming that behind the graphemes אכלה and שתה are respectively the roots אכל ("to eat") and שתה ("to drink") in a pre-vocalized archetypical text, the following is an attempt to alleviate grammatical inconsistencies and generate better understanding of this section.

One possibility is to read אָכְלָה as a feminine noun; a problem with this reading is one would expect the same with שָׁתֹה, yet there are no nouns under the verbal root שתה with these three letters. One could also read אַחֲרֵי אָכְלָה as אַחֲרֵי followed by a perfect verb, since this syntagm does occur elsewhere in classical Hebrew (e.g. Lev 25:48; 1 Sam 5:9). If indeed אָכְלָה is a perfect, one might assume the same behind the phrase וְאַחֲרֵי שָׁתֹה, with שָׁתֹה, pointed as an infinitive absolute, probably being שָׁתָת (from the root שתה), a 3f.s. suffix conjugation verb.[1] But reading אָכְלָה as a perfect does not accord with the previous verse (v. 8) which clearly indicates Hannah abstained from eating. Furthermore, the rarity of such a syntagm, the great preponderance of verbal

---

1. Assuming a scribal error of the *tav* and *he* graphical confusion.

forms following the preposition אַחֲרֵי being infinitive constructs, suggests both אחרי אכלה and אחרי שתה are better read as verbal noun constructions. Reading אַחֲרֵי אָכְלָה as a verbal noun construction, one could argue there is a vocalic mispointing of the phrase; it should be אַחֲרֵי אָכְלָהּ ("after her eating"), an infinitive construct with a 3f.s. suffix. But again, an obvious weakness in such a Hebrew repointing is that the previous verse (v. 8) has Hannah refraining from eating (the same semantic problem when reading אָכְלָה as a 3f.s. *qal* perfect). Not reading Hannah as eating, and according with the previous verse wherein her husband remarks on her abstinence, the LXX μετὰ τὸ φαγεῖν αὐτούς ("after they had eaten") suggests that αὐτούς ("they," 3 masculine plural, i.e. Elkanah, Peninnah and the rest of the family) are the ones who participated in the eating in Shiloh with no allusion to Hannah joining in the feasting. According with this, not marking Hannah as eating, אָכְלָה could be a feminine form of the *qal* infinitive construct with no suffix,[2] with אַחֲרֵי אָכְלָה בְשִׁלֹה meaning "after eating in Shiloh." Thus, the subject of eating could be anyone, as the infinitive has no genitive potentially functioning as the subject. But the problem is no other *qal* infinitive constructs of אכל in classical Hebrew have this ending.[3]

The current text, if read as "after eating in Shiloh and after drinking," sounds odd to readers (it would read more smoothly if the prepositional phrase "in Shiloh" were placed at the end, i.e. "after eating and after drinking in Shiloh"). Thus McCarter emends בְשִׁלֹה to בַּשֶּׁלִי ("privately") to make sense of such an oddity, suggesting Hannah as the subject of eating.[4] Alternatively, the LXX's omission of drinking might suggest that וְאַחֲרֵי שָׁתֹה is a later addition to the original text. But the fragment of 4QSam^a, . . .]וא ה[. . . , retains the final letter of possibly "[Shilo]h" and the first two letters of the next word (possibly "and a[fter]"). As such, the evidence for removing ואחרי שתה from the original text is not so strong, whatever the unpointed ואחרי שתה in fact denotes.[5] Klein, following Wellhausen, conjectures a different word הַבְּשֵׁלָה ("the boiled flesh") by moving the ה from אכלה to the next word בשלה.[6] In

---

2. See GKC, § 45d; Joüon-Muraoka, § 49d.
3. See GKC, § 45d for an explanation of this particular form with examples.
4. See McCarter, *1 Samuel*, 53.
5. See Steinmann, *1 Samuel*, 47.
6. See Klein, *1 Samuel*, 1, 3.

this case, Hannah is not necessarily part of the eating, "Then Hannah arose after the eating of the boiled flesh . . . ," although Klein translates it as if she is part of the meal. It seems to me Klein's word reconstruction is plausible.

The retrojection of the unpointed letters שתה remains disputed. The MT, reflecting the lemma שתה "to drink," requires further examination due in part to its grammatically problematic phrase וְאַחֲרֵי שָׁתֹה.[7] The LXX, however, does not render it with πίνω, "to drink," but has καθίστημι (potentially reflecting the Hebrew roots יצב, שׂים or שׁית). The last word שׁית (καθίστημι also translates שׁית in Gen 41:33, Ps 9:21 and 45:17) would retain the same base letters as the MT and fit as an infinitive construct without the *mater lectionis hireq yod* and with a 3f.s. suffix pronoun, namely, שְׁתָהּ, providing a syntactical balance of two infinitive constructs with their respective genitives, assuming one reads אֲכֹל הַבְּשֵׁלָה for the first of the infinitive phrases. Thus, וַתָּקָם חַנָּה אַחֲרֵי אֲכֹל הַבְּשֵׁלָה וְאַחֲרֵי שְׁתָהּ, "So Hannah arose after the eating of the boiled meat and after the taking of her position."[8] One merit of such a rendition is that the context does not suggest drinking – the previous verse (v. 8) only references eating, not drinking; likewise, only eating is alluded to in the custom of the priests (1 Sam 2:12–17). Thus, the LXX reading has its own merits.

However, if one makes a comparison between the LXX and Codex L, one would naturally expect to see the occurrence of another μετά ("after") with καθίστημι used in an infinitive phrase – μετὰ τὸ καταστῆσαι αὐτήν – concurring with the earlier infinitive τὸ φαγεῖν ("the eating"). The LXX, however, presents καθίστημι as a finite verb (κατέστη) balancing syntactically with the earlier verb ἀνέστη (in Hebrew וַתָּקָם), not τὸ φαγεῖν (אֲכֹל). If using the lemma שׁית, one might expect וַתֵּשֶׁת לִפְנֵי יְהוָה ("and she took her position before the Lord") as a possible retrojection of the LXX καὶ κατέστη ἐνώπιον κυρίου. Thus, it might seem that the reconstruction of וְאַחֲרֵי שְׁתָהּ is less likely in light of the syntax of the LXX. But a strict word by word correspondence may not be

---

7. An infinitive absolute never immediately follows a preposition; GKC, § 113e considers this example as "impossible Hebrew." A grammatically correct infinitive construct here should be שְׁתֹת and requires emendation from the letter ה to ת, functioning as a substantive.

8. Assuming the intransitive use of the verb שׁית as a potential emendation (see Isa 22:7; Ps 3:7). However, it should be stated that the local adverbial phrase that is present in Isaiah 22:7 and Psalm 3:7 is missing in the emendation above.

necessary. What is important is generating meaningful sense in the passage as based on at least one verb necessarily retrojected from the LXX.

Similar to the MT, both the readings of the Syriac Peshitta translation and the Targums (documents with a tradition reaching back as early as the 2nd century CE) have שתי ("to drink"); but unlike the MT, both are with correct grammar. It is uncertain whether the Peshitta and Targums have שתי because they are translating a Hebrew text with שתה, "to drink," but with correct grammar, or they read שתי because אכל with שתה is a common pair in the Tanakh, occurring elsewhere as many as 195 times. One needs to reckon with the possibility of a post-Second Temple period smoothening of an earlier text, due to the huge preponderance of אכל and שתה being linked together as complementary actions – as well as the requirement to point שתה as an infinite absolute in the MT to accommodate for what was arguably a different lemma in an unvocalized text of earlier antiquity. (As discussed, the unpointed שתה could be from a different verbal root – an infinitive construct of שית plus a 3f.s. suffix pronoun.) Plus, that שָׁתֹה might not be from שתה, "to drink," presents a more difficult text, the science of textual criticism operating under the philosophy that readings typically degenerate from the more complex to the more simple in an attempt by scribes to make the text more understandable.

There is no easy solution to the problem. But given the evidence thus far, it seems that the reading of a base Hebrew text retrojected from the LXX καθίστημι is more favorable. Similarly, Klein and McCarter also entertain such a reading.[9]

---

9. See Klein, *1 Samuel*, 1; McCarter, *1 Samuel*, 53.

APPENDIX 4

Notes on מָעוֹן in 1 Samuel 2:29

The MT's reading, לָמָּה תִבְעֲטוּ בְּזִבְחִי וּבְמִנְחָתִי אֲשֶׁר צִוִּיתִי מָעוֹן ("Why do you [pl.] kick at my sacrifice and my offering which I commanded dwelling place?"), is widely thought to be a corrupted text. In the history of interpretation, others have attempted to smooth the text in order to make better sense of the MT מעון. Rashi, a medieval Jewish rabbi, commented by explaining מעון as equivalent to במעוני ("in my sanctuary"), adding a preposition before מעון and a first person suffix after it. Similarly, Gesenius's *Handwörterbuch* (up to the 1883 edition) assumed a locative adverbial function of the accusative מָעוֹן, "in the sanctuary."[1] Likewise, Keil followed Gesenius's tradition by reading מָעוֹן as an accusative, suggesting it is "in the dwelling" (the tabernacle) in v. 29 and "oppression of the dwelling" in v. 32.[2] The advantage of reading מעון as a noun is that one can try to make sense of the MT without emending the text. But the problem is that מָעוֹן, with its literal meaning "dwelling, habitation," is limited mostly to poetry for the meaning "temple."[3]

Seebass tries to make better sense of the MT by revocalizing מָעוֹן and emending it to מֵעָוֹן (*um der Schuld willen* ["because of sin/guilt"]).[4] But such an emendation is very unlikely as it would require a major emendation in

---

1. After the 1883 edition, this tradition moved toward emending the noun to a verb. The later editions (e.g. 1905, 1915) seem to adopt the emendation מָעוֹיֵן (a *pōʿel* participle of עין) as suggested by Budde. Ges[18] (p. 708), following the influence of Stoebe, refrains from emending the text, listing מָעוֹן in 1 Samuel 2:29, 32, under the meaning "Wohnung, Wohnsitz" ("abode, dwelling").

2. Keil, *Biblical Commentary*, 38–48.

3. Ehrlich, *Randglossen zur Hebräischen Bibel*, 175; Stoebe, *Das erste Buch Samuelis*, 116; Driver, *Notes*, 37–38.

4. Seebass, "Zum Text," 77.

v. 32a from בכל אשר ייטיב את ישראל to בכל אשר חֲטָאתֶם אֶל קָדְשִׁי ("all which you have sinned toward my holy [place]").[5]

Generally speaking, reading מעון as a noun with the meaning "temple" in v. 29 and v. 32 lost acceptance in mainstream scholarship in the late nineteenth and twentieth centuries.[6] In his article "Eli, 'Enemy of a Temple'?," Kim tries to reconcile the interpretive conundrum by reading מָעוֹן as "in a temple" (taking מעון as an adverb of the main verb בעט)[7] in v. 29a and צַר מָעוֹן as "enemy of a temple" (thus a vocative as the subject of the verb נבט) in v. 32a.[8] Nevertheless, his statement, that תבעטו ("making light of" God's sacrifices and offerings) in v. 29a is in sharp contrast to the motif of ותכבד ("honoring" God more than his sons) in v. 29b, is problematic.[9]

---

5. Seebass, 77. Koowon Kim in a recent article points out that עָוֹן and its required guilt offering (אָשָׁם), as suggested in Leviticus 5, conflict with the broad range of sacrifices seen in מִנְחָה and זֶבַח; see Kim, "Eli," 52.

6. Many have embraced instead the emendation of מָעוֹן to מְעִיֵן, a pōʿel participle from the root עין, which I will discuss in the following paragraphs.

7. Reading it this way, one could express Kim's rendition of this sentence as "Why do you trample on my sacrifices and my offerings which I have commanded, [doing so] in my temple?" Alternatively, the noun מָעוֹן could be part of an elliptical expression אֲשֶׁר צִוִּיתִי מָעוֹן, rendered "which I have commanded to bring into a temple." Such is buttressed by the interpretation of Targum Jonathan as דפקידית לקרבא קדמי בבית מקדשי, "that I commanded to bring before me into my holy house." See Kim, "Eli," 56–58, 61.

8. Kim, 50–63. Reading it as a vocative, the subject of the verb is Eli himself, and according to this reading, he is being seen as the enemy of the temple and its sacrificial system. Kim's handling of this in the entire narrative would give credence to מָעוֹן having the meaning of temple, rather than simply a dwelling. What seems to be a problem, however, is that it puts Eli into a situation wherein he will live to see all the good which (God) is portrayed as yet to exhibit toward Israel (v. 32b), when only his descendants following his death (not Eli himself) would be the ones viewing the prosperity coming to Israel. Kim attempts to alleviate this problem by arguing that Eli represents his entire line and that v. 32 reflects the judgment on "the accursed Elides who will look on the bountiful table prepared by Yahweh, without really participating in it" (p. 58–59). Note, however, that the plural verb תִּבְעֲטוּ is used in v. 29 wherein it encompasses both Eli and his sons and their trampling of the sacrifices in the temple precinct. If the entire Elide line is to be part also of the verb נבט in v. 32a, one would by the same token expect a plural verb וְהִבַּטְתֶּם and arguably also a plural vocative subject, צָרֵי מָעוֹן. Seen this way, the use of the singular verb וְהִבַּטְתָּ in the text would seem to limit the recipient of the prophecy to one individual, Eli.

9. Kim, 57. These two verbs (בעט and כבד and their verbal complements) are actually part of a parallel structure, both pointing to the fault of the Elides. Or, more plausibly, as I will argue, the emendation of looking at (נבט) the sacrifices (as per the reading of Qumran and the LXX), desirably eyeing them with an expectation of getting them (emendation based on the LXX and Talmud Berachot 55a), fits into the context of accusing Eli of honoring (כבד) his sons more than God in v. 29b.

On the other hand, the LXX reads καὶ ἵνα τί ἐπέβλεψας ἐπὶ τὸ θυμίαμά μου καὶ εἰς τὴν θυσίαν μου ἀναιδεῖ ὀφθαλμῷ ("and for the purpose of what did you look at my incense and my sacrifice with shameless eye. . . ?"). It seems the LXX translator(s) saw the verb הִבַּטְתָּ (from the root נבט, "look at") rather than the MT תִבְעֲטוּ (from the root בעט, "kick") and either an adverbial adjunct such as רַע עַיִן (cf. Prov 23:6 and 28:22 for its function as the genitive of a construct noun object of the verb and the subject of an independent clause, respectively)[10] or some form of the verb עין rather than the noun מָעוֹן. Buttressing this reading is that the verb וְהִבַּטְתָּ occurs just a few verses later in v. 32, although I consider v. 32a in the MT (וְהִבַּטְתָּ צַר מָעוֹן בְּכֹל אֲשֶׁר־יֵיטִיב אֶת־יִשְׂרָאֵל) as corrupted text (both the LXX and 4QSam[a] omit it).[11] According with the reading נבט, is 4QSam[a] which reads ולמה תביט בזבחי ובמנחתי ("and why do you look at my sacrifice and my offering. . . ?"). This rendition would concur also with the priestly family's greedy observation of the people's sacrifices in 2:13–16 and makes better sense than the word בעט, "to kick [at sacrifices]," which does not make sense literally, generating meaning only figuratively.[12] The suffix conjugation (perfect) הִבַּטְתָּ, following the LXX in tense-aspect, would agree in aspect and number with the imperfect consecutive וַתְּכַבֵּד which follows later in the verse.

Following the reading of the LXX, many have chosen to emend the MT מָעוֹן to מְעַיֵּן ("eyeing jealously"), thus a pōʿel participle,[13] theoretically generating a meaning analogous to the postulated qal עֹיֵן, the qere for the עָוֵן of 1 Samuel 18:9. Such an emendation seems to have been brought out first by Klostermann[14] and was accepted by Budde, Smith and Dhorme.[15] Such a

---

10. The first one who suggested צר עין as an emendation of the MT צִוִּיתִי מָעוֹן seems to be Ehrlich; I will discuss the weakness of such an emendation shortly.

11. Wellhausen suggests that MT v. 32a presumes that Eli sees the demise of his line when he only lives to witness the sign of it, i.e. the death of his two sons. Wellhausen, Der Text, 48–49.

12. Kim's translation of בעט ("to make light of") has blurred the meaning of the verb. See also HALOT 1, 142 for a metaphorical meaning of "to despise."

13. BDB, 733; HALOT 2, 610. GKC, § 55c addresses this form (based nevertheless on the qere reading of 1 Sam 18:9) as the "pōʿel proper."

14. Klostermann does not give a grammatical rationale for his reading the letters מעון as a pōʿel participle in v. 29. Possibly such a reading is to parallel his emendation of components of the immediately preceding אשר צויה to אִישׁ מְרַצֵּד (a man watching stealthily), forming a grammatical as well as a synonymous parallelism, with the reconstruction איש מרצד ומעין (in Klostermann's own rendition: "ein Mann neidisch u. scheelsehend," namely, "an envious and malevolent man"); see Klostermann, Die Bücher Samuelis, 9.

15. See, for example, Smith, Samuel, 24.

reading seems to make better sense in the context of the text, pointing out the greediness of the Elides and thereafter their judgment. But such a *pō'el* participle form is not attested in Biblical and Rabbinic Hebrew for any of the so-called middle weak verbs, all of which follow the *polel* and/or *piel* pattern.[16] Segal also calls this *pō'el* form "un-hebraic."[17] Having said that, one should not totally close the door on the possibility that this rare form could be an idiosyncratic expression of the author.[18]

To complicate the situation further, Ehrlich suggests an emendation of צר עין for the MT מָעוֹן צִוִּיתִי.[19] This is certainly a possibility. But the phrase צר עין is never attested in Biblical Hebrew (צר never occurs as the predicate of עין).[20] Meanwhile, the lexical denotations of צרת עין ("distress of eye") would probably not give the sense of the greediness of eye of the LXX ἀναιδεῖ ὀφθαλμῷ ("with shameless eye").[21]

One other possibility is to emend the MT מעון to מְעַיֵּן (a *piel* participle). The use of the *piel* participle of the stem עין is brought out by Jastrow (entry #3) where he cites Berakot 55a – המאריך בתפלתו ומעיין בה – with his translation "he who stays long in prayer and speculates on it (expecting its fulfillment as a reward for his lengthy prayer)."[22] Imported into 1 Samuel 2:29, this lexical semantic and precise verb-complement syntax seen in נבט... ב of 1 Samuel 2:32 might convey the sense of Eli observing (נבט) the sacrifice and offering, anticipating getting them. However, one would expect an additional בָּהֶם or בָּם following the participle for perfect syntactical accordance ("speculating on them," that is, "speculating on attaining them"). The OT is replete though

---

16. Driver refers to it as a "doubtful restoration"; Driver, *Notes*, 38. Blau is also skeptical about the existence of the *pō'el* stem; see Blau, *Biblical Hebrew*, 237. For more information on the *pō'el* conjugation, see Joüon-Muraoka, § 55a.

17. Segal, "Studies," 208.

18. The existence of the *poel* (or possibly a *poal*) elsewhere in 1 Samuel 21:3 serves to show this *binyan* (although very rarely attested) was in the use of the writer/redactor of Samuel, and in theory only adds support to it possibly occurring elsewhere.

19. Ehrlich, *Randglossen zur Hebräischen Bibel*, 175. Similarly, צרת עין in McCarter, *1 Samuel*, 87, citing Frank M. Cross in personal correspondence; Klein, *1 Samuel*, 22–23. Such an emendation is also suggested by the editors of DJD 17 in the restoration of the lacuna. See Cross, et al., *Qumran Cave 4*, 40.

20. The closest pattern one can compare with is צרת נפש in Genesis 42:21. For the listing of צר(י) עין and עין צרה in post-biblical Hebrew, see Kim, "Eli," 53.

21. Greediness of eye would be better expressed by the lexeme רע from the root רעע I (see רע עין, "evil of eye," in Prov 23:6 and 28:22).

22. Jastrow, *Dictionary*, 1053. See also Levy, *Neuhebräisches*, 645.

with such elliptical verbal complements. One might assume that this could be one such ellipsis.

The challenge of reading מְעַיֵּן (a *piel* participle) as an emended text from the MT מָעוֹן is that there is an almost non-existent use of the *piel* for hollow verbs in classical Hebrew; the *piel* form of עין is only attested in Rabbinic Hebrew.

Nevertheless, it seems to me that the conjecture of מְעַיֵּן as the *piel* of the root עין is more favorable as a solution for the Hebrew מעון in this difficult section. First, beside the problematic *pōʿel*, only the *piel* would work graphically with the letters מעון (assuming a *waw* and *yod* graphical confusion). Second, the *piel* participle works with an existing stem for hollow verbs (the ע-ו category), doing so in the broader family of Hebrew, albeit with as much as a millennium (and maybe longer) between the Talmud and Samuel.

This being said, there seems to be no prevailing conclusion[23] to this textual problem, a *crux interpretum*.

---

23. Wellhausen, Thenius (3rd ed., edited by Löhr, 1898) and Stoebe all refrain from emending the text. Stoebe and Thenius simply leave a blank in their translation.

Bibliography

Aberbach, David. "מנה אחת אפים (1 Sam. I 5): A New Interpretation." *Vetus Testamentum* 24 (1974): 350–353.

Ackerman, James S. "Who Can Stand before YHWH, This Holy God: A reading of 1 Samuel 1–15." *Proof* 11 (1991): 1–24.

Ackerman, Susan. "Who Is Sacrificing at Shiloh? The Priesthoods of Ancient Israel's Regional Sanctuaries." In *Levites and Priests in Biblical History and Tradition*, edited by Mark A. Leuchter and Jeremy M. Hutton, 25–44. Atlanta: Society of Biblical Literature, 2011.

Ackroyd, P. R. *The First Book of Samuel*. Cambridge: Cambridge University Press, 1971.

Adair, James R. *An Inductive Method for Reconstructing the Biblical Text: Illustrated by an Analysis of I Samuel 3*. JNSLMS 2. Stellenbosch: University of Stellenbosch Department of Ancient Studies, 2000.

Albright, William F. *Yahweh and the Gods of Canaan: A Historical Analysis of Two Contrasting Faiths*. Garden City: Doubleday, 1969.

Alter, Robert. *The Art of Biblical Narrative*. New York: Basic Books, 1981.

———. *The David Story: A Translation with Commentary of 1 and 2 Samuel*. New York: W. W. Norton & Company, 2009.

Amit, Yairah. *Reading Biblical Narratives: Literary Criticism and the Hebrew Bible*. Minneapolis: Fortress, 2001.

Andersson, Greger. *Untamable Texts: Literary Studies and Narrative Theory in the Books of Samuel*. The Library of Hebrew Bible/Old Testament Studies. New York: T&T Clark, 2009.

Arnold, Bill T. *1 and 2 Samuel*. The NIV Application Commentary. Grand Rapids: Zondervan, 2014.

The Assyrian Dictionary of the Oriental Institute of the University of Chicago. Chicago: The Oriental Institute, 1956–2011.

Auld, Graeme. *Samuel at the Threshold: Selected Works of Graeme Auld*. Society for Old Testament Study. Aldershot: Ashgate Publishing, 2004.

———. *I & II Samuel: A Commentary*. The Old Testament Library. Louisville: Westminster John Knox, 2011.

Avrahami, Yael. "בוש in the Psalms: Shame or Disappointment?" *Journal for the Study of the Old Testament* 34 (2010): 295–313.

Bailey, Randall C. "The Redemption of YHWH: A Literary Critical Function of the Songs of Hannah and David." *Bibint* 3 (1995): 213–231.

Bal, Mieke. *Narratology: Introduction to the Theory of Narrative*. Toronto: University of Toronto Press, 1985.

Baldwin, Joyce G. *1 and 2 Samuel*. Downers Grove: InterVarsity Press, 2008.

Bar, Shaul. "Grave Matters: Sheol in the Hebrew Bible." *JBQ* 43 (2015): 145–153.

Bar-Efrat, Shimon. *Narrative Art in the Bible*. Sheffield: Sheffield Academic, 1997.

Barr, James. *The Semantics of Biblical Language*. Oxford: Oxford University Press, 1961.

Barton, John. "Reflections on Literary Criticism." In *Method Matters, Essays on the Interpretation of the Hebrew Bible in Honor of David L. Petersen*, edited by Joel M. LeMon and Kent Harold Richards, 523–540. Atlanta: Society of Biblical Literature, 2009.

Bechtel, Lyn M. "The Biblical Experience of Social Shame/Shaming." PhD diss., Drew University, 1983.

———. "The Perception of Shame within the Divine-Human Relationship in Biblical Israel." In *Uncovering Ancient Stones: Essays in Memory of H. Neil Richardson*, edited by Lewis M. Hopfe, 79–92. Winona Lake, IN: Eisenbrauns, 1994.

———. "Shame as a Sanction of Social Control in Biblical Israel: Judicial, Political, and Social Shaming." *Journal for the Study of the Old Testament* 16 (1991): 76–47.

———. "What if Dinah Is Not Raped? (Genesis 34)." *Journal for the Study of the Old Testament* 62 (1994): 19–36.

Bedford, Olwen, and Kwang-Kuo Kwang. "Guilt and Shame in Chinese Culture: A Cross-Cultural Framework from the Perspective of Morality and Identity." *Journal of the Theory of Social Behaviour* 33 (2003): 127–144.

Berding, Kenneth. "The Hermeneutical Framework of Social-Scientific Criticism: How Much Can Evangelicals Get Involved?" *Evangelical Quarterly* 75 (2005): 3–22.

Bergant, Dianne. "'My Beloved Is Mine and I Am His' (Song 2:16): The Song of Songs and Honor and Shame." In *Semeia 68: Honor and Shame in the World of the Bible*, edited by Victor H. Matthews, Don C. Benjamin, and Claudia Camp, 23–40. Atlanta: SBL Press, 1996.

Bergen, Robert D. *1, 2 Samuel*. The New American Commentary 7. Nashville: Broadman & Holman, 1996.

Betsworth, Sharon. *The Reign of God Is Such as These: A Socio-Literary Analysis of Daughters in the Gospel of Mark*. London: T&T Clark, 2010.

Birch, Bruce C. *The Rise of the Israelite Monarchy: The Growth and Development of I Samuel 7–15*. Society of Biblical Literature Dissertation Series 27. Missoula: Scholars Press, 1976.

———. "Samuel." In *Eerdmans Dictionary of the Bible*, edited by David N. Freedman, Allen C. Mayers, and Astrid B. Beck, 1161–1162. Grand Rapids: Eerdmans, 2000.

———. "1 and 2 Samuel." In *New Interpreter's Bible*, edited by Leander E. Keck, 947–1383. Vol. 2. Nashville: Abingdon Press, 1998.

Blau, Joshua. *Biblical Hebrew Phonology and Morphology: An Introduction*. Linguistic Studies in Ancient West Semitic 2. Winona Lake: Eisenbrauns, 2010.

Blenkinsopp, Joseph. "Kiriath-Jearim and the Ark." *Journal of Biblical Literature* 88 (1969): 143–56.

Block, Daniel I. "Beyond the Grave: Ezekiel's Vision of Death and Afterlife." *Bulletin for Biblical Research* 2 (1992): 113–141.

Bock, Darrell L. *Luke 9:51–24:53*. Baker Exegetical Commentary on the New Testament. Grand Rapids: Baker Academic, 2007.

Bodner, Keith. *1 Samuel: A Narrative Commentary*. Hebrew Bible Monographs 19. Sheffield: Sheffield Phoenix, 2009.

Boiger, Michael, Derya Güngör, Mayumi Karasawa, and Batja Mesquita. "Defending Honour, Keeping Face: Interpersonal Affordances of Anger and Shame in Turkey and Japan." *Cognition and Emotion* 28 (2014): 1255–1269.

Borooah, Vani Kant, Nidhi S. Sabharwal, Dilip G. Diwakar, Vinod Kumar Mishra, and Ajaya Kumar Naik. *Caste, Discrimination, and Exclusion in Modern India*. New Delhi: SAGE Publications, 2015.

Botha, P. J. "Honour and Shame as Keys to the Interpretation of Malachi." *Old Testament Essays* 14 (2001): 392–403.

———. "Isaiah 37:21–35: Sennacherib's Siege of Jerusalem as a Challenge to the Honour of Yahweh." *Old Testament Essays* 13 (2000): 269–282.

Botterweck, G. J., and H. Ringgren. *Theological Dictionary of the Old Testament*. Translated by J. T. Willis, G. W. Bromiley, and D. E. Green. 8 vols. Grand Rapids: Eerdmans, 1974–2006.

Brettler, Marc. "The Composition of 1 Samuel 1–2." *Journal of Biblical Literature* 116 (1997): 601–612.

Briscoe, David Owen. "The Implications of Samuel's Priestly Functions in the Setting of the Former Prophets." PhD diss., New Orleans Baptist Theological Seminary, 1988.

Brown, A. Philip, II. "Point of View in the Book of Ezra." *Bibliotheca Sacra* 162 (2005): 310–330.

Brown, Francis, S. R. Driver, and C. A. Briggs, eds. *Hebrew and English Lexicon of the Old Testament*. Oxford: Clarendon Press, 1906.

Brueggemann, Walter. *First and Second Samuel*. Louisville: Westminster John Knox Press, 1990.

———. *Ichabod toward Home: The Journey of God's Glory*. Grand Rapids: Eerdmans, 2002.

———. "I Samuel 1: A Sense of a Beginning." *Zeitschrift für die alttestamentliche Wissenschaft* 102 (1990): 33–48.

Budde, Karl. *Die Bücher Samuel erklärt*. Tübingen and Leipzig: Mohr (Siebeck), 1902.

Byron, John. "Childlessness and Ambiguity in the Ancient World." *Proceedings* 30 (2010): 17–46.

Callaham, Scott N. *Modality and the Biblical Hebrew Infinitive Absolute*. Abhandlungen für die Kunde des Morgenlandes 71. Wiesbaden: Harrasowitz, 2010.

Campbell, Antony F. *The Ark Narrative (1 Sam 4–6; 2 Sam 6): A Form-Critical and Traditio-Historical Study*. Society of Biblical Literature Dissertation Series 16. Missoula: Scholars Press, 1975.

———. *Of Prophets and Kings: A Late Ninth-Century Document (1 Samuel 1–2 Kings 10)*. CBQMS 17. Washington, DC: Catholic Biblical Association of America, 1986.

———. "Yahweh and the Ark: A Case Study in Narrative." *Journal of Biblical Literature* 98 (1979): 31–43.

Campbell, Barth. *Honor, Shame, and the Rhetoric of 1 Peter*. Society of Biblical Literature Dissertation Series 160. Atlanta: Scholars Press, 1998.

Campbell, J. K. *Honour, Family and Patronage: A Study of Institutions and Moral Values in a Greek Mountain Community*. Oxford: Clarendon Press, 1964.

Caquot, André, and Philippe de Robert. *Les Livres de Samuel*. Commentaire de l'Ancien Testament VI. Genève: Labor et Fides, 1994.

Cartledge, Tony W. *Vows in the Hebrew Bible and the Ancient Near East*. JSOTSup 147. Sheffield: Sheffield Academic, 1993.

Chalcraft, David J., ed. *Social-Scientific Old Testament Criticism*. Sheffield: Sheffield Academic, 1997.

Chalcraft, David J., Frauke Uhlenbruch, and Rebecca Sally Watson, eds. *Methods, Theories, Imagination: Social Scientific Approaches in Biblical Studies*. Sheffield: Sheffield Phoenix Press, 2014.

Cheng, Chung-Ying. "The Concept of Face and Its Confucian Roots." *Journal of Chinese Philosophy* 13 (1986): 329–348.

Chia, Philip. "Biblical Studies in the Rising Asia: An Asian Perspective on the Future of the Biblical Past." *Sino-Christian Studies* 12 (2011): 329–348.

Childs, Brevard S. *Introduction to the Old Testament as Scripture.* Philadelphia: Fortress, 1979.

Choi, Shin-Ho, and Michael A. Rynkiewich. "Face and the Loss of Reputation in the Korean Protestant Church." *Missio Dei: A Journal of Missional Theology and Praxis* 11 (2020): http://missiodeijournal.com/issues/md-11/authors/md-11-choi-rynkiewich.

Clines, D. J. A., ed. *Dictionary of Classical Hebrew.* 8 vols. Sheffield: Sheffield Academic, 1993–2011.

Coggins, Richard, Anthony Phillips, and Michael Knibb, eds. *Israel's Prophetic Tradition: Essays in Honour of Peter R. Ackroyd.* Cambridge: Cambridge University Press, 1982.

Cole, Alan. *Exodus.* Edited by Donald J. Wiseman. Tyndale Old Testament Commentaries. London: InterVarsity Press, 1973.

Cook, Joan E. *Hannah's Desire, God's Design: Early Interpretations of the Story of Hannah.* JSOTSup 282. Sheffield: Sheffield Academic, 1999.

Cook, Ryan. "Pious Eli? The Characterization of Eli in 1 Samuel 3:18." *Horizons in Biblical Theology* 40 (2018): 166–182.

Corrigan, Gregory M. "Paul's Shame for the Gospel." *Biblical Theology Bulletin* 16 (1986): 22–27.

Crook, Zeba A. "Honor, Shame, and Social Status Revisited." *Journal of Biblical Literature* 128 (2009): 591–611.

———. "Structure versus Agency in Studies of the Biblical Social World: Engaging with Louise Lawrence." *Journal for the Study of the New Testament* (2007): 251–275.

Cross, Frank Moore, Donald W. Parry, Richard J. Saley, and Eugene Ulrich, eds. *Qumran Cave 4, XII: 1–2 Samuel.* Discoveries in the Judaean Desert 17. Oxford: Clarendon, 2005.

Cowley, A. ed. *Aramaic Papyri of the Fifth Century B.C.* Oxford: Clarendon Press, 1923.

Daley, Brian E. "Position and Patronage in the Early Church: The Original Meaning of Primacy of Honour." *JTS* 44 (1993): 529–553.

Daniels, John W. "Engendering Gossip in Galatians 2:11–14: The Social Dynamics of Honor, Shame, Performance, and Gossip." *Biblical Theology Bulletin* 47 (2017): 171–179.

Daube, D. "The Culture of Deuteronomy." *Orita: Ibadan Journal of Religious Studies* 3 (1969): 27–52. Reprinted in vol. 3 of *Biblical Law and Literature: Collected Essays of David Daube,* edited by Calum Carmichael, 995–1013. Berkeley: University of California Press, 2003.

Day, John, ed. *Prophecy and Prophets in Ancient Israel.* New York: T&T Clark, 2010.

———. *Yahweh and the Gods and Goddesses of Canaan*. JSOTSup 265. Sheffield: Sheffield Academic, 2000.

Deist, Ferdinand. "'ΛPPΛYIM (1 Sam. I 5) < *PYM?" *Vetus Testamentum* 27 (1977): 205–209.

deSilva, David. *Bearing Christ's Reproach: The Challenge of Hebrews in an Honor Culture*. North Richland Hills, TX: Bibal Press, 1999.

———. *Despising Shame: Honor Discourse and Community Maintenance in the Epistle to the Hebrews*. Society of Biblical Literature Dissertation Series 152. Atlanta: Scholars Press, 1995.

———. *Honor, Patronage, Kinship & Purity: Unlocking New Testament Culture*. Downers Grove, IL: InterVasity Press, 2000.

———. *The Hope of Glory: Honor Discourse and New Testament Interpretation*. Collegeville, MN: Liturgical Press, 1999.

Dietrich, Walter. *The Early Monarchy in Israel: The Tenth Century B.C.E.* Translated by Joachim Vette. Leiden: Brill, 2007.

———. "Samuel – ein Prophet?" In *Prophets and Prophecy in Jewish and Early Christian Literature*, edited by Joseph Verheyden, Korinna Zamfir, and Tobias Nicklas, 1–17. Wissenschaftliche Untersuchungen zum Neuen Testament 2/286. Tübingen: Mohr Siebeck, 2010.

Dillard, Raymond B., and Tremper Longman III. *An Introduction to the Old Testament*. 2nd ed. Grand Rapids: Zondervan, 2009.

Downing, F. Gerald. "'Honor' among Exegetes." *Catholic Biblical Quarterly* 61 (1999): 53–73.

Dozeman, Thomas B. *Commentary on Exodus*. Grand Rapids: Eerdmans, 2009.

Driesbach, Jason K. *4QSamuel^a and the Text of Samuel*. Leiden: Brill, 2016.

Driver, G. R. "The Plague of the Philistines (1 Samuel v, 6–vi, 16)." *Journal of the Royal Asiatic Society* 82, no. 1/2 (1950): 50–52.

Driver, Samuel R. *Notes on the Hebrew Text and the Topography of the Books of Samuel*. Oxford: Clarendon, 1913.

Duff, Paul Brooks. "Honor or Shame: The Language of Processions and Perception in 2 Cor. 2:14–6:13; 7:2–4." PhD diss., University of Chicago, 1988.

Dumbrell, W. J. "'In Those Days There Was No King in Israel; Every Man Did What Was Right in His Own Eyes': The Purpose of the Book of Judges Reconsidered." *Journal for the Study of the Old Testament* 25 (1983): 23–33.

Dunn, David M. "New Directions in the Study of Biblical Hebrew Narrative." In *Beyond Form Criticism: Essays in Old Testament Literary Criticism*, edited by Paul R. House, 412–422. Winona Lake, Eisenbrauns, 1992.

Durham, John. *Exodus*. Word Biblical Commentary 3. Dallas: Word, 1998.

Edelman, Diana V. *King Saul in the Historiography of Judah*. JSOTSup 121. Sheffield: JSOT Press, 1991.

Ehrlich, Arnold B. *Randglossen zur Hebräischen Bibel: Textkritisches, Sprachliches und Sachliches*. Vol. 3. Leipzig: J. C. Hinrichs, 1912.

Elliger, K., and W. Rudolph, eds. *Biblia Hebraica Stuttgartensia*. Stuttgart: Deutsche Bibelstiftung, 1977.

Elliott, John. *Conflict, Community, and Honor: 1 Peter in Social-Scientific Perspective*. Eugene: Wipf & Stock, 2007.

———. *A Home for the Homeless: A Social-Scientific Criticism of 1 Peter, Its Situation and Strategy*. Philadelphia: Fortress, 1981.

———. *What Is Social-Scientific Criticism?* Minneapolis: Fortress, 1993.

Ellison, H. L. *The Centrality of the Messianic Idea for the Old Testament*. Tyndale Monographs. London: Tyndale Press, 1953.

Engineer, Asghar Ali. "Politics of Identity Caste and Religion in India." *Hamdard Islamicus* 33 (2010): 186–190.

Emerton, J. A. "Sheol and the Sons of Belial." *Vetus Testamentum* 37 (1987): 214–218.

Esler, Philip H., ed. *Ancient Israel: The Old Testament in Its Social Context*. London: SCM, 2006.

Eslinger, Lyle Mark. *Kingship of God in Crisis: A Close Reading of 1 Samuel 1–12*. Bible and Literature Series 10. Decatur: Almond, 1985.

———. "Viewpoints and Points of View in 1 Samuel 8–12." *Journal for the Study of the Old Testament* 26 (1983): 61–76.

Evans, Mary J. *The Message of Samuel: Personalities, Potential, Politics and Power*. Downers Grove: InterVarsity Press, 2004.

Exum, J. Cheryl. *Tragedy and Biblical Narrative: Arrows of the Almighty*. Cambridge: Cambridge University Press, 1992.

Fernandez, Eleazar S. *Toward a Theology of Struggle*. Eugene, OR: Wipf and Stock, 1994.

Firth, David G. "Parallelismus Memborum in Prose Narrative: The Function of Repetition in 1 Samuel 5–6." *Old Testament Essays* 15 (2002): 647–656.

———. "'Play It Again, Sam': The Poetics of Narrative Repetition in 1 Samuel 1–7." *Tyndale Bulletin* 56 (2005): 1–17.

———. Review of *Ichabod Toward Home: The Journey of God's Glory*, by Walter Brueggemann. *Review of Biblical Literature* 5 (2003): 253–255.

———. *1 & 2 Samuel*. Apollos Old Testament Commentary. Downers Grove: InterVarsity, 2009.

Fitzmyer, Joseph A. *The Gospel according to Luke I–IX*. The Anchor Bible 28. New York: Doubleday, 1979.

Fleming, Daniel E. *The Installation of Baal's High Priestess at Emar: A Window on Ancient Syrian Religion*. Harvard Semitic Studies 42. Atlanta: Scholars Press, 1992.

Fokkelman, Jan P. "Desire Divine: Poems – Pillars – Pivots." In *Characters and Characterization in the Book of Samuel*, edited by Keith Bodner and Benjamin J. M. Johnson, 14–24. London: T&T Clark, 2020.

———. *Narrative Art and Poetry in the Books of Samuel: Vow and Desire (I Sam. 1-12)*. Studia Semitica Neerlandica 31. Assen: Van Gorcum, 1993.

———. *Reading Biblical Narrative: An Introductory Guide*. Louisville: Westminster John Knox, 1999.

Fouts, David M. "Added Support for Reading '70 Men' in 1 Samuel VI:19." *Vetus Testamentum* 42 (1992): 394.

———. "A Defense of the Hyperbolic Interpretation of Large Numbers in the Old Testament." *The Journal of the Evangelical Theological Society* 40 (1997): 377–387.

Frolov, Serge. *The Turn of the Cycle: 1 Samuel 1-8 in Synchronic and Diachronic Perspectives*. Berlin: Walter de Gruyter, 2014.

———. "1 Samuel 1-8: The Prophet as Agent Provocateur." In *Constructs of Prophecy in the Former and Latter Prophets and Other Texts*, edited by Lester L. Grabbe and Martti Nissinen, 77–85. Atlanta: Society of Biblical Literature, 2011.

Funk, Robert W. *The Poetics of Biblical Narrative*. Sonoma, CA: Polebridge Press, 1988.

Garsiel, Moshe. *The First Book of Samuel: A Literary Study of Comparative Structures, Analogies and Parallels*. Ramat-Gan: Revivim, 1985.

Georges, Jayson, and Mark D. Baker. *Ministering in Honor-Shame Cultures: Biblical Foundations and Practical Essentials*. Downers Grove: InterVarsity Press, 2016.

Gener, Timoteo D., and Stephen T. Pardue, eds. *Asian Christian Theology: Evangelical Perspectives*. London: Langham Global Library, 2019.

Gesenius, Wilhelm. *Geschichte der hebräischen Sprache und Schrift: Eine philologisch-historische Einleitung in die Sprachlehren und Wörterbücher der hebräischen Sprache*. Leipzig: Vogel, 1815.

———. *Hebräisches und Aramäisches Handwörterbuch über das Alte Testament*. Auflage 18. Bearbeitet und herausgegeben von Herbert Donner. Heidelberg: Springer, 2013.

Geyer, John B. "Mice and Rites in 1 Samuel V–VI." *Vetus Testamentum* 31 (1981): 293–304.

Gilkey, Langdon. "Interpretation of Faith for Church and World." In *The Vocation of the Theologian*, edited by Theodore Jennings, 95–112. Philadelphia: Fortress, 1985.

Gilmour, Rachelle. *Representing the Past: A Literary Analysis of Narrative Historiography in the Book of Samuel*. VTSup 143. Leiden: Brill, 2011.

Gitay, Yehoshua. "Reflections on the Poetics of the Samuel Narrative: The Question of the Ark Narrative." *Catholic Biblical Quarterly* 54, no. 2 (1992): 221–230.

Glatt-Gilad, David A. "Yahweh's Honor at Stake: A Divine Conundrum." *Journal for the Study of the Old Testament* 98 (2002): 63–74.

Glueck, Nelson. *Hesed in the Bible*. Translated by Alfred Gottschalk. Edited by Elisas L. Epstein. Cincinnati: Hebrew Union College, 1967.

Gnuse, Robert. *The Dream Theophany of Samuel: Its Structure in Relation to Ancient Near Eastern Dreams and Its Theological Significance*. Lanham: University Press of America, 1984.

———. "A Reconsideration of the Form-Critical Structure in 1 Samuel 3: An Ancient Near Eastern Dream Theophany." *Zeitschrift für die alttestamentliche Wissenschaft* 94 (1982): 379–390.

———. Review of *Ichabod toward Home: The Journey of God's Glory*, by Walter Brueggemann. *Catholic Biblical Quarterly* 65 (2003): 103–4.

Goetze, Albrecht. "The So-Called Intensive of the Semitic Languages." *Journal of the American Oriental Society* 62 (1942): 1–8.

Gordon, Robert P., ed. *The Place Is Too Small for Us: The Israelite Prophets in Recent Scholarship*. Winona Lake: Eisenbrauns, 1995.

———. "'Who Made the Kingmaker?' Reflections on Samuel and the Institution of the Monarchy." In *Faith, Tradition, and History: Old Testament Historiography in Its Near Eastern Context*, edited by A. R. Millard, James K. Hoffmeier, and David W. Baker, 255–270. Winona Lake: Eisenbrauns, 1994.

———. *1 and 2 Samuel*. Old Testament Guides. Sheffield: Sheffield Academic, 1984.

Gottwald, Norman K. *The Hebrew Bible: A Socio-Literary Introduction*. Minneapolis: Augsburg Fortress, 1985.

Guha, Sumit. *Beyond Caste: Identity and Power in South Asia, Past and Present*. Leiden: Brill, 2013.

Gunn, David M. *Fate of King Saul: An Interpretation of a Biblical Story*. JSOTSup 14. Sheffield: JSOT Press, 1980.

Halbertal, Moshe, and Stephen Holmes. *The Beginning of Politics: Power in the Biblical Book of Samuel*. Princeton: Princeton University Press, 2017.

Halpern, Baruch. *David's Secret Demons: Messiah, Murderer, Traitor, King*. Grand Rapids: Eerdmans, 2001.

Hanley, Ryan Cole. "The Use of Nakedness Imagery as Theological Language in the Old Testament." PhD diss., Southern Baptist Theological Seminary, 2019.

Hare, John Allen. "The Literary Portrait of Samuel: A Spiritual Biography." PhD diss., Emory University, 1972.

Hasel, Gerhard. *Old Testament Theology: Basic Issues in the Current Debate*. 4th ed. Grand Rapids: Eerdmans, 1991.

Hellerman, Joseph. "Challenging the Authority of Jesus: Mark 11:27–33 and Mediterranean Notions of Honor and Shame." *The Journal of the Evangelical Theological Society* 43, no. 2 (2000): 213–228.

Hertzberg, Hans Wilhelm. *I & II Samuel: A Commentary*. Translated by J. S. Bowden. Old Testament Library. Philadelphia: Westminster Press, 1964.

Hoffner, Harry A. *1 & 2 Samuel: Evangelical Exegetical Commentary*. Bellingham: Lexham Press, 2015.

Hornkohl, Aaron D. "Her Word versus His: Establishing the Underlying Text in 1 Samuel 1:23." *Journal of Biblical Literature* 133 (2014): 465–477.

Horrell, David G., ed. *Social-Scientific Approaches to New Testament Interpretation*. Edinburgh: T&T Clark, 1999.

Houston, Walter. "Tragedy in the Courts of the Lord: A Socio-Literary Reading of the Death of Nadab and Abihu." *Journal for the Study of the Old Testament* 90 (2000): 31–39.

Howard, David M. *An Introduction to the Old Testament Historical Books*. Chicago: Moody Press, 1993.

Hu, Hsien-Chin. "The Chinese concepts of 'face'". In *Face: Power game of Chinese people*, 40–62. [In Chinese] Beijing: China Renmin University Press, 2004.

Huang, Guang Guo. "Face in Chinese Society and Its Communication." In *Face: Power Game of Chinese People*, 63–87. [In Chinese] Beijing: China Renmin University Press, 2004

Hundley, Michael. "To Be or Not to Be: A Reexamination of Name Language in Deuteronomy and the Deuteronomistic History." *Vetus Testamentum* 59 (2009): 533–555.

Hutzli, Jürg. "Role and Significance of Ancestors in the Books of Samuel." In *The Books of Samuel: Stories – History – Reception History*, edited by Walter Dietrich, 424–437. Leuven: Peeters, 2016.

Hwang, Jerry. "'How Long Will My Glory Be Reproach?' Honour and Shame in Old Testament Lament Traditions." *Old Testament Essays* 30, no. 3 (2017): 684–706.

Janzen, J. G. "'Samuel Opened the Doors of the House of Yahweh' (1 Samuel 3:15)." *Journal for the Study of the Old Testament* 26 (1983): 89–96.

Jastrow, Marcus. *A Dictionary of the Targumim, the Talmud Babli and Yerushalmi, and the Midrashic Literature*. Vol. 2. London: Luzac, 1903.

Jenni, Ernst. *Das hebräische Piel: Syntaktisch-semasiologische Untersuchung einer Verbalform im Alten Testament*. Zürich: EVZ-Verlag, 1968.

———. "Nifal und Hitpael im Biblisch-Hebräischen." In *Studien zur Sprachwelt des Alten Testaments III*, 131–303. Stuttgart: Kohlhammer, 2012.

Jewett, Robert. *Saint Paul Returns to the Movies: Triumph over Shame*. Grand Rapids: Eerdmans, 1999.

Jobes, Karen. Review of *Shame and Honor in the Book of Esther*, by T. S. Laniak. *Review of Biblical Literature* 2 (2000): 273–275.

Jobling, David. *The Sense of Biblical Narrative: Structural Analyses in the Hebrew Bible*. 2nd ed. JSOTSup 7. Sheffield: JSOT Press, 1986.

---. *1 Samuel*. Edited by David W. Cotter. Berit Olam. Collegeville, MN: Liturgical Press, 1998.

Johnson, Dave. "The Biblical Reflections on Shame and Honor in Asia." *Asian Journal of Pentecostal Studies* 21 (2018): 1–3.

Josephus, Flavius. *The Antiquities of the Jews*. Translated by William Whiston. London: Wordsworth Classics, 2006.

Joubert, S. J. "The Jerusalem Community as Role-Model for a Cosmopolitan Christian Group: A Socio-Literary Analysis of Luke's Symbolic Universe." *Neotestamentica* 29 (1995): 49–59.

Joüon, Paul, and T. Muraoka. *A Grammar of Biblical Hebrew*. Subsidia Biblica 27. Roma: Editrice Pontificio Istituto Biblico, 2006.

Jumper, James Nicholas. "Honor and Shame in the Deuteronomic Covenant and the Deuteronomistic Presentation of the Davidic Covenant." Ph.D. diss., Harvard University, 2013.

Kaiser, Walter C. *A History of Israel, from the Bronze Age through the Jewish Wars*. Nashville: Broadman & Holman, 1998.

Kang, Bin. "The Positive Role of Shame for Post-Exilic Returnees in Ezra/Nehemiah." *Old Testament Essays* 33 (2020): 250–265.

---. "The Rhetoric of Honor and Shame as a Significant Role in Understanding the Judgment Oracle against Tyre in Ezekiel 28:1–19." ThM thesis, Asia Graduate School of Theology, 2019.

Kasle, Annette Levinson. "An Analysis of the Role of Shaming and Shame in the Tanakh: The Divine Response to Arrogance." PhD diss., Jewish Theological Seminary of America, 2019.

Kautzsch, E., ed. *Gesenius' Hebrew Grammar*. Translated by A. E. Cowley. 2nd ed. Oxford: Clarendon Press, 1910.

Keddie, Gordon J. *Dawn of a Kingdom: The Message of 1 Samuel*. Darlington, Durham: Evangelical Press, 1988.

Keil, C. F. *Biblical Commentary on the Books of Samuel*. Grand Rapids: Eerdmans, 1956.

Kim, Koowon. "Eli, 'Enemy of a Temple'? A Study of מעון in 1 Samuel 2.29 and 3.32." *The Bible Translator* 70 (2019): 50–63.

---. *1 Samuel*. Asia Bible Commentary Series. Carlisle Langham Global Library, 2018.

Kim, Sebastian C. H., ed. *Christian Theology in Asia*. Cambridge: Cambridge University Press, 2008.

Kim, Seong-Kwang Kevin. "Paragraph Delimitation in 1 Samuel 1–7." PhD diss., Dallas Theological Seminary, 2019.

Kiraz, George A., and Joseph Bali. *The Syriac Peshitta Bible with English Translation: Samuel*. Translated by Donald M. Walter and Gillian Greenberg. Piscataway: Gorgias Press, 2015.

Kirkpatrick, Shane. *Competing for Honor: A Social-Scientific Reading of Daniel 1–6*. Leiden: Brill, 2005.

Kittel, G., and G. Friedrich, eds. *Theological Dictionary of the New Testament*. Translated by G. W. Bromiley. 10 vols. Grand Rapids: Eerdmans, 1964–1976.

Klopfenstein, Martin A. *Scham and Schande nach dem Alten Testament*. Abhandlungen zur Theologie des Alten und Neuen Testaments 62. Zurich: Theologischer Verlag Zürich, 1972.

Klostermann, August. *Die Bücher Samuelis und der Könige*. Nördlingen: C. H. Beck, 1887.

Koehler, L., W. Baumgartner, and J. J. Stamm. *The Hebrew and Aramaic Lexicon of the Old Testament*. Trans. and ed. under the supervision of M. E. J. Richardson. Study ed. 2 vols. Leiden: Brill, 2001.

Kratz, Reinhard G. *The Prophets of Israel*. Critical Studies in the Hebrew Bible 2. Winona Lake: Eisenbrauns, 2015.

Labuschagne, C. J. *The Incomparability of Yahweh in the Old Testament*. Leiden: Brill, 1966.

Lambdin, Thomas O. *Introduction to Biblical Hebrew*. London: Darton, Longman & Todd, 1973.

Landry, David. "Honor Restored: New Light on the Parable of the Prudent Steward (Luke 16:1–8a)." *Journal of Biblical Literature* 119 (2000): 287–309.

Laniak, Timothy S. *Shame and Honor in the Book of Esther*. Society of Biblical Literature Dissertation Series 165. Atlanta: Scholars Press, 1998.

Lapsley, Jacqueline E. "Shame and Self-Knowledge: The Positive Role of Shame in Ezekiel's View of the Moral Self." In *The Book of Ezekiel: Theological and Anthropological Perspectives*, edited by Margaret S. Odell and John T. Strong, 143-173. Atlanta: Society of Biblical Literature, 2000.

Lawrence, Louise Joy. "'For Truly, I Tell You, They Have Received Their Reward' (Matt 6:2): Investigating Honor Precedence and Honor Virtue." *Catholic Biblical Quarterly* 64 (2002): 687–702.

Lemche, Niels P. *Ancient Israel: A New History of Israel*. 2nd ed. London: Bloomsbury T&T Clark, 2015.

LeMon, Joel M., and Kent Harold Richards, eds. *Method Matters, Essays on the Interpretation of the Hebrew Bible in Honor of David L. Petersen*. Atlanta: Society of Biblical Literature, 2009.

Lemos, T. M. "Shame and Mutilation of Enemies in the Hebrew Bible." *Journal of Biblical Literature* 125 (2006): 229–232.

Lendon, J. E. *Empire of Honour: The Art of Government in the Roman World*. Oxford: Oxford University Press, 2002.

Leuchter, Mark. "Something Old, Something Older: Reconsidering 1 Sam. 2:27–36." *Journal of Hebrew Scriptures* 4 (2003): art. 6. www.jhsonline.org.

———. *Samuel and the Shaping of Tradition*. Oxford: Oxford University Press, 2013.

———. "Samuel: A Prophet Like Moses or a Priest Like Moses?" In *Israelite Prophecy and the Deuteronomistic History: Portrait, Reality, and the Formation of a History*, edited by Mignon R. Jacobs and Raymond F. Person, 147–168. Atlanta: Society of Biblical Literature, 2013.

Levasheff, Drake. "Jesus of Nazareth, Paul of Tarsus, and the Early Christian Challenge to Honor and Shame Values." PhD diss., UCLA, 2013.

Levy, Jacob. *Neuhebräisches und chaldäisches Wörterbuch über die Talmudim und Midraschim*. Leipzig: Brockhaus, 1876–1889.

Lewis, Theodore J. "The Textual History of the Song of Hannah: 1 Samuel II 1–10." *Vetus Testamentum* 44 (1994): 18–46.

Long, V. Philips. *1 and 2 Samuel: An Introduction and Commentary*. Tyndale Old Testament Commentaries 8. Downers Grove: InterVarsity Press, 2020.

Mahlangu, E. "The ancient Mediterranean Values of Honour and Shame as a Hermeneutical Procedure: A Social-Scientific Criticism in an African Perspective." *Verbum Et Ecclesia* 22 (2001): 85–100.

Malessa, Michael. *Untersuchungen zur verbalen Valenz im biblischen Hebräisch*. Studia Semitica Neerlandica 49. Assen: Van Gorcum, 2006.

Malina, Bruce J. "The Bible, Witness, or Warrant: Reflections on Daniel Patte's Ethics of Biblical Interpretation." *Biblical Theology Bulletin* 26 (1996): 82–87.

———. *The New Testament World: Insights from Cultural Anthropology*. Atlanta: John Knox Press, 1981.

———. "Rhetorical Criticism and Social-Scientific Criticism: Why Don't Romanticism Leave Us Alone." In *The Social World of the New Testament, Insights and Models*, edited by Jerome H. Neyrey and Eric C. Stewart, 5–21. Peabody: Hendrikson, 2008.

Malina, Bruce J., and John J. Pilch, eds. *Social Scientific Models for Interpreting the Bible: Essays by the Context Group in Honor of Bruce J. Malina*. Boston: Brill, 2001.

Manley, G. T., and D. J. Wiseman. "Judges." In *New Bible Dictionary*, 627. Downers Grove: InterVarsity Press, 1996.

Marcus, David. *Jephthah and His Vow*. Lubbock, TX: Texas Tech Press, 1986.

Maré, Leonard P. "Honour and Shame in Psalm 44." *Scriptura* 113 (2014): 1–12.

Marshall, Howard. *The Gospel of Luke: A Commentary on the Greek Text*. New International Greek Testament Commentary 13. Grand Rapids: Eerdmans, 1978.

Marshall, Peter. "A Metaphor of Social Shame: THRIAMBEUEIN in 2 Cor. 2:14." *Novum Testamentum* 25 (1983): 302–317.

Marsman, Hennie J. *Women in Ugarit and Israel: Their Social and Religious Position in the Context of the Ancient Near East*. Old Testament Studies 46. Leiden: Brill, 2003.

Matthews, Victor H. "Honor and Shame in Gender Related Legal Situation in the Hebrew Bible." In *Gender and Law in the Hebrew Bible and the Ancient Near East*, edited by Victor H. Matthews, Bernard M. Levinson, and Tikva Frymer Kensky, 97–112. Sheffield: Sheffield Academic, 1998.

Matthews, Victor H., and Don C. Benjamin. *Social World of Ancient Israel, 1250–587 BCE*. Peabody, MA: Hendrickson, 1993.

Matthews, Victor H., Don C. Benjamin, and Claudia Camp, eds. *Semeia 68: Honor and Shame in the World of the Bible*. Atlanta: SBL Press, 1996.

Mbuvi, Andrew M. "The Ancient Mediterranean Values of Honour and Shame as a Hermeneutical Lens for Reading the Book of Job." *Old Testament Essays* 23 (2010): 752–768.

McCarter, Peter Kyle. *I Samuel: A New Translation with Introduction, Notes, and Commentary*. The Anchor Bible 8. New York: Doubleday, 1995.

McKenzie, Steven L. *King David: A Biography*. Oxford: Oxford University Press, 2000.

McVann, M. "Reading Mark Ritually: Honor-Shame and the Ritual of Baptism." In *Semeia 67: Transformations, Passages, and Processes: Ritual Approaches to Biblical Texts*, edited by Mark McVann and Bruce Malina, 179–198. Atlanta: SBL Press, 1994.

Milgrom, Jacob. "Further on the Expiatory Sacrifices." *Journal of Biblical Literature* 115 (1996): 511–514.

———. *Leviticus 1–16: A New Translation with Introduction and Commentary*. Edited by W. F. Albright and D. N. Freedman. The Anchor Bible 3. New York: Doubleday, 1991.

Miller, Patrick D., and J. J. M. Roberts. *The Hand of the Lord: A Reassessment of the "Ark Narrative" of 1 Samuel*. Baltimore: Johns Hopkins University Press, 1977.

Minschke, Werner. *The Global Gospel: Achieving Missional Impact in Our Multicultural World*. Scottsdale: Mission One, 2014.

Miscall, Peter D. *1 Samuel: A Literary Reading*. Bloomington, IN: Indiana University Press, 1986.

Moberly, R. W. L. *Old Testament Theology: Reading the Hebrew Bible as Christian Scripture*. Grand Rapids: Baker Academic, 2013.

Moon, Joshua. "Honor and Shame in Hosea's Marriage." *Journal for the Study of the Old Testament* 39 (2015): 335–351.

Moxnes, Halvor. "Honor and Righteousness in Romans." *Journal for the Study of the New Testament* 32 (1988): 61–77.

———. "Honor and Shame." In *The Social Sciences and New Testament Interpretation*, edited by Richard L. Rohrbaugh, 19–40. Peabody: Hendrickson, 1996.

Muenchow, Charles. "Dust and Dirt in Job 42:6." *Journal of Biblical Literature* 108 (1989): 597–611.

Muilenburg, James. "Form Criticism and Beyond." *Journal of Biblical Literature* 88 (1969): 1–18.

Müller, Reinhard. "1 Samuel 1 as the Opening Chapter of the Deuteronomistic History." In *Is Samuel among the Deuteronomists? Current Views on the Place of Samuel in a Deuteronomistic History*, edited by Cynthia Eden Burg and Juha Pakkala, 207–224. Atlanta: SBL Press, 2013.

Muraoka, Takamitsu. *A Greek-English Lexicon of the Septuagint*. Leuven: Peeters, 2009.

———. "1 Sam 1, 15 Again." *Biblica* 77 (1996): 98–99.

Murphy, Francesca A. *1 Samuel*. Brazos Theological Commentary on the Bible. Grand Rapids: Brazos, 2010.

Myers, Allen C., ed. *The Eerdmans Bible Dictionary*. Grand Rapids: Eerdmans, 1987.

Na'aman, Nadav. "Samuel's Birth Legend and the Sanctuary of Shiloh." *Journal of Northwest Semitic Languages* 43 (2017): 51–61.

Neyrey, Jerome. "Despising the Shame of the Cross: Honor and Shame in the Johannine Passion Narrative." In *Semeia 68: Honor and Shame in the World of the Bible*, edited by Victor H. Matthews, Don C. Benjamin, and Claudia Camp, 113–137. Atlanta: SBL Press, 1996.

———. *Honor and Shame in the Gospel of Matthew*. Louisville: Westminster John Knox, 1998.

———, ed. *The Social World of Luke–Acts: Models for Interpretation*. Peabody, MA: Hendrickson, 1991.

Nissinen, Martti. "Prophets and Prophecy in Joshua–Kings, A Near Eastern Perspective." In *Israelite Prophecy and the Deuteronomistic History: Portrait, Reality, and the Formation of a History*, edited by Mignon R. Jacobs and Raymond F. Person, 103–128. Atlanta: Society of Biblical Literature, 2013.

Noth, Martin. *The Deuteronomistic History*. JSOTSup 15. Sheffield: Sheffield Academic, 1991.

———. *Die israelitischen Personennamen im Rahmen der gemeinsemitischen Namengebung*. Hildesheim: Georg Olms Verlag, 1980. First published 1928.

Olley, J. W. "A Forensic Connotation of *bôš*." *Vetus Testamentum* 26 (1976): 230–234.

Olyan, Saul M. "Honor, Shame, and Covenant Relations in Ancient Israel and Its Environment." *Journal of Biblical Literature* 115 (1996): 201–218.

Omanson, Roger Lee, and John Ellington. *A Handbook on the First and Second Books of Samuel*. New York: United Bible Societies, 2001.

Page, Margaret. "The Establishment of God's Word in Israel: A 'Reconsidered' Form-Critical Analysis of the Birth and Call Narratives of Samuel (1 Sam 1:1–4:1a)." PhD diss., Saint Paul University, 1984.

Pedersen, Johannes. *Israel, Its Life and Culture*. London: Oxford University Press, 1926.

Peristiany, J. G., ed. *Honour and Shame: The Values of Mediterranean Society*. London: Weidenfeld & Nicolson, 1965.

Petersen, David L. *The Roles of Israel's Prophets*. JSOTSup 17. Sheffield: JSOT Press, 1981.

Peterson, Eugene H. *First and Second Samuel*. Louisville: Westminster John Knox, 1999.

Pilch, John J. *Introducing the Cultural Context of the Old Testament*. Eugene: Wipf & Stock, 2007.

Pisano, Stephen. *Additions or Omissions in the Books of Samuel: The Significant Pluses and Minuses in the Massoretic, LXX and Qumran Texts*. Orbis Biblicus et Orientalis 57. Göttingen: Vandenhoeck & Ruprecht, 1984.

Pitt-Rivers, Julian. *The Fate of Shechem or the Politics of Sex: Essays in the Anthropology of the Mediterranean*. Cambridge: Cambridge University Press, 1977.

Plummer, Alfred. *A Critical and Exegetical Commentary on the Gospel according to St. Luke*. International Critical Commentary. London: T&T Clark, 1896.

Polzin, Robert. *Samuel and the Deuteronomist: A Literary Study of the Deuteronomic History Part Two: 1 Samuel*. Bloomington: Indiana University Press, 1993.

Powell, Mark Allan. *What Is Narrative Criticism?* Minneapolis: Fortress, 1990.

Provan, Iain W., V. Philips Long, and Tremper Longman III. *A Biblical History of Israel*. Louisville: Westminster John Knox, 2003.

Rabichev, Renata. "The Mediterranean Concepts of Honour and Shame as Seen in the Depiction of the Biblical Women." *Religion and Theology* 3 (1996): 51–63.

Ranke, Leopold von. *Geschichten der romanischen und germanischen Völker: Von 1494 Bis 1535*. Vol. 1. Leipzig: Reimer, 1824.

Ratner, Robert. "Three Bulls or One: A Reappraisal of 1 Samuel 1:24." *Biblica* 68 (1987): 98–102.

Resseguie, James L. *Narrative Criticism of the New Testament: An Introduction*. Grand Rapids: Baker Academic, 2005.

Rhoads, David M., and Donald Michie. *Mark as Story: An Introduction to the Narrative of a Gospel*. Minneapolis: Fortress, 1982.

Rivers, Pitt. *The Fate of Shechem or the Politics of Sex: Essays in the Anthropology of the Mediterranean*. Cambridge: Cambridge University Press, 1977.

Rodd, Cyril S. "On Applying a Sociological Theory to Biblical Studies." In *Social-Scientific Old Testament Criticism: A Sheffield Reader*, edited by David J. Chalcraft, 22–33. Sheffield: Sheffield Academic, 1997.

Rogala, Krystle. "Hinduism and the Origin of Caste in India." *Social Science Docket* 8 (2008): 40–41.

Rohrbaugh, Richard L., ed. *The Social Sciences and New Testament Interpretation.* Peabody: Hendrikson, 1996.

Ross, J. P. "Yahweh *Sebaʾot* in Samuel and Psalms." *Vetus Testamentum* 17 (1967): 76–92.

Rost, Leonhard. *Die Überlieferung von der Thronnachfolge Davids.* Beiträge zur Wissenschaft vom Alten und Neuen Testament 111/6. Stuttgart: Kohlhammer, 1926. Reprinted in *Das kleine Credo und andere Studien zum Alten Testament.* Heidelberg: Quelle & Meyer, 1965.

Salinas, Daniel. *Prosperity Theology and the Gospel: Good News or Bad News for the Poor?* Peabody: Hendrickson, 2017.

Santos, Narry F. *Transformation of the Filipino Hiya in the Light of Mark's Gospel.* Manila: Lifechange, 2003.

Sasson, Jack M. *Jonah.* The Anchor Yale Bible Commentaries 24B. New York: Doubleday, 1990.

———. "Circumcision in the Ancient Near East." *Journal of Biblical Literature* 85 (1996): 473–476.

———. "The Eyes of Eli: An Essay in Motif Accretion." In *Inspired Speech: Prophecy in the Ancient Near East; Essays in Honour of Herbert B. Huffmon*, edited by John Kaltner and Louis Stulman, 171–190. JSOTSup 378. London: T&T Clark, 2004.

Satterthwaite, P. E., R. S. Hess, and G. J. Wenham, eds. *The Lord's Anointed: Interpretation of Old Testament Messianic Texts.* Carlisle: Paternoster, 1995.

Savarikannu, Balu. "Expressions of Honor and Shame in Lamentations 1." *Asian Journal of Pentecostal Studies* 21 (2018): 81–94.

Schley, Donald G. *Shiloh: A Biblical City in Tradition and History.* JSOTSup 63. Sheffield: Sheffield Academic, 1989.

Schulz, Alfons. "Narrative Art in the Books of Samuel." In *Narrative and Novella in Samuel: Studies by Hugo Gressmann and Other Scholars 1906–1923*, translated by David E. Orton, edited by David M. Gunn, 119–170. Decatur, GA: Almond Press, 1991.

Schwartz, Seth. *Were the Jews a Mediterranean Society? Reciprocity and Solidarity in Ancient Judaism.* Princeton: Princeton University Press, 2010.

Seebass, H. "Zum Text von 1 Sam. XIV 23b–25a und II 29, 31–33." *Vetus Testamentum* 16 (1966): 74–82.

Segal, M. H. "Studies in the Books of Samuel. III." *Jewish Quarterly Review* 10 (1920): 203–236.

Sharma, Arvind. "Dr. B. R. Ambedkar on the Aryan Invasion and the Emergence of the Caste System in India." *Journal of the American Academy of Religion* 73 (2005): 843–870.

Simkins, Ronald A. "Return to Yahweh: Honor and Shame in Joel." In *Semeia 68: Honor and Shame in the World of the Bible*, edited by Victor H. Matthews, Don C. Benjamin, and Claudia Camp, 41–54. Atlanta: SBL Press, 1996.

Simkins, Ronald A., Stephen L. Cook, and Athalya Brenner, eds. *Semeia 87: The Social World of the Hebrew Bible: Twenty-Five Years of the Social Sciences in the Academy*. Atlanta: Society of Biblical Literature, 1999.

Smith, Henry P. *Samuel*. 4th ed. Edinburgh: T&T Clark, 1951. First published 1899.

Soggin, J. Alberto. *An Introduction to the History of Israel and Judah*. Translated by John Bowden. 3rd ed. London: SCM Press, 1999.

Spina, Frank Anthony. "Eli's Seat: The Transition from Priest to Prophet in 1 Samuel 1–4." *Journal for the Study of the Old Testament* 62 (1994): 67–75.

———. "A Prophet's 'Pregnant Pause': Samuel's Silence in the Ark Narrative (1 Sam 4:1–7:2)." *Horizons in Biblical Theology* 13 (1991): 59–73.

Spronk, Klaas. "Samuel as the Paradigm of the Judges: The Use of the Verb שפט in the Books of Judges and Samuel." In *Writing and Rewriting History in Ancient Israel and Near Eastern Cultures*, edited by Isaac Kalimi, 129–140. Wiesbaden: Harrassowitz Verlag, 2020.

Stansell, Gary. "Honor and Shame in the David Narratives." In *Semeia 68: Honor and Shame in the World of the Bible*, edited by Victor H. Matthews, Don C. Benjamin, and Claudia Camp, 55–79. Atlanta: SBL Press, 1996.

Steck, Odil Hannes. *Old Testament Exegesis, A Guide to the Methodology*. Edited by Marvin A. Sweeney. Translated by James D. Nogalski. 2nd ed. Atlanta: Scholars Press, 1998.

Steinmann, Andrew E. *1 Samuel*. Edited by Christopher W. Mitchell. Concordia Commentary. Saint Louis, MO: Concordia Publishing House, 2016.

Sternberg, Meir. *The Poetics of Biblical Narrative: Ideological Literature and the Drama of Reading*. Bloomington: Indiana University Press, 1985.

Steussy, Marti J., and James L. Crenshaw. *Samuel and His God*. Columbia: University of South Carolina Press, 2013.

Stiebert, Johanna. *The Construction of Shame in the Hebrew Bible: The Prophetic Contribution*. JSOTSup 346. London: Sheffield Academic, 2002.

———. "Shame and Prophecy: Approaches Past and Present." *Biblical Interpretation* 8 (2000): 255–275.

Still, Clarinda. *Dalit Women: Honour and Patriarchy in South India*. New York: Routledge, 2017.

Stirrup, A. "'Why Has Yahweh Defeated Us Today before the Philistines?' The Question of the Ark Narrative." *Tyndale Bulletin* 51 (2000): 81–100.

Stoebe, Hans J. *Das erste Buch Samuelis*. Kommentar zum Alten Testament 8.1. Gütersloh: Mohn, 1973.

Stol, Marten. *Women in the Ancient Near East*. Translated by Helen and Mervyn Richardson. Berlin: de Gruyter, 2016.

Stone, Ken. "Gender and Homosexuality in Judges 19: Subject-Honor, Object-Shame?" *Journal for the Study of the Old Testament* 67 (1995): 87–107.

———. *Sex, Honor and Power in the Deuteronomistic History*. JSOTSup 234. Sheffield: Sheffield Academic, 1996.

Sturhahn, Herbert. "An Investigation of the Literary Artistry of the Final Composer of the Narrative of 1 Samuel 1–8." PhD diss., Fuller Theological Seminary, 1995.

Sweeney, Marvin. "Eli: A High Priest Thrown under the Wheels of the Ox Cart." In *Characters and Characterization in the Book of Samuel*, edited by Keith Bodner and Benjamin J. M. Johnson, 59–75. London: T&T Clark, 2020.

———. "Samuel's Institutional Identity in the Deuteronomistic History." In *Constructs of Prophecy in the Former and Latter Prophets and Other Texts*, edited by Lester L. Grabbe and Martti Nissinen, 165–174. Atlanta: Society of Biblical Literature, 2011.

Thenius, Otto. *Die Bücher Samuels*. Edited by Löhr. 3rd ed. Leipzig: S. Hirzel, 1898.

Thomas, D. W. "בְּלִיַּעַל in the Old Testament." In *Biblical and Patristic Studies in Memory of Robert Pierce Casey*, edited by J. N. Birdsall and R. W. Thomson, 11–19. Freiburg: Herder, 1963.

Thorat, Sukhadeo. *Dalits in India: Search for a Common Destiny*. Los Angeles: SAGE Publications, 2009.

Tov, Emmanuel. *The Text-Critical Use of the Septuagint in Biblical Research*. 3rd ed. Winona Lake: Eisenbrauns, 2015.

———. *Textual Criticism of the Hebrew Bible*. 3rd ed. Minneapolis: Fortress, 2012.

Trebolle, Julio. "Textual Criticism and the Composition History of Samuel: Connections between Pericopes in 1 Samuel 1–4." In *Archaeology of the Books of Samuel: The Entangling of the Textual and Literary History*, edited by Philippe Hugo and Adrian Schenker, 261–285. VTSup 132. Leiden: Brill, 2009.

Tsevat, Mattitiahu. "Interpretation of I Sam. 2:27–36: The Narrative of *Kareth*." *Hebrew Union College Annual* 32 (1961): 191–216.

Tsumura, David Toshio. *The First Book of Samuel*. New International Commentary on the Old Testament. Grand Rapids: Eerdmans, 2007.

Tur-Sinai, N. H. "The Ark of God at Beit Shemesh (1 Sam. VI) and Peres 'Uzza (2 Sam. VI; 1 Chron. XIII)." *Vetus Testamentum* 1 (1951): 275–286.

Tushima, Cephas T. A. *The Fate of Saul's Progeny in the Reign of David*. Cambridge: James Clarke, 2012.

Uspensky, Boris. *A Poetics of Composition: The Structure of the Artistic Text and Typology of a Compositional Form*. Translated by Valentina Zavarin and Susan Wittig. London: University of California Press, 1973.

Van der Merwe, Christo H. J. "The Elusive Biblical Hebrew Term *Wayehi*. A Perspective in Terms of Its Syntax, Semantics, and Pragmatics in 1 Samuel." *Hebrew Studies* 40 (1999): 83–114.

Van der Merwe, Christo H. J., Jacobus A. Naudé, and Jan H. Kroeze. *A Biblical Hebrew Reference Grammar*. 2nd ed. Sheffield: Sheffield Academic, 2017.

Van der Toorn, Karel. "Female Prostitution in Payment of Vows in Ancient Israel." *Journal of Biblical Literature* 108 (1989): 193–205.

Van der Toorn, Karel, Bob Becking, and Pieter W. van der Horst, eds. *Dictionary of Deities and Demons in the Bible*. 2nd ed. Leiden: Brill, 1999.

Van Rooy, H. F. "Prophetic Utterances in Narrative Texts, with Reference to 1 Samuel 2:27–36." *Old Testament Essays* 3 (1990): 203–218.

Van Seters, John. "The Problem of Childlessness in Near Eastern Law and the Patriarchs of Israel." *Journal of Biblical Literature* 87 (1968): 401–408.

Van Staalduine-Sulman, Eveline. *The Targum of Samuel*. Studies in the Aramaic Interpretation of Scripture 1. Leiden: Brill, 2002.

Van Wijk-Bos, Johanna W. H. *Reading Samuel: A Literary and Theological Commentary*. Macon: Smyth & Helwys, 2011.

Van Wolde, Ellen. "The Niphal as Middle Voice and Its Consequence for Meaning." *Journal for the Study of the Old Testament* 43 (2019): 453–478.

Vannoy, J. Robert. *1–2 Samuel*. Cornerstone Biblical Commentary 4a. Carol Stream: Tyndale House, 2009.

Villanueva, Federico. "The Calling of an Asian Evangelical Scholar: A Biblical Scholar's Perspective." Paper presented at ATA Theological Consultation, Malang, Indonesia, 18 July 18 2017.

———. "The Challenge of Asian Biblical Interpretation Today." *Journal of Asian Evangelical Theology* 18 (2014): 5–17.

———. *It's OK to Be Not OK: Preaching the Lament Psalms*. Carlisle Langham Preaching Resources, 2017.

———. *The 'Uncertainty of a Hearing': A Study of the Sudden Change of Mood in the Psalms of Lament*. Leiden: Brill, 2008.

Waltke, Bruce K., and Michael O'Connor. *An Introduction to Biblical Hebrew Syntax*. Winona Lake: Eisenbrauns, 1990.

Walton, John H., Victor H. Matthews, and Mark W. Chavalas, *The IVP Bible Background Commentary: Old Testament*. Downers Grove: InterVarsity Press, 2000.

Waters, Stanley D. "Hannah and Anna: The Greek and Hebrew texts of 1 Samuel 1." *Journal of Biblical Literature* 107 (1998): 385–412.

Watson, Wilfred G. E. *Classical Hebrew Poetry: A Guide to Its Techniques*. London: T&T Clark, 2005.
Webster, Brian L. *The Cambridge Introduction to Biblical Hebrew*. Cambridge: Cambridge University Press, 2009.
Weiser, Artur. *The Old Testament: Its Formation and Development*. New York: Association Press, 1961. First published 1948.
Weiss, Andrea L. *Figurative Language in Biblical Prose Narrative: Metaphor in the Book of Samuel*. VTSup 107. Leiden: Brill, 2006.
Wellhausen, Julius. *Der Text der Bücher Samuelis*. Göttingen: Vandenhoeck & Ruprecht, 1871.

———. *Die Composition des Hexateuchs und der historischen Bücher des Alten Testaments*. Berlin: Walter de Gruyter, 1963. First published 1899.
Wenham, John W. "Large Numbers in the Old Testament." *Tyndale Bulletin* 18 (1967): 19–53.
Wiggins, Steve A. "Old Testament Dagan in the Light of Ugarit." *Vetus Testamentum* 43 (1993): 268–274.
Wilkinson, J. "The Philistine Epidemic of I Samuel 5 and 6." *Expository Times* 88 (1977): 137–141.
Williams, James G. "The Beautiful and the Barren: Conventions in Biblical Type-Scenes." *JSOT* 17 (1980): 107–119.
Williams, Jenni. "Hannah: A Woman Deeply Troubled." In *Characters and Characterization in the Book of Samuel*, edited by Keith Bodner and Benjamin J. M. Johnson, 42–58. London: T&T Clark, 2020.
Williams, Joel. *Other Followers of Jesus: Minor Characters as Major Figures in Mark's Gospel*. JSNTSup 102. Sheffield: Sheffield Academic, 1994.
Willis, John T. "An Anti-Elide Narrative Tradition from a Prophetic Circle at the Ramah Sanctuary." *Journal of Biblical Literature* 90 (1971): 288–308.

———. "The Song of Hannah and Psalm 113." *Catholic Biblical Quarterly* 34 (1973): 139–154.

———. *1 & 2 Samuel*. Abilene: Abilene Christian University Press, 1984.
Wilson, Robert R. "Prophecy and Ecstasy: A Reexamination." *Journal of Biblical Literature* 98 (1979): 321–337.
Wolff, H. W. *Anthropology of the Old Testament*. Philadelphia: Fortress, 1974.
Wu, Daniel. *Honor, Shame, and Guilt: Social-Scientific Approaches to the Book of Ezekiel*. BBRSup 14. Winona Lake: Eisenbrauns, 2016.
Wu, Jackson. "Biblical Theology from a Chinese Perspective: Interpreting Scripture through the Lens of Honor and Shame." *Global Missiology* 4 (2013): 1–31.

———. *Saving God's Face: A Chinese Contextualization of Salvation through Honor and Shame*. Pasadena: William Carey International University Press, 2013.
Yamasaki, Gary. *Watching a Biblical Narrative: Point of View in Biblical Exegesis*. London: T&T Clark, 2007.

Yardney, Sarah Shaw. "Interpretation in the Septuagint of Samuel." PhD diss., University of Chicago, 2017.

Yee, Gale A. *Poor Banished Children of Eve*. Minneapolis, MN: Fortress, 2003.

Zimran, Yisca. "Divine vs. Human Authority in the Books of Samuel." In *The Books of Samuel: Stories – History – Reception History*, edited by Walter Dietrich, 403–411. Leuven: Peeters, 2016.

Langham Literature, with its publishing work, is a ministry of Langham Partnership.

Langham Partnership is a global fellowship working in pursuit of the vision God entrusted to its founder John Stott –

> *to facilitate the growth of the church in maturity and Christ-likeness through raising the standards of biblical preaching and teaching.*

Our vision is to see churches in the Majority World equipped for mission and growing to maturity in Christ through the ministry of pastors and leaders who believe, teach and live by the word of God.

Our mission is to strengthen the ministry of the word of God through:
- nurturing national movements for biblical preaching
- fostering the creation and distribution of evangelical literature
- enhancing evangelical theological education

especially in countries where churches are under-resourced.

Our ministry

Langham Preaching partners with national leaders to nurture indigenous biblical preaching movements for pastors and lay preachers all around the world. With the support of a team of trainers from many countries, a multi-level programme of seminars provides practical training, and is followed by a programme for training local facilitators. Local preachers' groups and national and regional networks ensure continuity and ongoing development, seeking to build vigorous movements committed to Bible exposition.

Langham Literature provides Majority World preachers, scholars and seminary libraries with evangelical books and electronic resources through publishing and distribution, grants and discounts. The programme also fosters the creation of indigenous evangelical books in many languages, through writer's grants, strengthening local evangelical publishing houses, and investment in major regional literature projects, such as one volume Bible commentaries like the *Africa Bible Commentary* and the *South Asia Bible Commentary*.

Langham Scholars provides financial support for evangelical doctoral students from the Majority World so that, when they return home, they may train pastors and other Christian leaders with sound, biblical and theological teaching. This programme equips those who equip others. Langham Scholars also works in partnership with Majority World seminaries in strengthening evangelical theological education. A growing number of Langham Scholars study in high quality doctoral programmes in the Majority World itself. As well as teaching the next generation of pastors, graduated Langham Scholars exercise significant influence through their writing and leadership.

To learn more about Langham Partnership and the work we do visit **langham.org**

www.ingramcontent.com/pod-product-compliance
Lightning Source LLC
Chambersburg PA
CBHW051537230426
43669CB00015B/2632

of Samuel is couched in a narrative ideology, which requires more than mere expertise in historical and literary-critical methodology to apprehend its ultimate message. The interpreter ideally also should be conscious of the presence and workings of social-cultural dynamics in society to penetrate properly those that were arguably resident in the ancient Palestinian world out of which the Old Testament arose, and which plausibly formed a foundation for the narrative therein. His confining his study primarily to the first seven chapters of 1 Samuel has not only allowed for in-depth analysis but prompts further research into this stimulating topic within the whole of the Samuelic corpus. I recommend this volume to anyone interested in the study of ancient Israel.

Tim Undheim, PhD
Asia Graduate School of Theology, Manila, Philippines

The volume offers a fresh approach to 1 Samuel that is methodologically sound and nuanced in order to gain a deeper understanding of the text in its own cultural context. The author's voice is an important one for scholars and pastors wishing to apply a social-scientific lens to the biblical text in order to hear its message afresh for today.

Bill T. Arnold, PhD
Paul S. Amos Professor of Old Testament Interpretation,
Asbury Theological Seminary, Kentucky, USA

Using the ideological perspective of honor and shame, this is a fresh understanding of the book of First Samuel, with a special treatment on the first seven chapters. Compulsively readable, the author interacts with a stunning amount of research and cautiously interprets the texts. His analyses of the neglected biblical concept of honor and shame, reflecting the social-cultural values of the Global South, will surely steer more scholarly debate and understanding. We are proud of his significant contribution to OT studies.

Joseph Shao, PhD
President Emeritus, Biblical Seminary of the Philippines
Former General Secretary, Asia Theological Association

In this close analysis of 1 Samuel 1–7, Kang Bin employs "socio-literary criticism" in demonstrating both the validity and the value of reading these chapters through an ideological "lens" of honor and shame, as developed by the narrator throughout 1 Samuel. He convincingly draws attention to the thematic centrality of these polar concepts in Hannah's journey from shame to honor, in the contrasting characters and outcomes of the Elides and Samuel, and in YHWH's defense of his own glory in the ark narrative. The author concludes by suggesting some implications of his study for the "honor and shame culture" in Asia, including the Chinese concept of "face" (*mianzi*).

Richard Schultz, PhD
Blanchard Professor of Old Testament,
Wheaton College, Illinois, USA

This volume is a unique contribution to biblical studies. Crafted, researched and written by a scholar well cognizant of and sensitive to the honor-shame culture common to much of Asia, Kang Bin argues that the first of the books